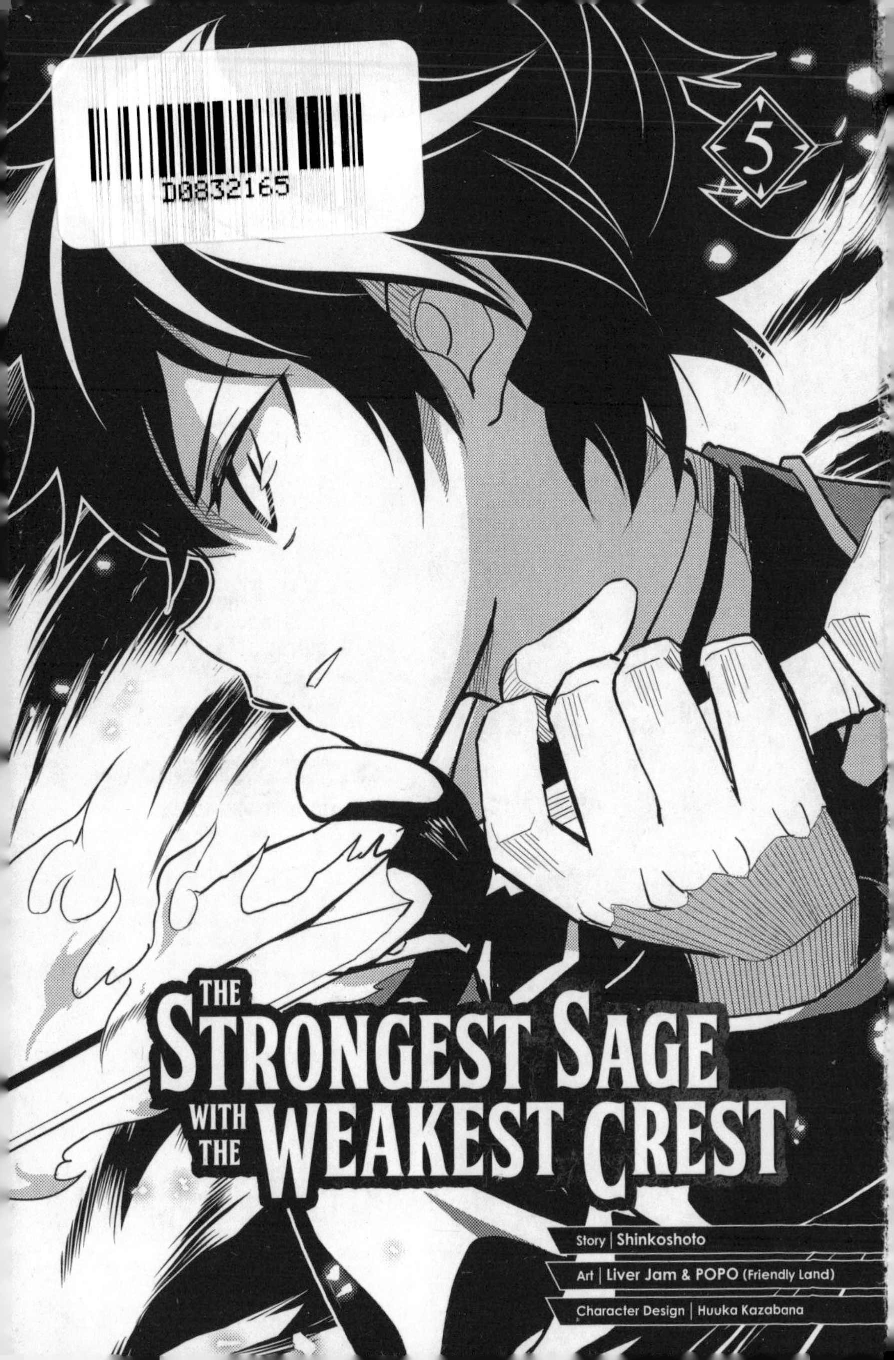
5
THE STRONGEST SAGE WITH THE WEAKEST CREST
Story | Shinkoshoto
Art | Liver Jam & POPO (Friendly Land)
Character Design | Huuka Kazabana

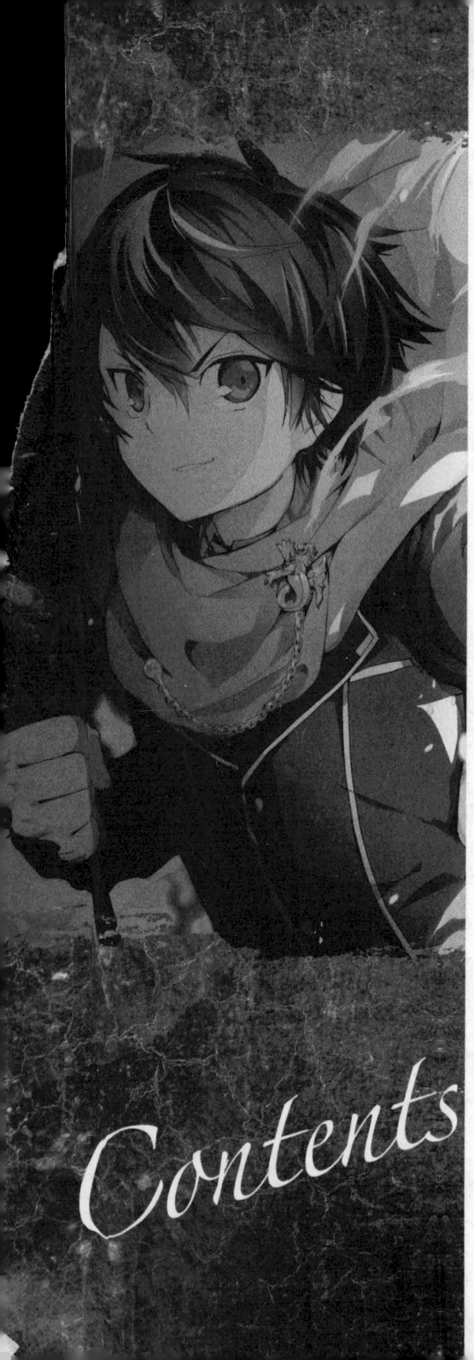

Contents

THE STRONGEST SAGE WITH THE WEAKEST CREST

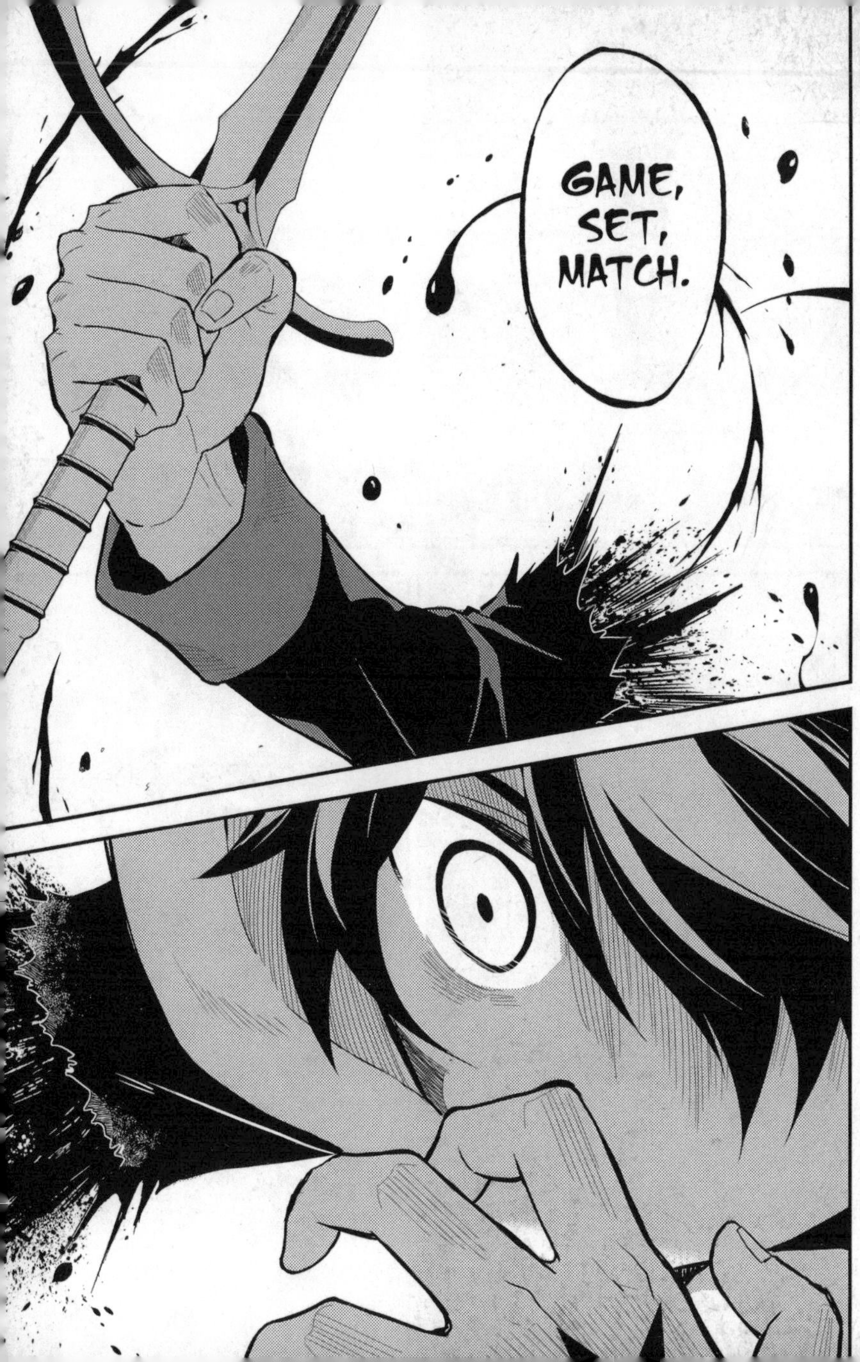
GAME, SET, MATCH.

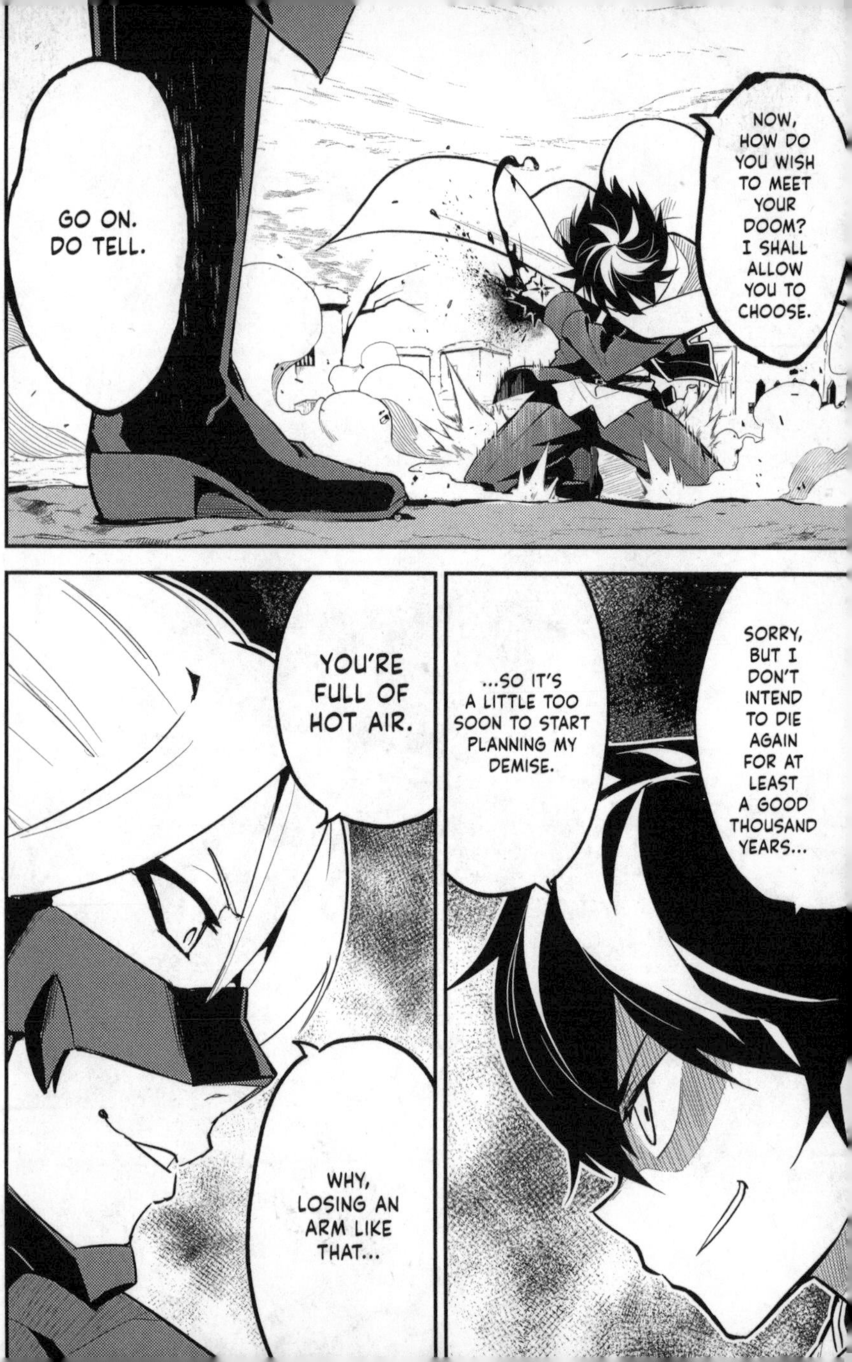
NOW, HOW DO YOU WISH TO MEET YOUR DOOM? I SHALL ALLOW YOU TO CHOOSE.
GO ON. DO TELL.
SORRY, BUT I DON'T INTEND TO DIE AGAIN FOR AT LEAST A GOOD THOUSAND YEARS...
...SO IT'S A LITTLE TOO SOON TO START PLANNING MY DEMISE.
YOU'RE FULL OF HOT AIR.
WHY, LOSING AN ARM LIKE THAT...

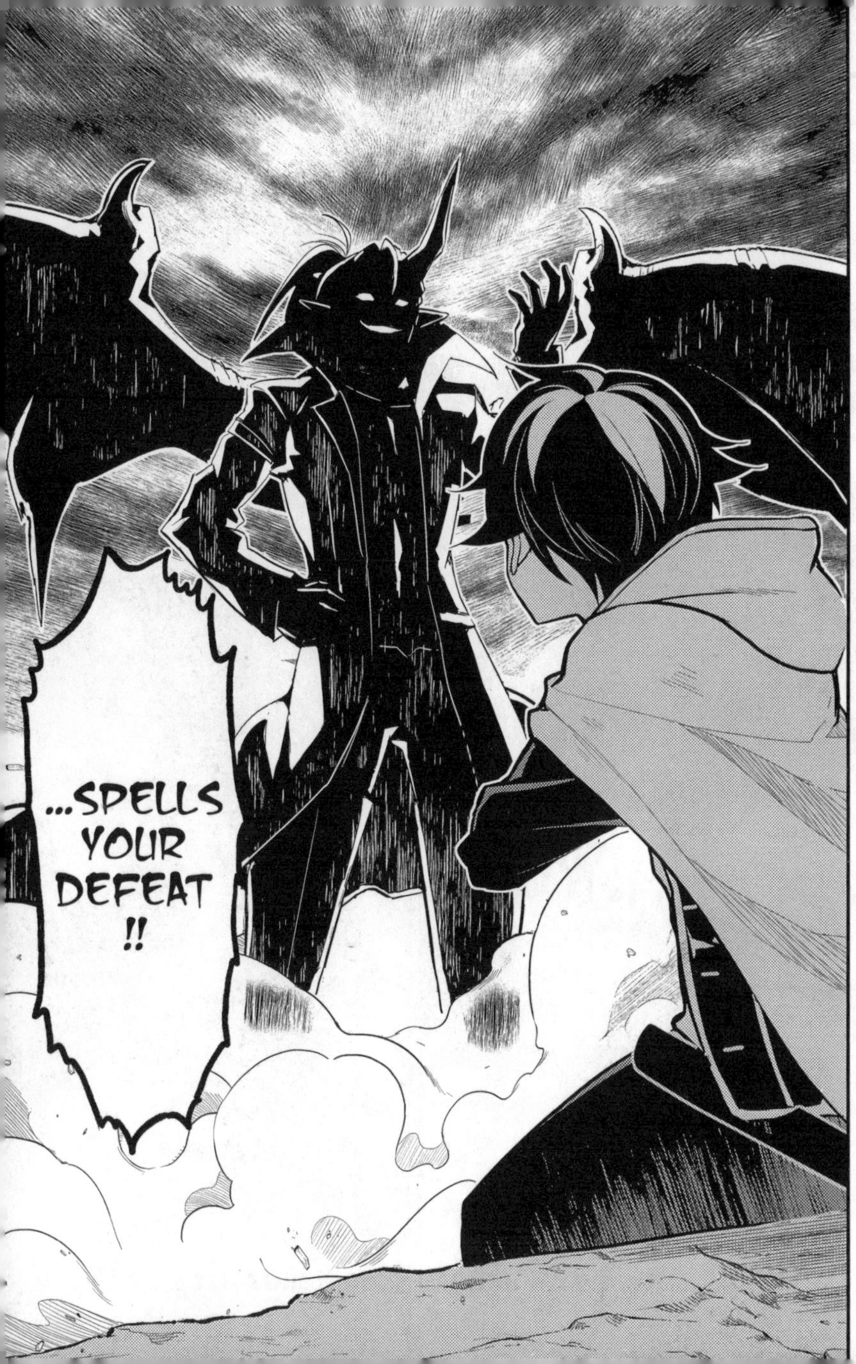
...SPELLS YOUR DEFEAT !!

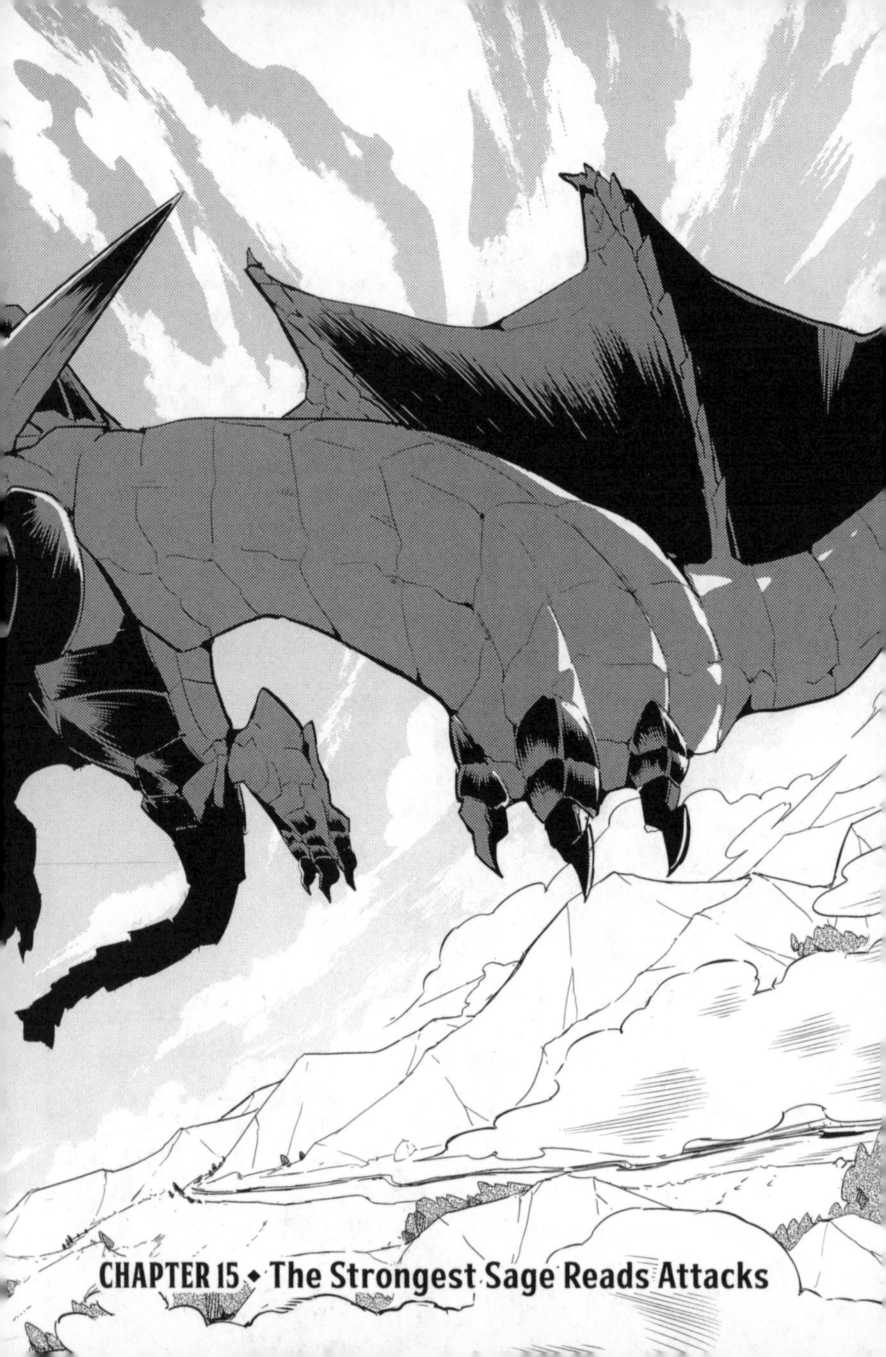

CHAPTER 15 ◆ The Strongest Sage Reads Attacks

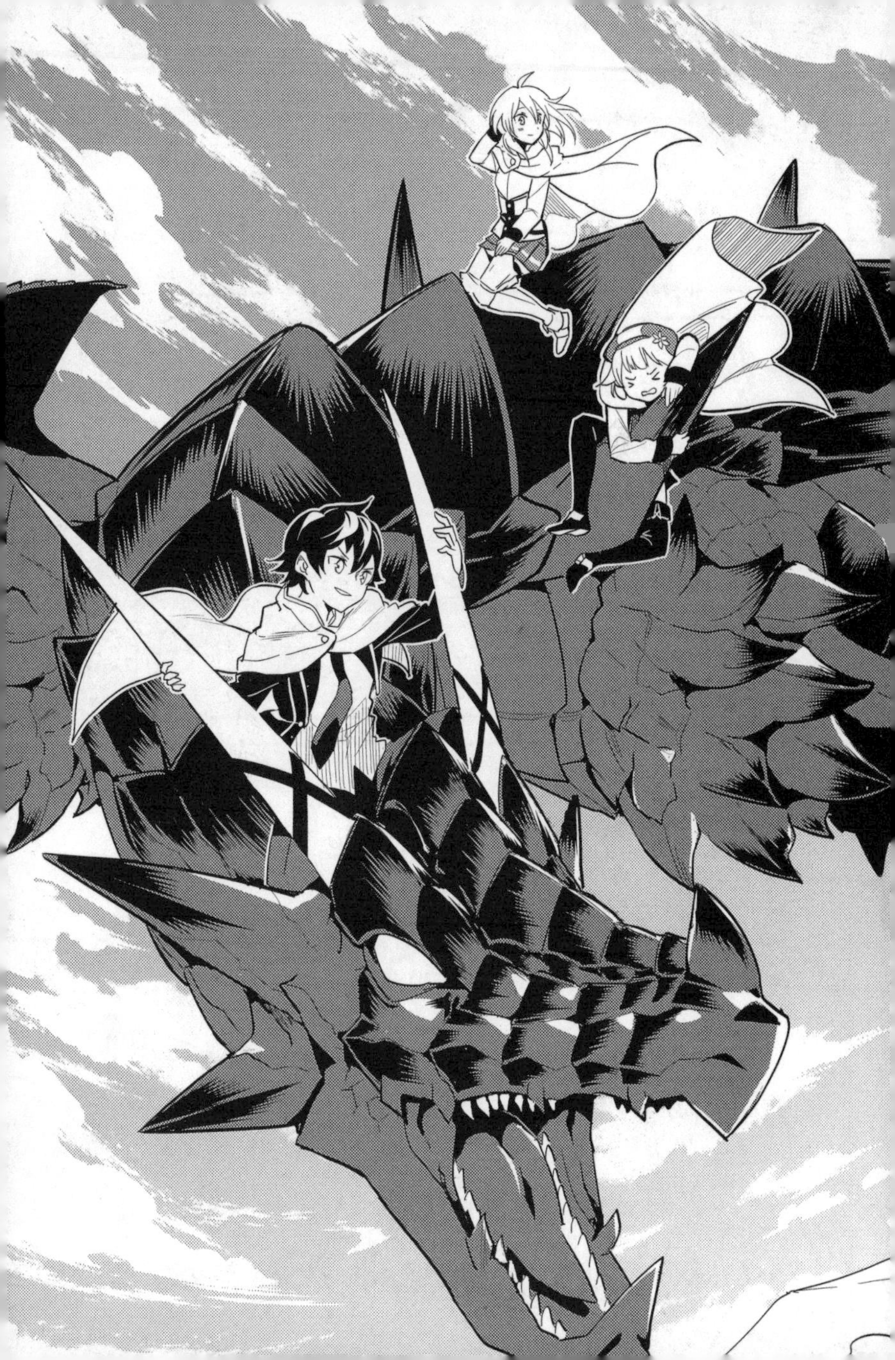

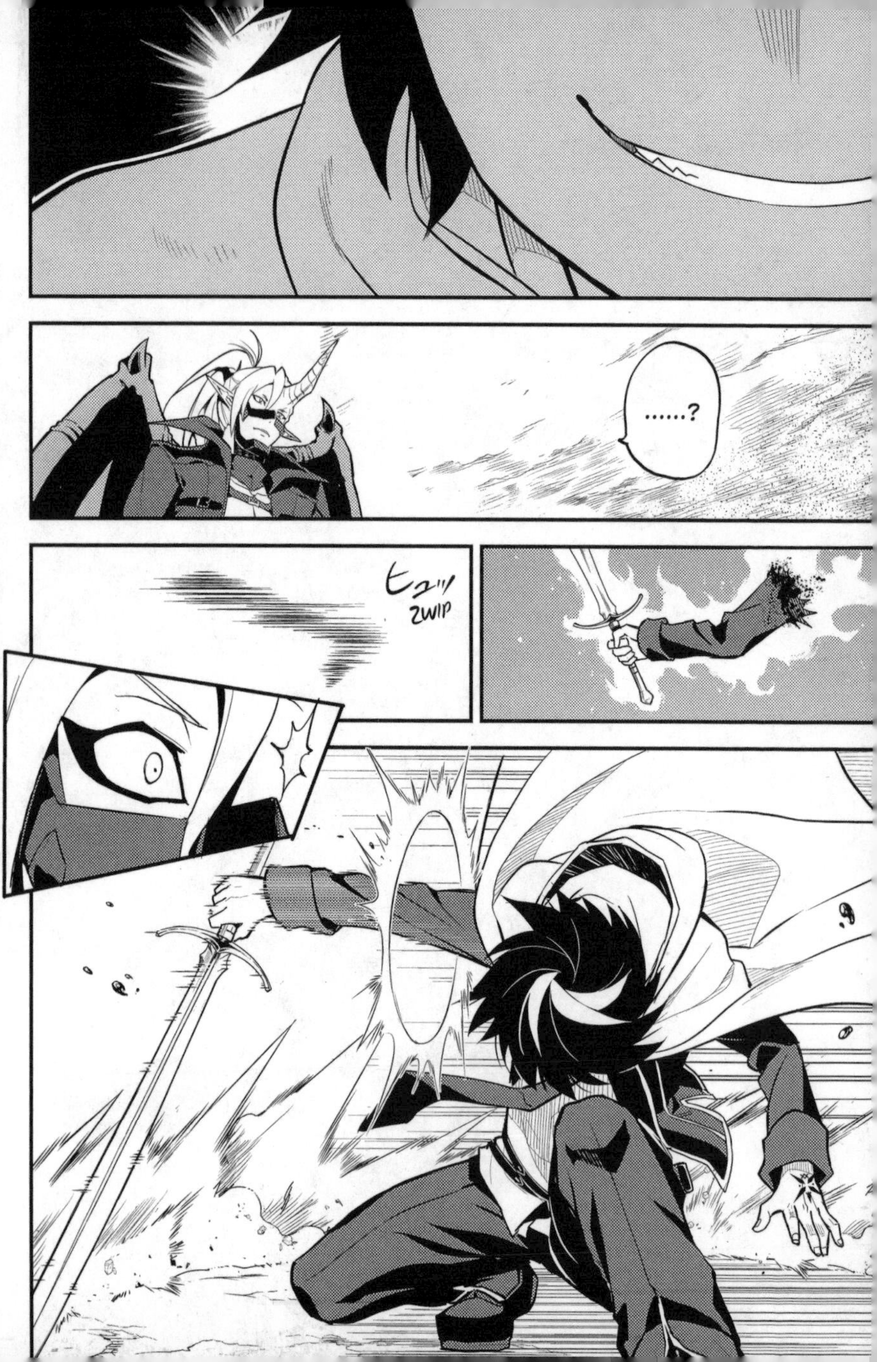
......?
ヒュッ
ZWIP

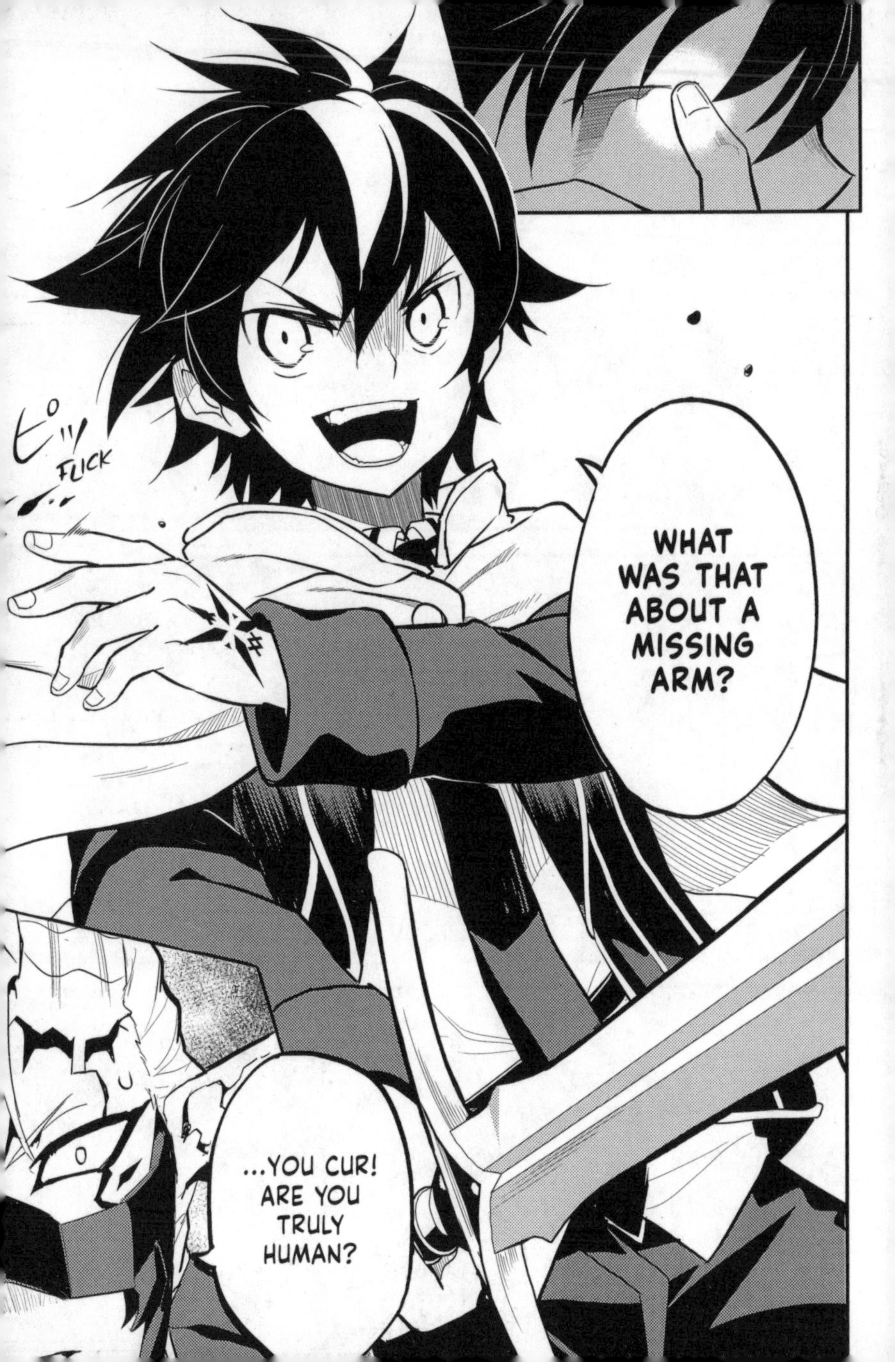
WHAT WAS THAT ABOUT A MISSING ARM?
FLICK
...YOU CUR! ARE YOU TRULY HUMAN?

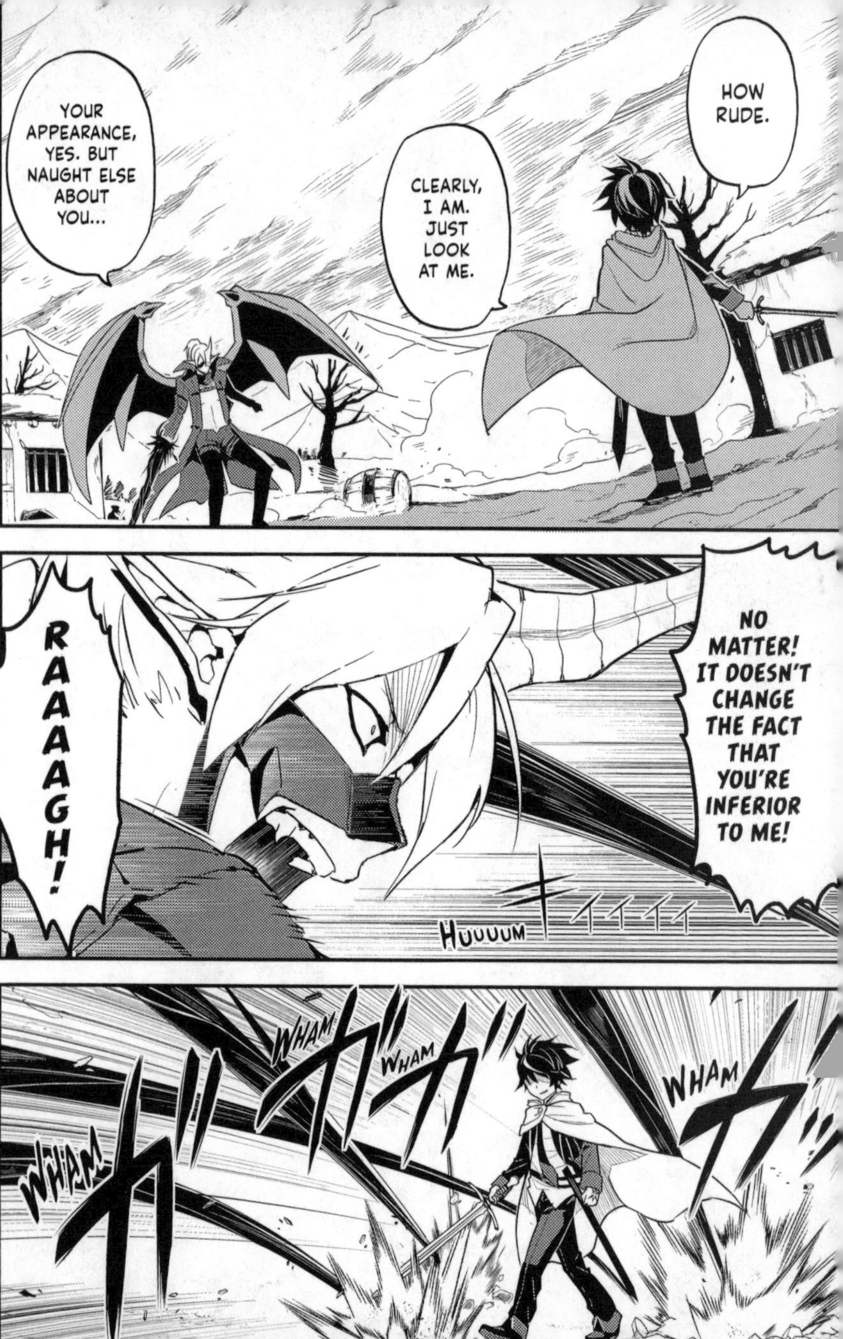
HOW RUDE.
CLEARLY, I AM. JUST LOOK AT ME.
YOUR APPEARANCE, YES. BUT NAUGHT ELSE ABOUT YOU...
NO MATTER! IT DOESN'T CHANGE THE FACT THAT YOU'RE INFERIOR TO ME!
HUUUUM
RAAAAGH!
WHAM
WHAM
WHAM
WHAM

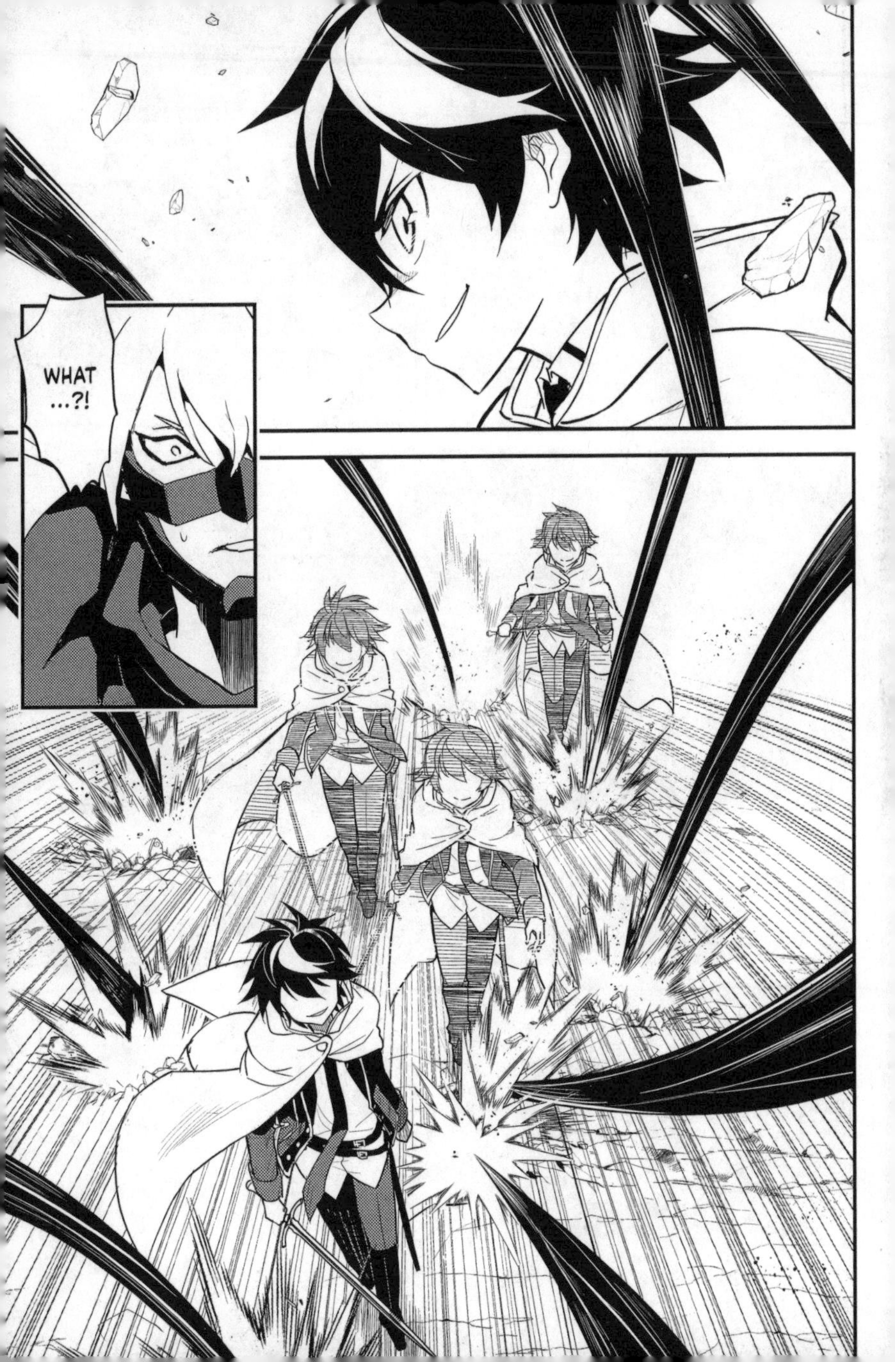
WHAT ...?!

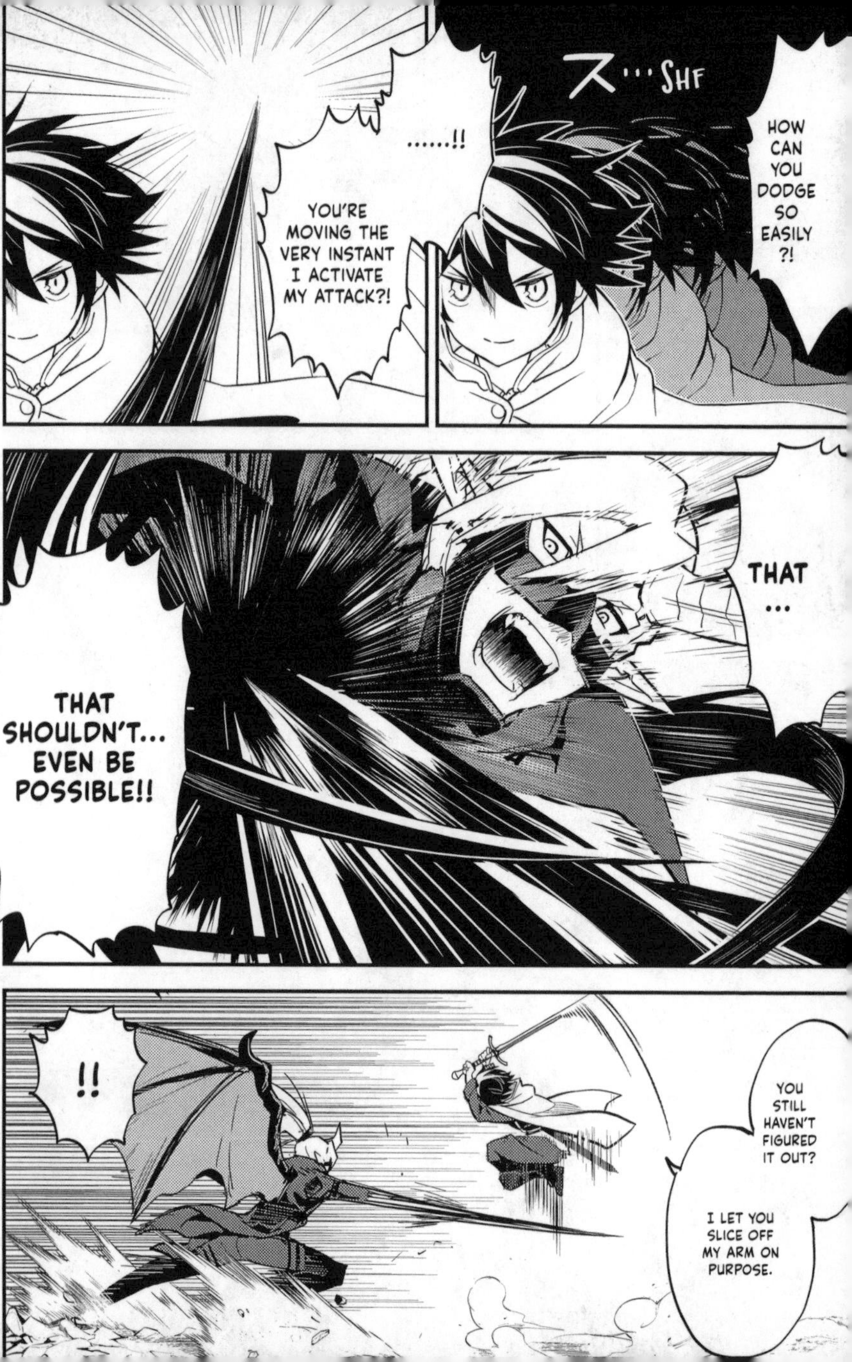
ス…SHF
HOW CAN YOU DODGE SO EASILY?!
......!!
YOU'RE MOVING THE VERY INSTANT I ACTIVATE MY ATTACK?!
THAT ...
THAT SHOULDN'T... EVEN BE POSSIBLE!!
YOU STILL HAVEN'T FIGURED IT OUT?
I LET YOU SLICE OFF MY ARM ON PURPOSE.
!!

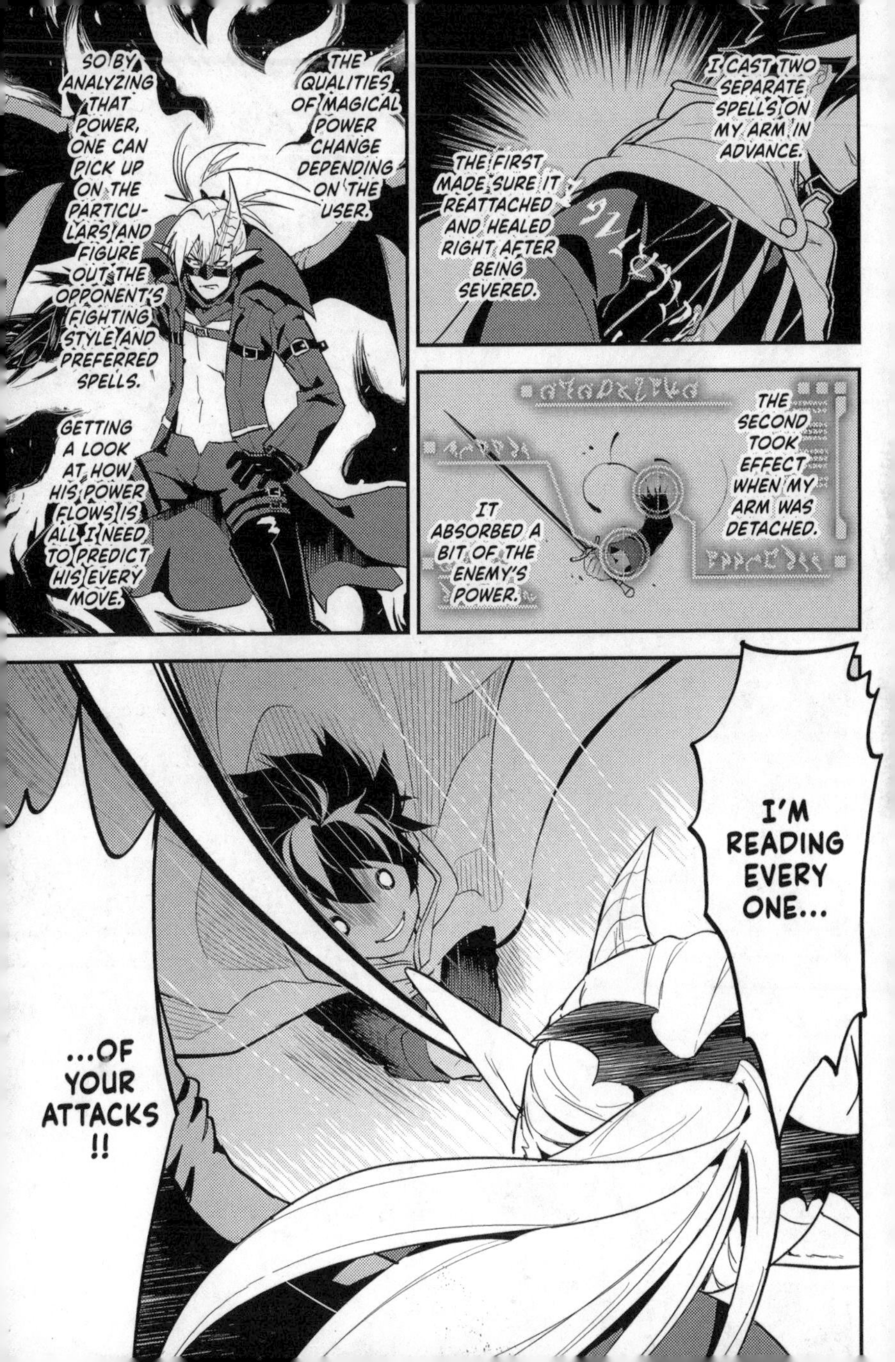
I CAST TWO SEPARATE SPELLS ON MY ARM IN ADVANCE.
THE FIRST MADE SURE IT REATTACHED AND HEALED RIGHT AFTER BEING SEVERED.
THE SECOND TOOK EFFECT WHEN MY ARM WAS DETACHED.
IT ABSORBED A BIT OF THE ENEMY'S POWER.
THE QUALITIES OF MAGICAL POWER CHANGE DEPENDING ON THE USER.
SO BY ANALYZING THAT POWER, ONE CAN PICK UP ON THE PARTICU-LARS AND FIGURE OUT THE OPPONENT'S FIGHTING STYLE AND PREFERRED SPELLS.
GETTING A LOOK AT HOW HIS POWER FLOWS IS ALL I NEED TO PREDICT HIS EVERY MOVE.
I'M READING EVERY ONE...
...OF YOUR ATTACKS !!

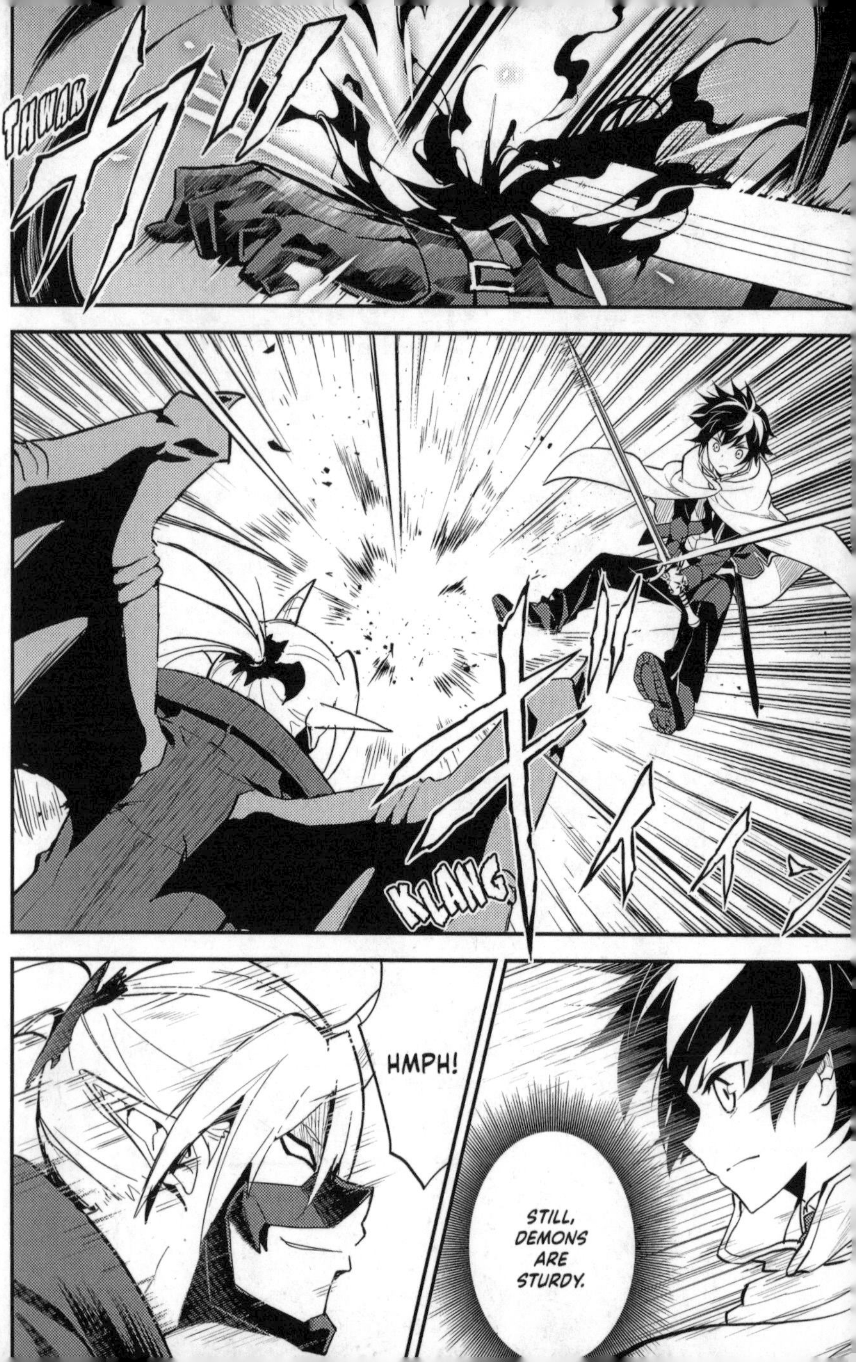
THWAK
KLANG
STILL, DEMONS ARE STURDY.
HMPH!

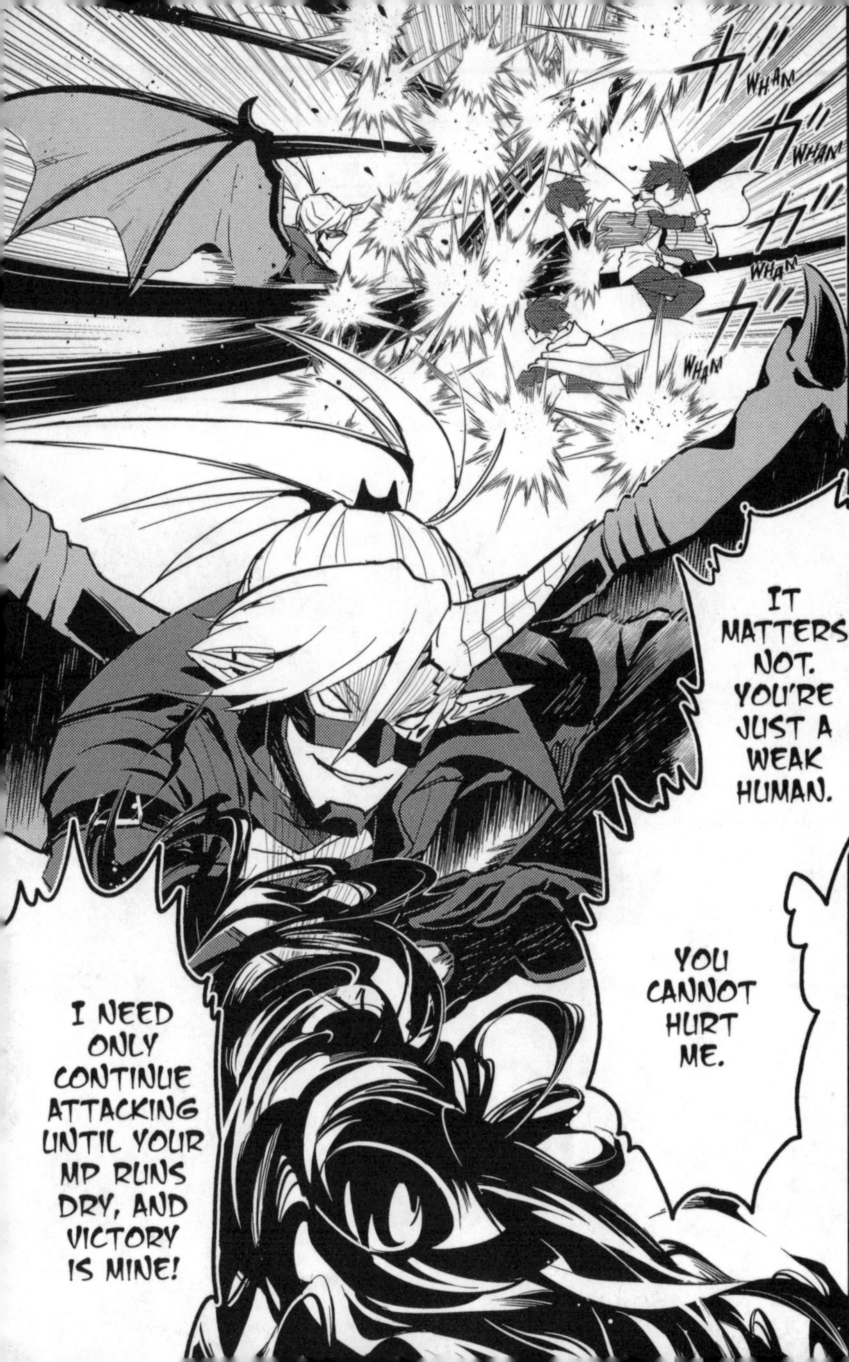
WHAM
WHAM
WHAM
WHAM
IT MATTERS NOT. YOU'RE JUST A WEAK HUMAN.
YOU CANNOT HURT ME.
I NEED ONLY CONTINUE ATTACKING UNTIL YOUR MP RUNS DRY, AND VICTORY IS MINE!

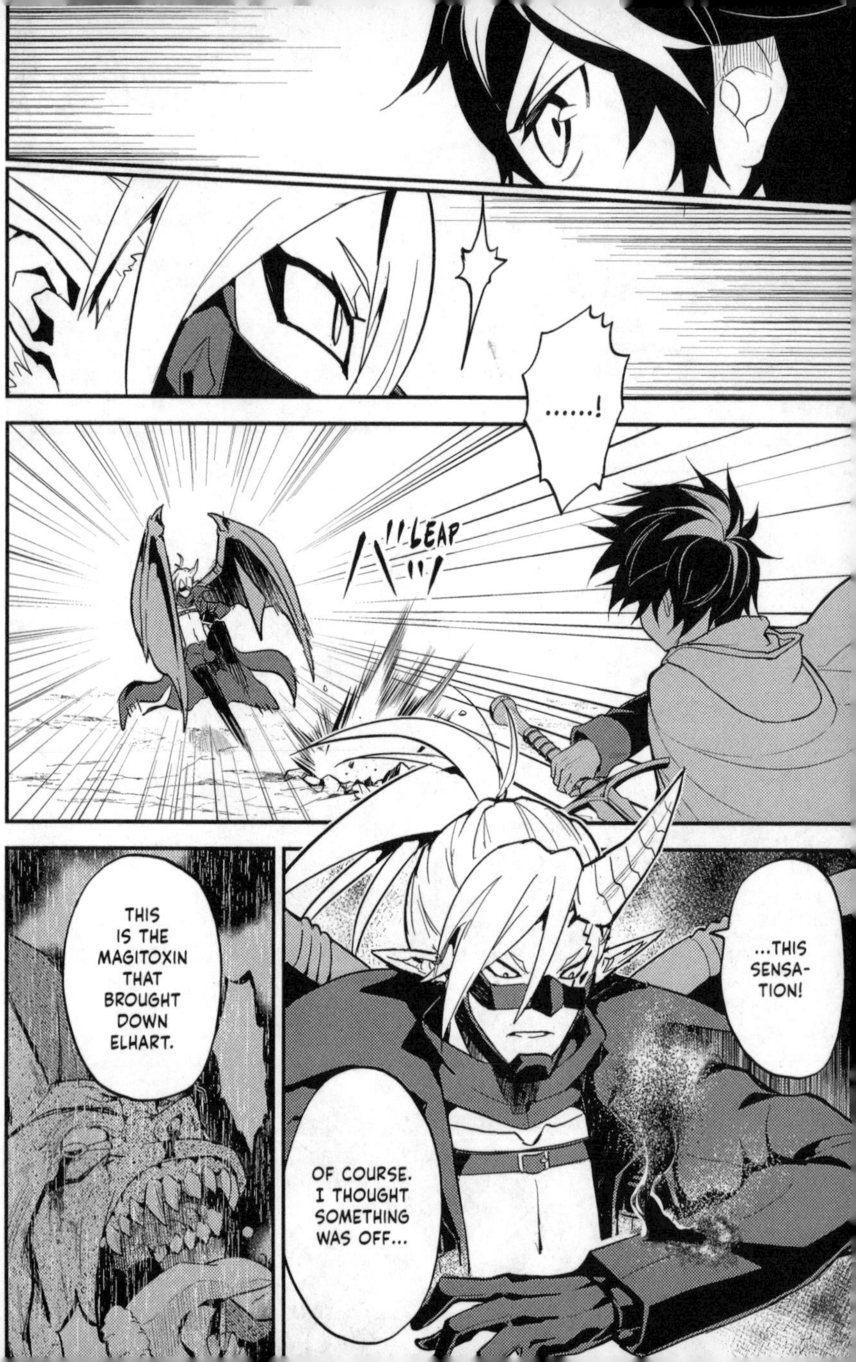
......!
LEAP
...THIS SENSA-TION!
OF COURSE. I THOUGHT SOMETHING WAS OFF...
THIS IS THE MAGITOXIN THAT BROUGHT DOWN ELHART.

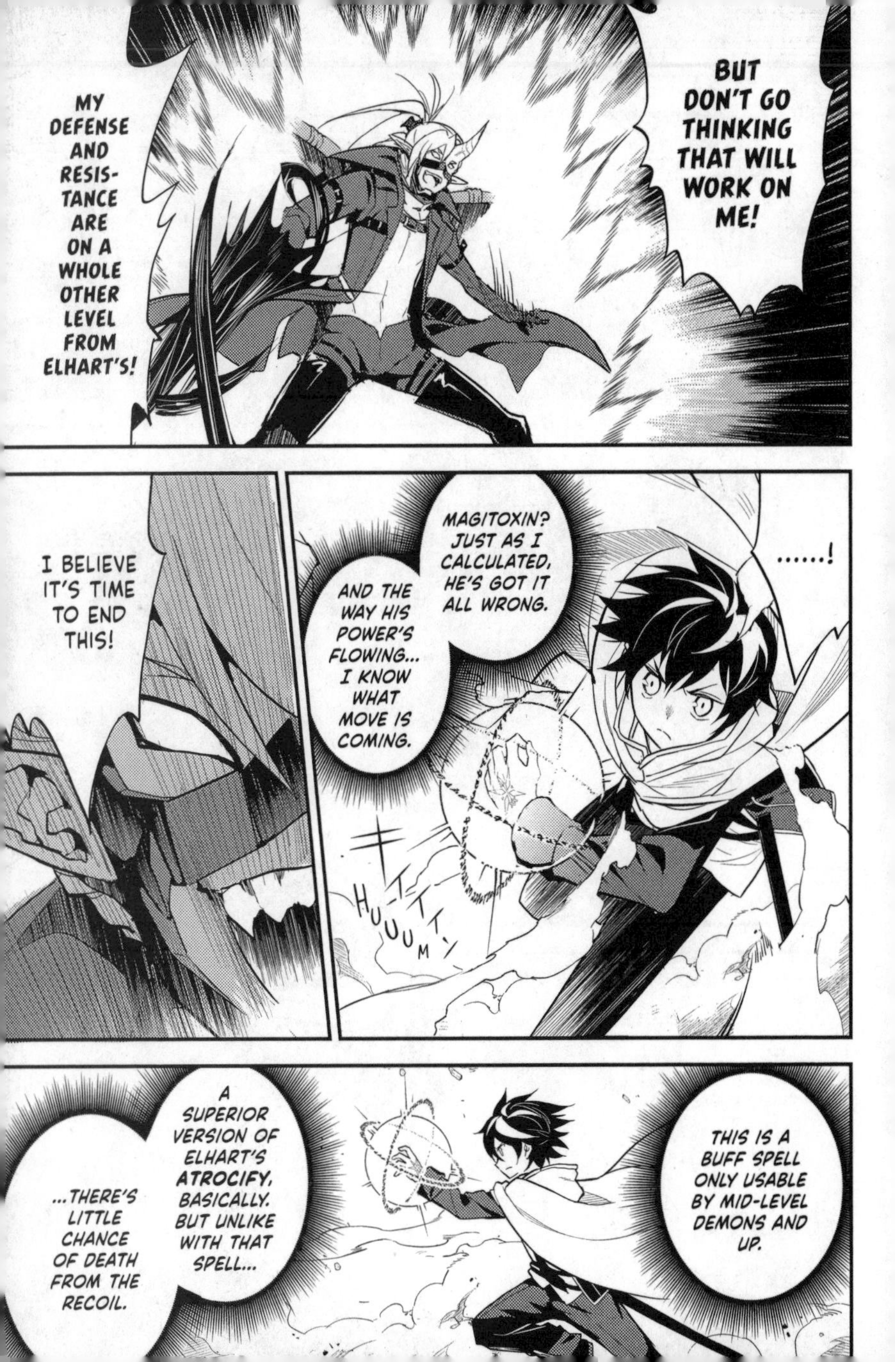
BUT DON'T GO THINKING THAT WILL WORK ON ME!
MY DEFENSE AND RESISTANCE ARE ON A WHOLE OTHER LEVEL FROM ELHART'S!
......!
MAGITOXIN? JUST AS I CALCULATED, HE'S GOT IT ALL WRONG.
AND THE WAY HIS POWER'S FLOWING... I KNOW WHAT MOVE IS COMING.
HUUUM
I BELIEVE IT'S TIME TO END THIS!
THIS IS A BUFF SPELL ONLY USABLE BY MID-LEVEL DEMONS AND UP.
A SUPERIOR VERSION OF ELHART'S ATROCIFY, BASICALLY. BUT UNLIKE WITH THAT SPELL...
...THERE'S LITTLE CHANCE OF DEATH FROM THE RECOIL.

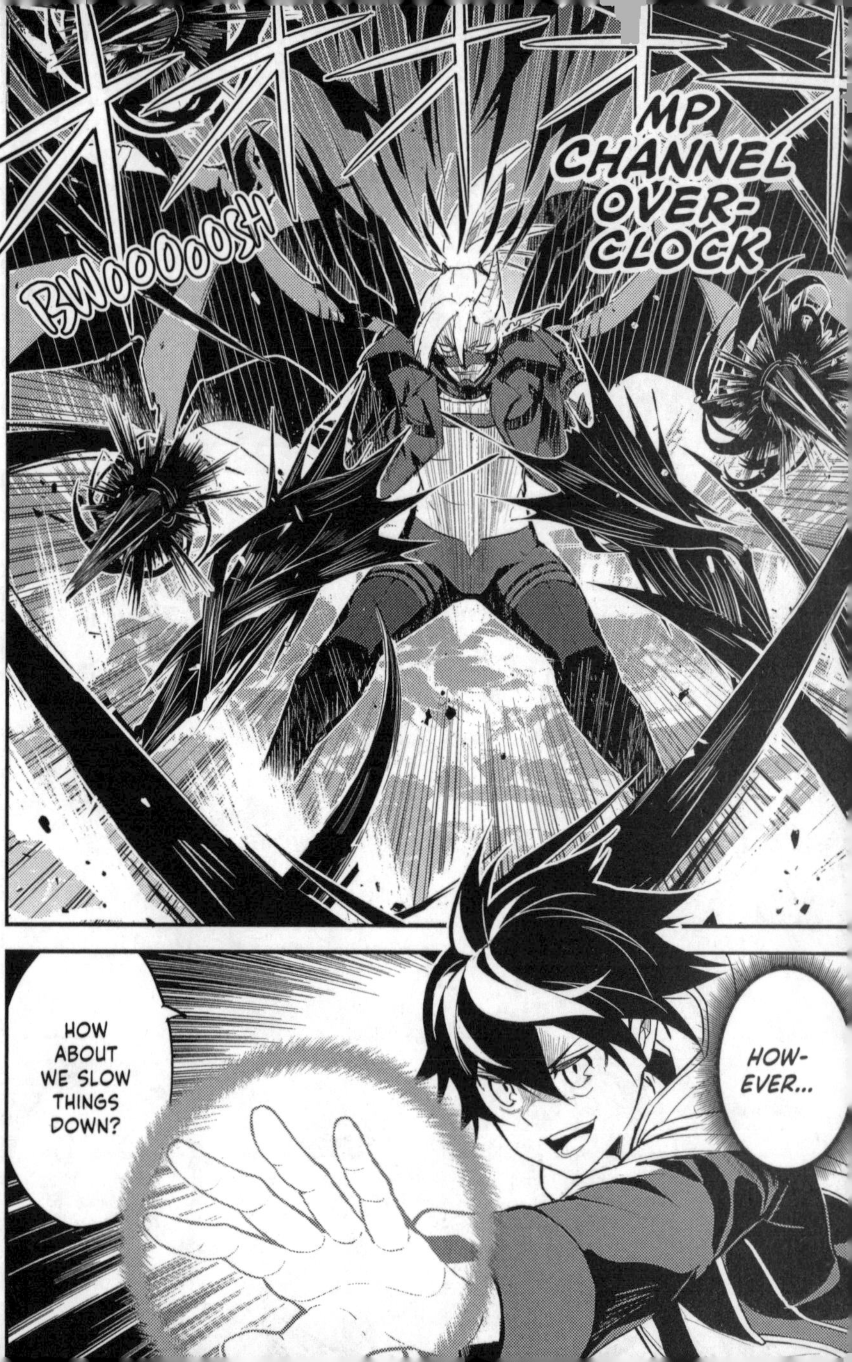
MP CHANNEL OVER-CLOCK
BWOOOOOSH
HOW-EVER...
HOW ABOUT WE SLOW THINGS DOWN?

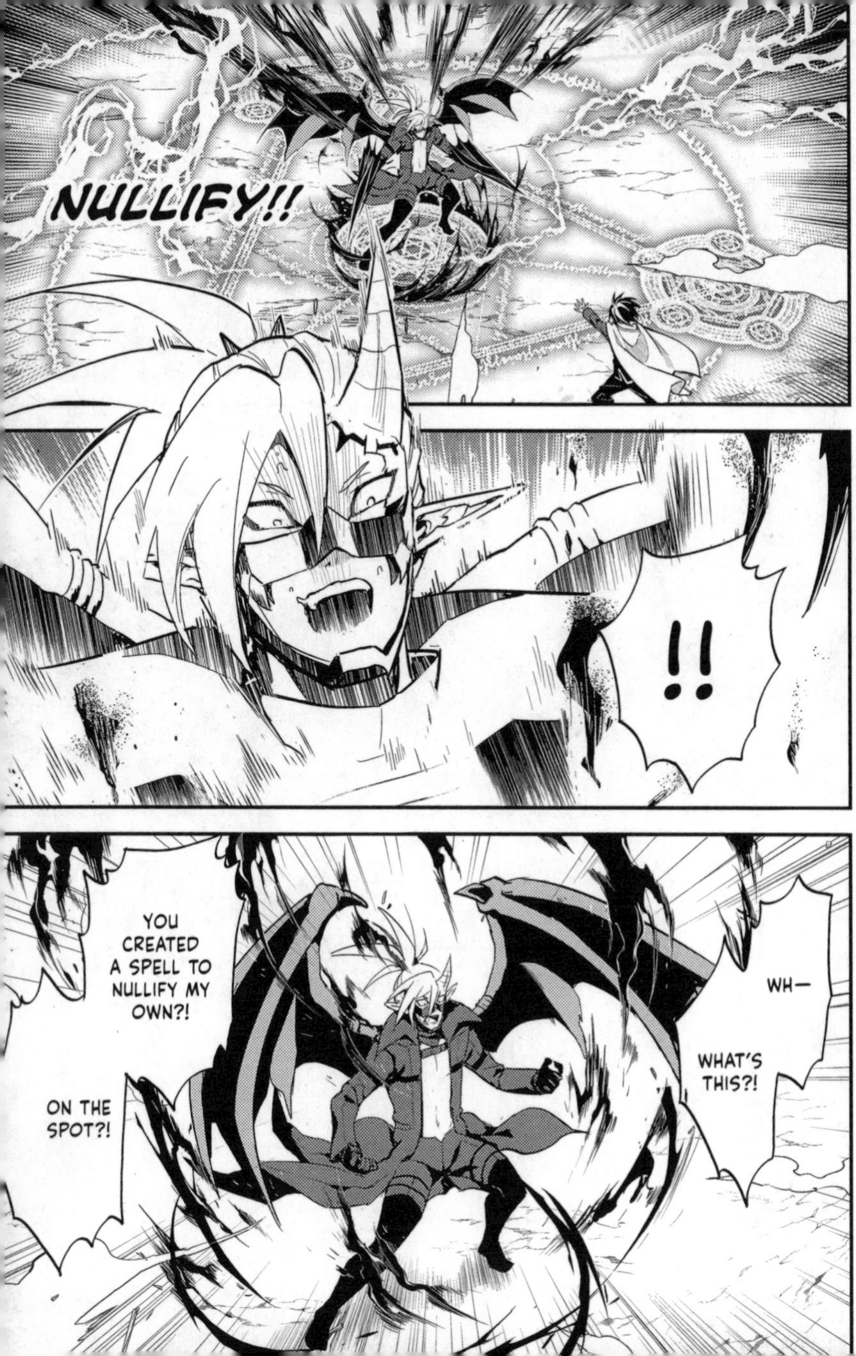
NULLIFY!!
!!
WH—
WHAT'S THIS?!
YOU CREATED A SPELL TO NULLIFY MY OWN?!
ON THE SPOT?!

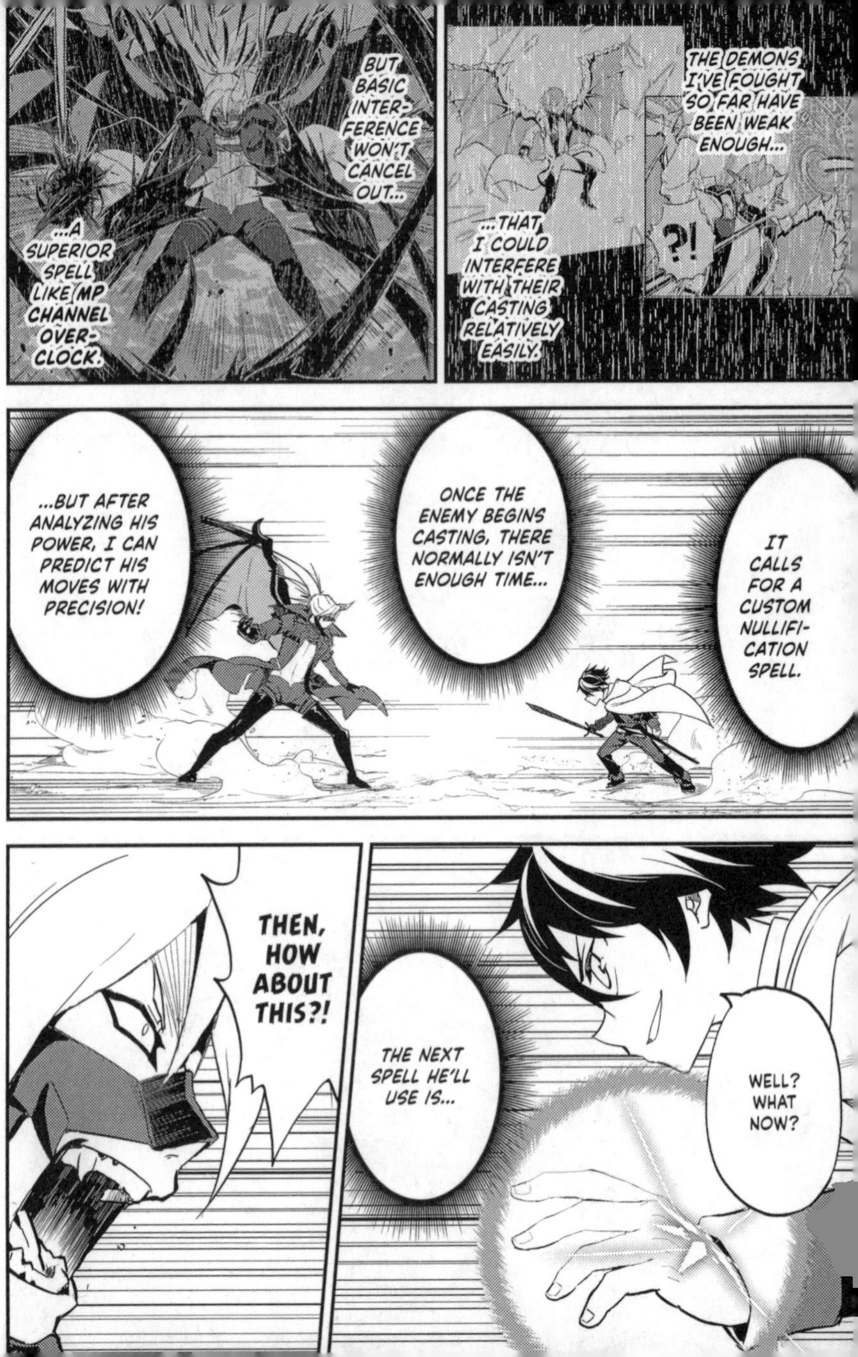
THE DEMONS I'VE FOUGHT SO FAR HAVE BEEN WEAK ENOUGH...
?!
...THAT I COULD INTERFERE WITH THEIR CASTING RELATIVELY EASILY.
BUT BASIC INTERFERENCE WON'T CANCEL OUT...
...A SUPERIOR SPELL LIKE MP CHANNEL OVERCLOCK.
IT CALLS FOR A CUSTOM NULLIFICATION SPELL.
ONCE THE ENEMY BEGINS CASTING, THERE NORMALLY ISN'T ENOUGH TIME...
...BUT AFTER ANALYZING HIS POWER, I CAN PREDICT HIS MOVES WITH PRECISION!
WELL? WHAT NOW?
THE NEXT SPELL HE'LL USE IS...
THEN, HOW ABOUT THIS?!

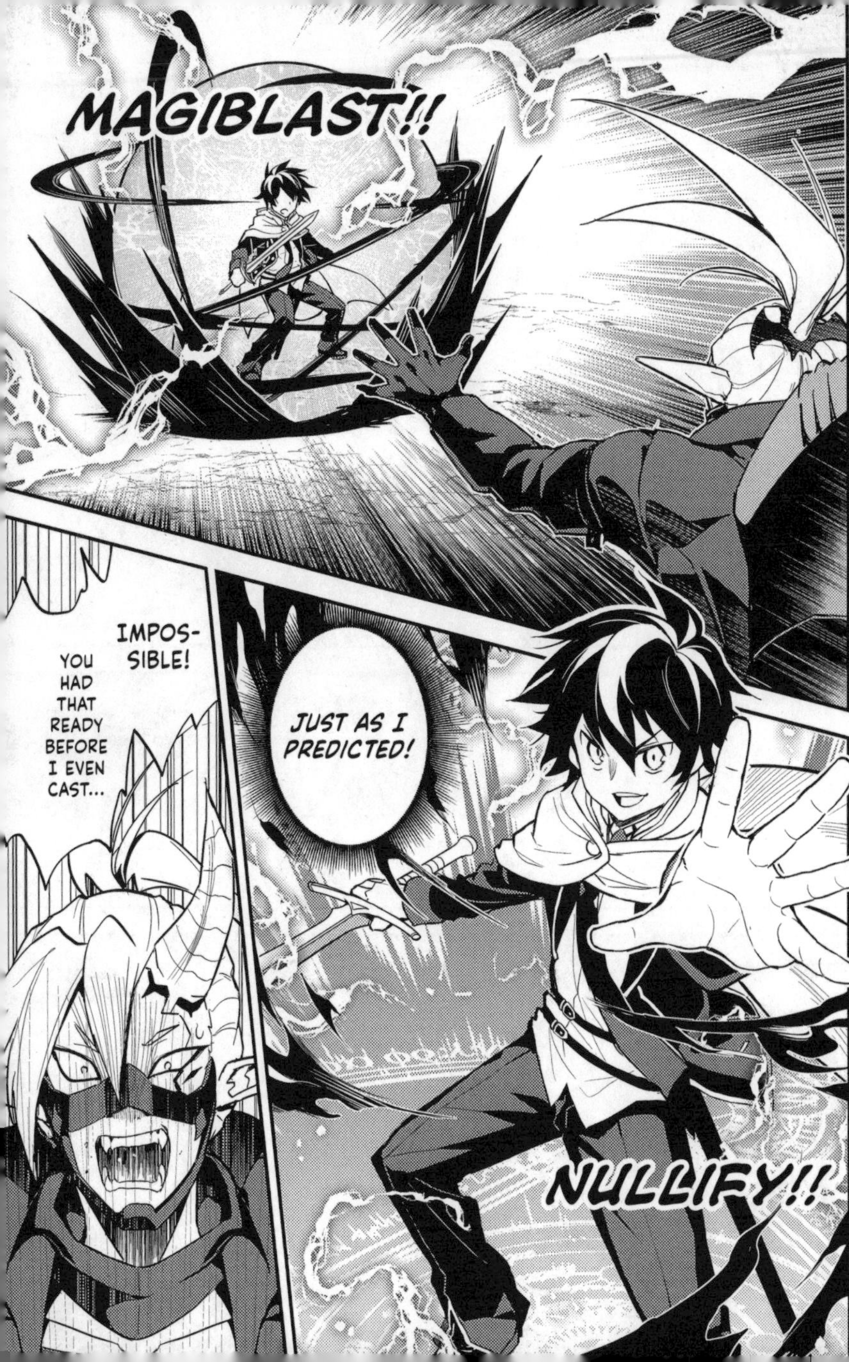
MAGIBLAST!!
JUST AS I PREDICTED!
NULLIFY!!
IMPOS-SIBLE!
YOU HAD THAT READY BEFORE I EVEN CAST...

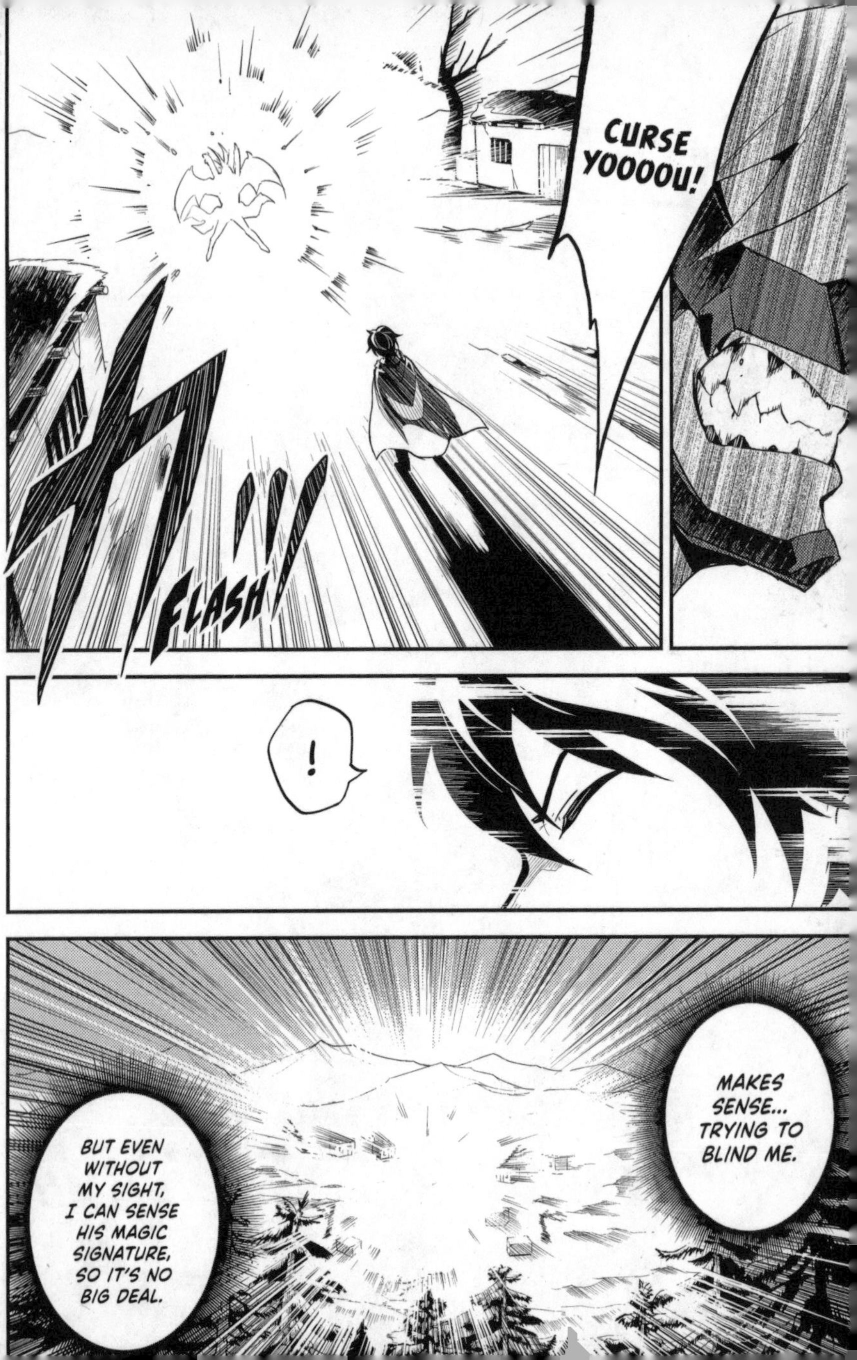
CURSE YOOOOU!
FLASH
!
MAKES SENSE... TRYING TO BLIND ME.
BUT EVEN WITHOUT MY SIGHT, I CAN SENSE HIS MAGIC SIGNATURE, SO IT'S NO BIG DEAL.

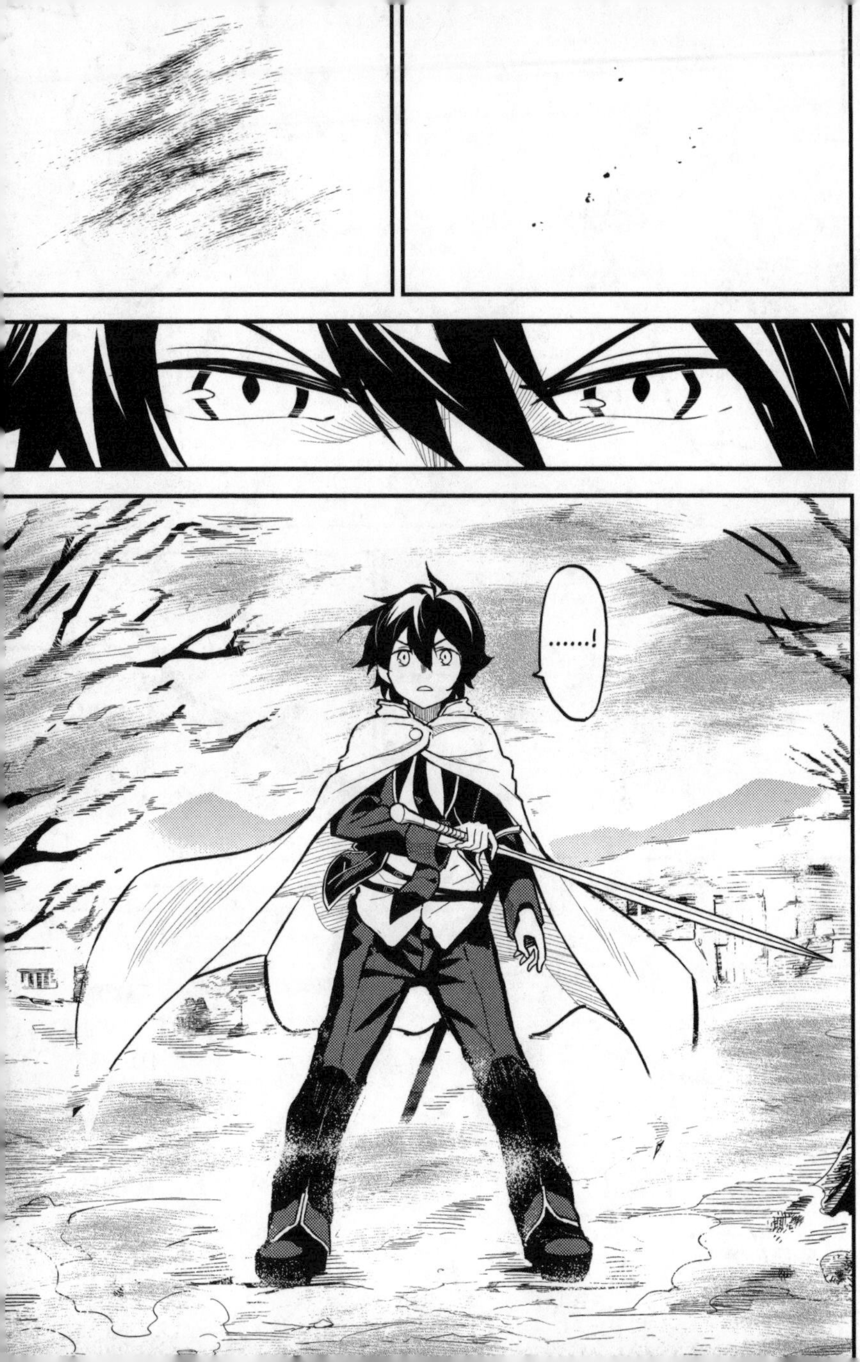
......!

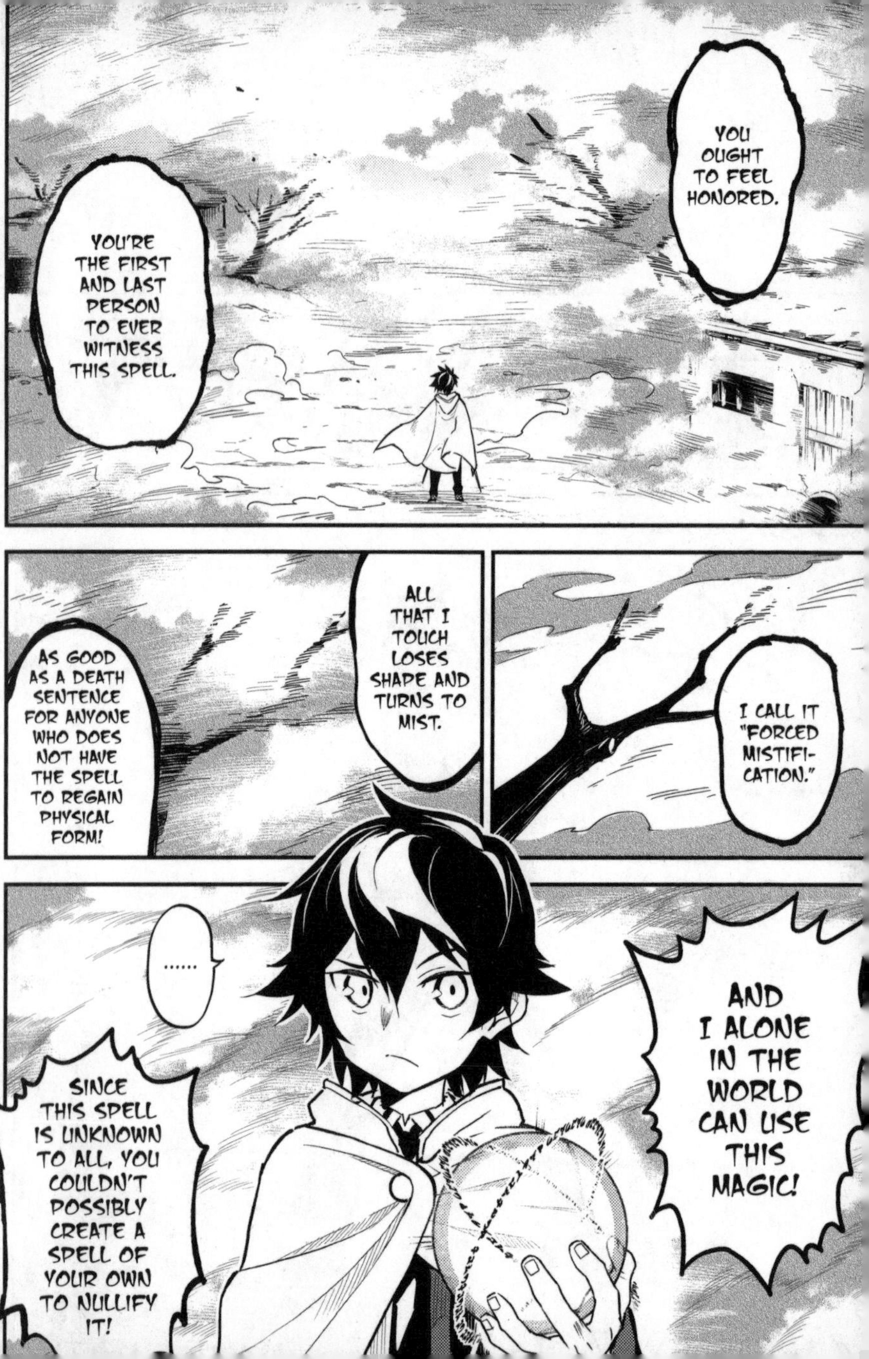
YOU OUGHT TO FEEL HONORED.
YOU'RE THE FIRST AND LAST PERSON TO EVER WITNESS THIS SPELL.
I CALL IT "FORCED MISTIFI-CATION."
ALL THAT I TOUCH LOSES SHAPE AND TURNS TO MIST.
AS GOOD AS A DEATH SENTENCE FOR ANYONE WHO DOES NOT HAVE THE SPELL TO REGAIN PHYSICAL FORM!
AND I ALONE IN THE WORLD CAN USE THIS MAGIC!
......
SINCE THIS SPELL IS UNKNOWN TO ALL, YOU COULDN'T POSSIBLY CREATE A SPELL OF YOUR OWN TO NULLIFY IT!

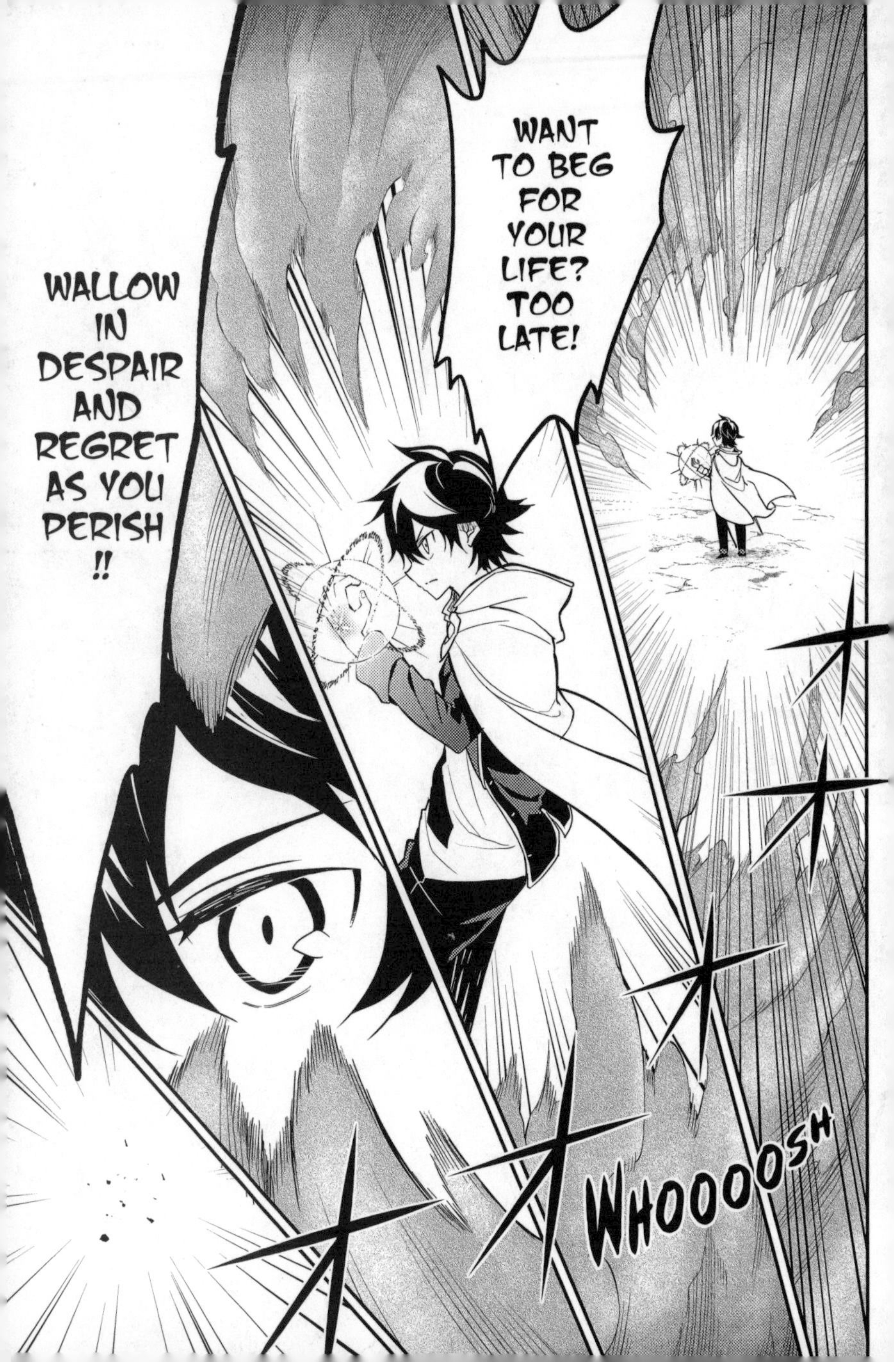
WANT TO BEG FOR YOUR LIFE? TOO LATE!
WALLOW IN DESPAIR AND REGRET AS YOU PERISH!!
WHOOOOOSH

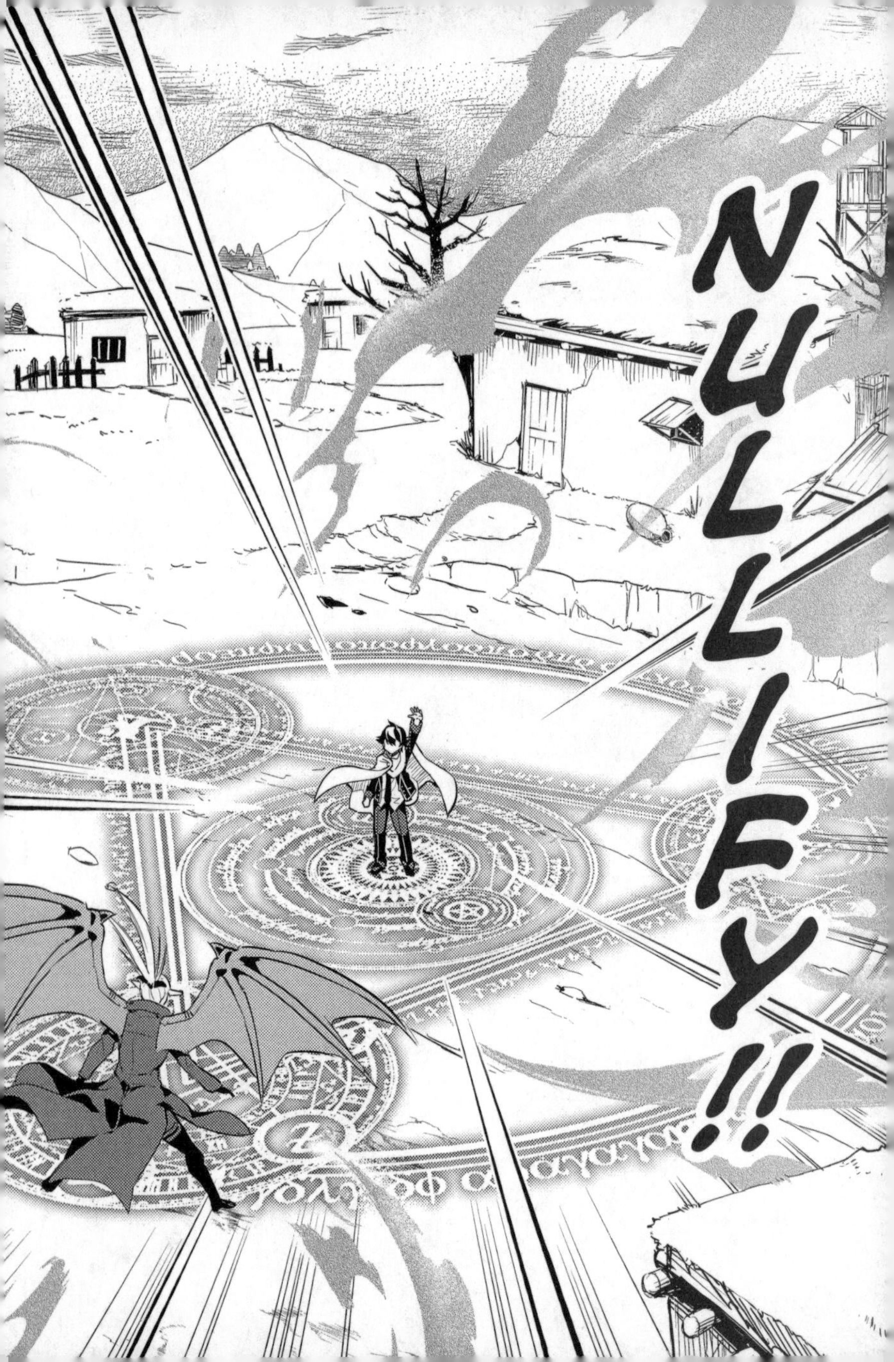
NULLIFY!!

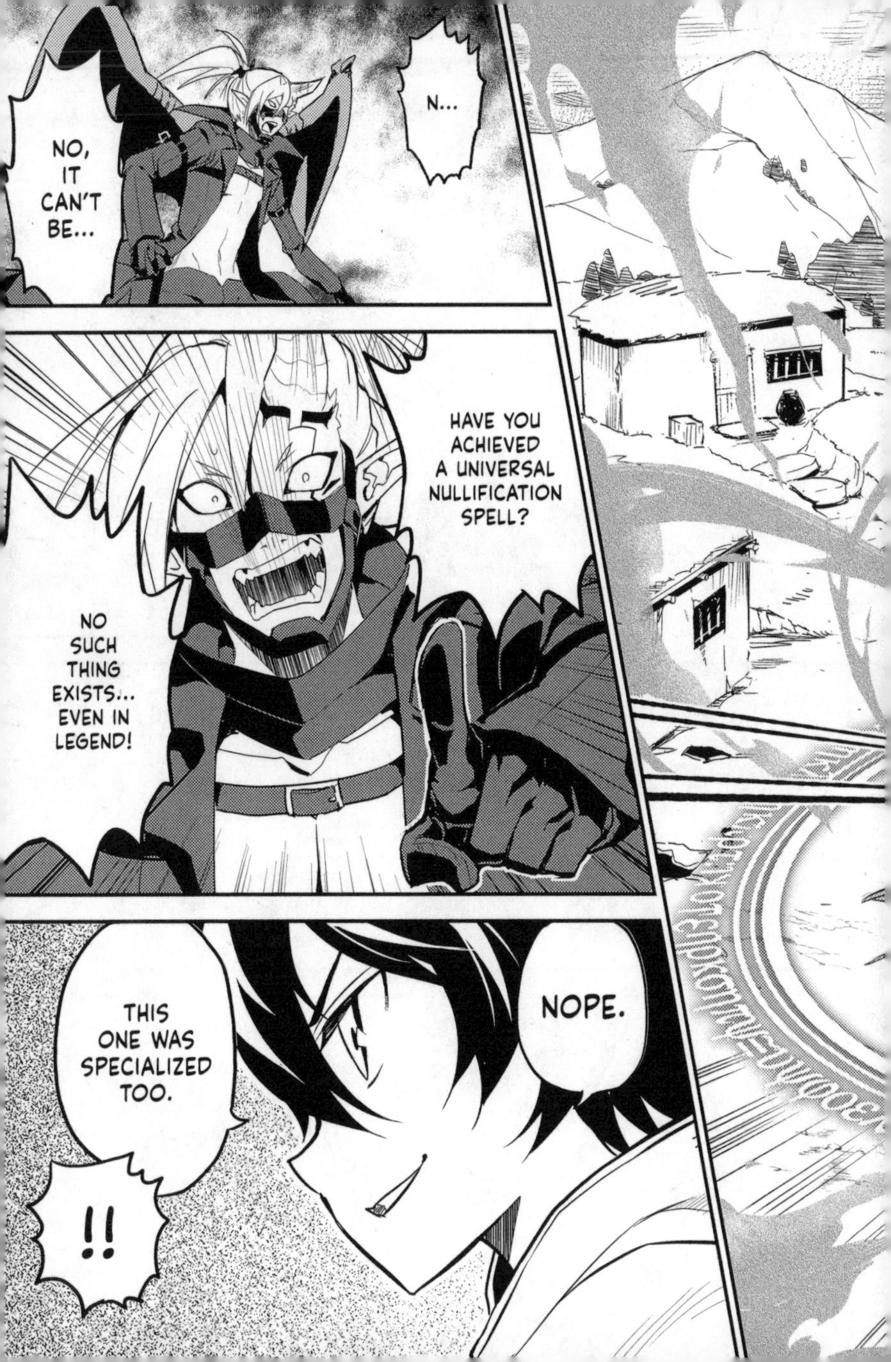
N...
NO, IT CAN'T BE...
HAVE YOU ACHIEVED A UNIVERSAL NULLIFICATION SPELL?
NO SUCH THING EXISTS... EVEN IN LEGEND!
NOPE.
THIS ONE WAS SPECIALIZED TOO.
!!

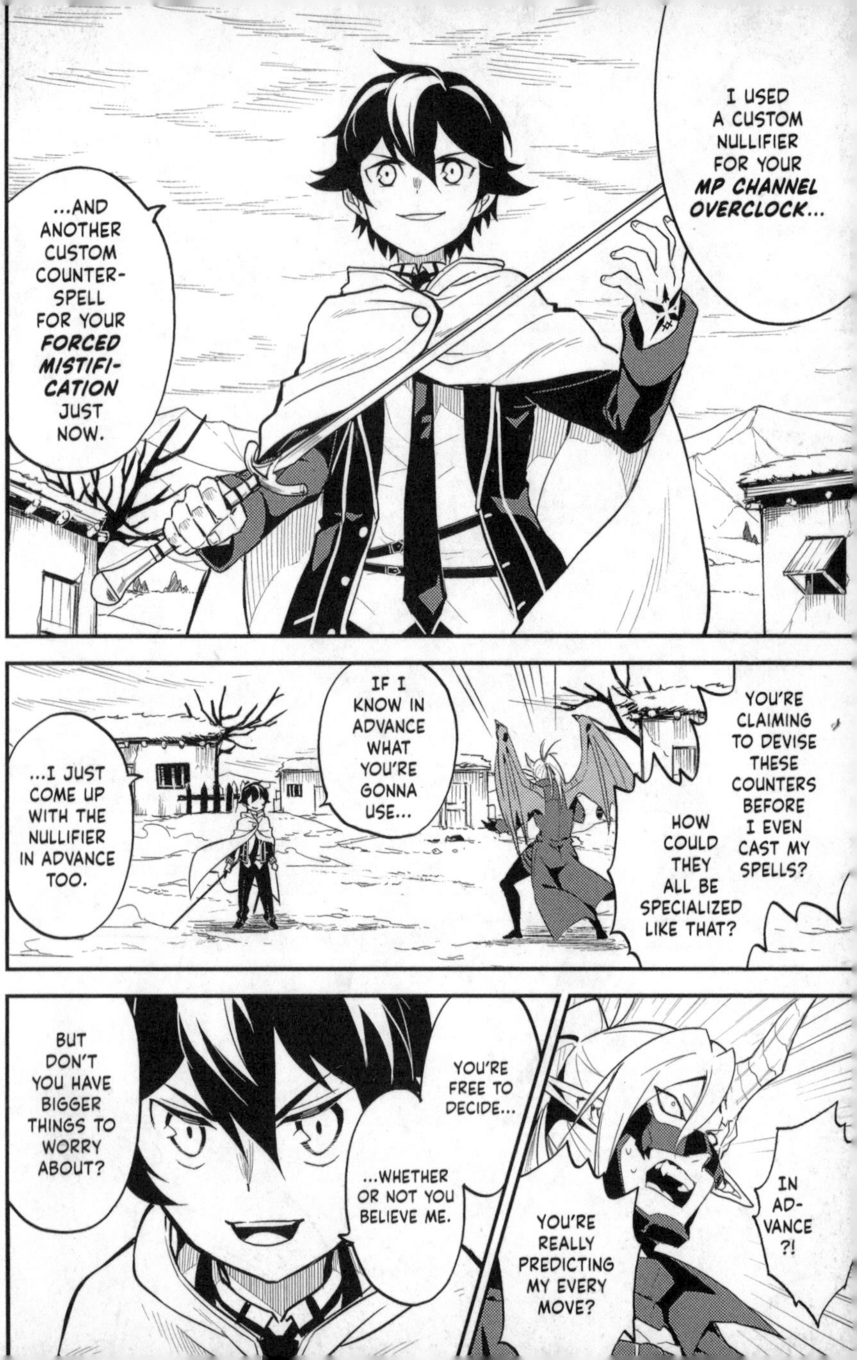
I USED A CUSTOM NULLIFIER FOR YOUR **MP CHANNEL OVERCLOCK**...
...AND ANOTHER CUSTOM COUNTER-SPELL FOR YOUR **FORCED MISTIFICATION** JUST NOW.
YOU'RE CLAIMING TO DEVISE THESE COUNTERS BEFORE I EVEN CAST MY SPELLS?
HOW COULD THEY ALL BE SPECIALIZED LIKE THAT?
IF I KNOW IN ADVANCE WHAT YOU'RE GONNA USE...
...I JUST COME UP WITH THE NULLIFIER IN ADVANCE TOO.
IN ADVANCE?!
YOU'RE REALLY PREDICTING MY EVERY MOVE?
YOU'RE FREE TO DECIDE...
...WHETHER OR NOT YOU BELIEVE ME.
BUT DON'T YOU HAVE BIGGER THINGS TO WORRY ABOUT?

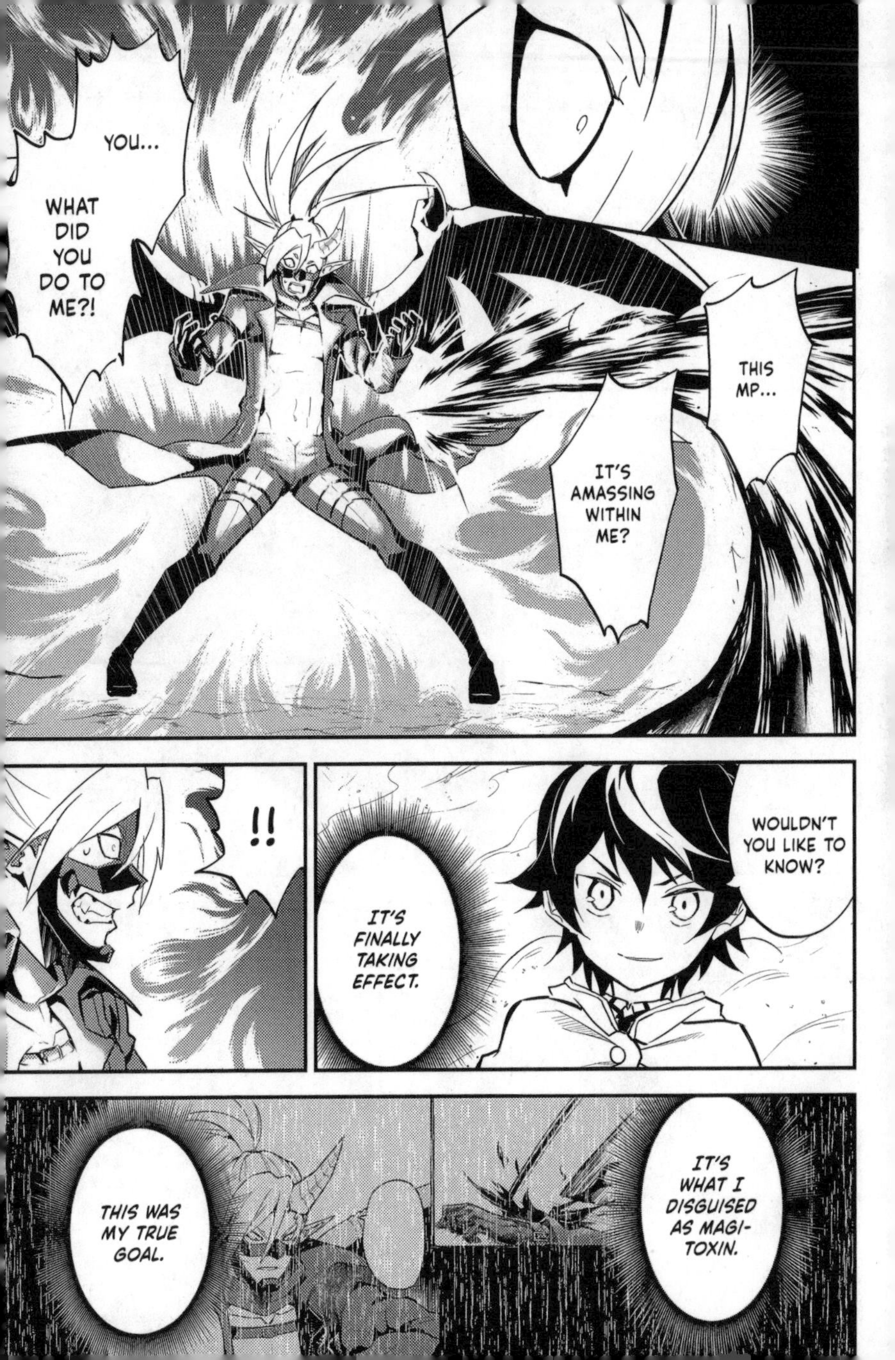
THIS MP...
IT'S AMASSING WITHIN ME?
YOU...
WHAT DID YOU DO TO ME?!
WOULDN'T YOU LIKE TO KNOW?
IT'S FINALLY TAKING EFFECT.
!!
IT'S WHAT I DISGUISED AS MAGI-TOXIN.
THIS WAS MY TRUE GOAL.

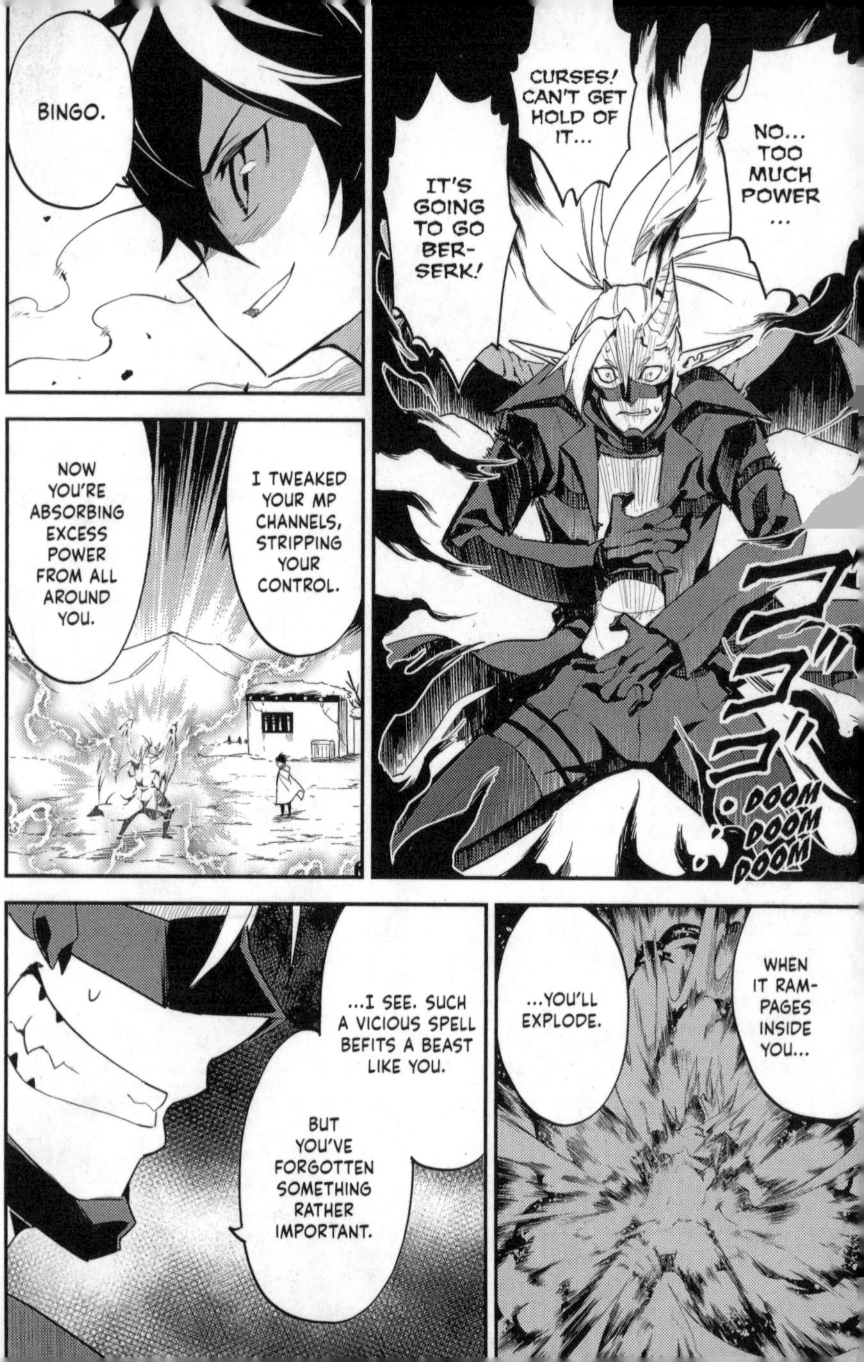
NO... TOO MUCH POWER ...
CURSES! CAN'T GET HOLD OF IT...
IT'S GOING TO GO BER-SERK!
DOOM DOOM DOOM
BINGO.
I TWEAKED YOUR MP CHANNELS, STRIPPING YOUR CONTROL.
NOW YOU'RE ABSORBING EXCESS POWER FROM ALL AROUND YOU.
WHEN IT RAM-PAGES INSIDE YOU...
...YOU'LL EXPLODE.
...I SEE. SUCH A VICIOUS SPELL BEFITS A BEAST LIKE YOU.
BUT YOU'VE FORGOTTEN SOMETHING RATHER IMPORTANT.

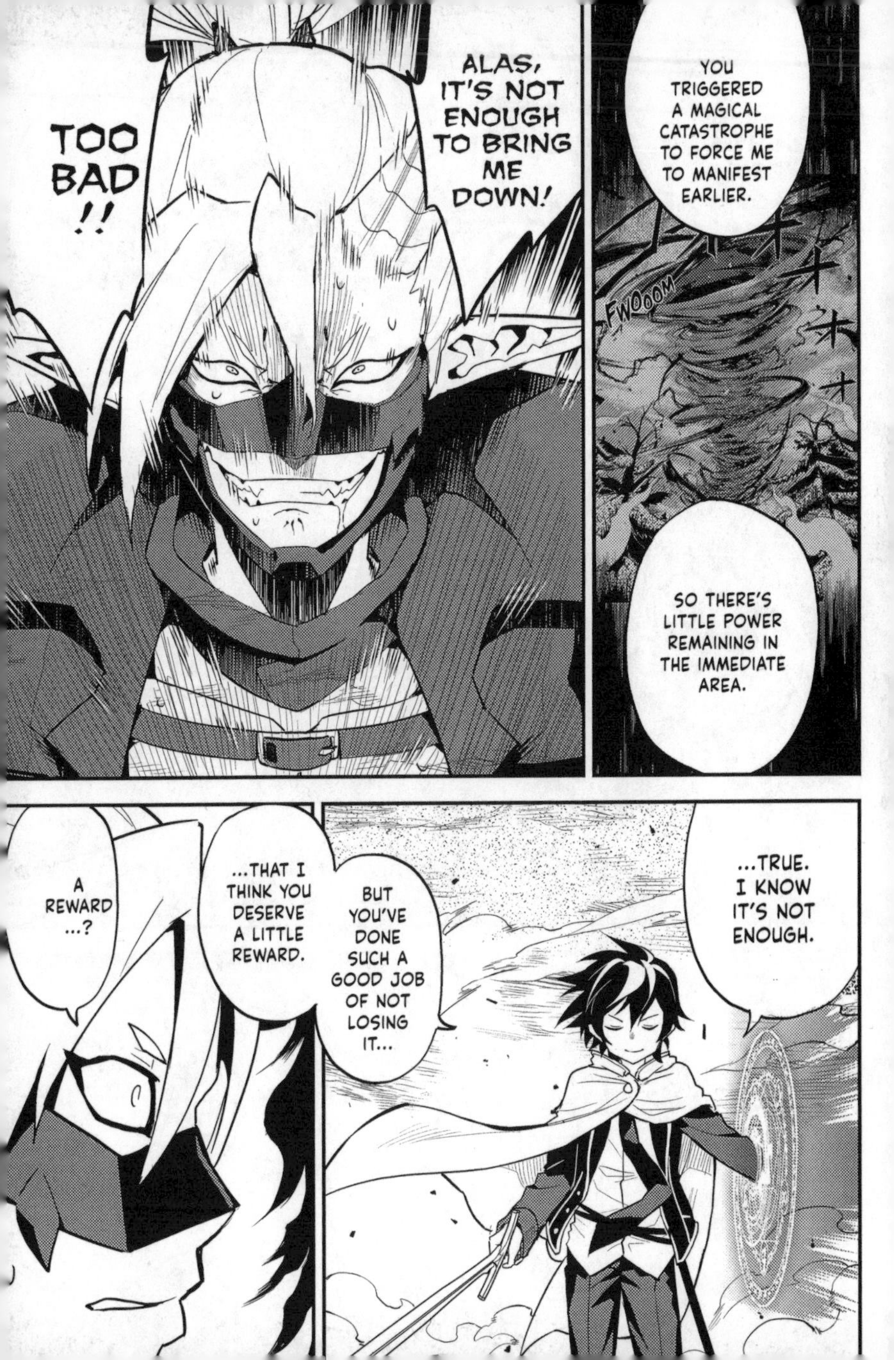
YOU TRIGGERED A MAGICAL CATASTROPHE TO FORCE ME TO MANIFEST EARLIER.
FWOOOM
SO THERE'S LITTLE POWER REMAINING IN THE IMMEDIATE AREA.
ALAS, IT'S NOT ENOUGH TO BRING ME DOWN!
TOO BAD!!
...TRUE. I KNOW IT'S NOT ENOUGH.
BUT YOU'VE DONE SUCH A GOOD JOB OF NOT LOSING IT...
...THAT I THINK YOU DESERVE A LITTLE REWARD.
A REWARD ...?

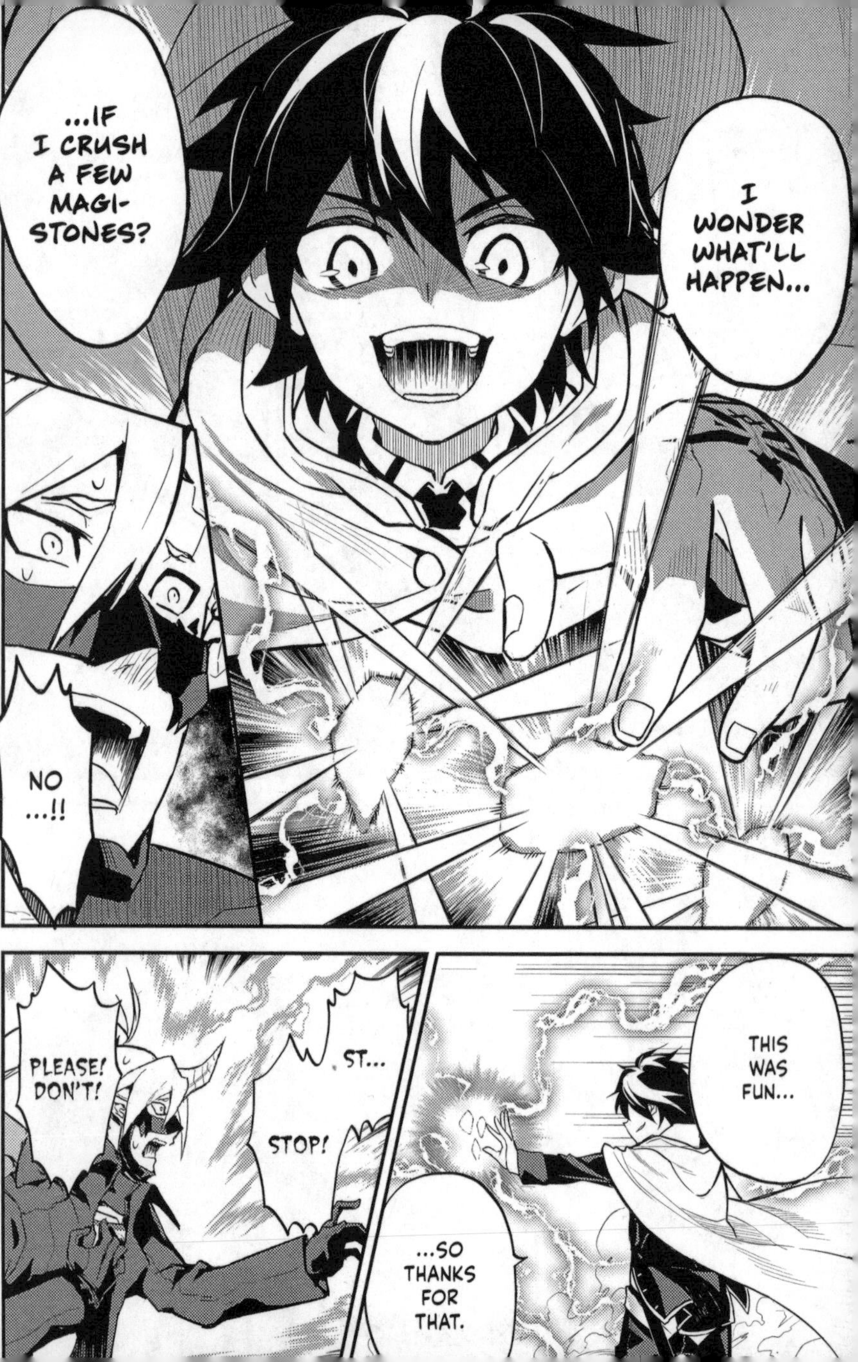
I WONDER WHAT'LL HAPPEN...
...IF I CRUSH A FEW MAGI-STONES?
NO...!!
THIS WAS FUN...
...SO THANKS FOR THAT.
ST...
STOP!
PLEASE! DON'T!

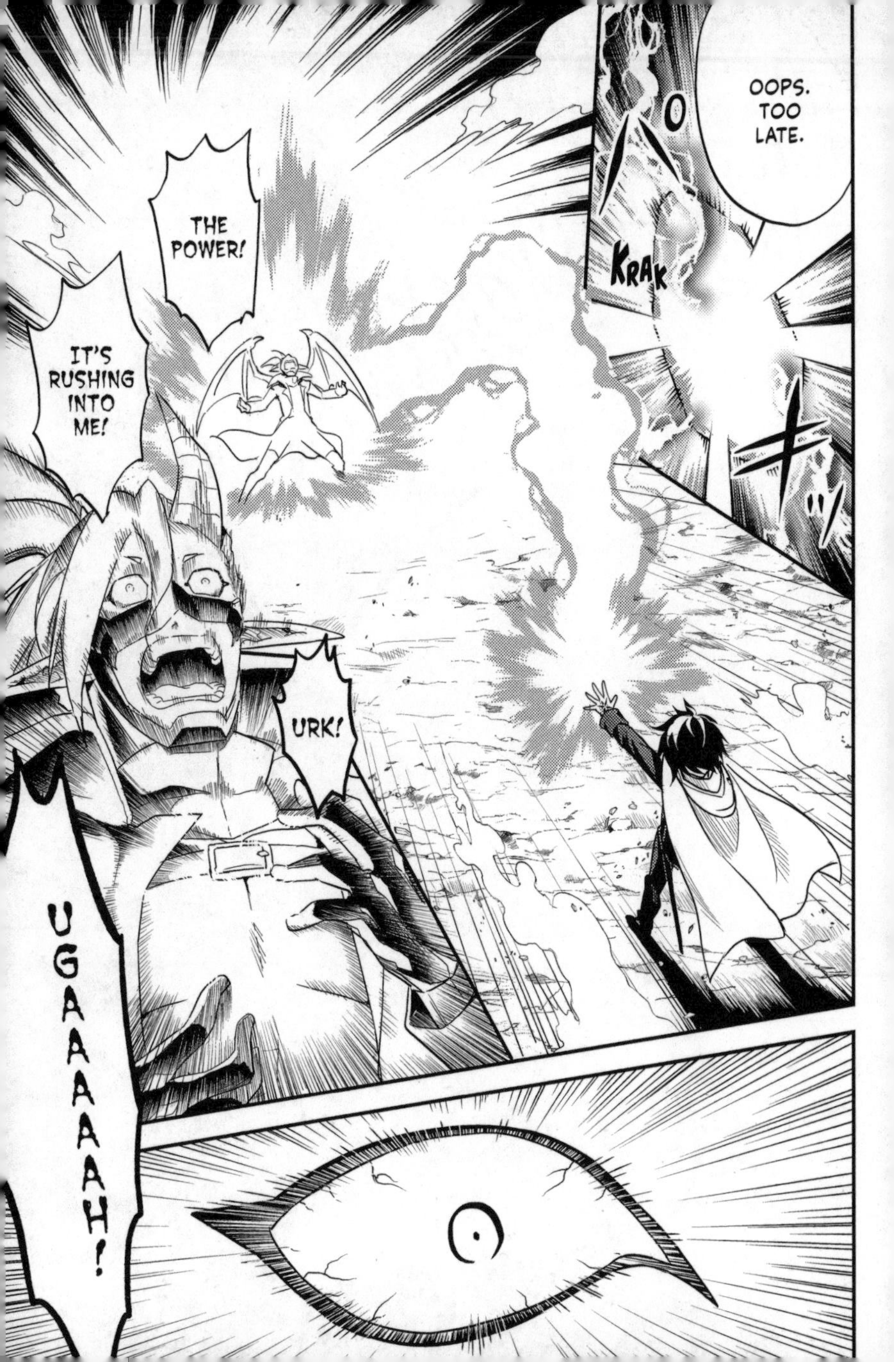
OOPS. TOO LATE.
KRAK
THE POWER!
IT'S RUSHING INTO ME!
URK!
UGAAAAAAH!

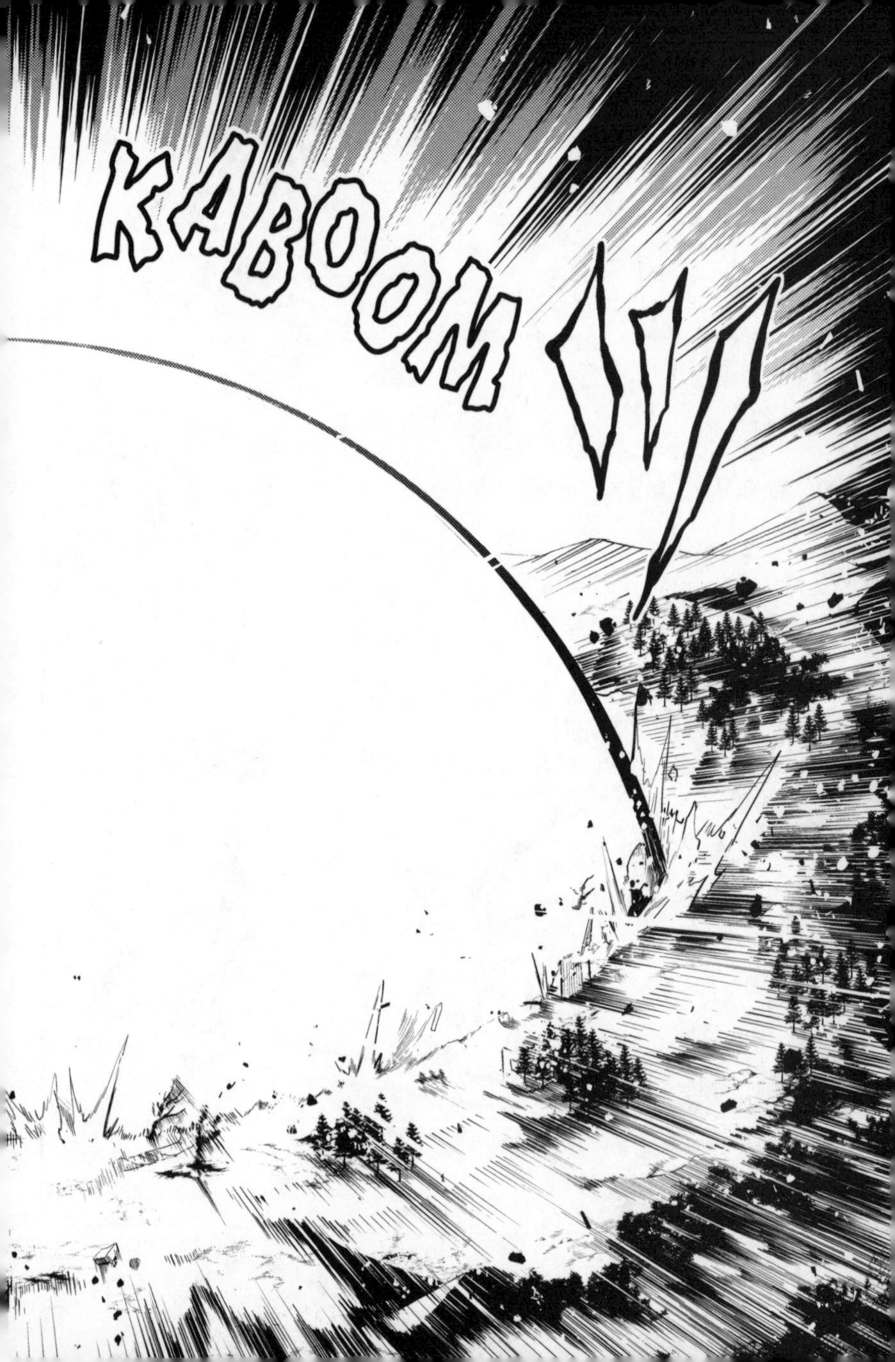
KABOOM

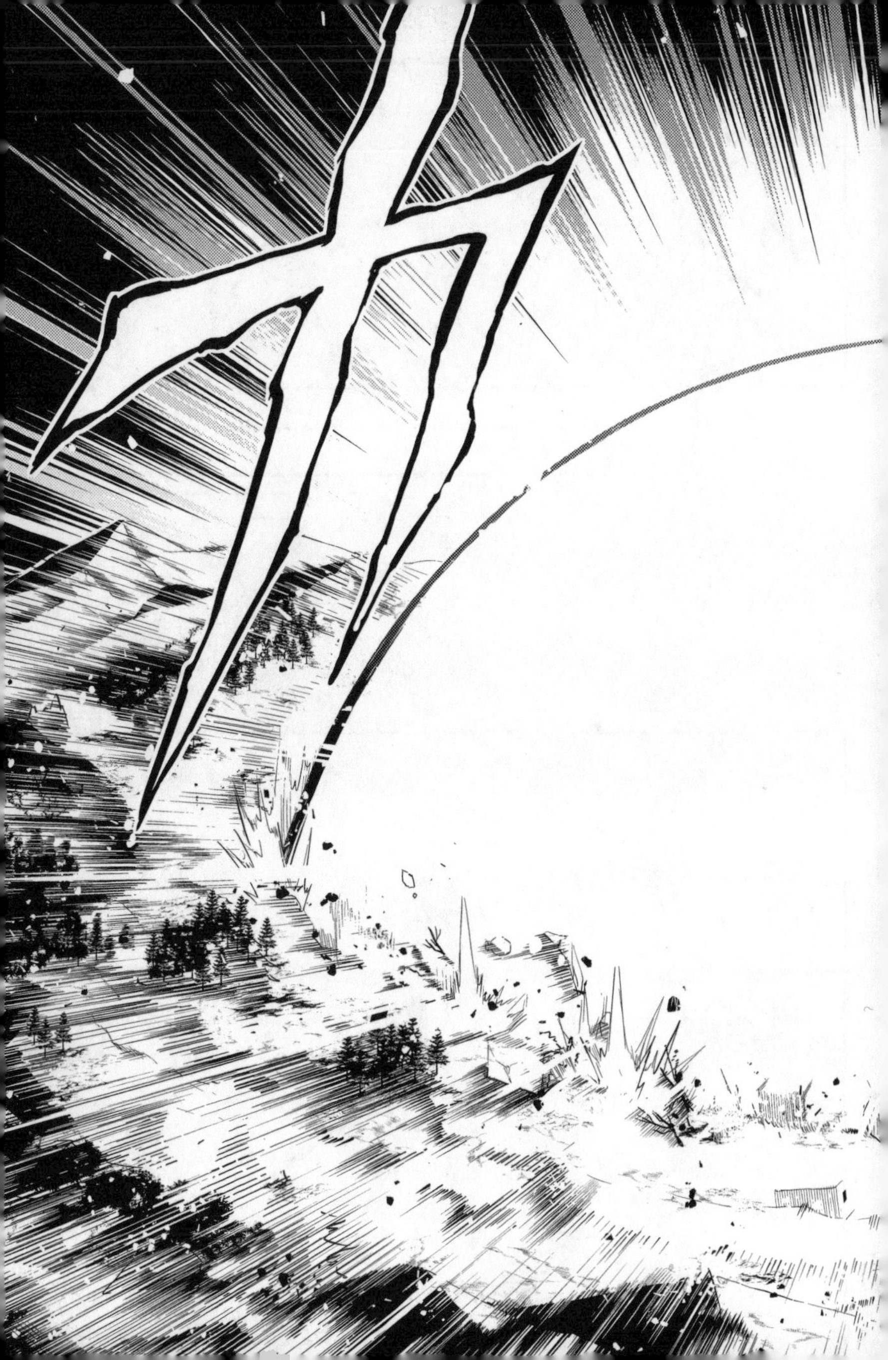

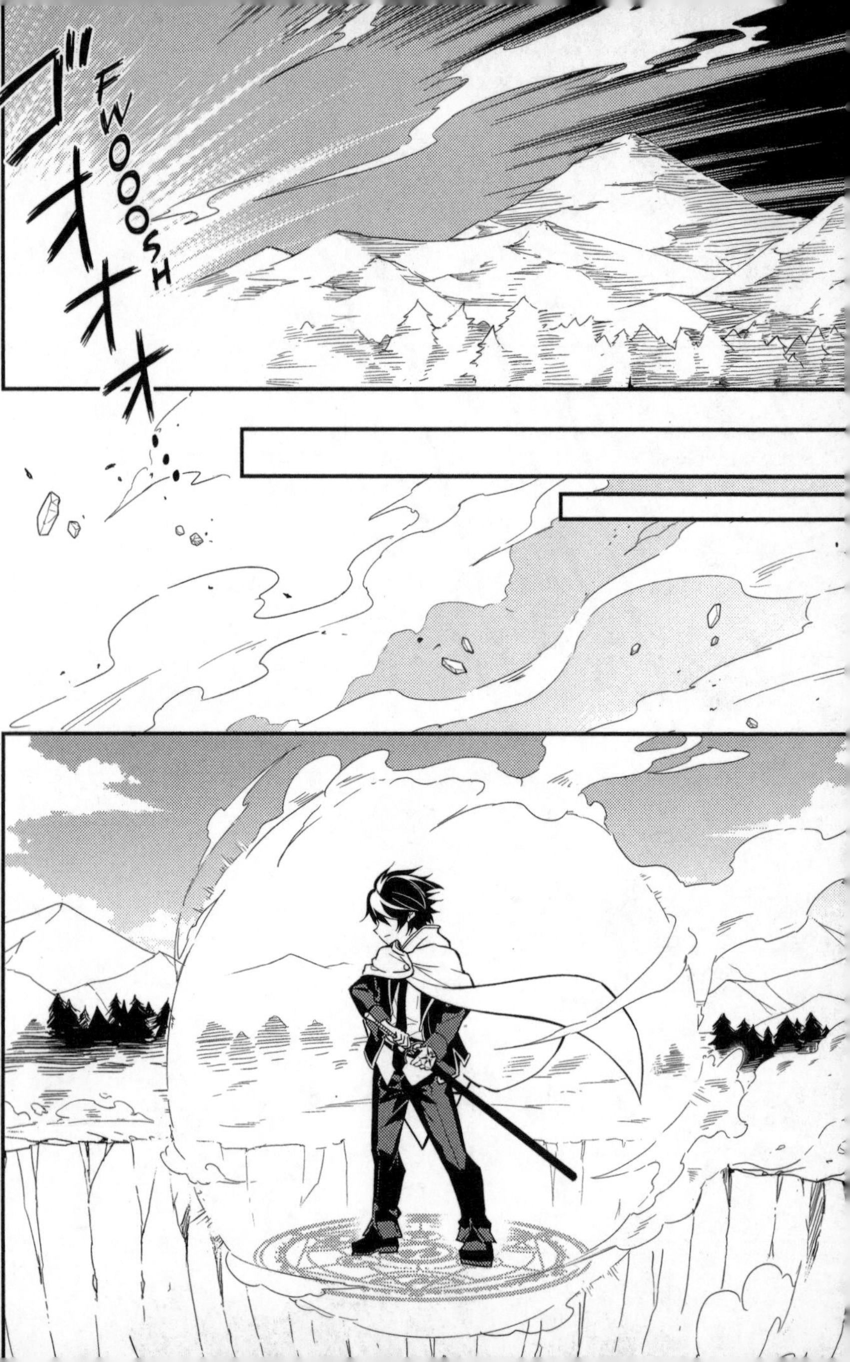
ゴオオオ
FWOOOSH

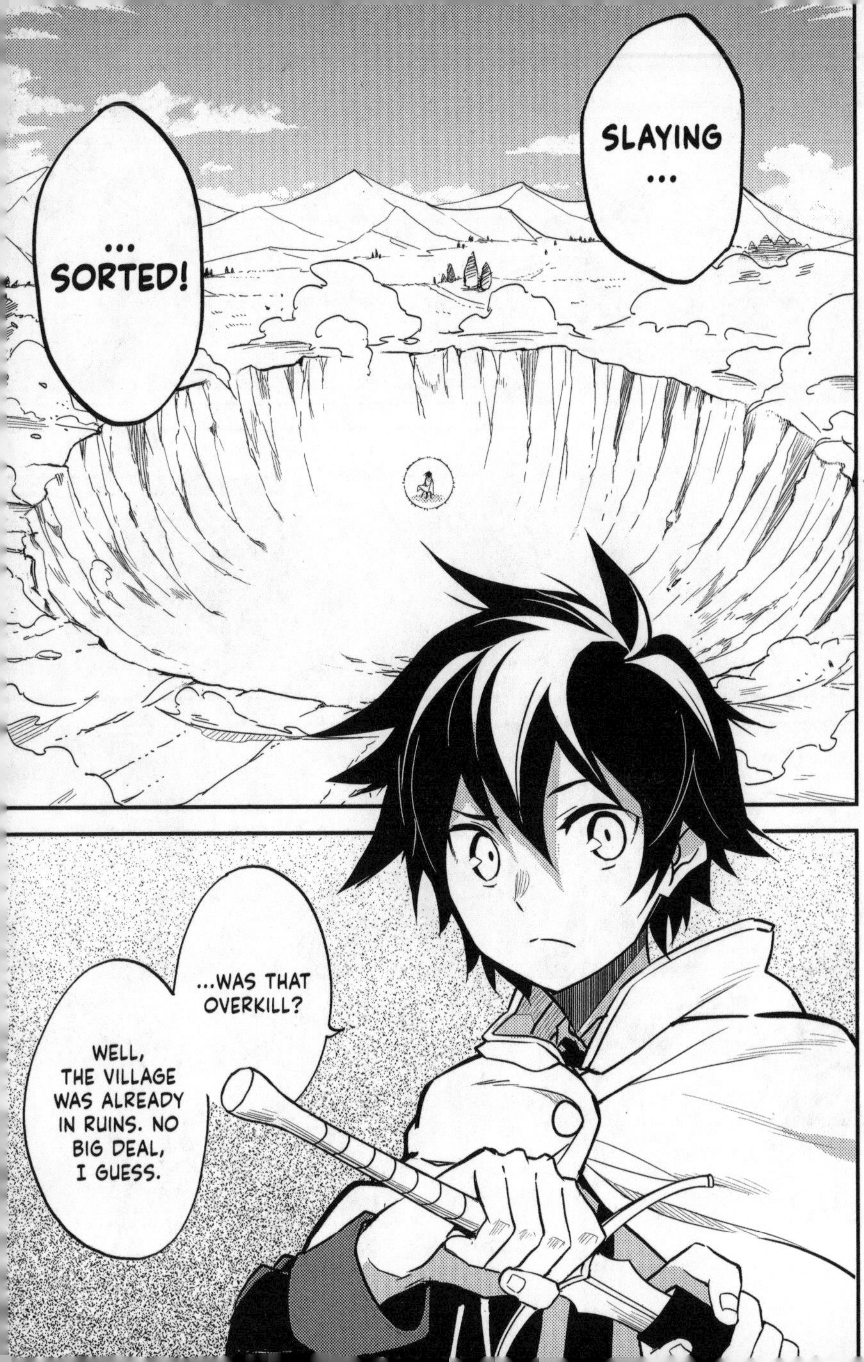
SLAYING ...
... SORTED!
...WAS THAT OVERKILL?
WELL, THE VILLAGE WAS ALREADY IN RUINS. NO BIG DEAL, I GUESS.

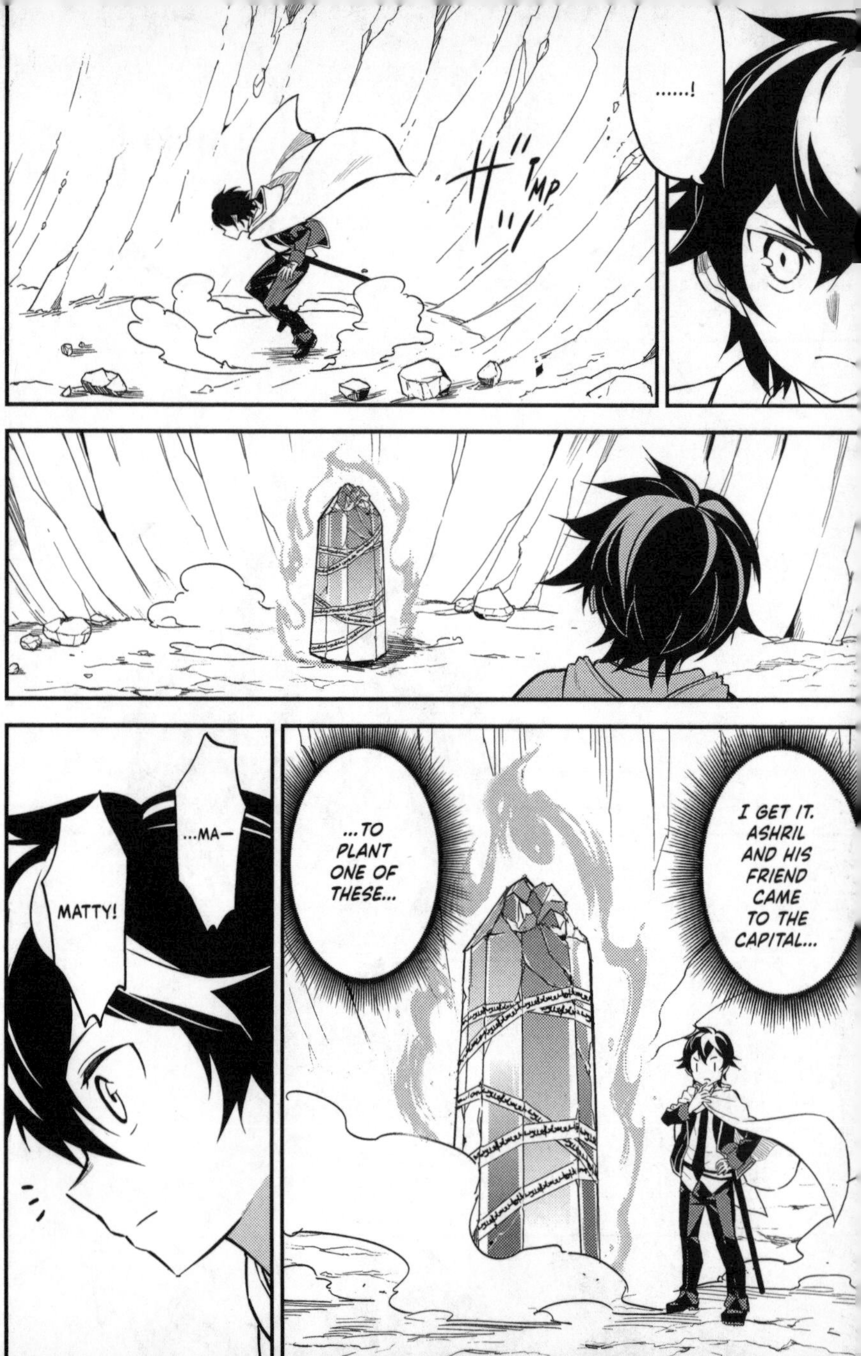
......!
TMP
I GET IT. ASHRIL AND HIS FRIEND CAME TO THE CAPITAL...
...TO PLANT ONE OF THESE...
...MA—
MATTY!

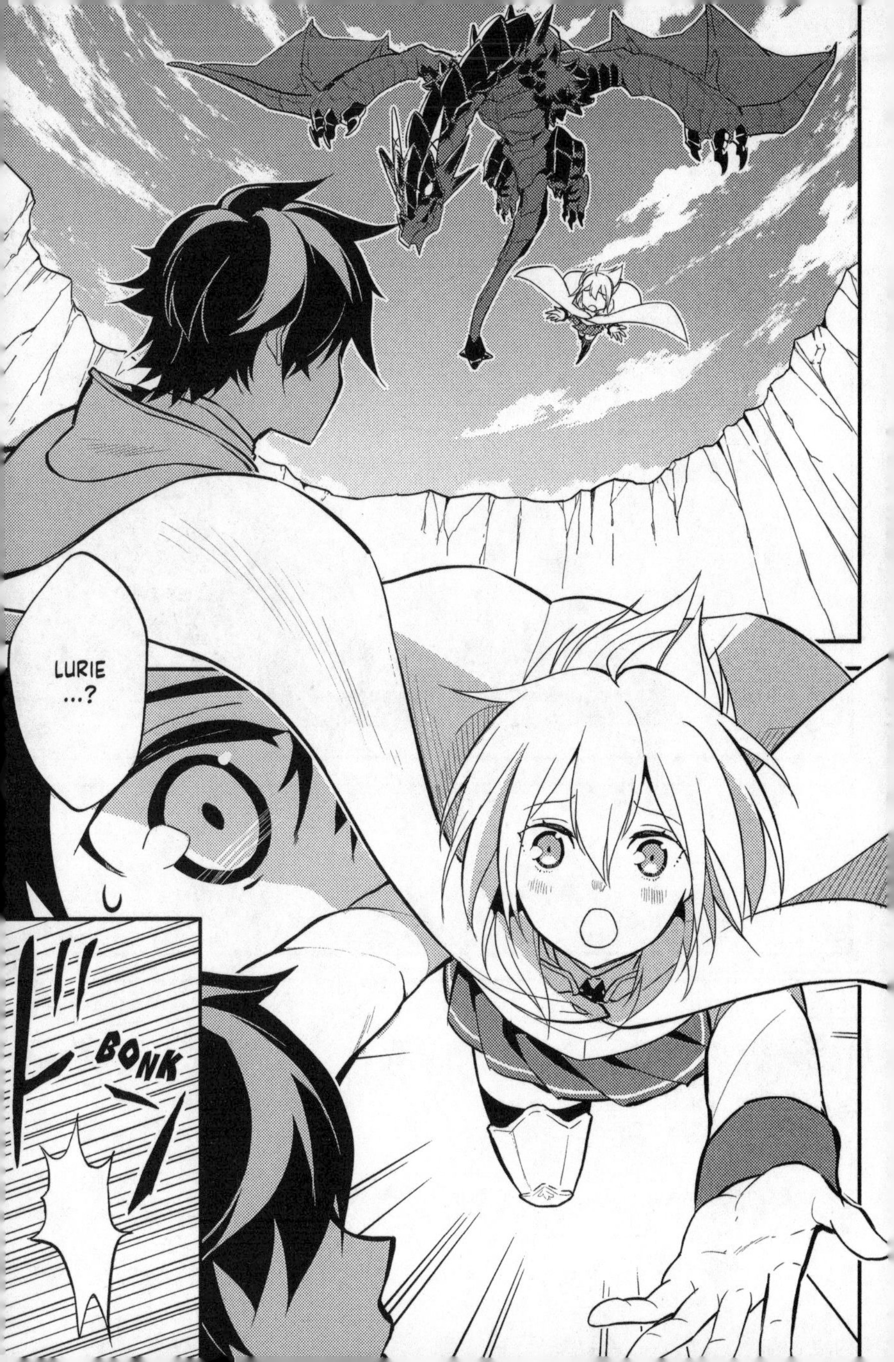
LURIE ...?
BONK

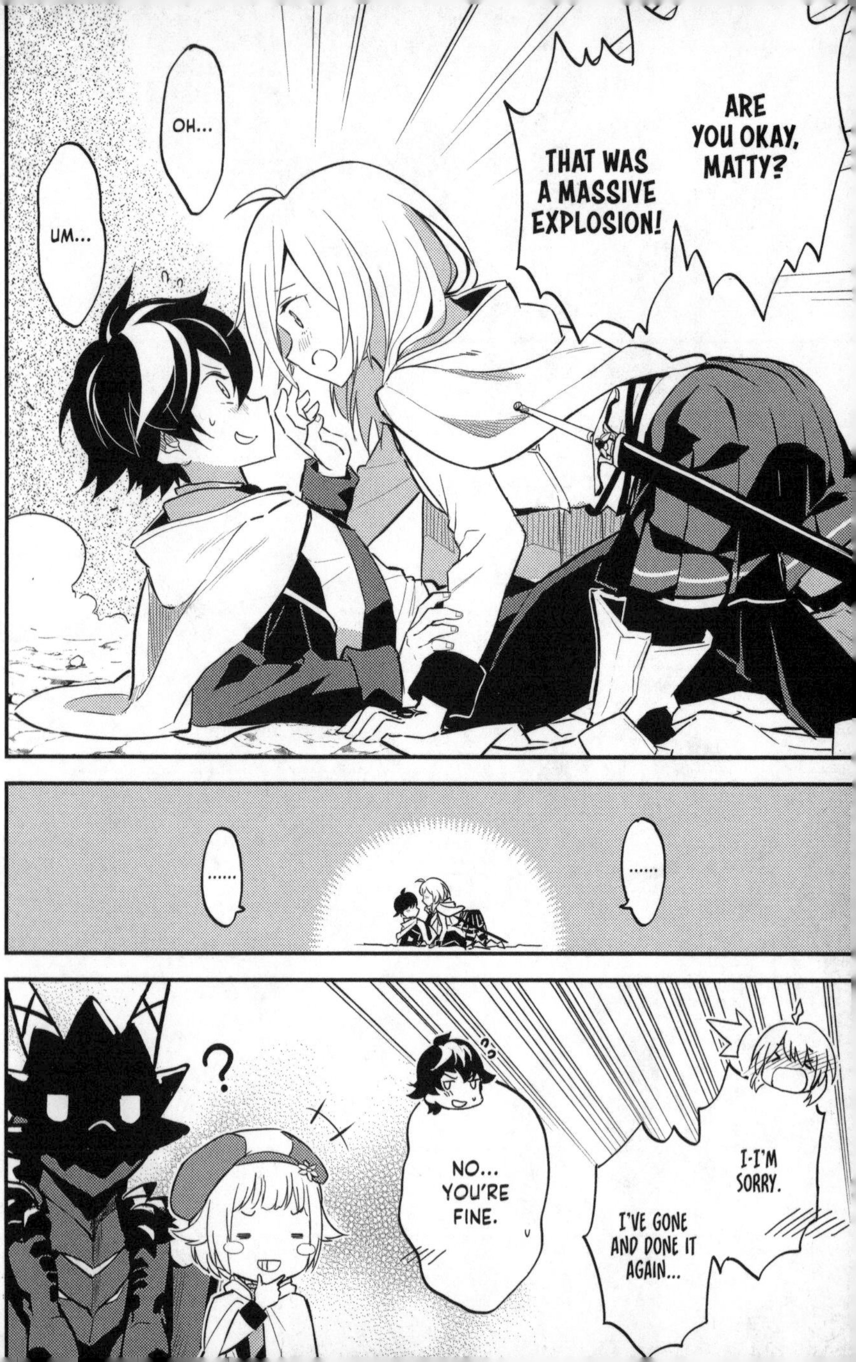
ARE YOU OKAY, MATTY?
THAT WAS A MASSIVE EXPLOSION!
OH...
UM...
......
......
I-I'M SORRY.
I'VE GONE AND DONE IT AGAIN...
NO... YOU'RE FINE.

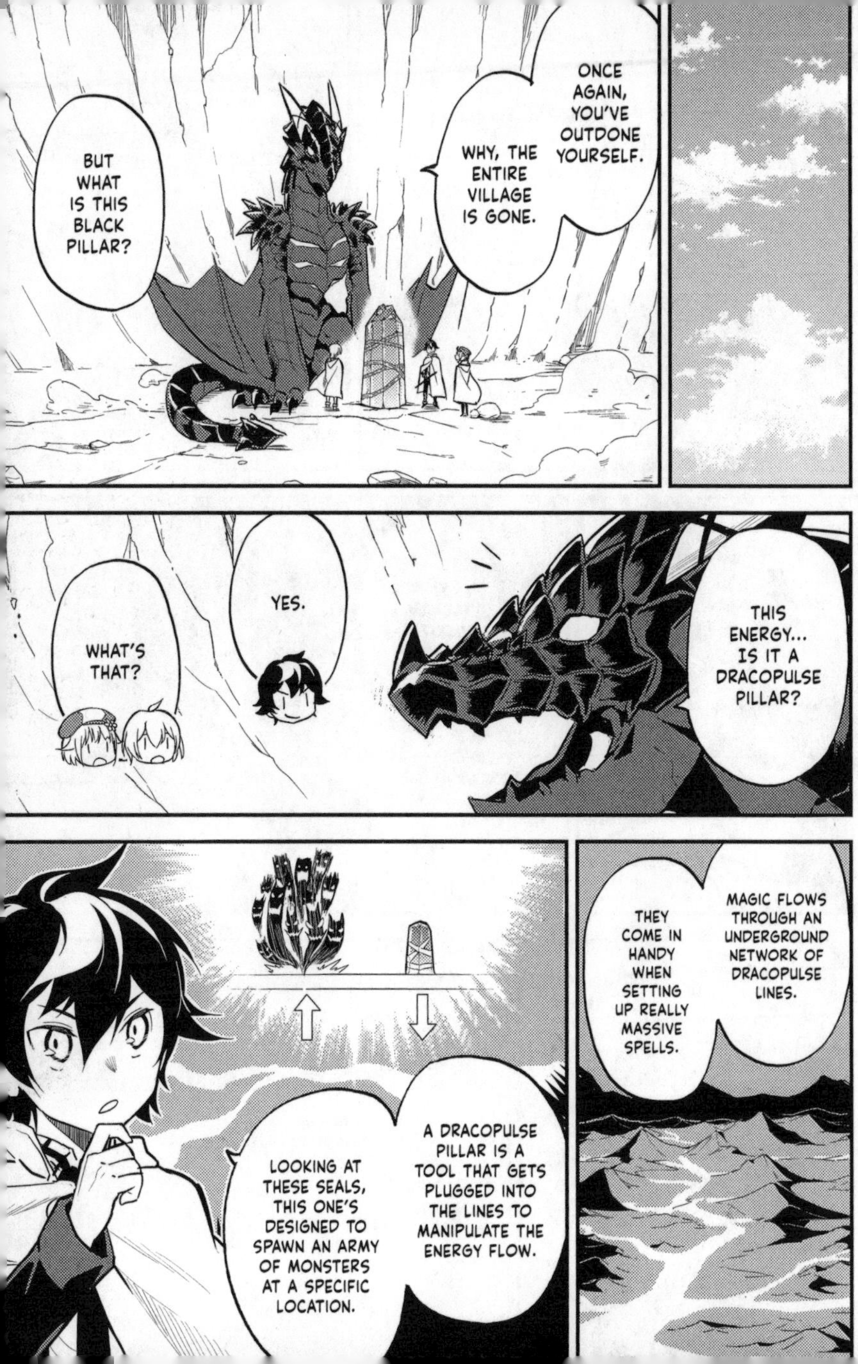

ONCE AGAIN, YOU'VE OUTDONE YOURSELF.
WHY, THE ENTIRE VILLAGE IS GONE.
BUT WHAT IS THIS BLACK PILLAR?
THIS ENERGY... IS IT A DRACOPULSE PILLAR?
YES.
WHAT'S THAT?
MAGIC FLOWS THROUGH AN UNDERGROUND NETWORK OF DRACOPULSE LINES.
THEY COME IN HANDY WHEN SETTING UP REALLY MASSIVE SPELLS.
A DRACOPULSE PILLAR IS A TOOL THAT GETS PLUGGED INTO THE LINES TO MANIPULATE THE ENERGY FLOW.
LOOKING AT THESE SEALS, THIS ONE'S DESIGNED TO SPAWN AN ARMY OF MONSTERS AT A SPECIFIC LOCATION.

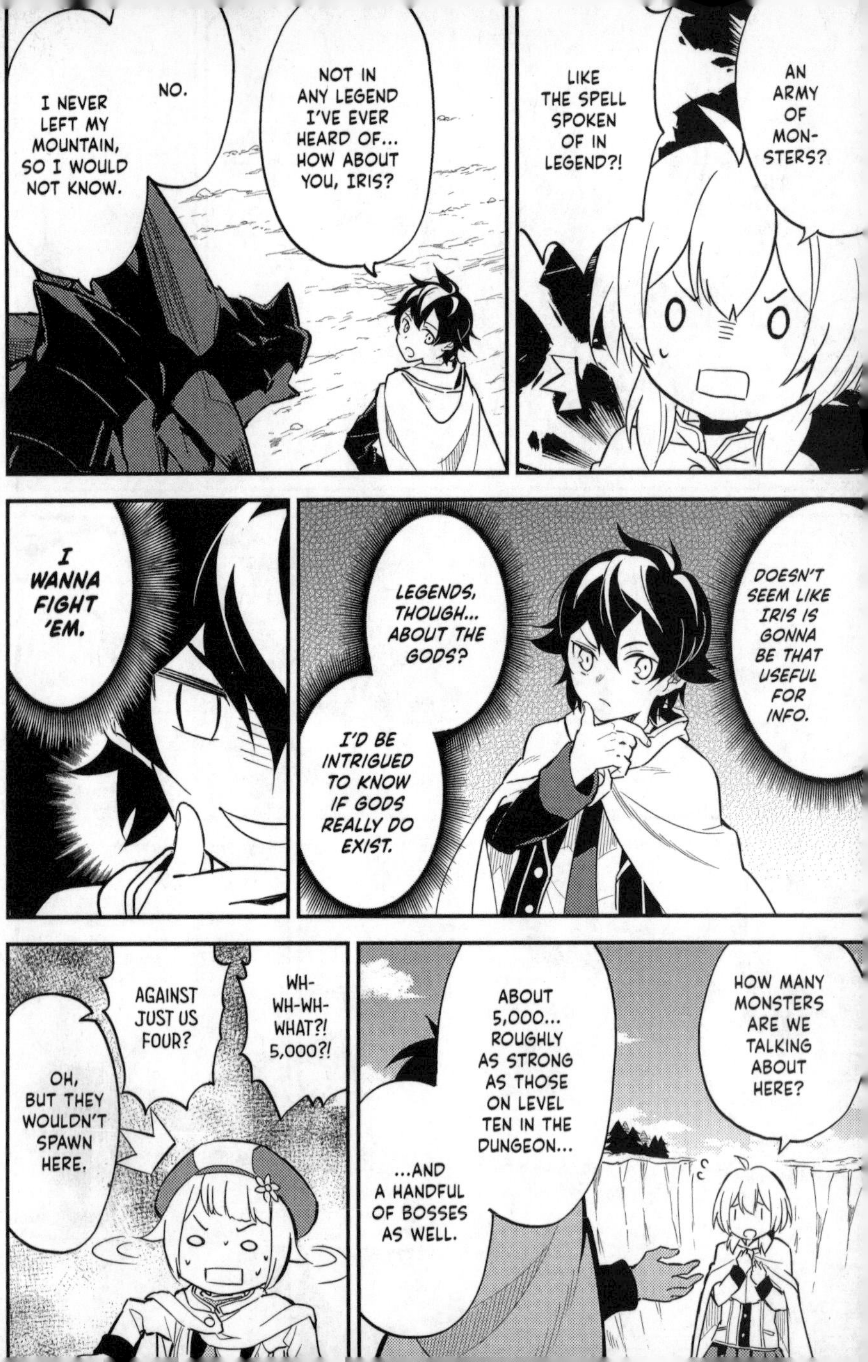
AN ARMY OF MON-STERS?
LIKE THE SPELL SPOKEN OF IN LEGEND?!
NOT IN ANY LEGEND I'VE EVER HEARD OF... HOW ABOUT YOU, IRIS?
NO.
I NEVER LEFT MY MOUNTAIN, SO I WOULD NOT KNOW.
DOESN'T SEEM LIKE IRIS IS GONNA BE THAT USEFUL FOR INFO.
LEGENDS, THOUGH... ABOUT THE GODS?
I'D BE INTRIGUED TO KNOW IF GODS REALLY DO EXIST.
I WANNA FIGHT 'EM.
HOW MANY MONSTERS ARE WE TALKING ABOUT HERE?
ABOUT 5,000... ROUGHLY AS STRONG AS THOSE ON LEVEL TEN IN THE DUNGEON...
...AND A HANDFUL OF BOSSES AS WELL.
WH-WH-WH-WHAT?! 5,000?!
AGAINST JUST US FOUR?
OH, BUT THEY WOULDN'T SPAWN HERE.

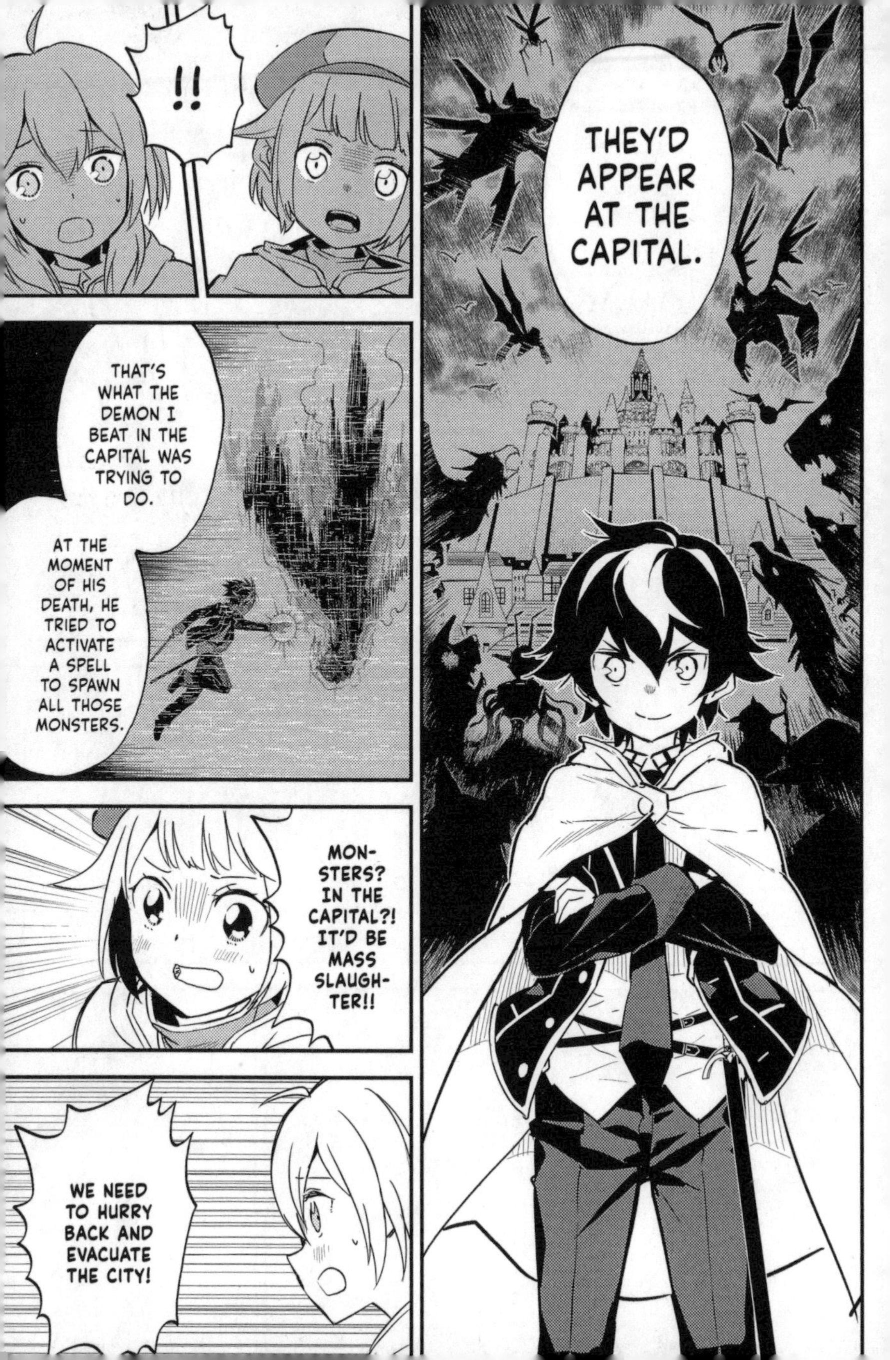
THEY'D APPEAR AT THE CAPITAL.
!!
THAT'S WHAT THE DEMON I BEAT IN THE CAPITAL WAS TRYING TO DO.
AT THE MOMENT OF HIS DEATH, HE TRIED TO ACTIVATE A SPELL TO SPAWN ALL THOSE MONSTERS.
MON-STERS? IN THE CAPITAL?! IT'D BE MASS SLAUGH-TER!!
WE NEED TO HURRY BACK AND EVACUATE THE CITY!

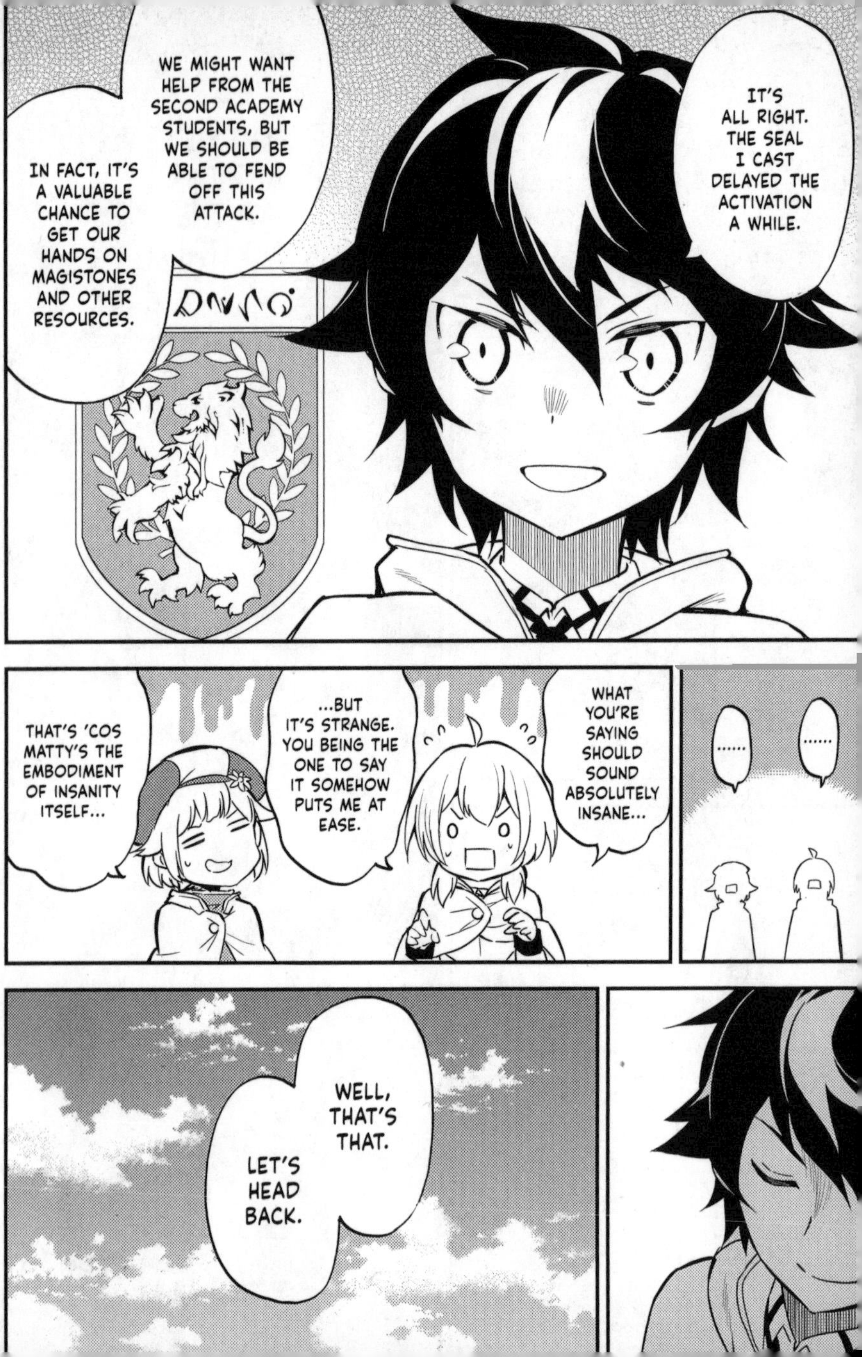
IT'S ALL RIGHT. THE SEAL I CAST DELAYED THE ACTIVATION A WHILE.
WE MIGHT WANT HELP FROM THE SECOND ACADEMY STUDENTS, BUT WE SHOULD BE ABLE TO FEND OFF THIS ATTACK.
IN FACT, IT'S A VALUABLE CHANCE TO GET OUR HANDS ON MAGISTONES AND OTHER RESOURCES.
......
......
WHAT YOU'RE SAYING SHOULD SOUND ABSOLUTELY INSANE...
...BUT IT'S STRANGE. YOU BEING THE ONE TO SAY IT SOMEHOW PUTS ME AT EASE.
THAT'S 'COS MATTY'S THE EMBODIMENT OF INSANITY ITSELF...
WELL, THAT'S THAT.
LET'S HEAD BACK.

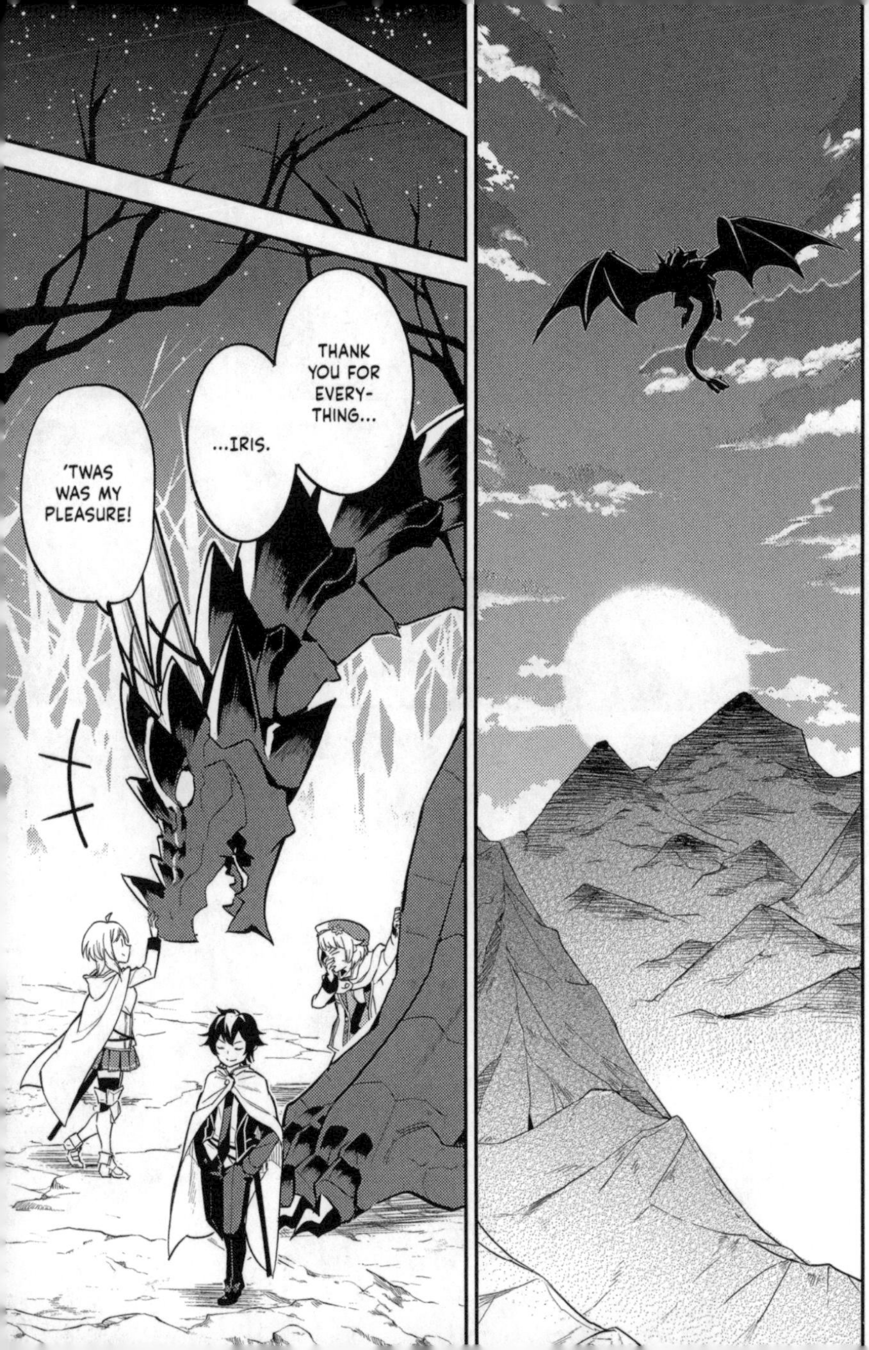
THANK YOU FOR EVERY-THING...
...IRIS.
'TWAS WAS MY PLEASURE!

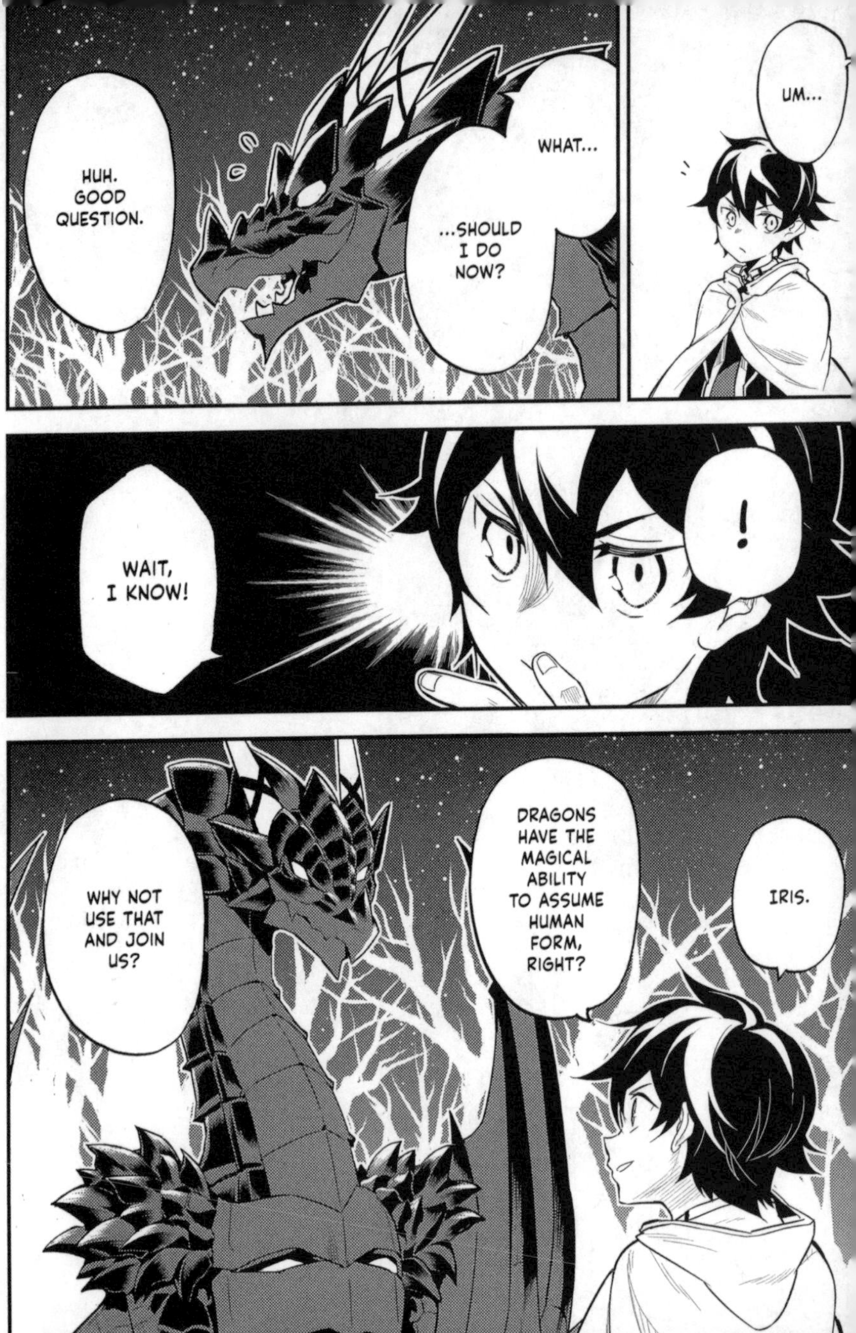
UM...
WHAT...
...SHOULD I DO NOW?
HUH. GOOD QUESTION.
!
WAIT, I KNOW!
IRIS.
DRAGONS HAVE THE MAGICAL ABILITY TO ASSUME HUMAN FORM, RIGHT?
WHY NOT USE THAT AND JOIN US?

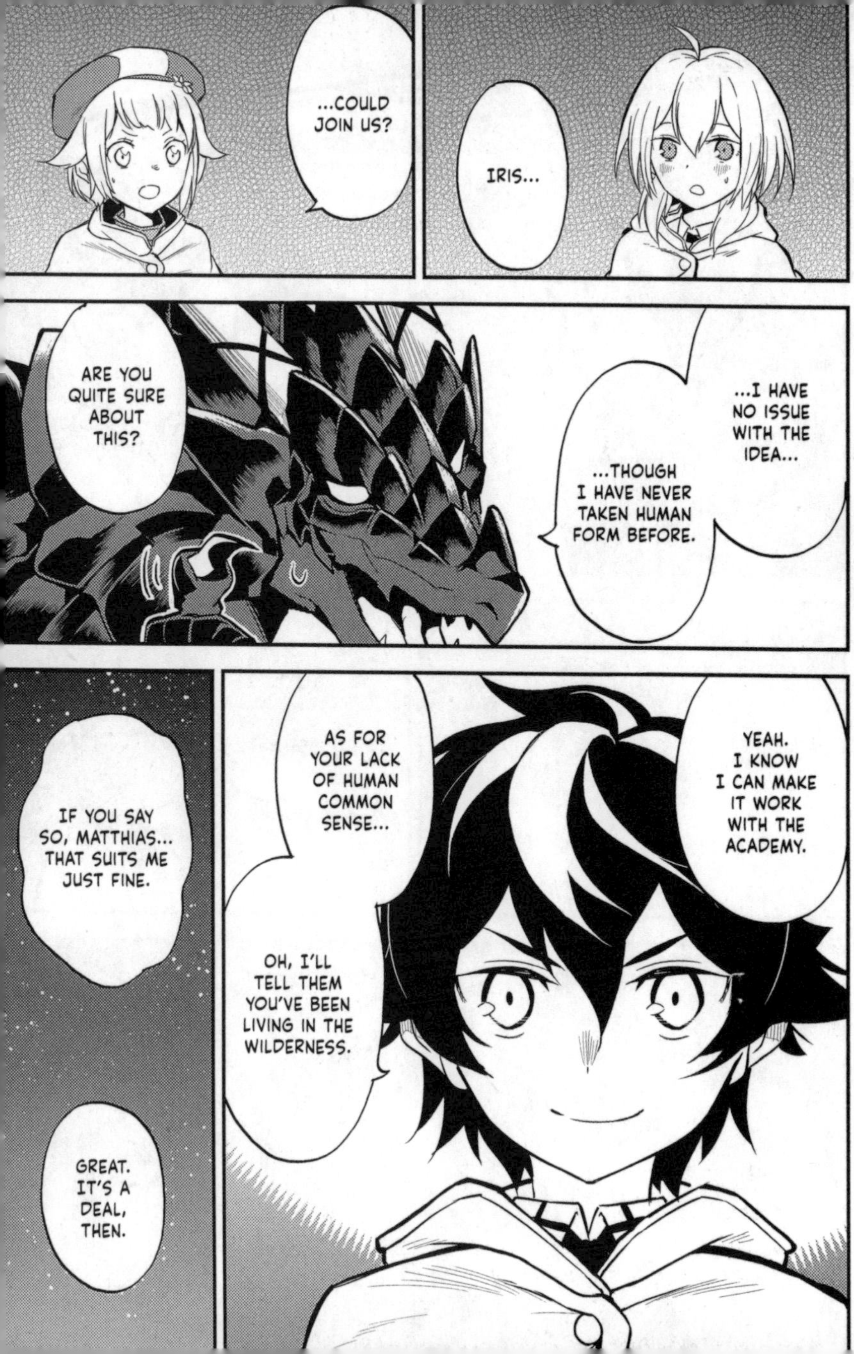
IRIS...
...COULD JOIN US?
...I HAVE NO ISSUE WITH THE IDEA...
...THOUGH I HAVE NEVER TAKEN HUMAN FORM BEFORE.
ARE YOU QUITE SURE ABOUT THIS?
YEAH. I KNOW I CAN MAKE IT WORK WITH THE ACADEMY.
AS FOR YOUR LACK OF HUMAN COMMON SENSE...
OH, I'LL TELL THEM YOU'VE BEEN LIVING IN THE WILDERNESS.
IF YOU SAY SO, MATTHIAS... THAT SUITS ME JUST FINE.
GREAT. IT'S A DEAL, THEN.

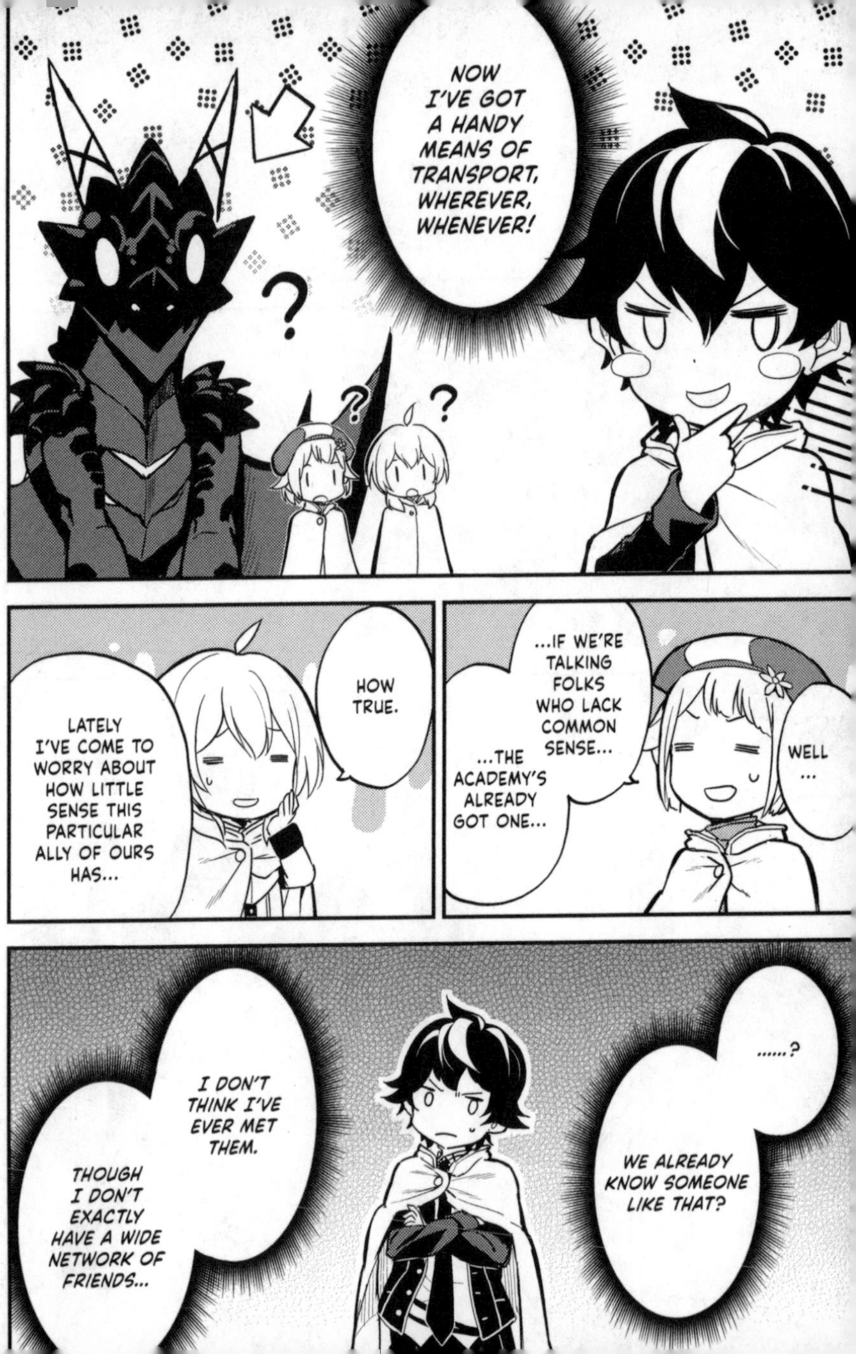
NOW I'VE GOT A HANDY MEANS OF TRANSPORT, WHEREVER, WHENEVER!
WELL ...
...IF WE'RE TALKING FOLKS WHO LACK COMMON SENSE...
...THE ACADEMY'S ALREADY GOT ONE...
HOW TRUE.
LATELY I'VE COME TO WORRY ABOUT HOW LITTLE SENSE THIS PARTICULAR ALLY OF OURS HAS...
......?
WE ALREADY KNOW SOMEONE LIKE THAT?
I DON'T THINK I'VE EVER MET THEM.
THOUGH I DON'T EXACTLY HAVE A WIDE NETWORK OF FRIENDS...

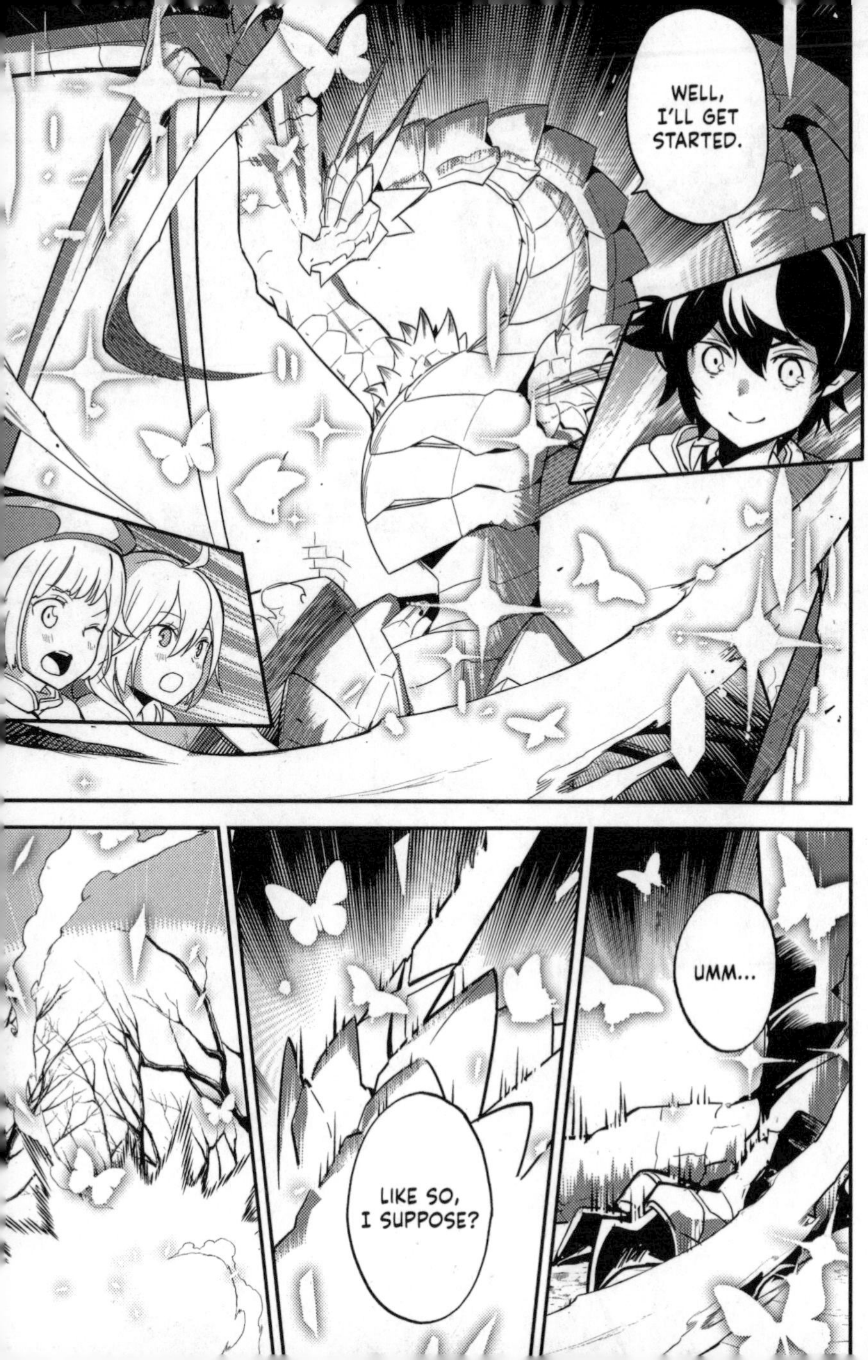
WELL, I'LL GET STARTED.
UMM...
LIKE SO, I SUPPOSE?

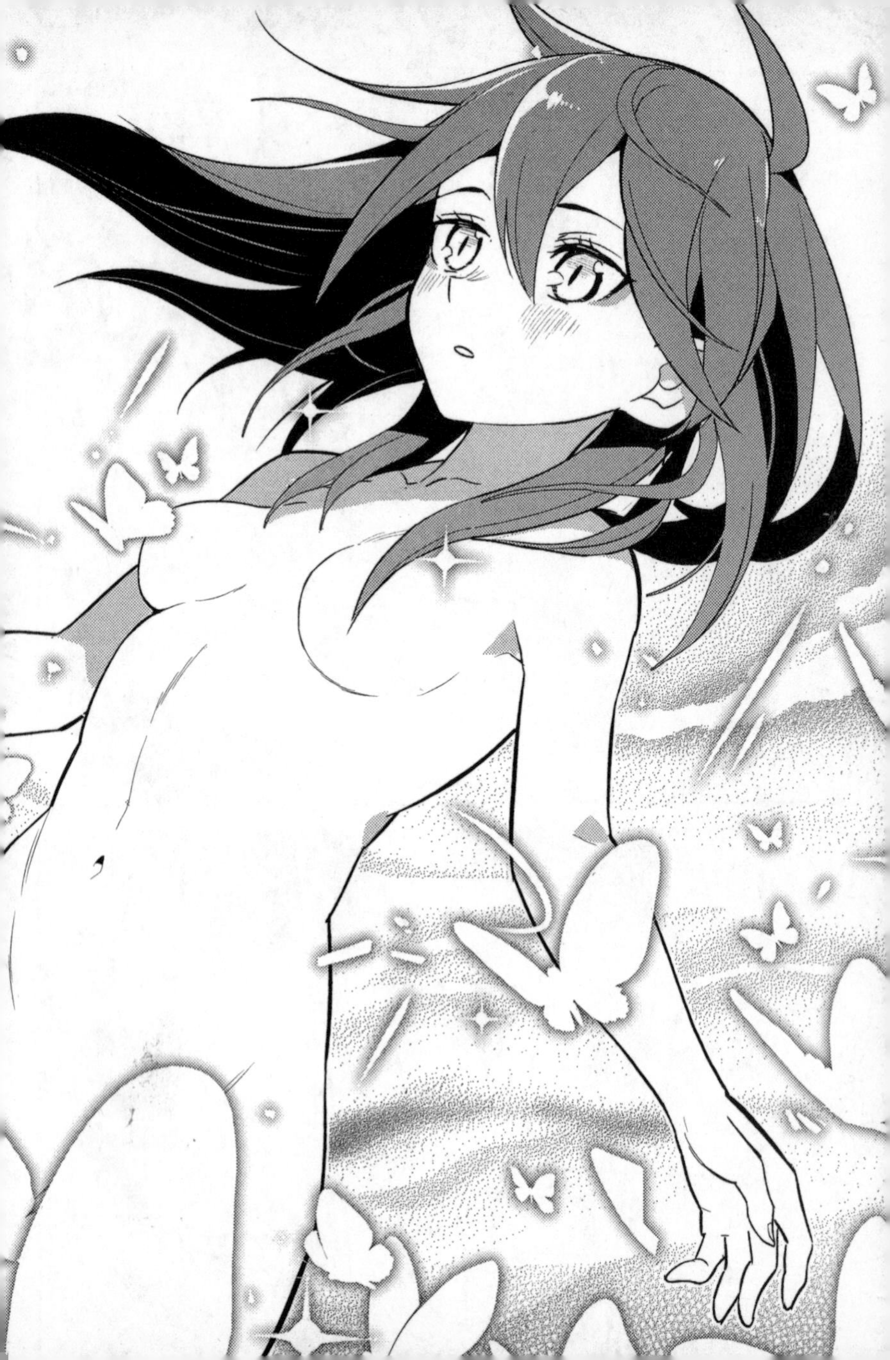

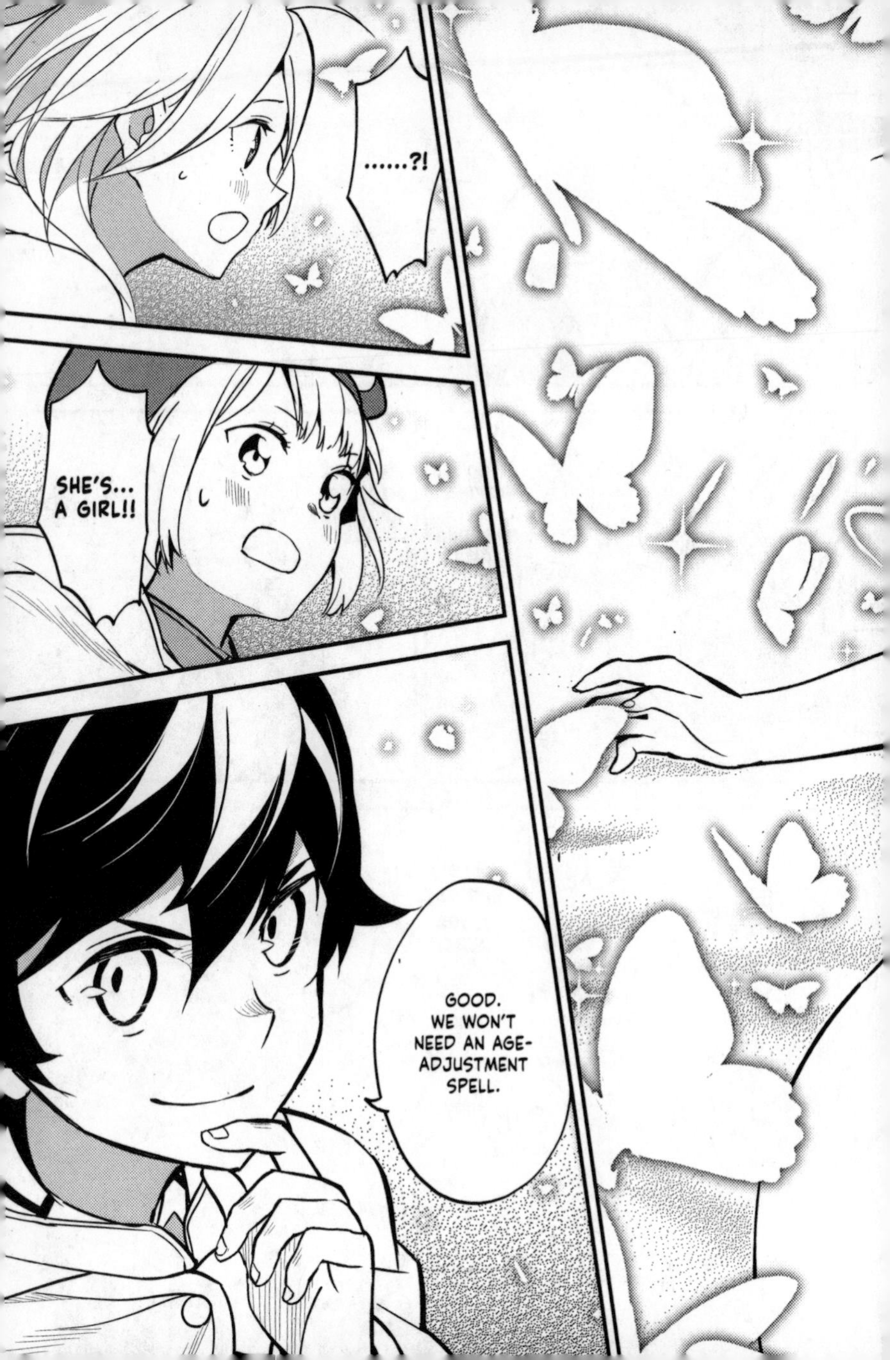
......?!
SHE'S... A GIRL!!
GOOD. WE WON'T NEED AN AGE-ADJUSTMENT SPELL.

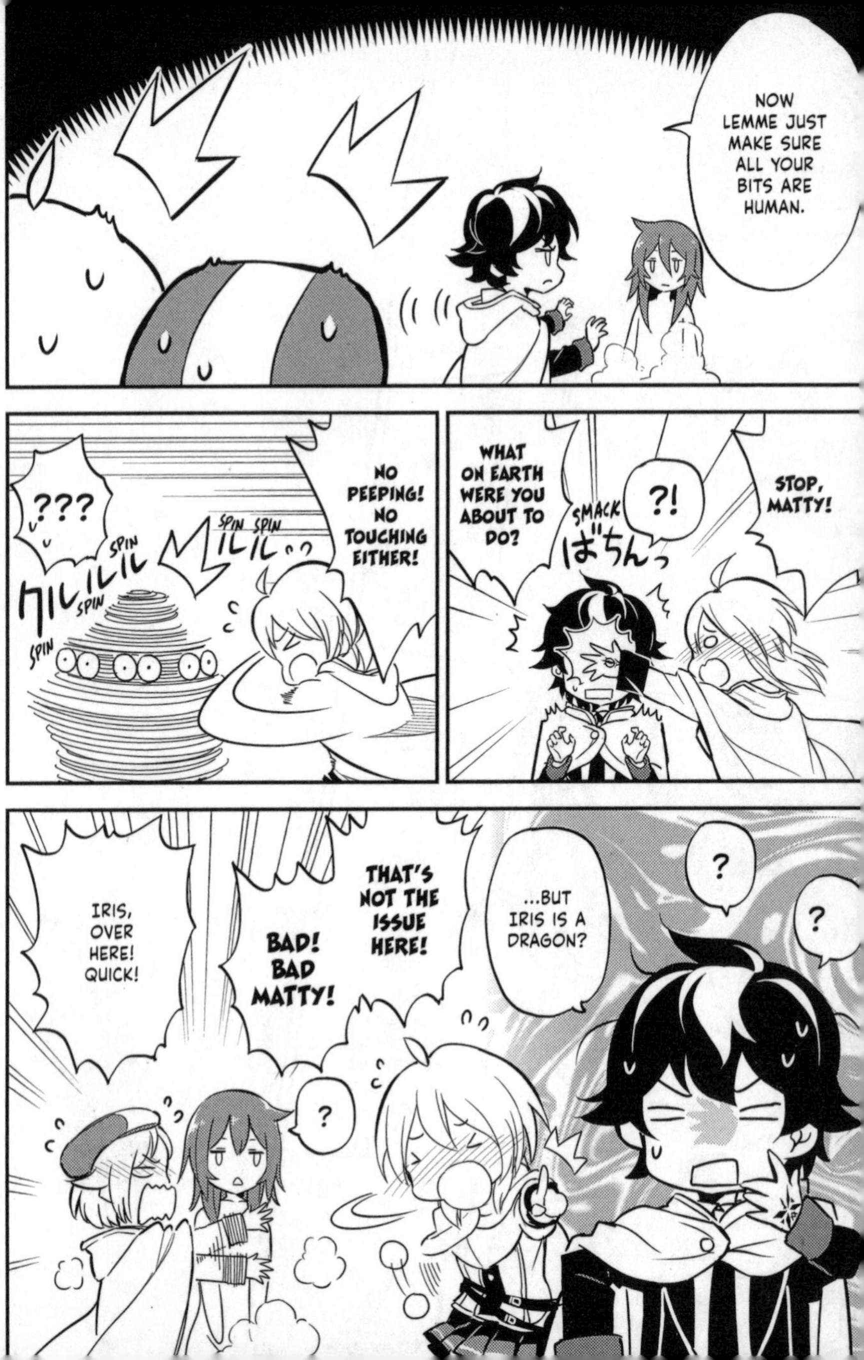
NOW LEMME JUST MAKE SURE ALL YOUR BITS ARE HUMAN.
STOP, MATTY!
?!
SMACK
ばちんっ
WHAT ON EARTH WERE YOU ABOUT TO DO?
NO PEEPING! NO TOUCHING EITHER!
SPIN SPIN
ルルっ
SPIN
クルルルル
SPIN
SPIN
???
?
?
...BUT IRIS IS A DRAGON?
THAT'S NOT THE ISSUE HERE!
BAD! BAD MATTY!
IRIS, OVER HERE! QUICK!
?

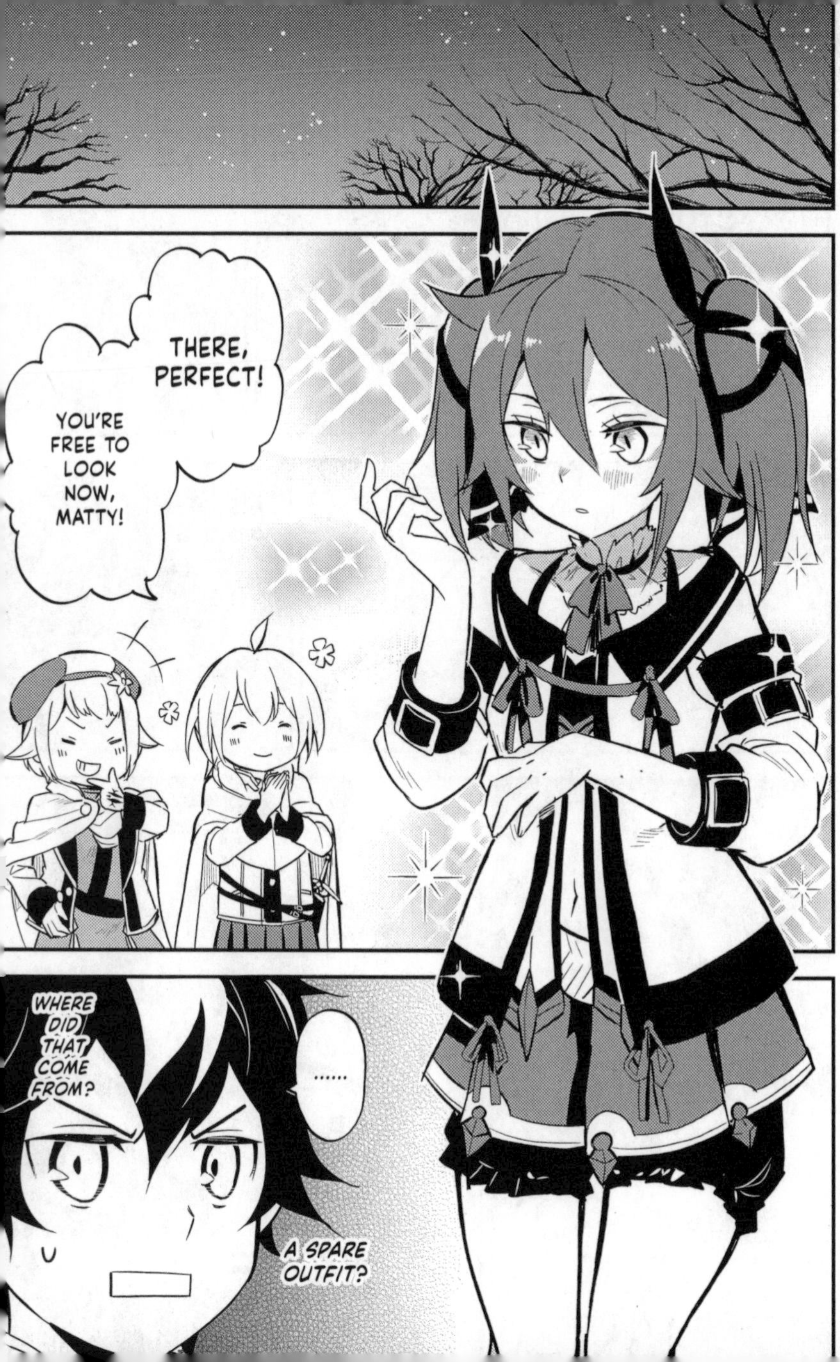
THERE, PERFECT!
YOU'RE FREE TO LOOK NOW, MATTY!
......
WHERE DID THAT COME FROM?
A SPARE OUTFIT?

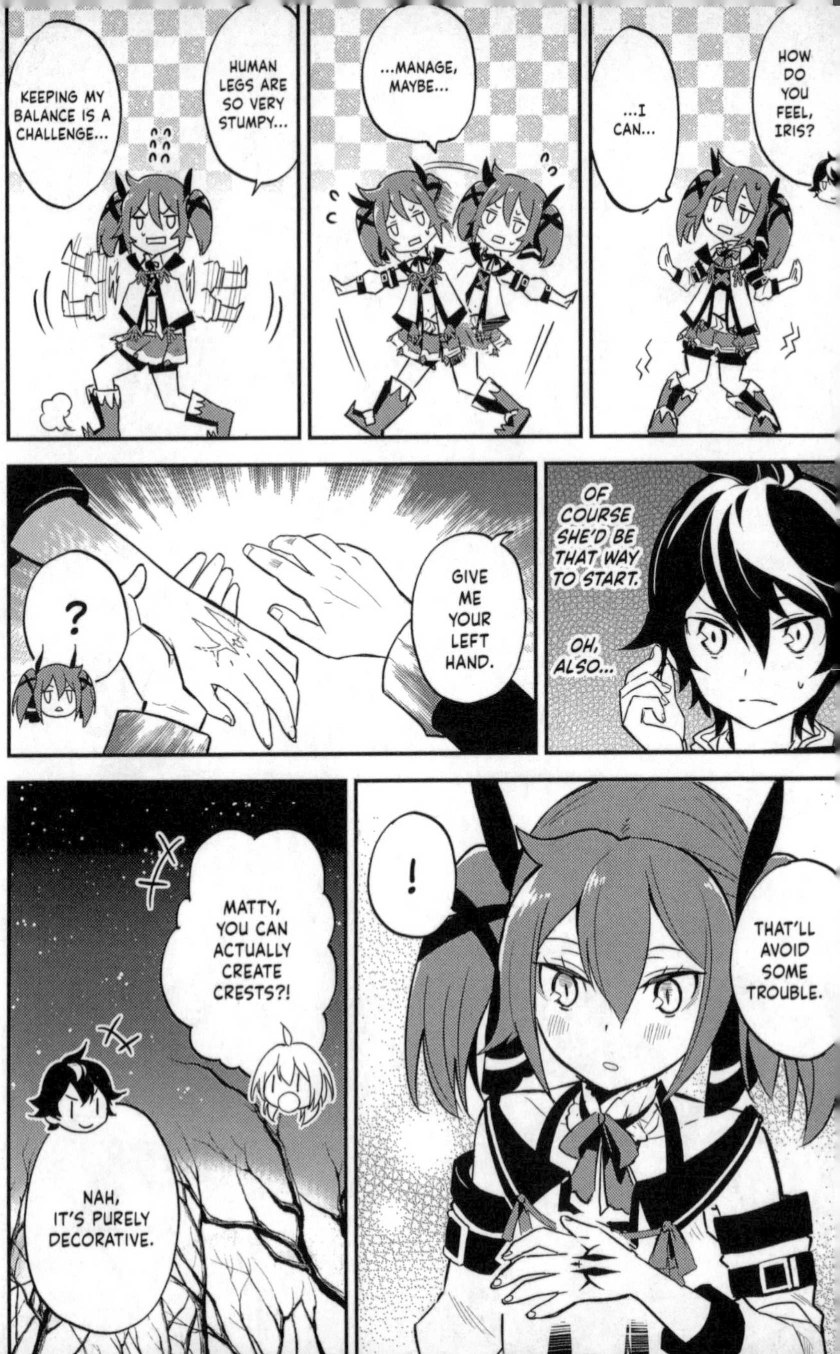
HOW DO YOU FEEL, IRIS?
...I CAN...
...MANAGE, MAYBE...
HUMAN LEGS ARE SO VERY STUMPY...
KEEPING MY BALANCE IS A CHALLENGE...
OF COURSE SHE'D BE THAT WAY TO START.
OH, ALSO...
GIVE ME YOUR LEFT HAND.
?
THAT'LL AVOID SOME TROUBLE.
!
MATTY, YOU CAN ACTUALLY CREATE CRESTS?!
NAH, IT'S PURELY DECORATIVE.

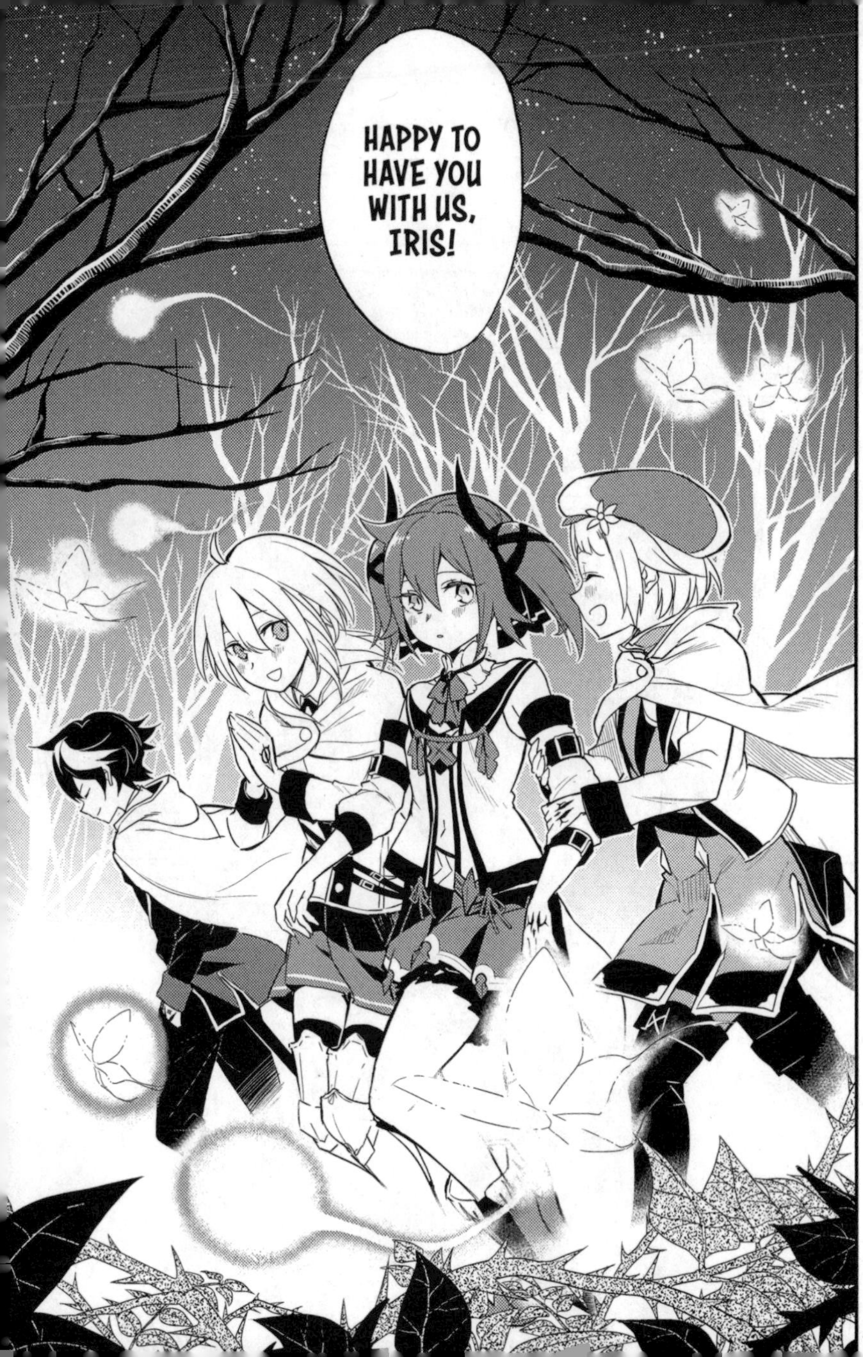
HAPPY TO HAVE YOU WITH US, IRIS!

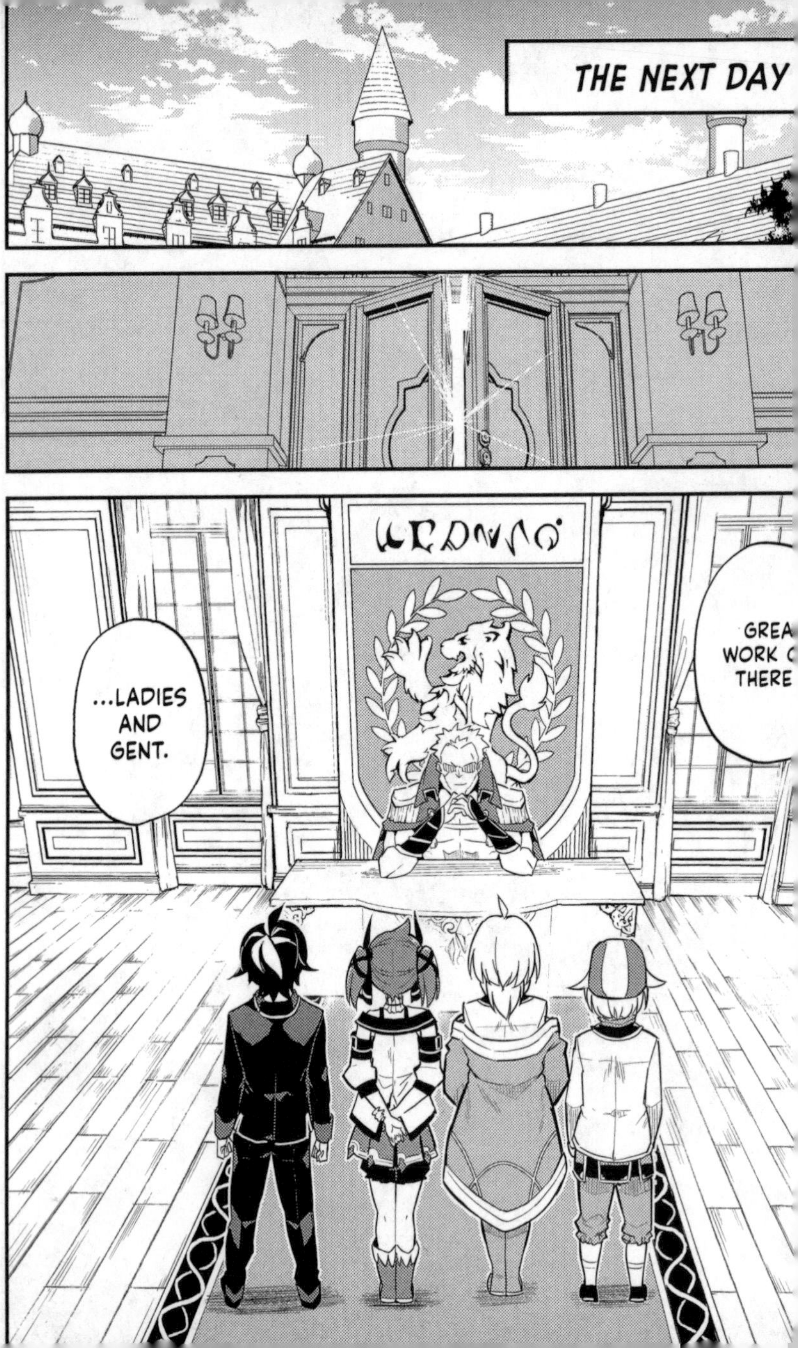
THE NEXT DAY
GREA WORK THERE
...LADIES AND GENT.

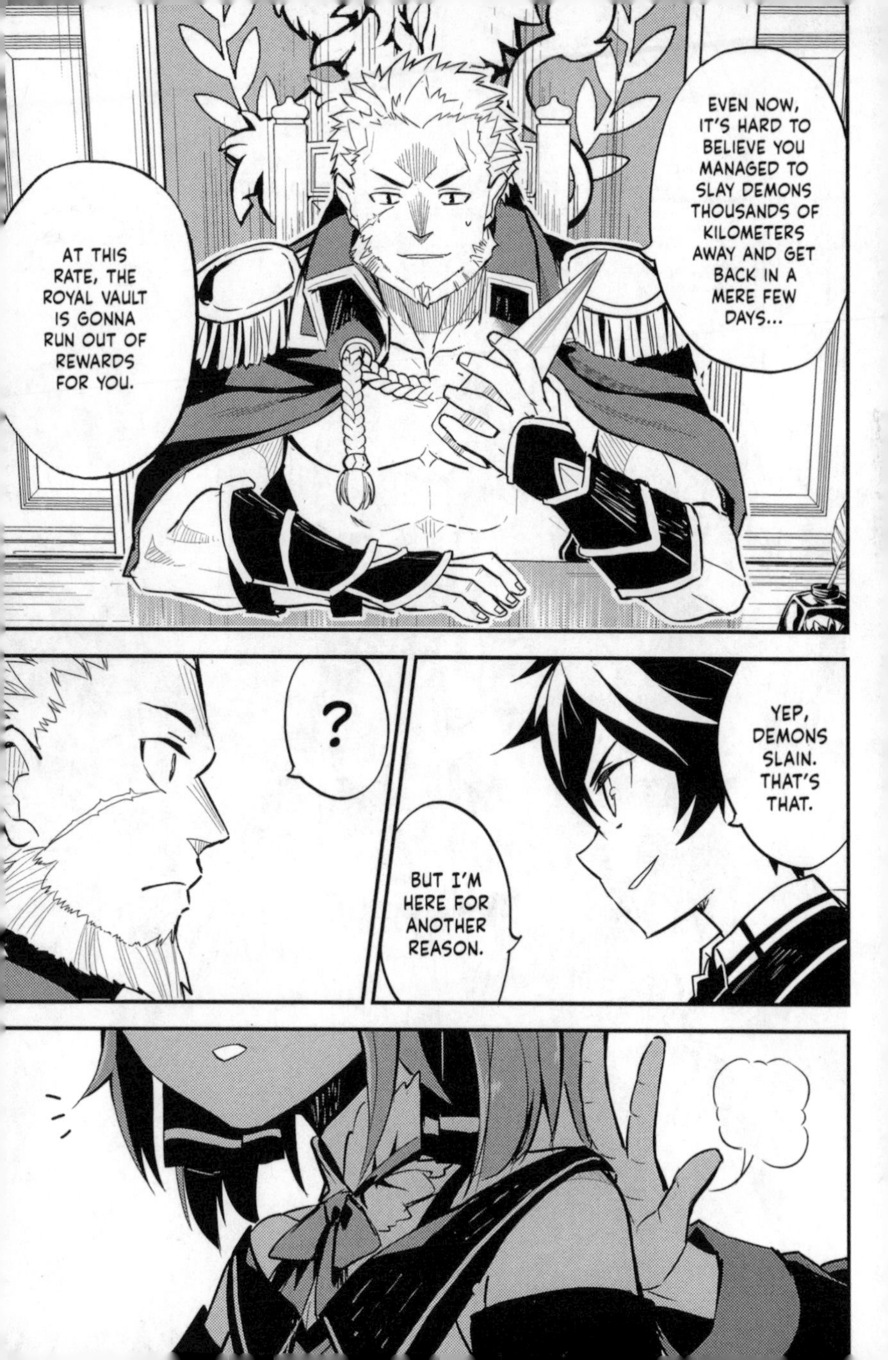
EVEN NOW, IT'S HARD TO BELIEVE YOU MANAGED TO SLAY DEMONS THOUSANDS OF KILOMETERS AWAY AND GET BACK IN A MERE FEW DAYS...
AT THIS RATE, THE ROYAL VAULT IS GONNA RUN OUT OF REWARDS FOR YOU.
YEP, DEMONS SLAIN. THAT'S THAT.
BUT I'M HERE FOR ANOTHER REASON.
?

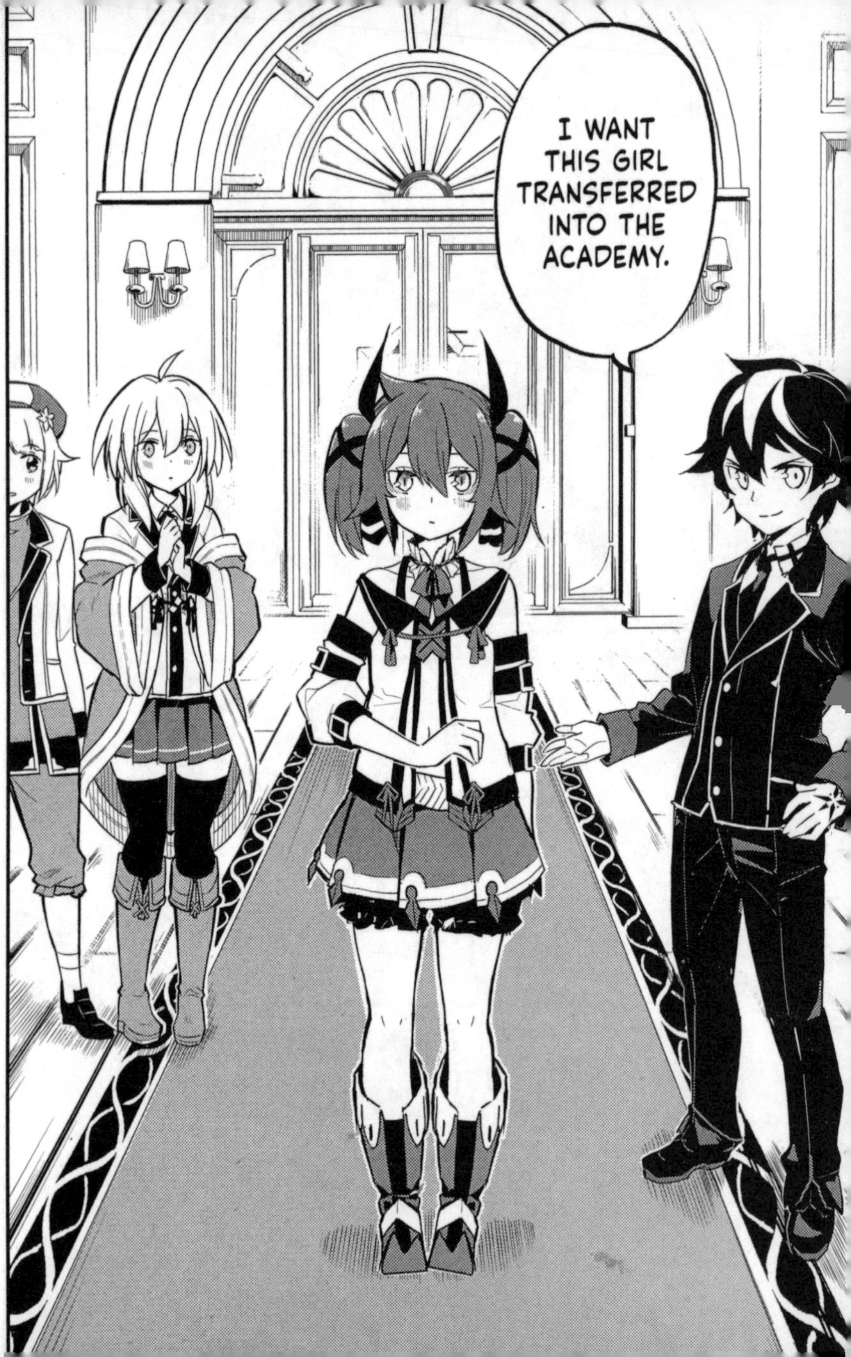
I WANT THIS GIRL TRANSFERRED INTO THE ACADEMY.

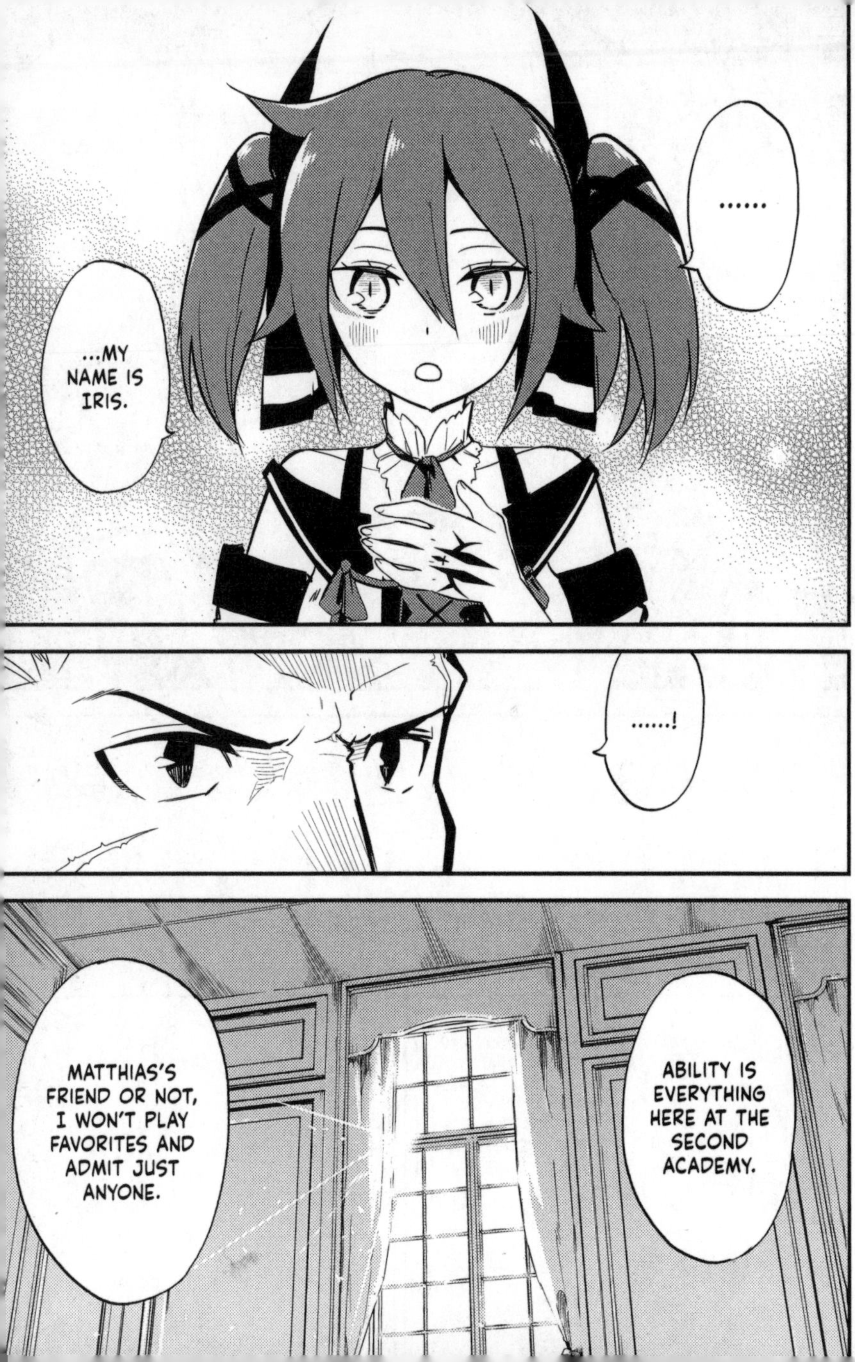
......
...MY NAME IS IRIS.
......!
ABILITY IS EVERYTHING HERE AT THE SECOND ACADEMY.
MATTHIAS'S FRIEND OR NOT, I WON'T PLAY FAVORITES AND ADMIT JUST ANYONE.

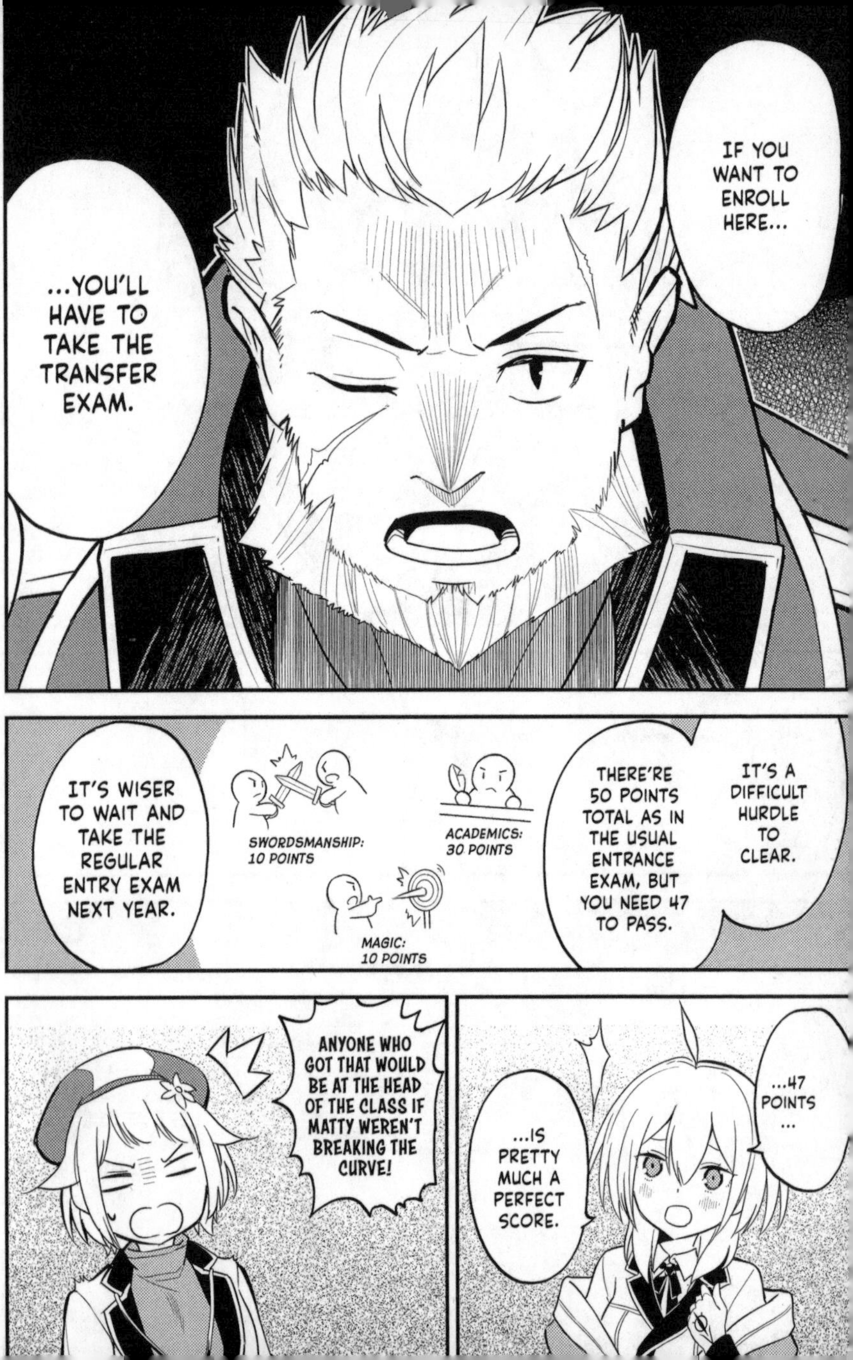
IF YOU WANT TO ENROLL HERE...
...YOU'LL HAVE TO TAKE THE TRANSFER EXAM.
IT'S A DIFFICULT HURDLE TO CLEAR.
THERE'RE 50 POINTS TOTAL AS IN THE USUAL ENTRANCE EXAM, BUT YOU NEED 47 TO PASS.
ACADEMICS: 30 POINTS
SWORDSMANSHIP: 10 POINTS
MAGIC: 10 POINTS
IT'S WISER TO WAIT AND TAKE THE REGULAR ENTRY EXAM NEXT YEAR.
...47 POINTS ...
...IS PRETTY MUCH A PERFECT SCORE.
ANYONE WHO GOT THAT WOULD BE AT THE HEAD OF THE CLASS IF MATTY WEREN'T BREAKING THE CURVE!

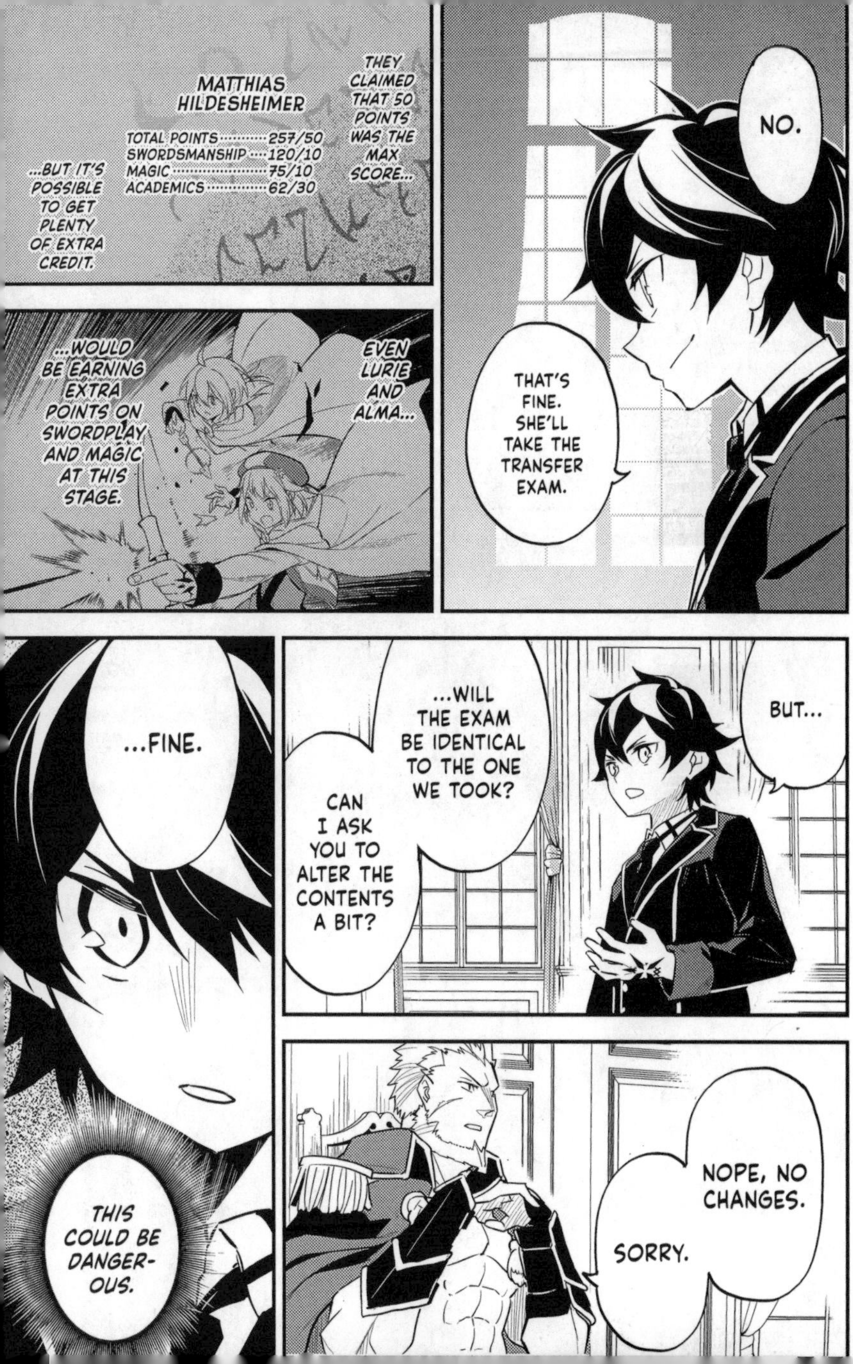
NO.
THAT'S FINE. SHE'LL TAKE THE TRANSFER EXAM.
THEY CLAIMED THAT 50 POINTS WAS THE MAX SCORE...
MATTHIAS HILDESHEIMER
TOTAL POINTS..........257/50
SWORDSMANSHIP....120/10
MAGIC..........75/10
ACADEMICS..........62/30
...BUT IT'S POSSIBLE TO GET PLENTY OF EXTRA CREDIT.
EVEN LURIE AND ALMA...
...WOULD BE EARNING EXTRA POINTS ON SWORDPLAY AND MAGIC AT THIS STAGE.
BUT...
...WILL THE EXAM BE IDENTICAL TO THE ONE WE TOOK?
CAN I ASK YOU TO ALTER THE CONTENTS A BIT?
NOPE, NO CHANGES.
SORRY.
...FINE.
THIS COULD BE DANGER-OUS.

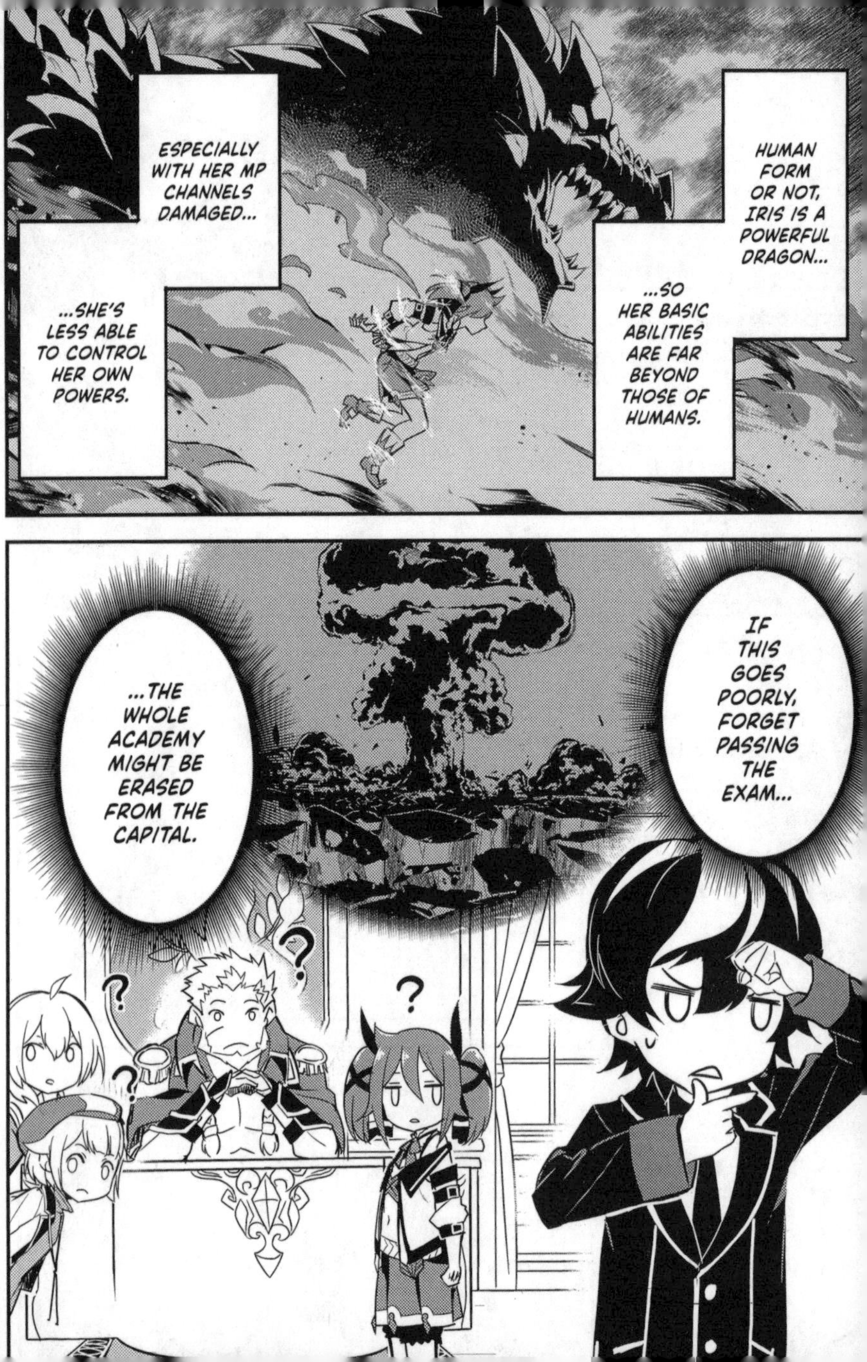
HUMAN FORM OR NOT, IRIS IS A POWERFUL DRAGON...
...SO HER BASIC ABILITIES ARE FAR BEYOND THOSE OF HUMANS.
ESPECIALLY WITH HER MP CHANNELS DAMAGED...
...SHE'S LESS ABLE TO CONTROL HER OWN POWERS.
IF THIS GOES POORLY, FORGET PASSING THE EXAM...
...THE WHOLE ACADEMY MIGHT BE ERASED FROM THE CAPITAL.
?
?
?
?

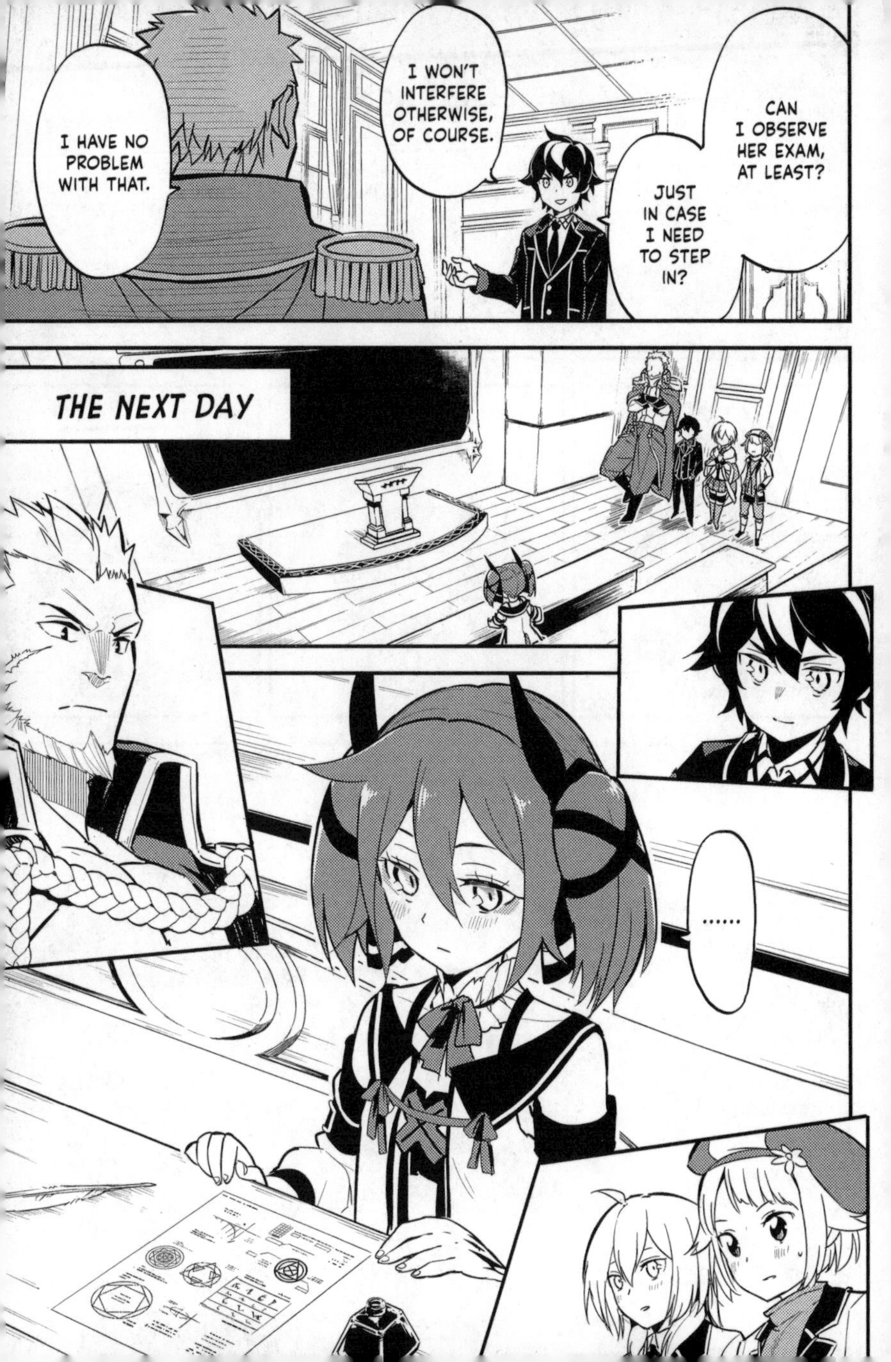
CAN I OBSERVE HER EXAM, AT LEAST?
JUST IN CASE I NEED TO STEP IN?
I WON'T INTERFERE OTHERWISE, OF COURSE.
I HAVE NO PROBLEM WITH THAT.
THE NEXT DAY
......

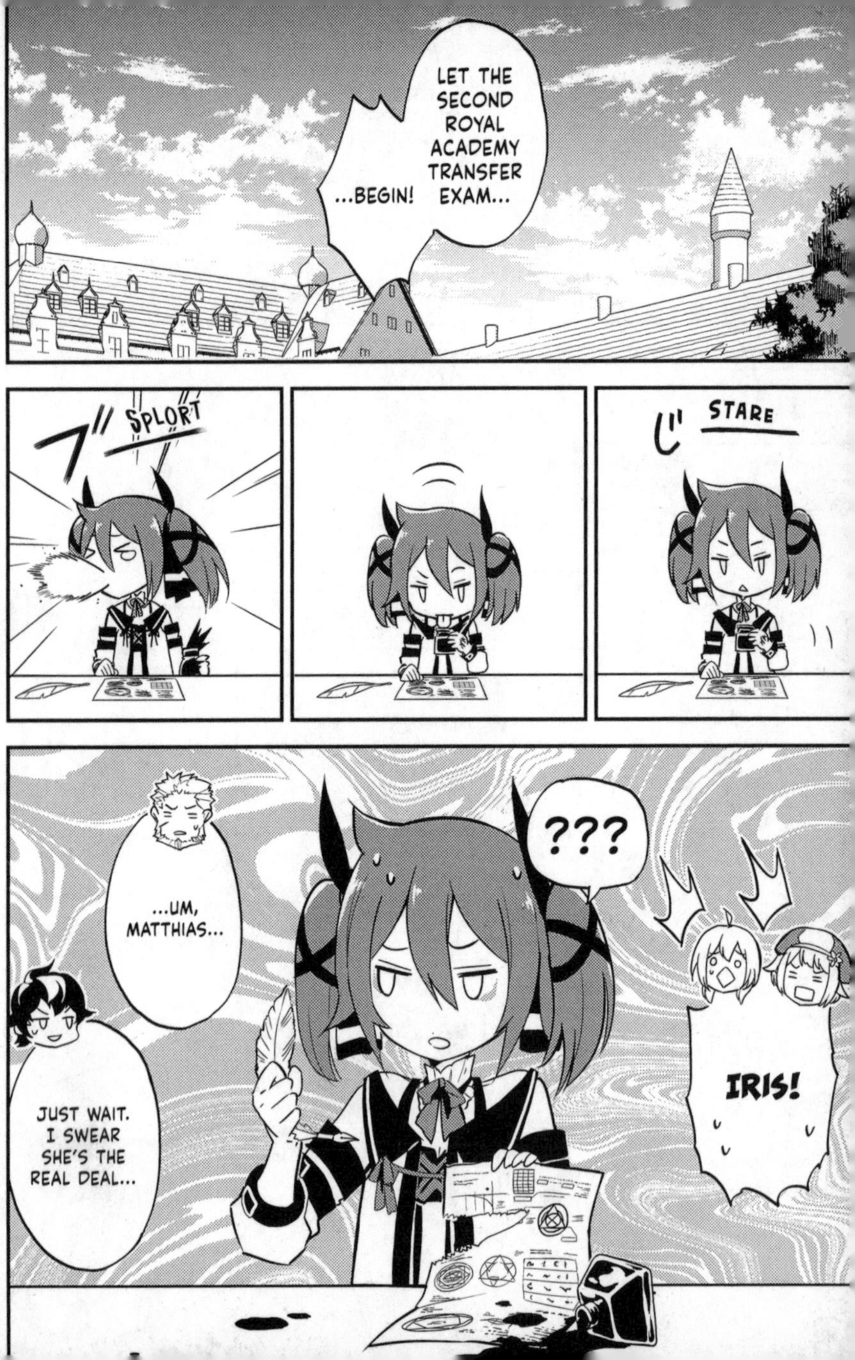
LET THE SECOND ROYAL ACADEMY TRANSFER EXAM...
...BEGIN!
じ
STARE
ブ
SPLORT
???
IRIS!
...UM, MATTHIAS...
JUST WAIT. I SWEAR SHE'S THE REAL DEAL...

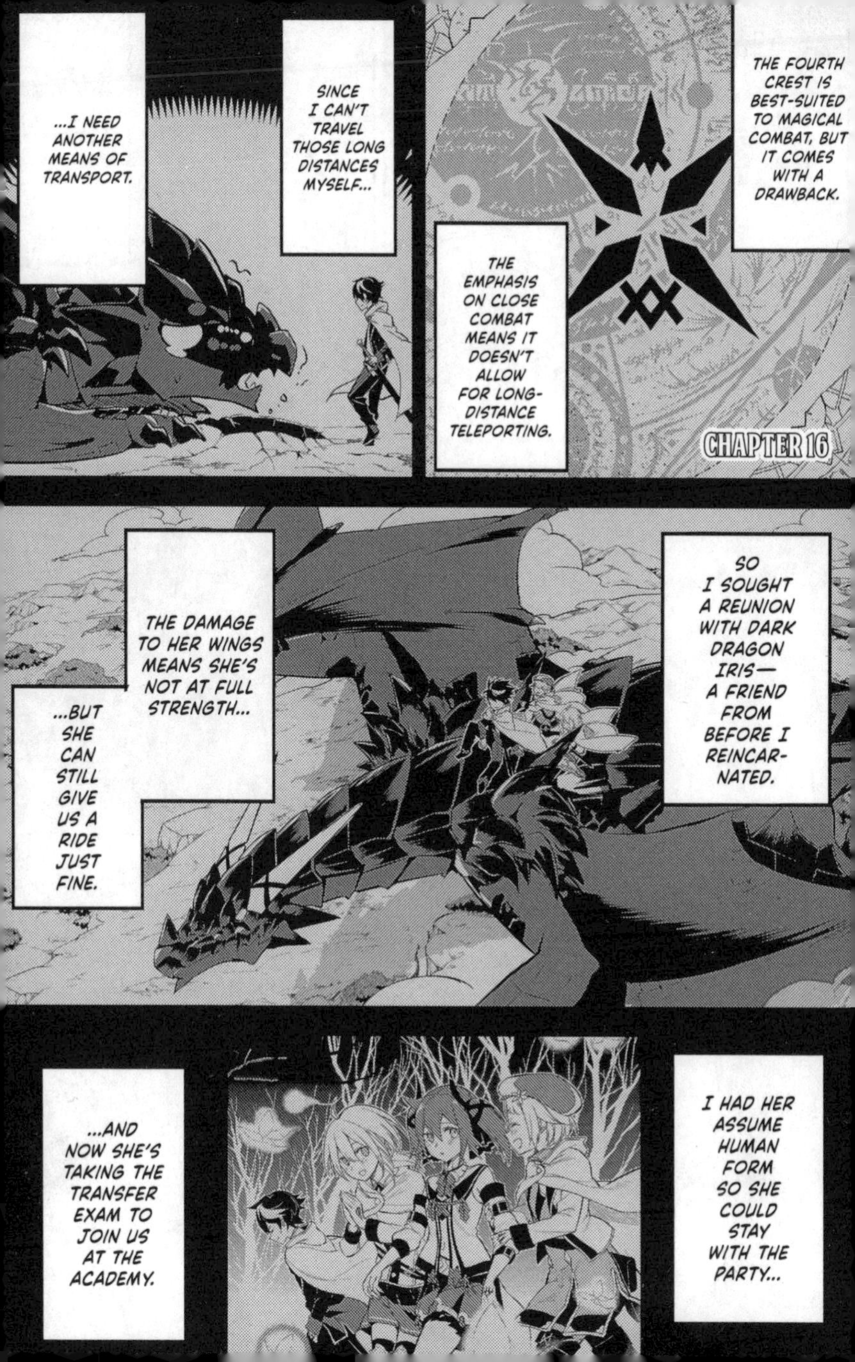
THE FOURTH CREST IS BEST-SUITED TO MAGICAL COMBAT, BUT IT COMES WITH A DRAWBACK.
THE EMPHASIS ON CLOSE COMBAT MEANS IT DOESN'T ALLOW FOR LONG-DISTANCE TELEPORTING.
CHAPTER 16
SINCE I CAN'T TRAVEL THOSE LONG DISTANCES MYSELF...
...I NEED ANOTHER MEANS OF TRANSPORT.
SO I SOUGHT A REUNION WITH DARK DRAGON IRIS—A FRIEND FROM BEFORE I REINCAR-NATED.
THE DAMAGE TO HER WINGS MEANS SHE'S NOT AT FULL STRENGTH...
...BUT SHE CAN STILL GIVE US A RIDE JUST FINE.
I HAD HER ASSUME HUMAN FORM SO SHE COULD STAY WITH THE PARTY...
...AND NOW SHE'S TAKING THE TRANSFER EXAM TO JOIN US AT THE ACADEMY.

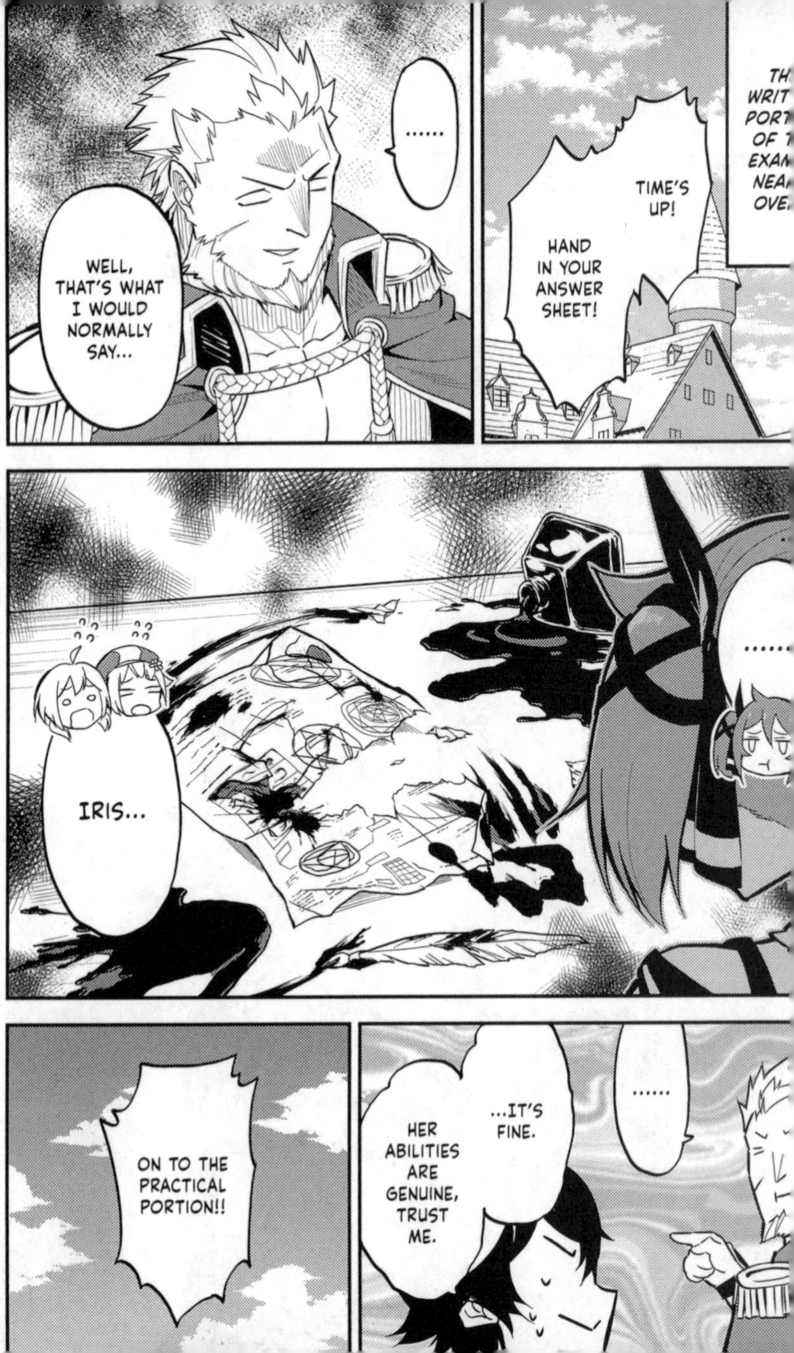
TIME'S UP!
HAND IN YOUR ANSWER SHEET!
......
WELL, THAT'S WHAT I WOULD NORMALLY SAY...
......
IRIS...
......
...IT'S FINE.
HER ABILITIES ARE GENUINE, TRUST ME.
ON TO THE PRACTICAL PORTION!!

CHAPTER 16 ◆ The Strongest Sage Sits In On an Exam

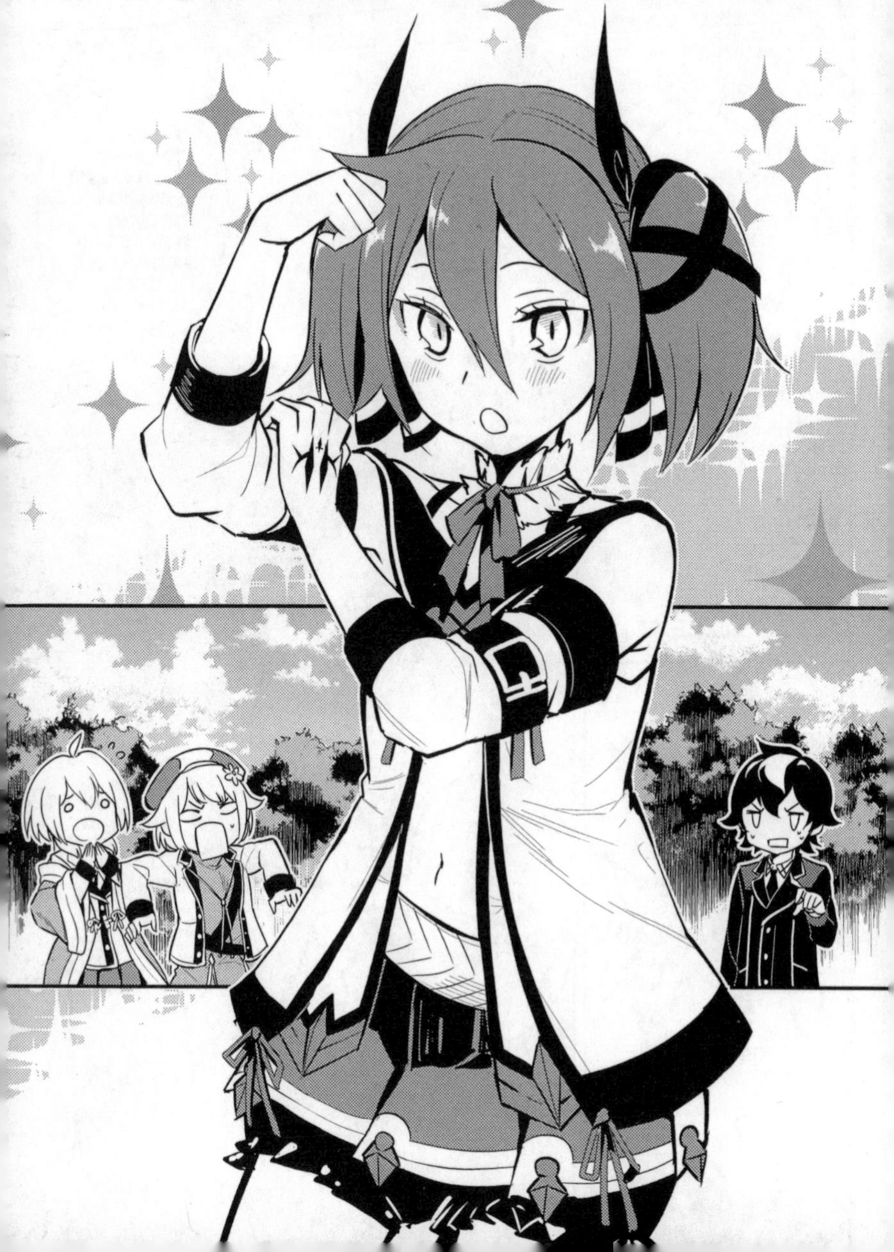

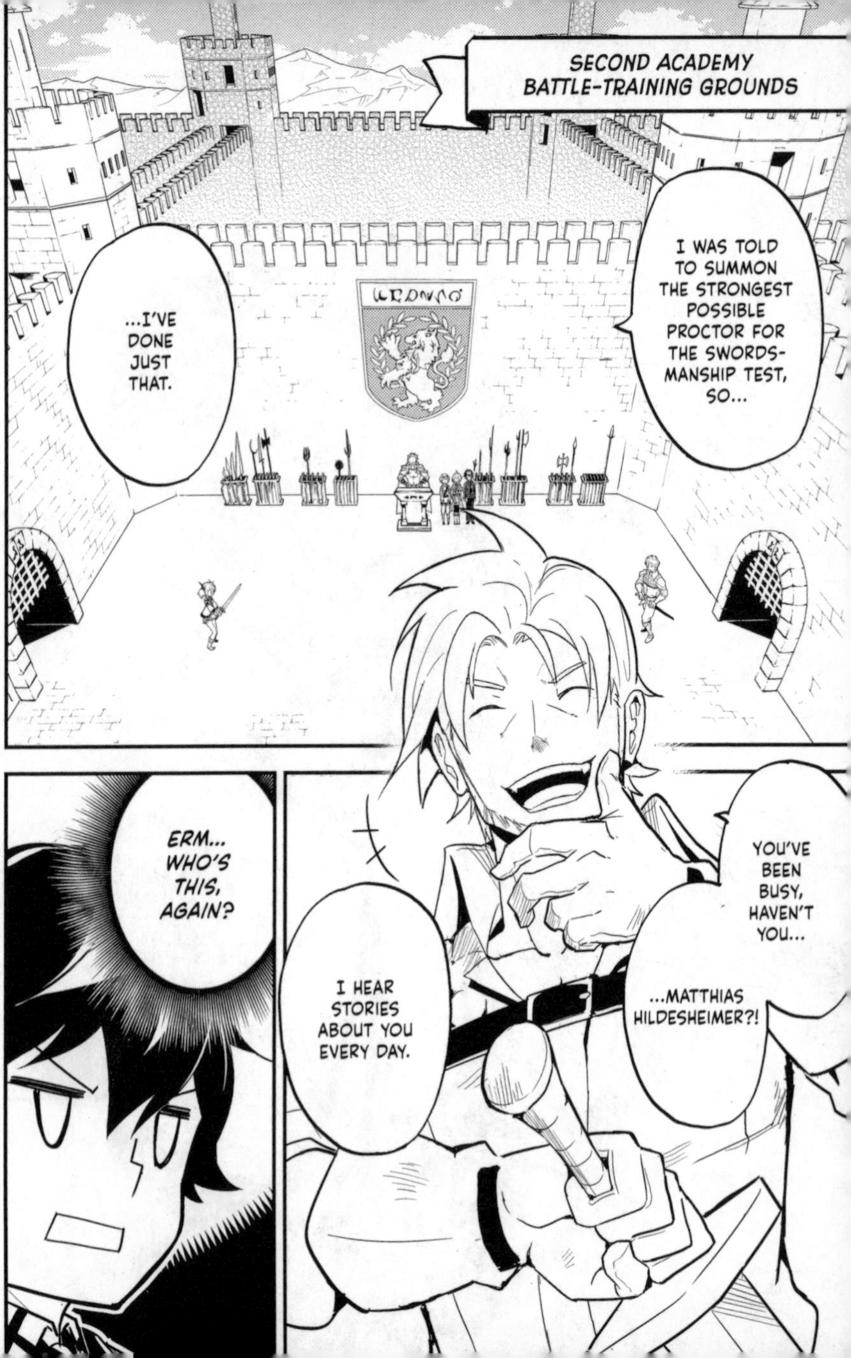
SECOND ACADEMY BATTLE-TRAINING GROUNDS
I WAS TOLD TO SUMMON THE STRONGEST POSSIBLE PROCTOR FOR THE SWORDS-MANSHIP TEST, SO...
...I'VE DONE JUST THAT.
YOU'VE BEEN BUSY, HAVEN'T YOU...
...MATTHIAS HILDESHEIMER?!
I HEAR STORIES ABOUT YOU EVERY DAY.
ERM... WHO'S THIS, AGAIN?

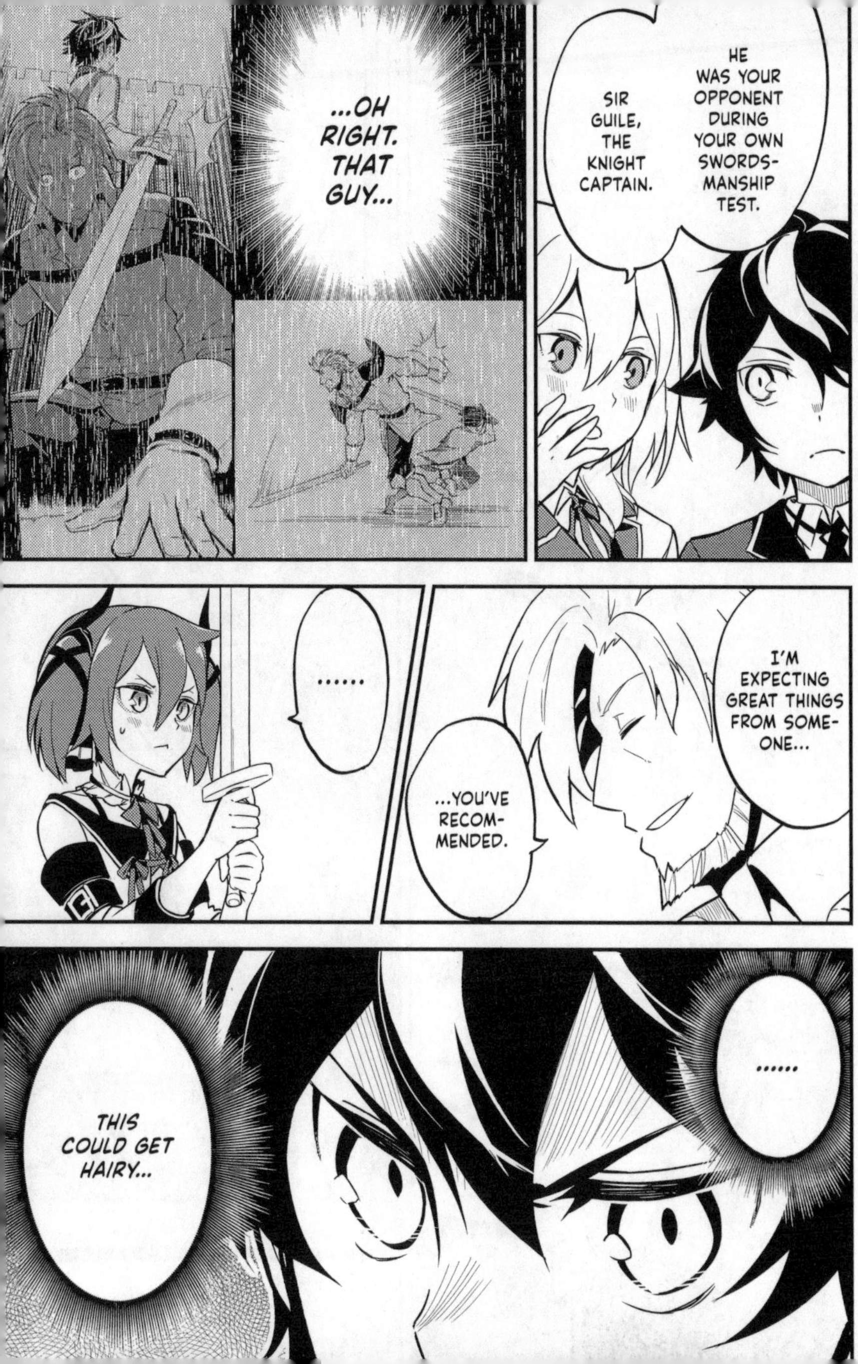
HE WAS YOUR OPPONENT DURING YOUR OWN SWORDS-MANSHIP TEST.
SIR GUILE, THE KNIGHT CAPTAIN.
...OH RIGHT. THAT GUY...
I'M EXPECTING GREAT THINGS FROM SOME-ONE...
...YOU'VE RECOM-MENDED.
......
......
THIS COULD GET HAIRY...

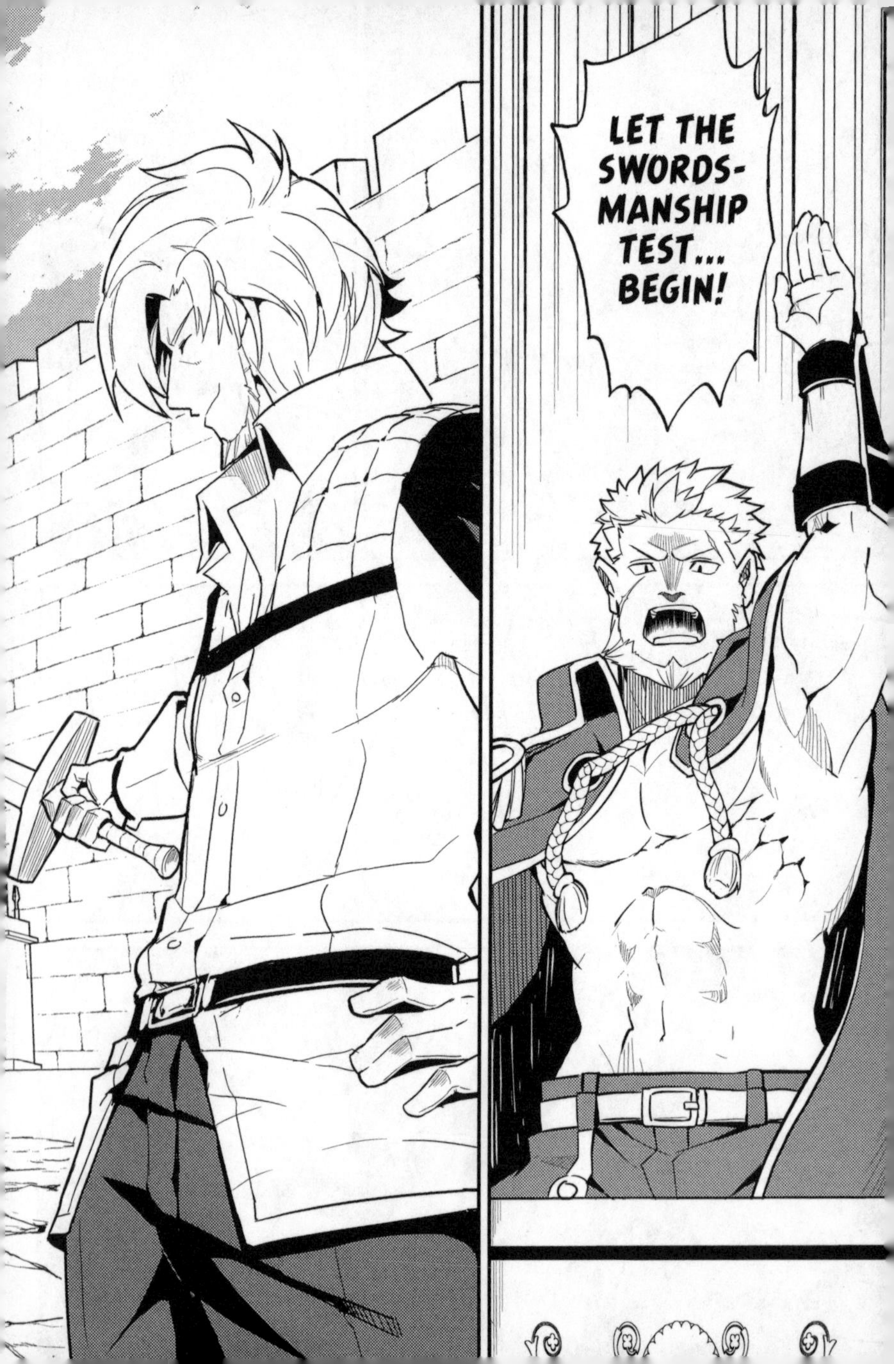
LET THE SWORDS-MANSHIP TEST.... BEGIN!

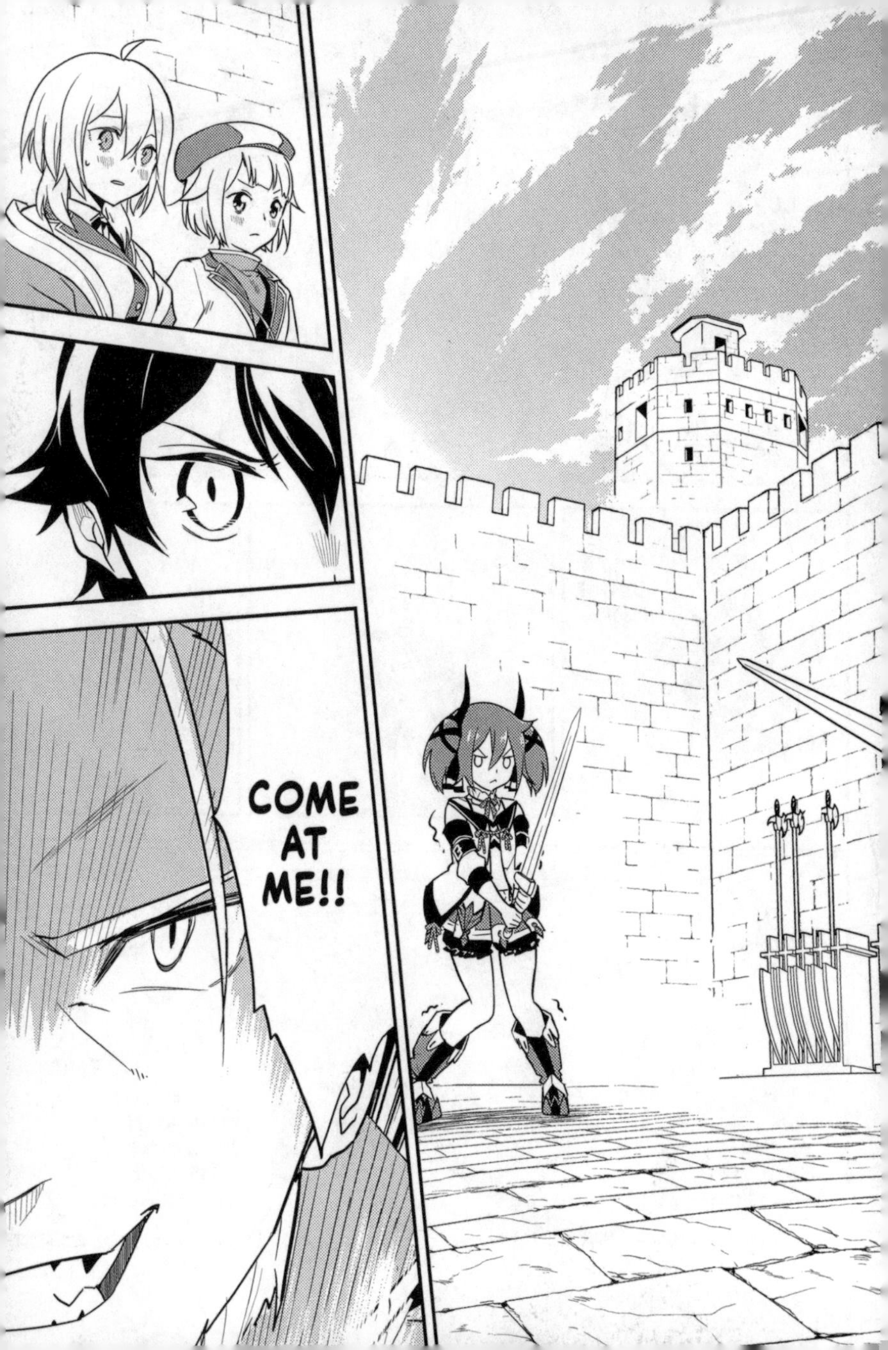
COME AT ME!!

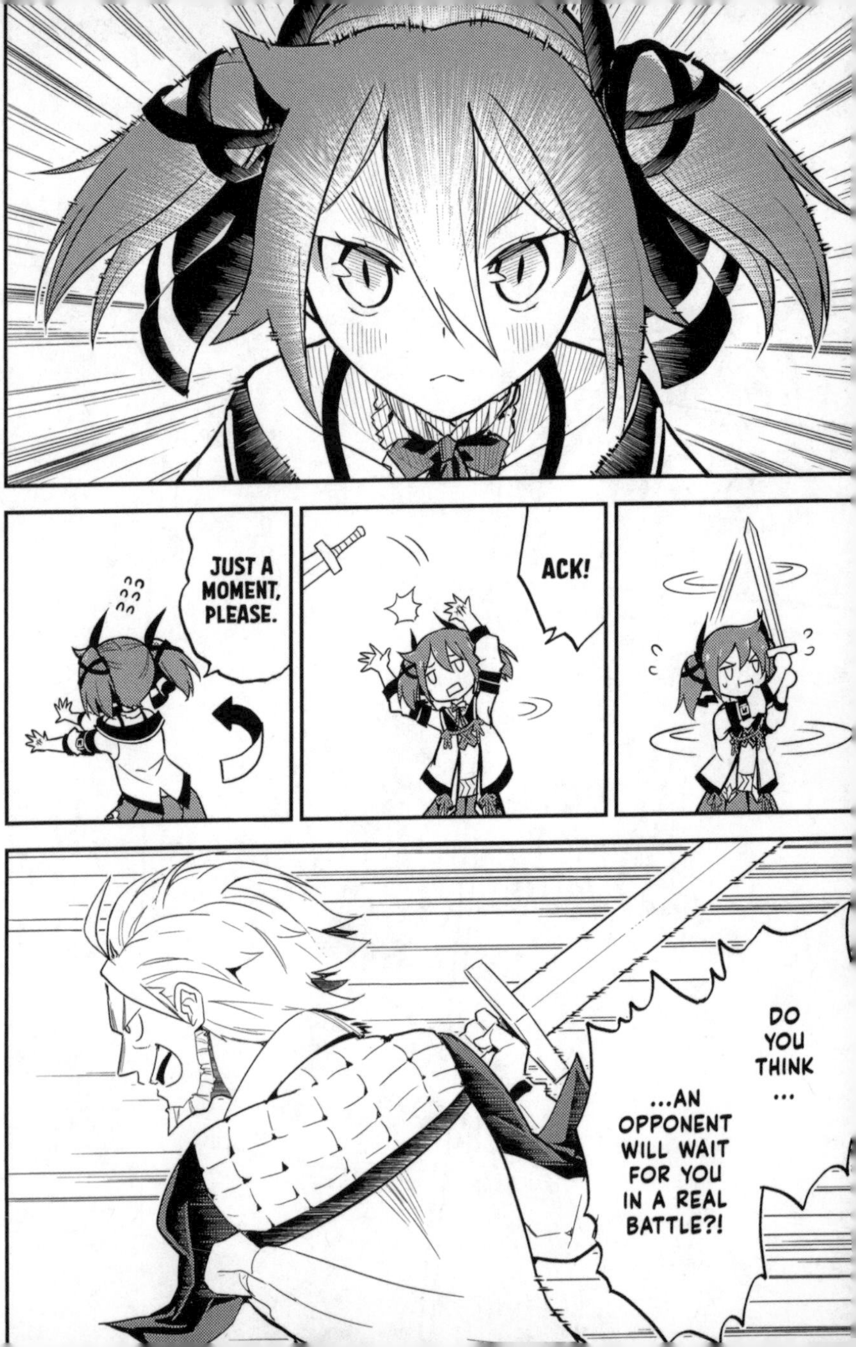
ACK!
JUST A MOMENT, PLEASE.
DO YOU THINK ...
...AN OPPONENT WILL WAIT FOR YOU IN A REAL BATTLE?!

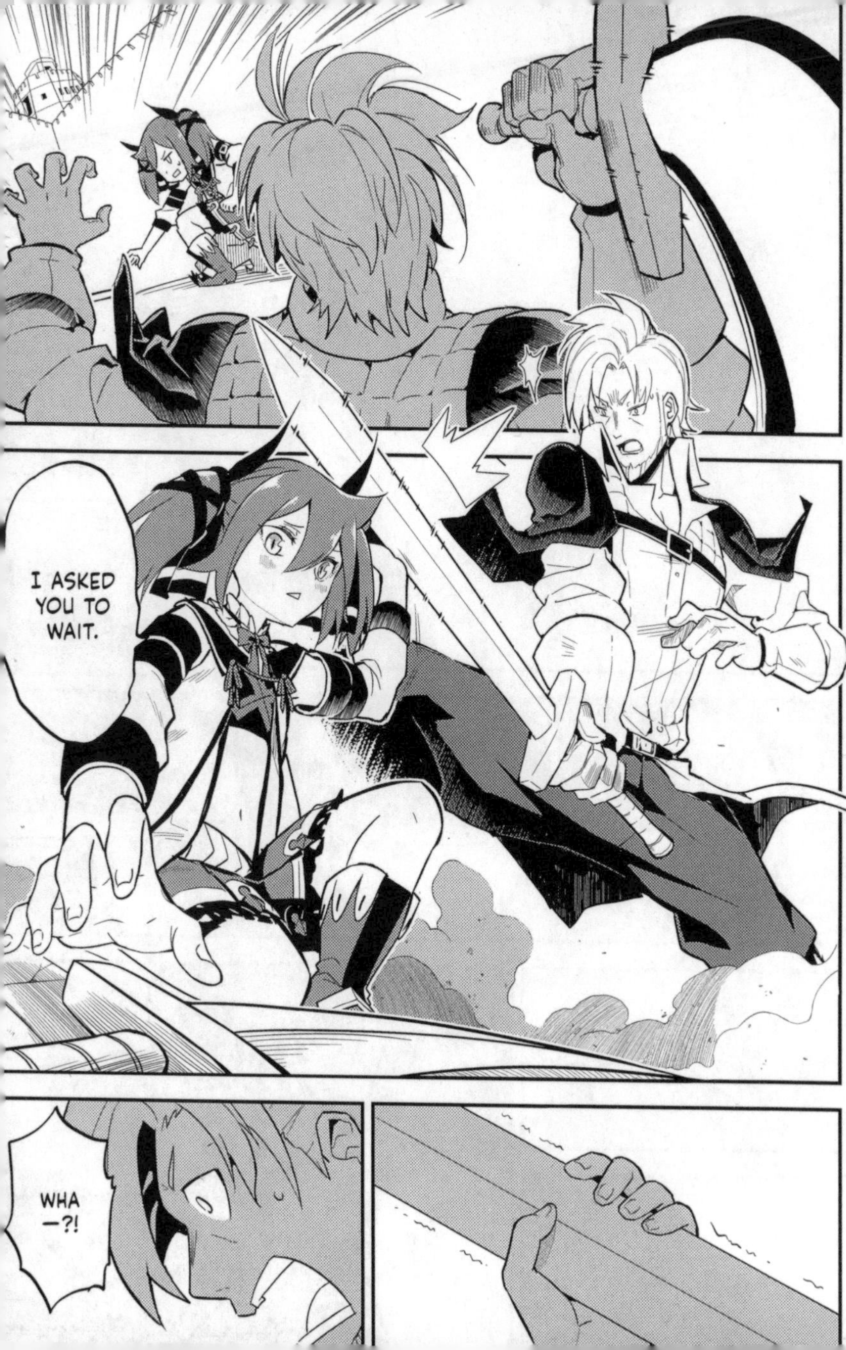
I ASKED YOU TO WAIT.
WHA —?!

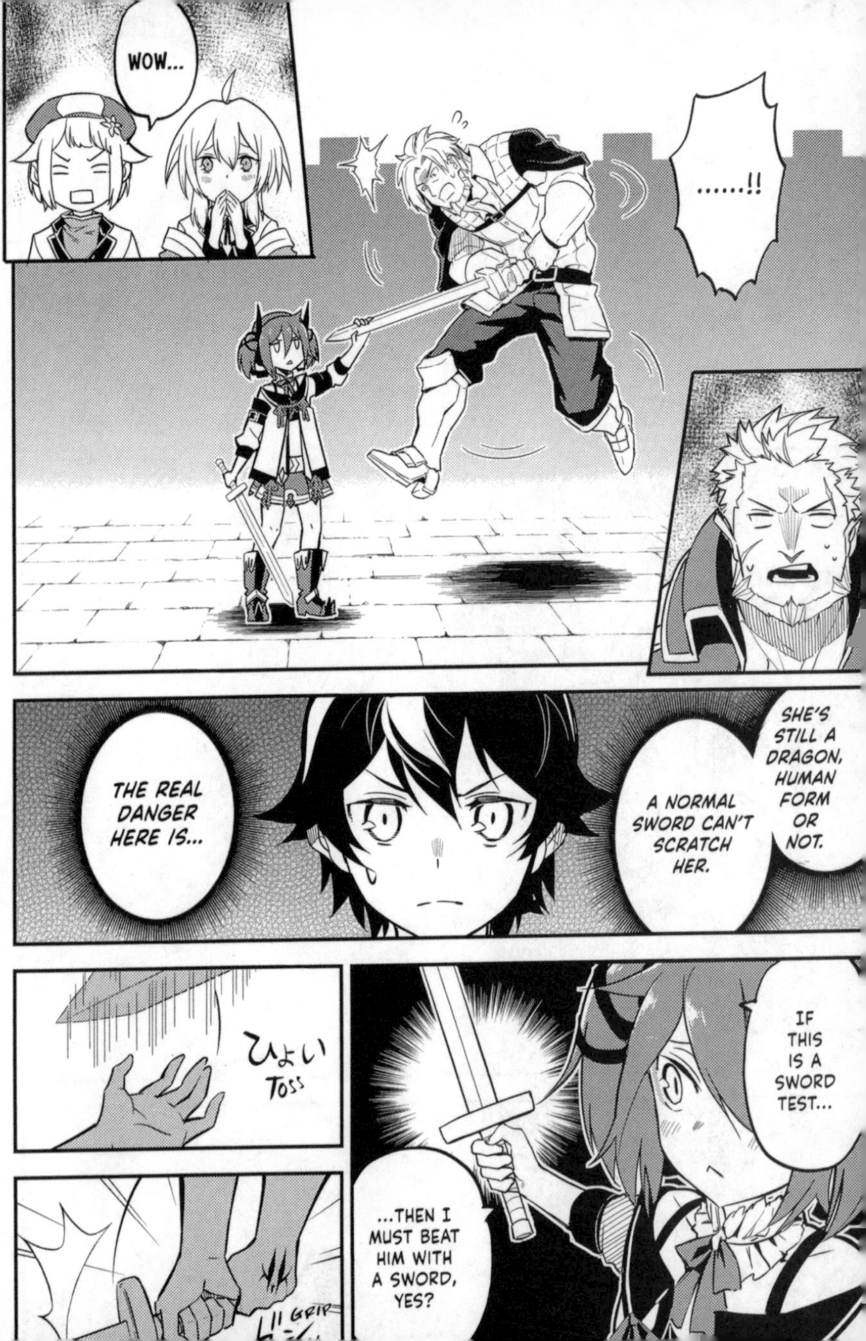
......!!
WOW...
SHE'S STILL A DRAGON, HUMAN FORM OR NOT.
A NORMAL SWORD CAN'T SCRATCH HER.
THE REAL DANGER HERE IS...
IF THIS IS A SWORD TEST...
...THEN I MUST BEAT HIM WITH A SWORD, YES?
ひょい
TOSS
GRIP

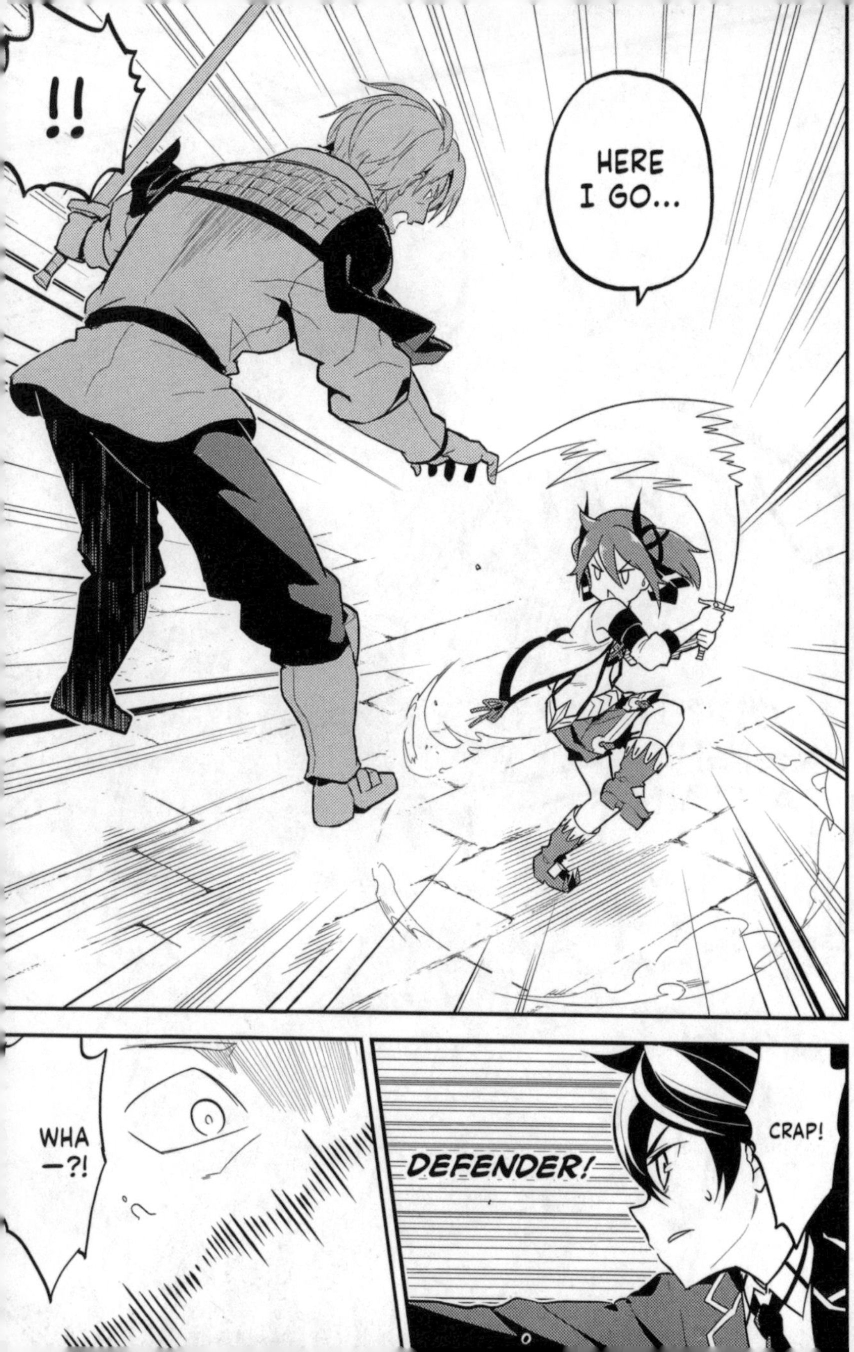
HERE I GO...
!!
CRAP!
DEFENDER!
WHA—?!

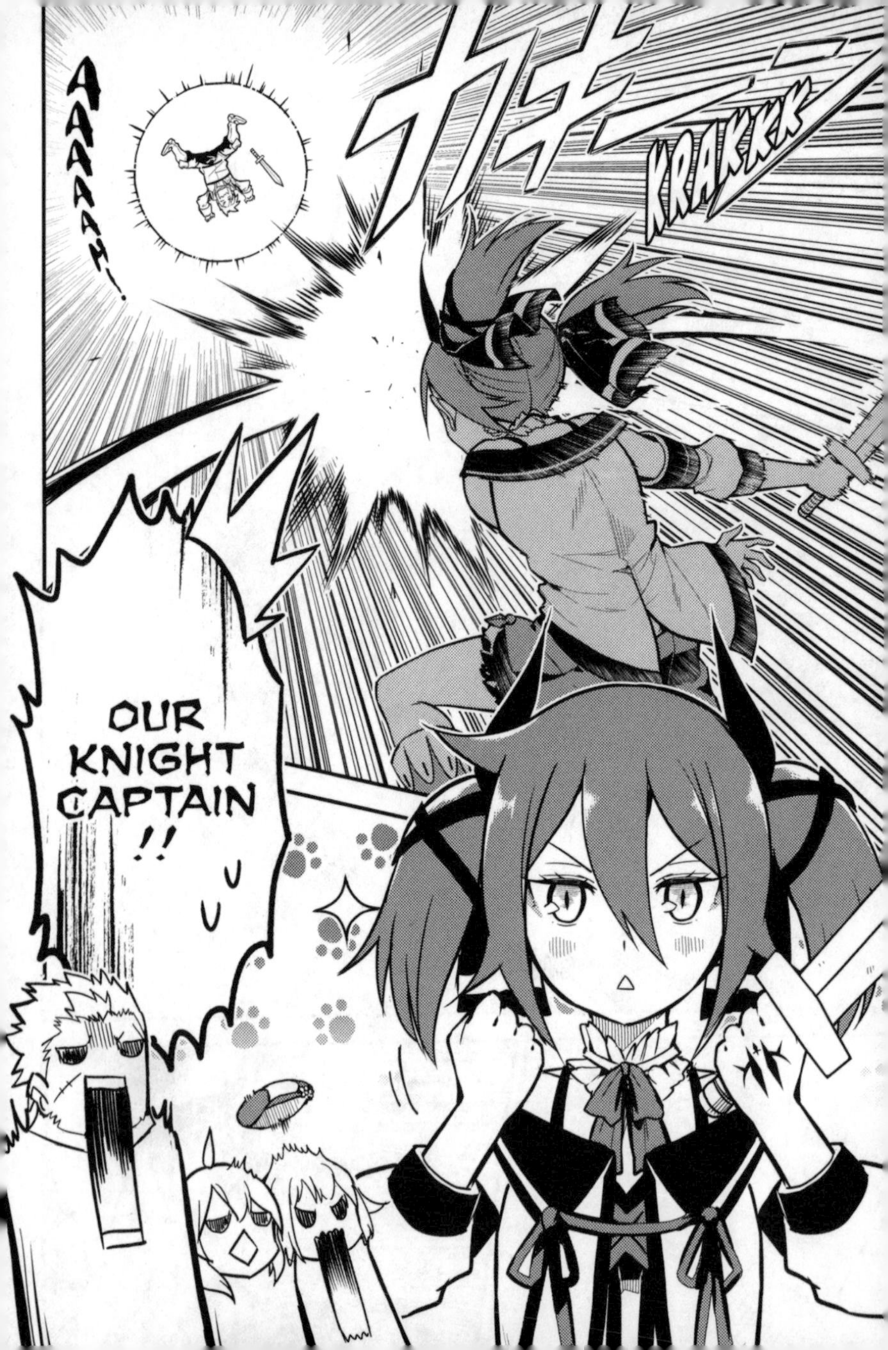
KRAKKK
AAAAAAH!
OUR KNIGHT CAPTAIN!!

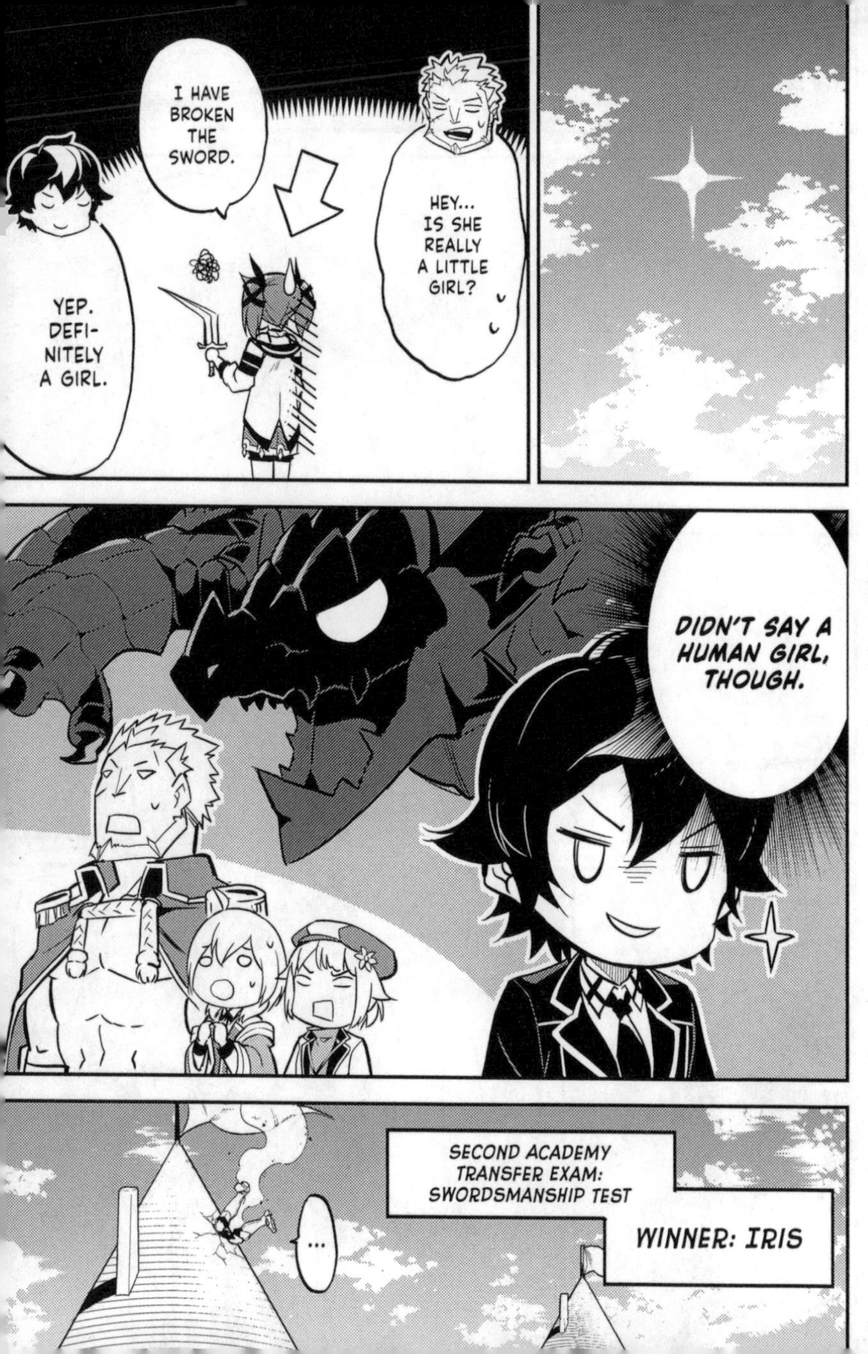
HEY... IS SHE REALLY A LITTLE GIRL?
I HAVE BROKEN THE SWORD.
YEP. DEFI-NITELY A GIRL.
DIDN'T SAY A HUMAN GIRL, THOUGH.
SECOND ACADEMY TRANSFER EXAM: SWORDSMANSHIP TEST
WINNER: IRIS
...

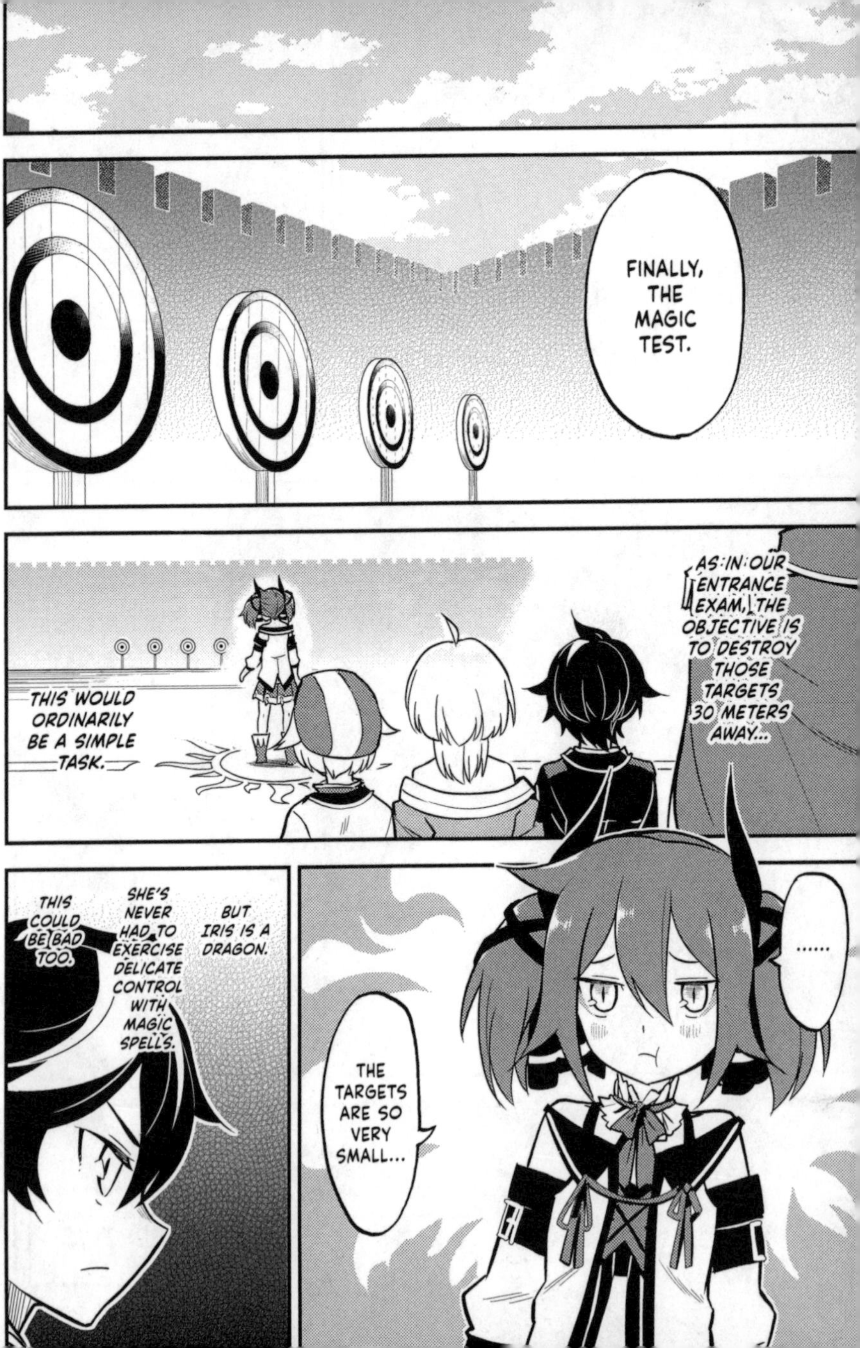
FINALLY, THE MAGIC TEST.
AS IN OUR ENTRANCE EXAM, THE OBJECTIVE IS TO DESTROY THOSE TARGETS 30 METERS AWAY...
THIS WOULD ORDINARILY BE A SIMPLE TASK.
......
THE TARGETS ARE SO VERY SMALL...
BUT IRIS IS A DRAGON.
SHE'S NEVER HAD TO EXERCISE DELICATE CONTROL WITH MAGIC SPELLS.
THIS COULD BE BAD TOO.

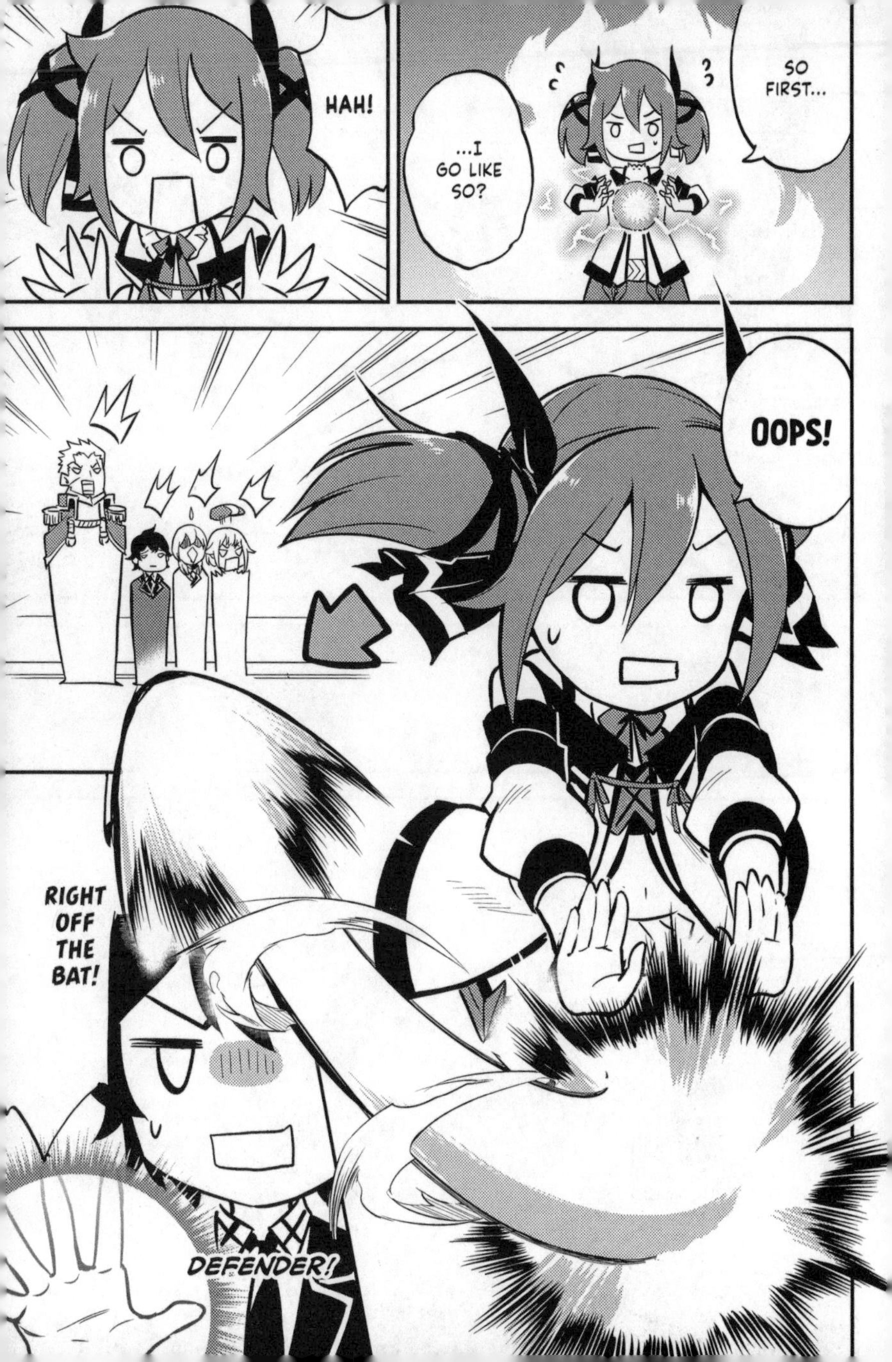
SO FIRST...
...I GO LIKE SO?
HAH!
OOPS!
RIGHT OFF THE BAT!
DEFENDER!

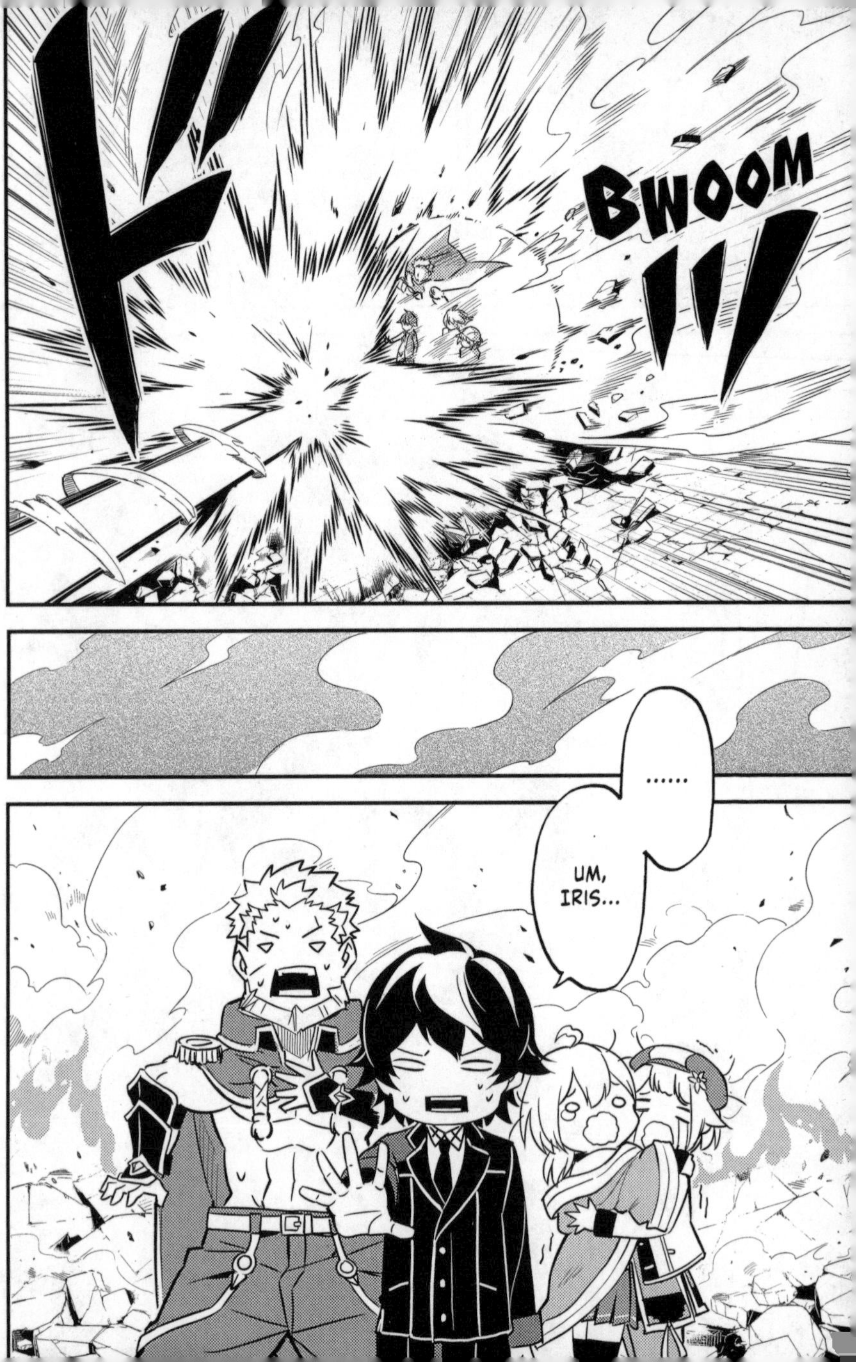
ド
BWOOM
......
UM, IRIS...

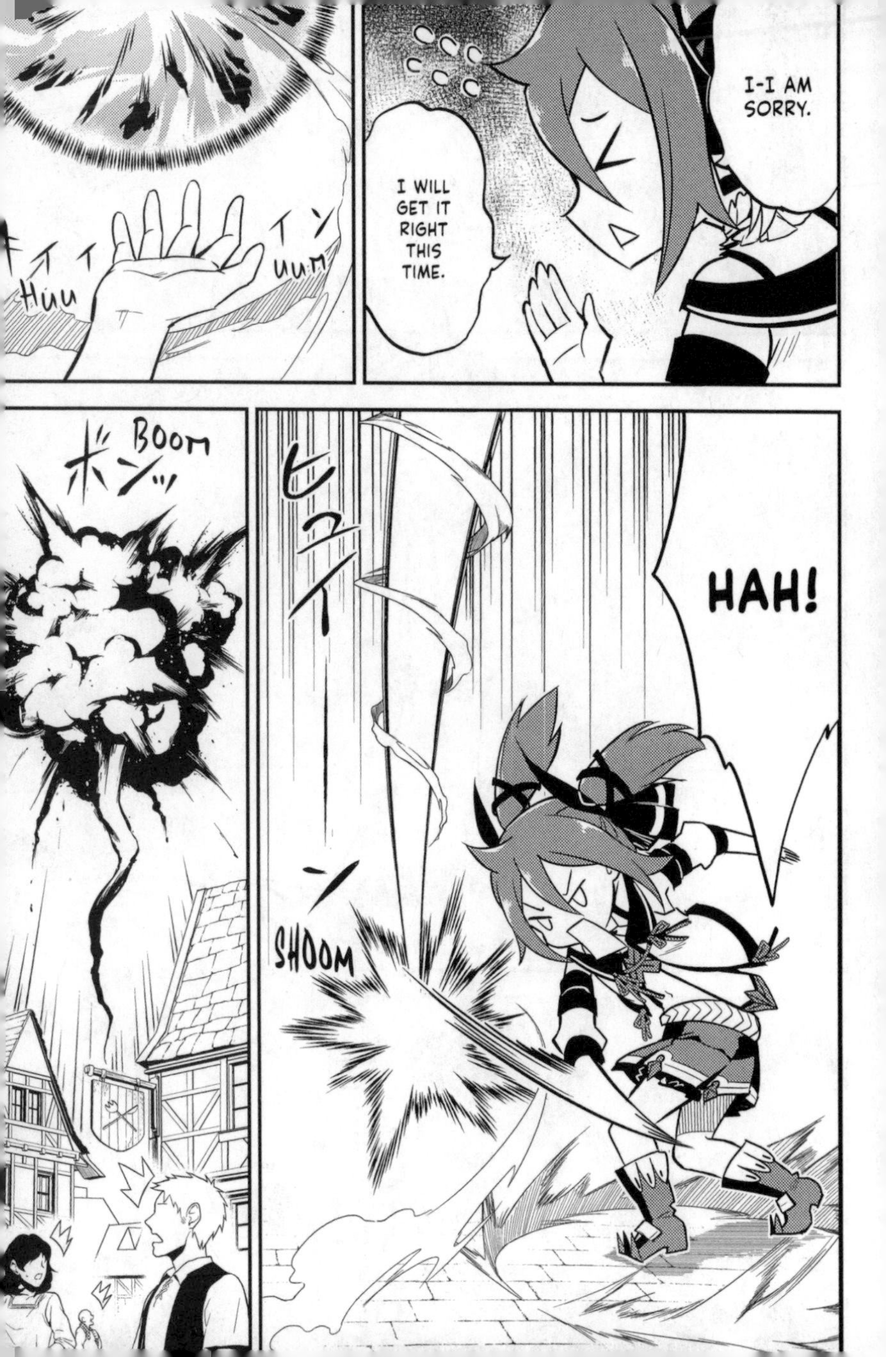

I-I AM SORRY.
I WILL GET IT RIGHT THIS TIME.
Huu uum
HAH!
SHOOM
ボンッ
BOOM

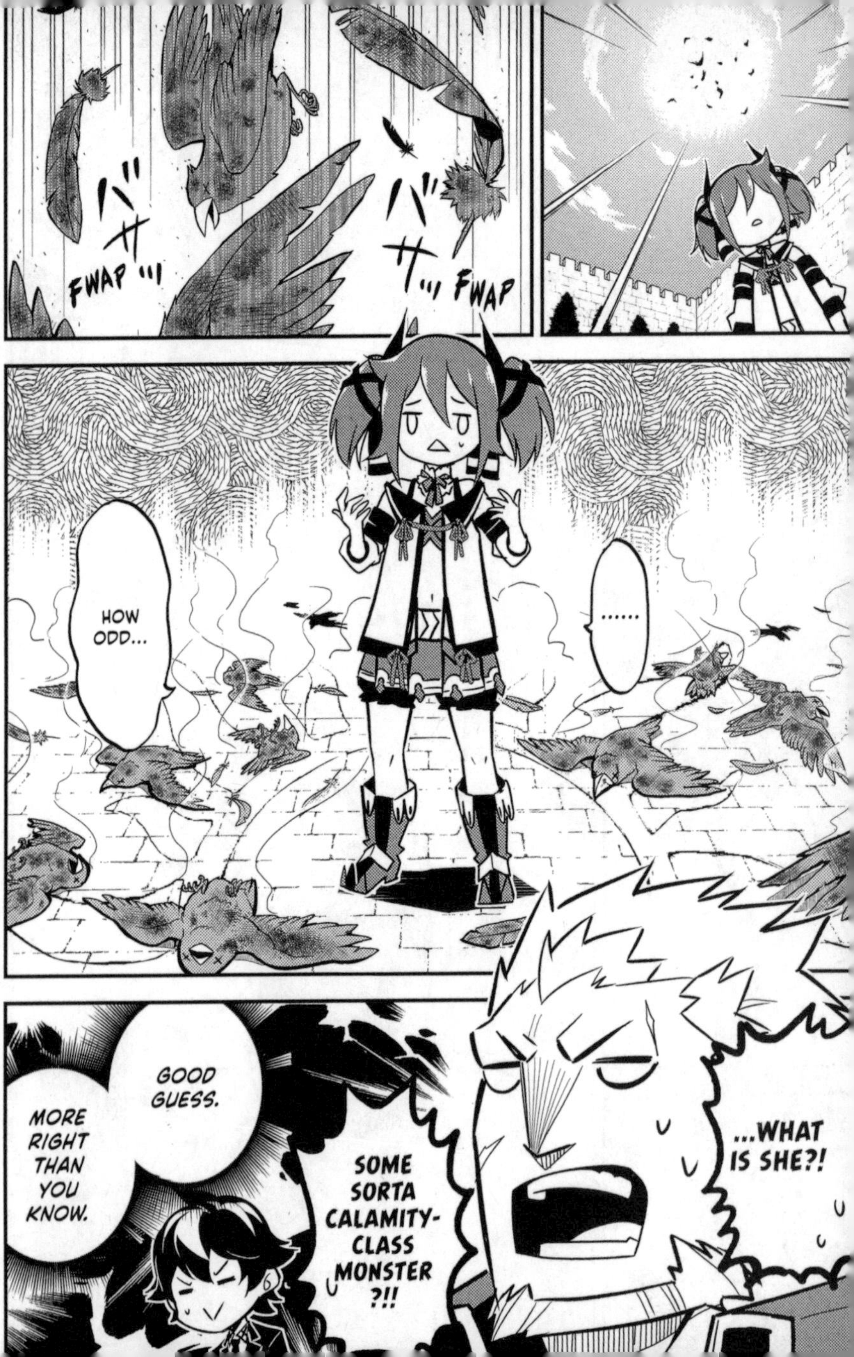
バサ FWAP
バサ FWAP
......
HOW ODD...
...WHAT IS SHE?!
SOME SORTA CALAMITY-CLASS MONSTER ?!!
GOOD GUESS.
MORE RIGHT THAN YOU KNOW.

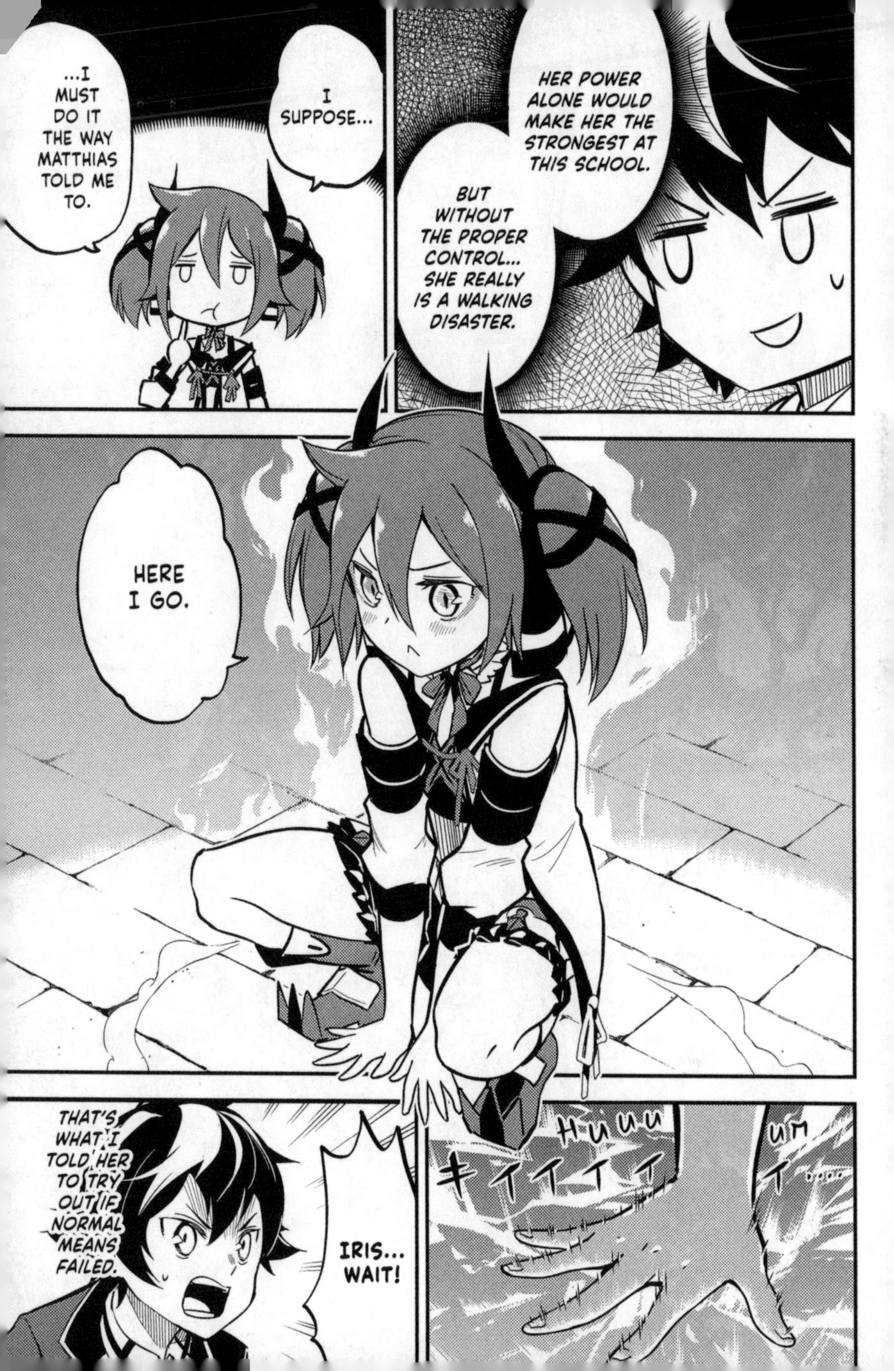
HER POWER ALONE WOULD MAKE HER THE STRONGEST AT THIS SCHOOL.
BUT WITHOUT THE PROPER CONTROL... SHE REALLY IS A WALKING DISASTER.
I SUPPOSE...
...I MUST DO IT THE WAY MATTHIAS TOLD ME TO.
HERE I GO.
HUUUUM
キイイイイ
イ…
IRIS... WAIT!
THAT'S WHAT I TOLD HER TO TRY OUT IF NORMAL MEANS FAILED.

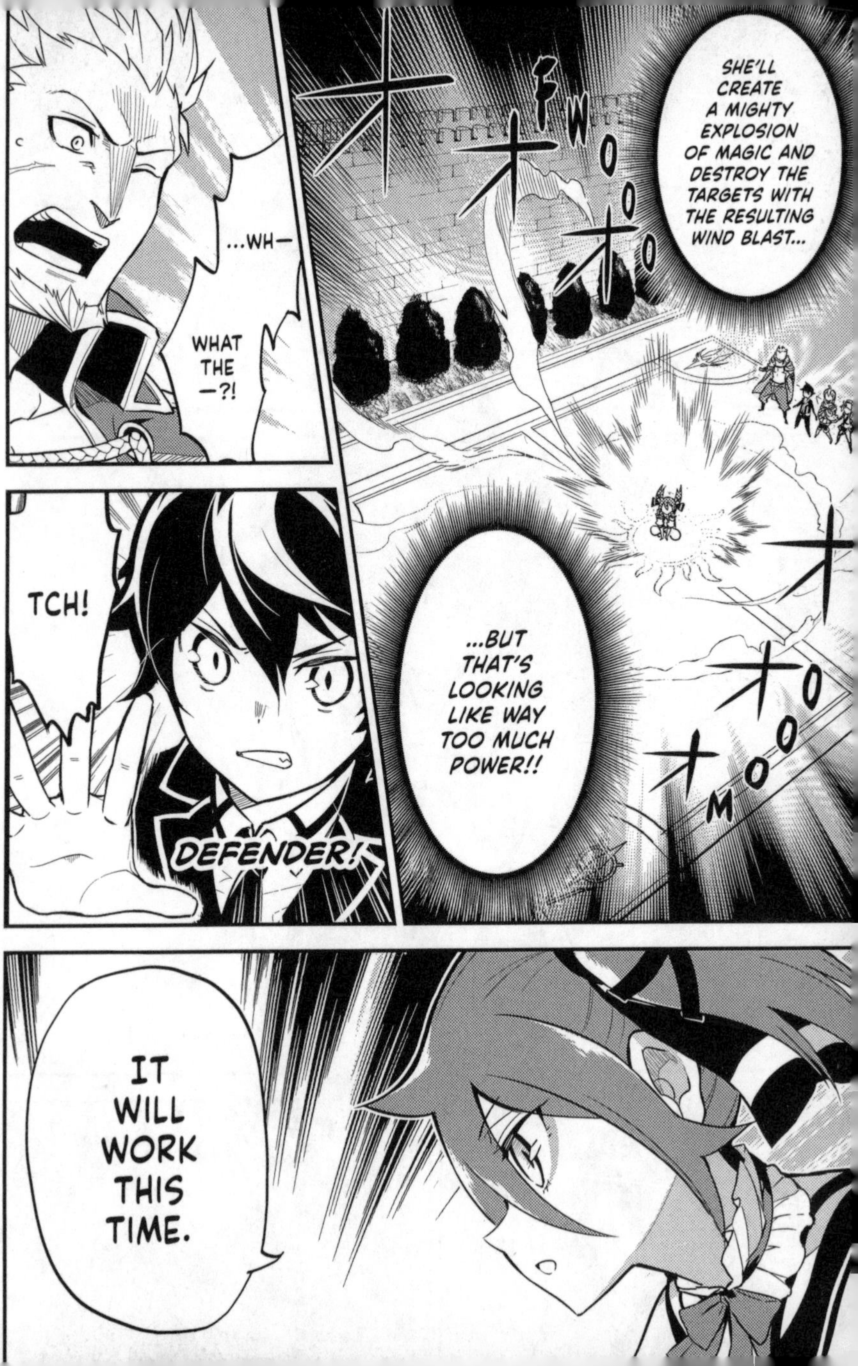
SHE'LL CREATE A MIGHTY EXPLOSION OF MAGIC AND DESTROY THE TARGETS WITH THE RESULTING WIND BLAST...
FWOOOO
...BUT THAT'S LOOKING LIKE WAY TOO MUCH POWER!!
OOOM
...WH—
WHAT THE —?!
TCH!
DEFENDER!
IT WILL WORK THIS TIME.

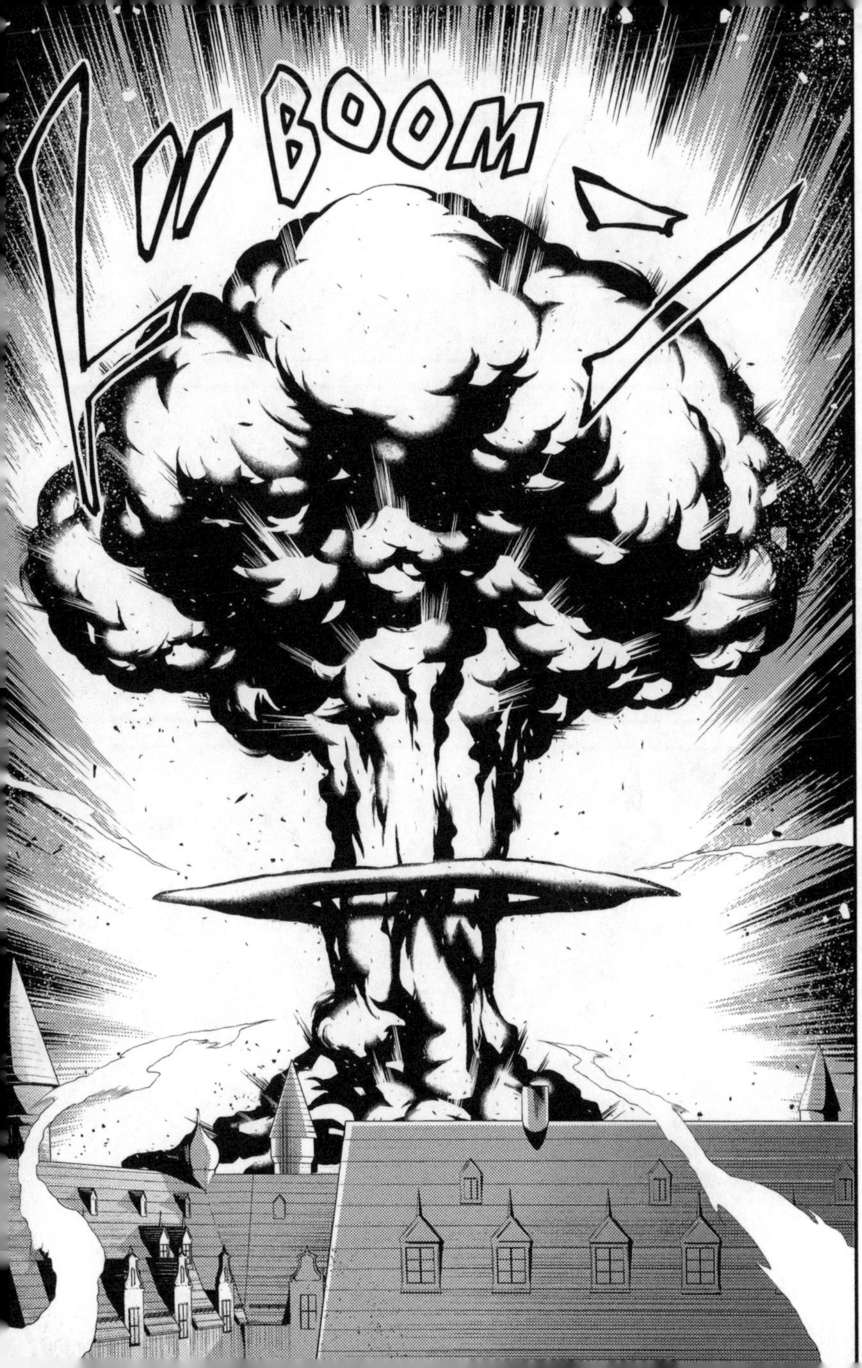
BOOM

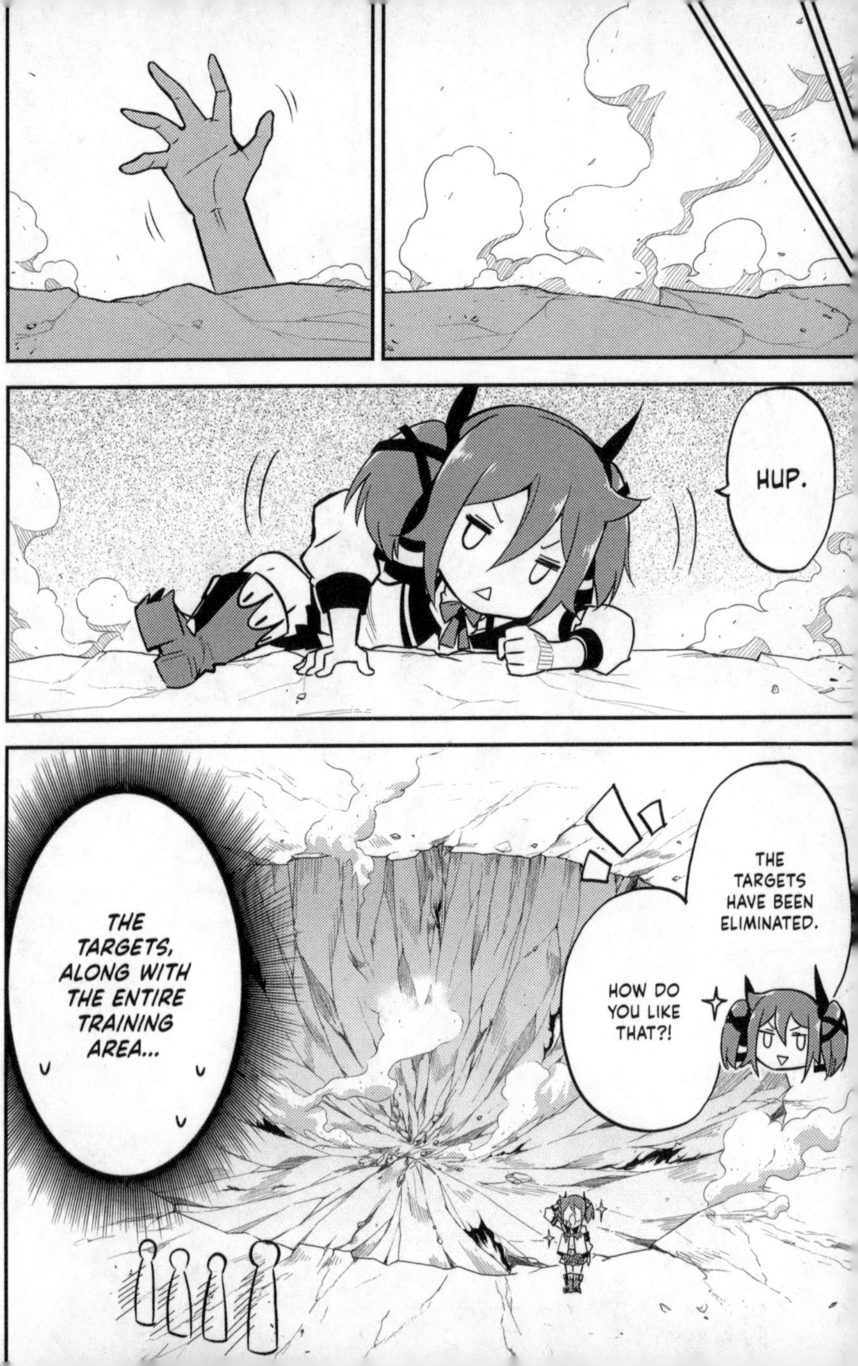
HUP.
THE TARGETS HAVE BEEN ELIMINATED.
HOW DO YOU LIKE THAT?!
THE TARGETS, ALONG WITH THE ENTIRE TRAINING AREA...

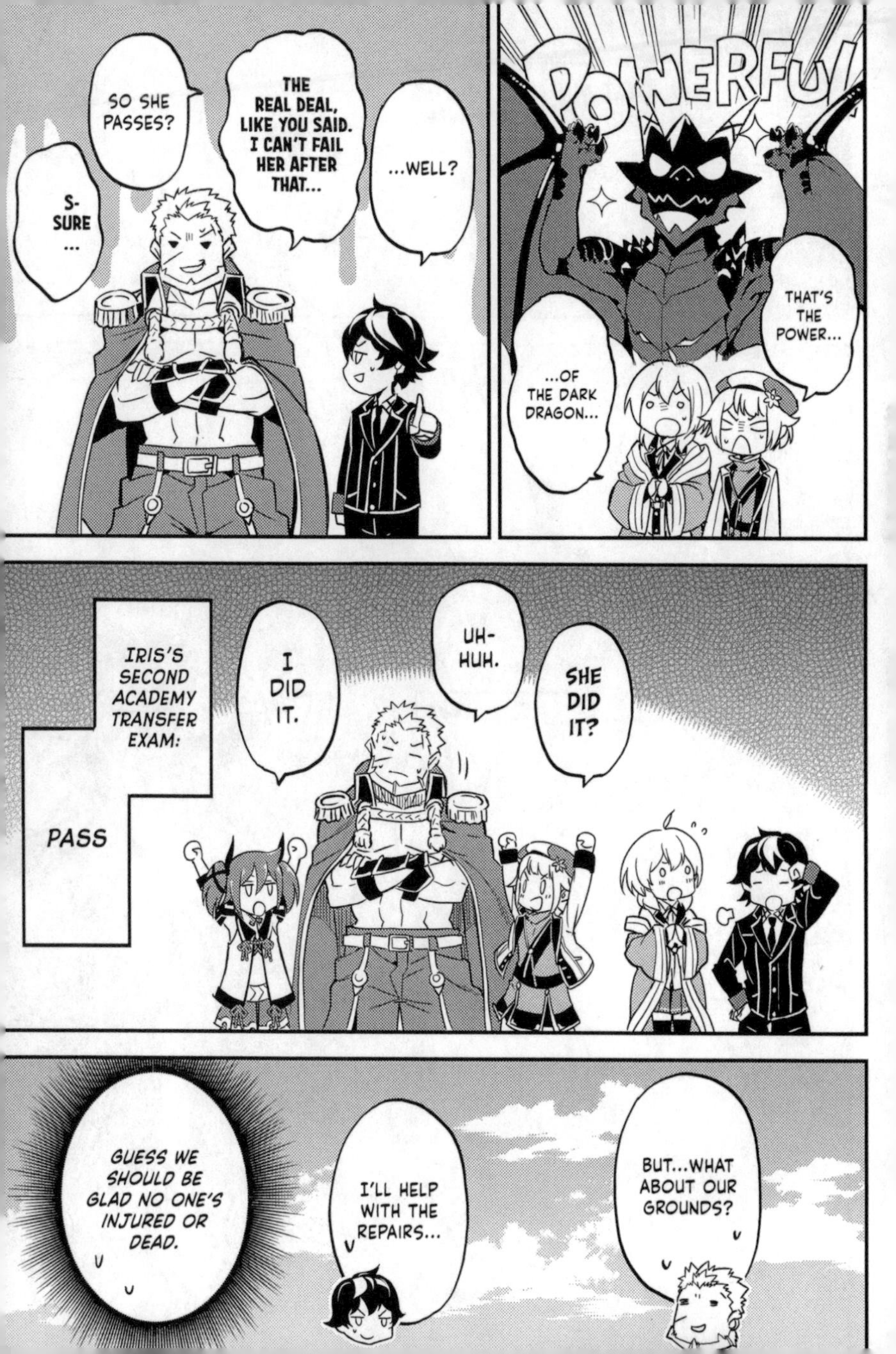

POWERFUL
THAT'S THE POWER...
...OF THE DARK DRAGON...
...WELL?
THE REAL DEAL, LIKE YOU SAID. I CAN'T FAIL HER AFTER THAT...
SO SHE PASSES?
S-SURE ...
SHE DID IT?
UH-HUH.
I DID IT.
IRIS'S SECOND ACADEMY TRANSFER EXAM:
PASS
BUT...WHAT ABOUT OUR GROUNDS?
I'LL HELP WITH THE REPAIRS...
GUESS WE SHOULD BE GLAD NO ONE'S INJURED OR DEAD.

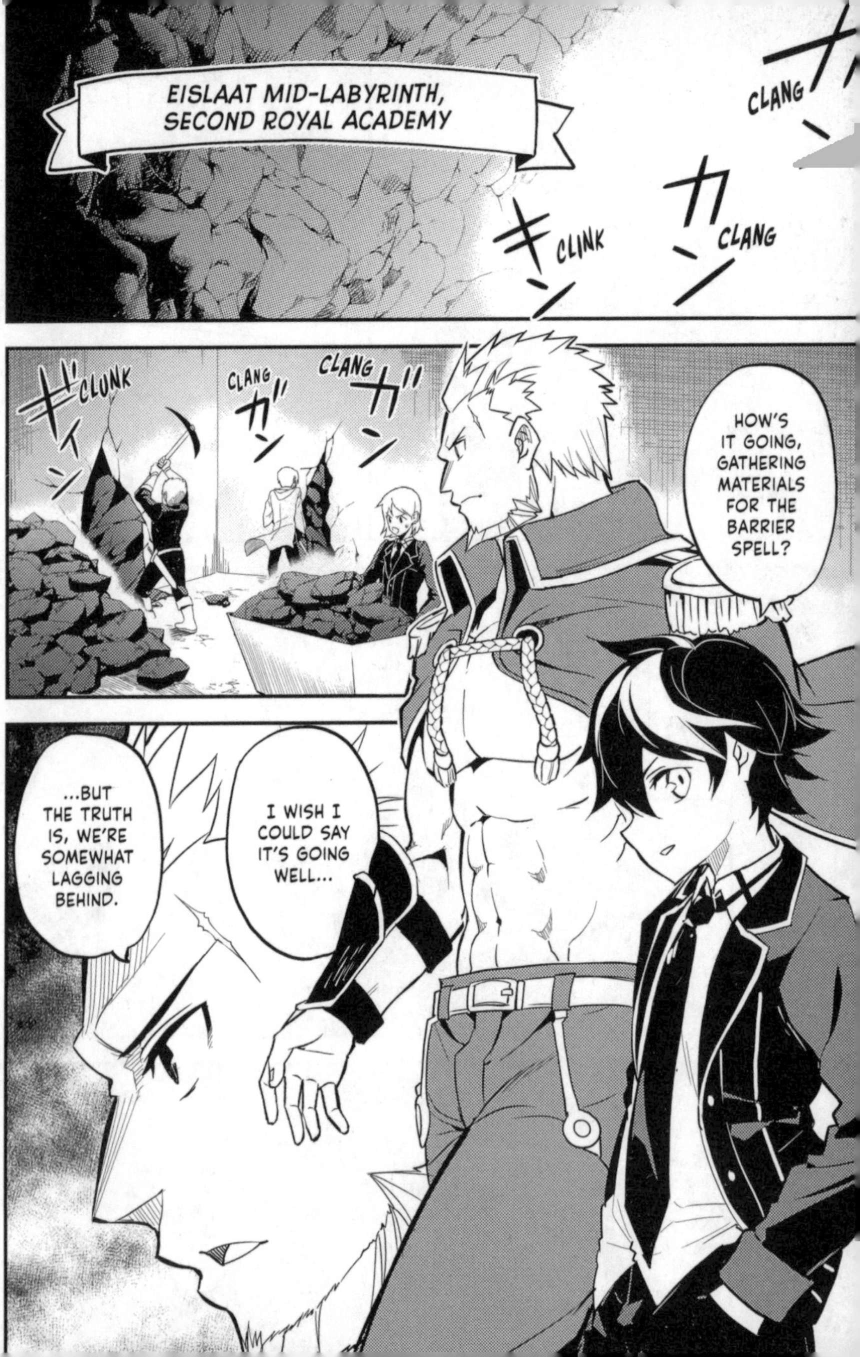
CLANG
カン CLANG
キン CLINK
EISLAAT MID-LABYRINTH, SECOND ROYAL ACADEMY
HOW'S IT GOING, GATHERING MATERIALS FOR THE BARRIER SPELL?
ガン CLANG
ガン CLANG
ギイン CLUNK
I WISH I COULD SAY IT'S GOING WELL...
...BUT THE TRUTH IS, WE'RE SOMEWHAT LAGGING BEHIND.

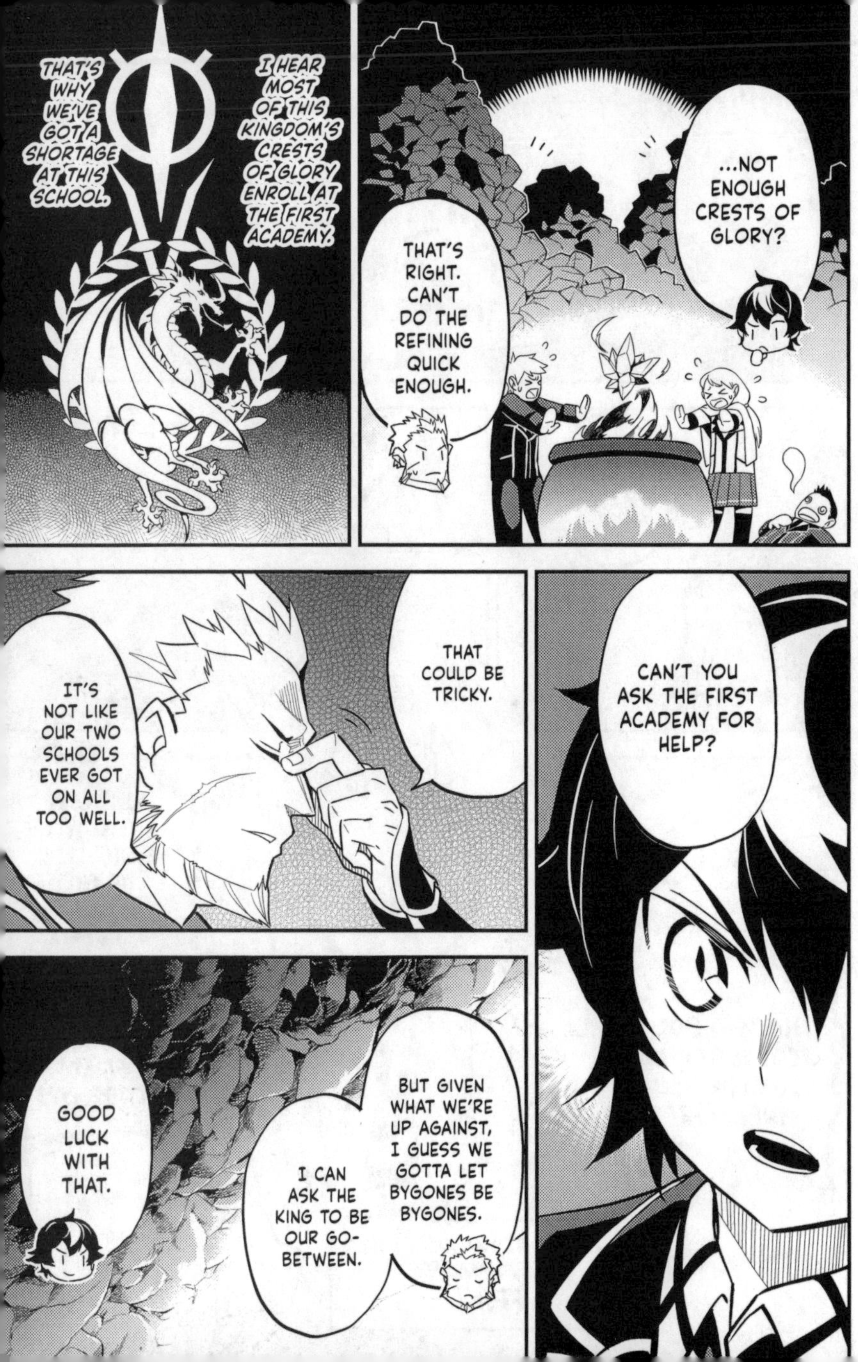
...NOT ENOUGH CRESTS OF GLORY?
THAT'S RIGHT. CAN'T DO THE REFINING QUICK ENOUGH.
I HEAR MOST OF THIS KINGDOM'S CRESTS OF GLORY ENROLL AT THE FIRST ACADEMY.
THAT'S WHY WE'VE GOT A SHORTAGE AT THIS SCHOOL.
CAN'T YOU ASK THE FIRST ACADEMY FOR HELP?
THAT COULD BE TRICKY.
IT'S NOT LIKE OUR TWO SCHOOLS EVER GOT ON ALL TOO WELL.
BUT GIVEN WHAT WE'RE UP AGAINST, I GUESS WE GOTTA LET BYGONES BE BYGONES.
I CAN ASK THE KING TO BE OUR GO-BETWEEN.
GOOD LUCK WITH THAT.

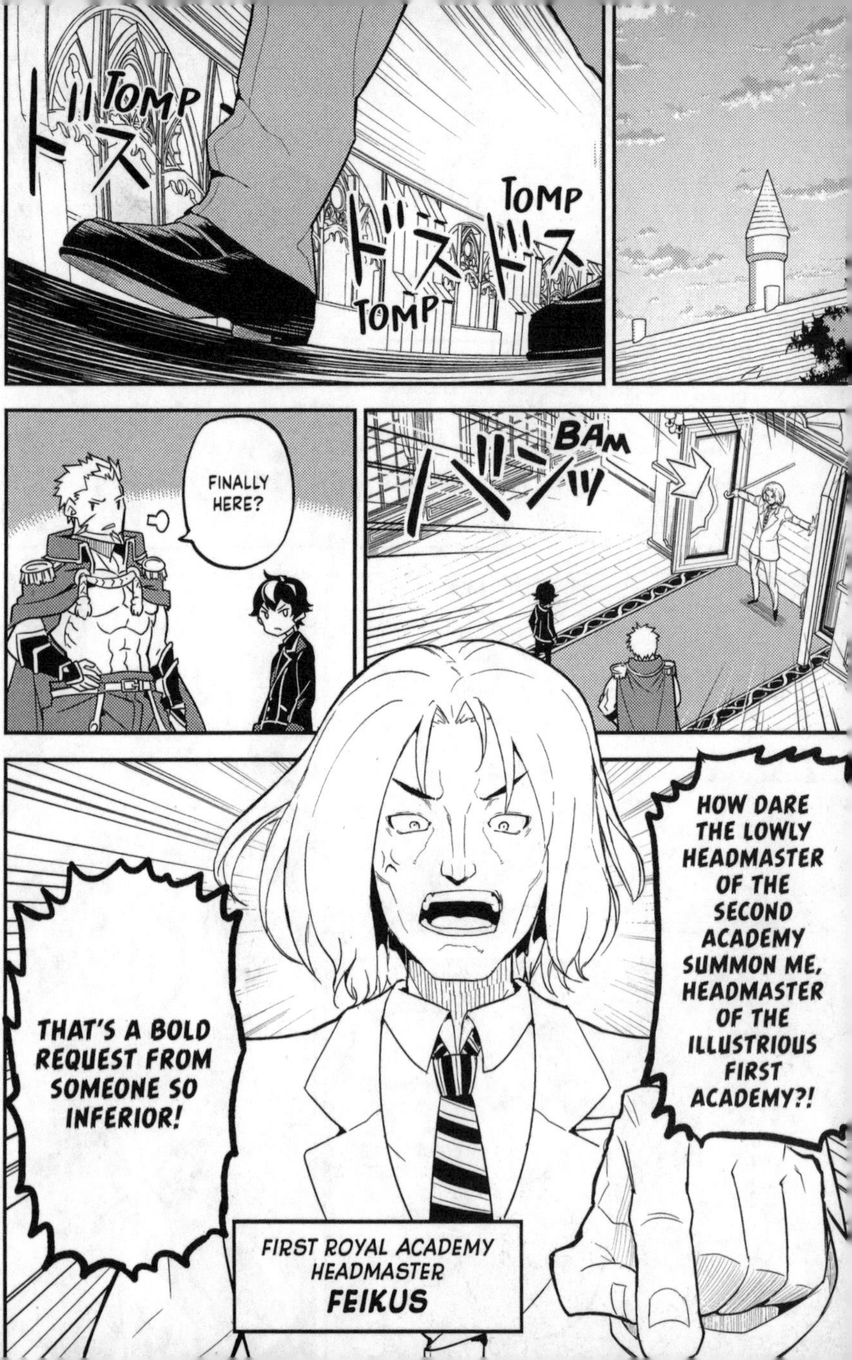
ドスドス
TOMP
TOMP
ドス
TOMP
バーンッ
BAM
FINALLY HERE?
HOW DARE THE LOWLY HEADMASTER OF THE SECOND ACADEMY SUMMON ME, HEADMASTER OF THE ILLUSTRIOUS FIRST ACADEMY?!
THAT'S A BOLD REQUEST FROM SOMEONE SO INFERIOR!
FIRST ROYAL ACADEMY HEADMASTER
FEIKUS

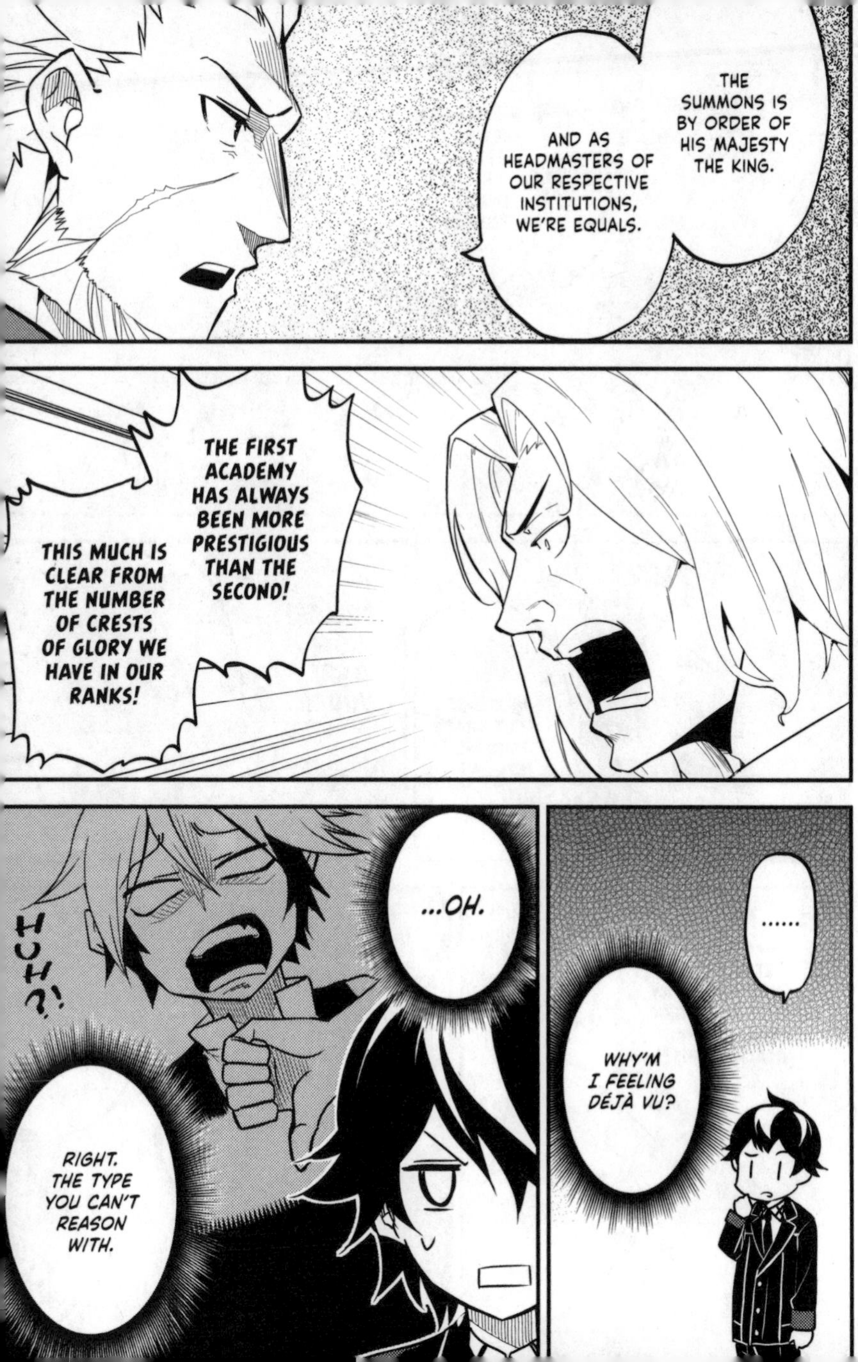
THE SUMMONS IS BY ORDER OF HIS MAJESTY THE KING.
AND AS HEADMASTERS OF OUR RESPECTIVE INSTITUTIONS, WE'RE EQUALS.
THE FIRST ACADEMY HAS ALWAYS BEEN MORE PRESTIGIOUS THAN THE SECOND!
THIS MUCH IS CLEAR FROM THE NUMBER OF CRESTS OF GLORY WE HAVE IN OUR RANKS!
......
WHY'M I FEELING DÉJÀ VU?
...OH.
HUH?!
RIGHT. THE TYPE YOU CAN'T REASON WITH.

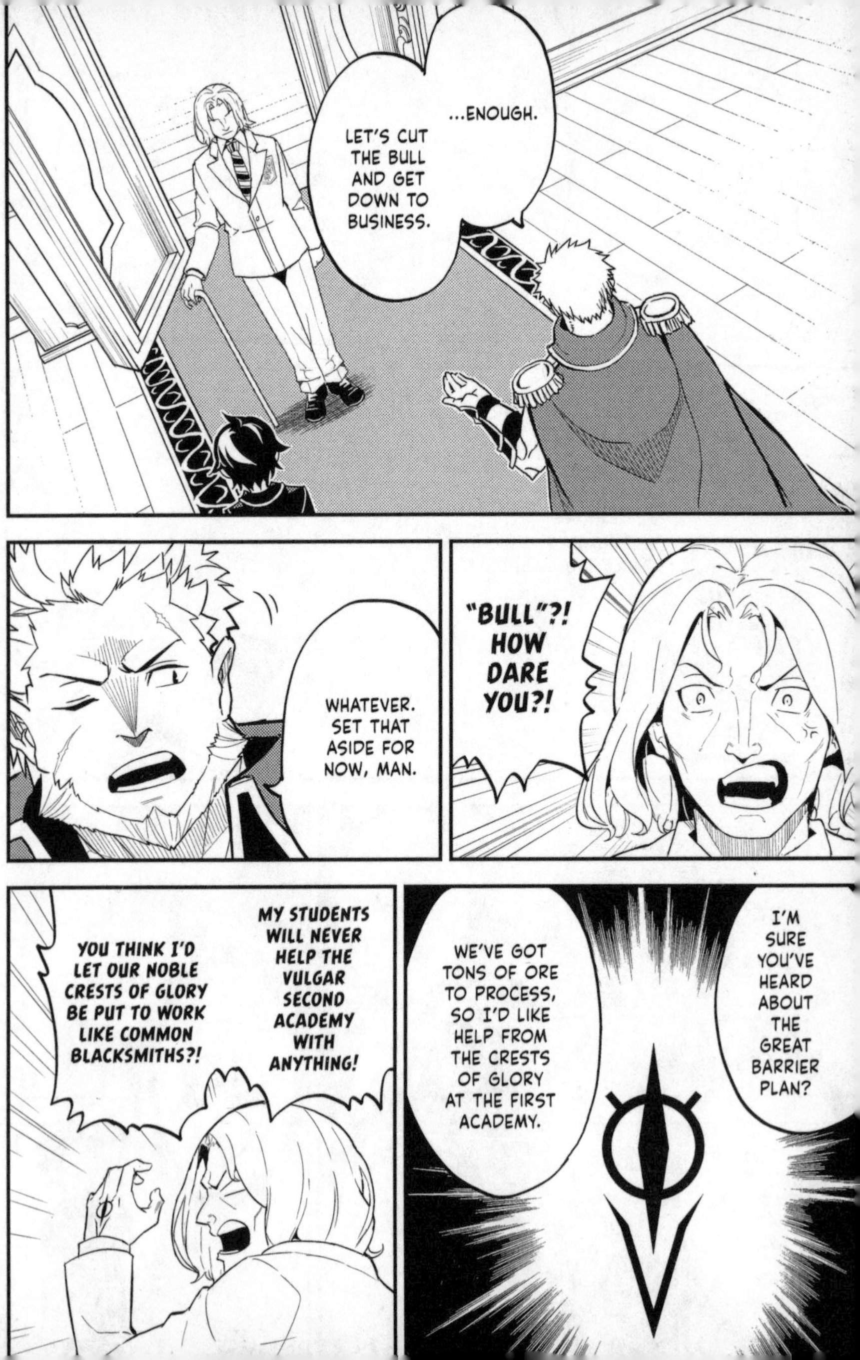
...ENOUGH.
LET'S CUT THE BULL AND GET DOWN TO BUSINESS.
"BULL"?! HOW DARE YOU?!
WHATEVER. SET THAT ASIDE FOR NOW, MAN.
I'M SURE YOU'VE HEARD ABOUT THE GREAT BARRIER PLAN?
WE'VE GOT TONS OF ORE TO PROCESS, SO I'D LIKE HELP FROM THE CRESTS OF GLORY AT THE FIRST ACADEMY.
MY STUDENTS WILL NEVER HELP THE VULGAR SECOND ACADEMY WITH ANYTHING!
YOU THINK I'D LET OUR NOBLE CRESTS OF GLORY BE PUT TO WORK LIKE COMMON BLACKSMITHS?!

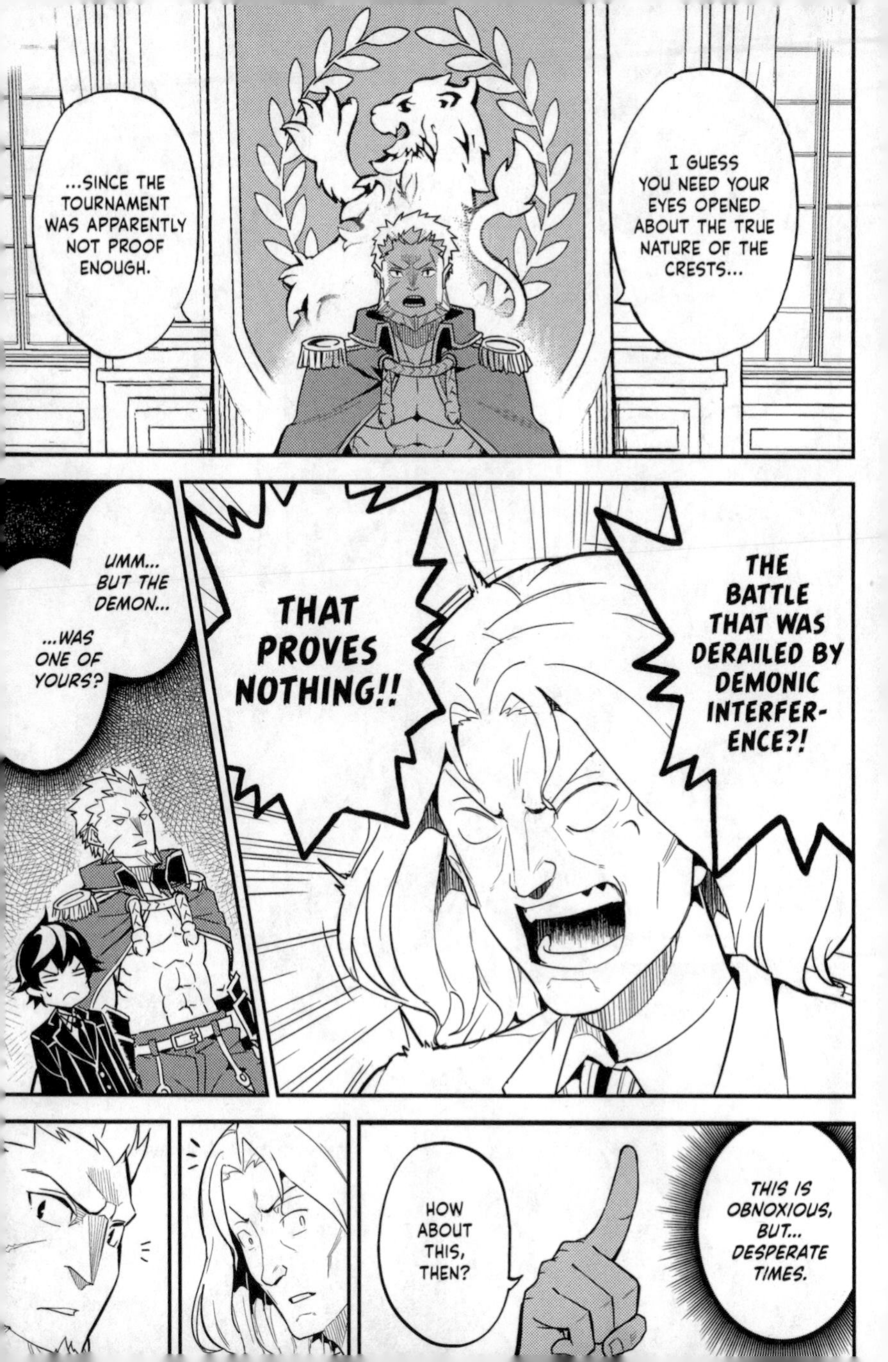
I GUESS YOU NEED YOUR EYES OPENED ABOUT THE TRUE NATURE OF THE CRESTS...
...SINCE THE TOURNAMENT WAS APPARENTLY NOT PROOF ENOUGH.
THE BATTLE THAT WAS DERAILED BY DEMONIC INTERFER-ENCE?!
THAT PROVES NOTHING!!
UMM... BUT THE DEMON...
...WAS ONE OF YOURS?
THIS IS OBNOXIOUS, BUT... DESPERATE TIMES.
HOW ABOUT THIS, THEN?

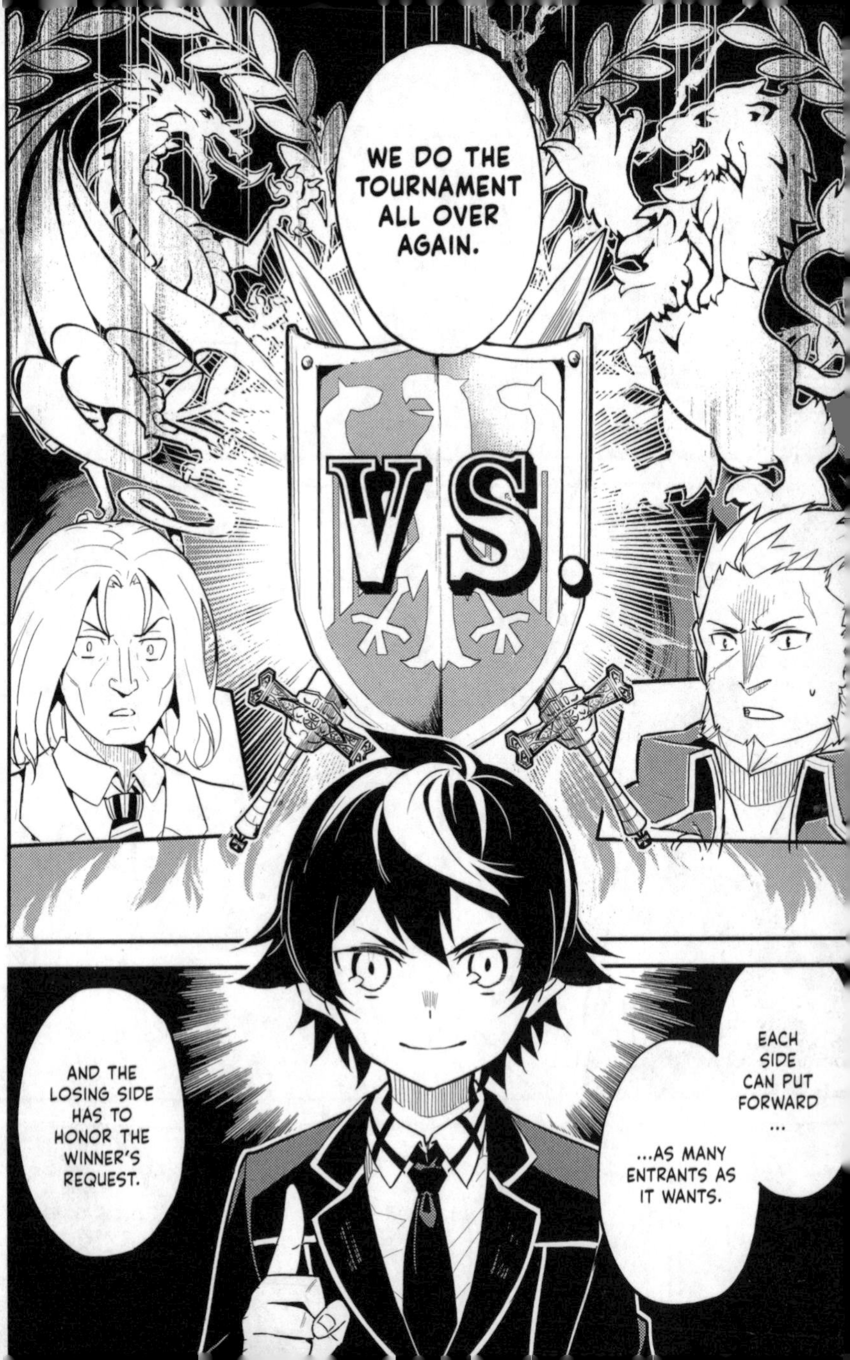
WE DO THE TOURNAMENT ALL OVER AGAIN.
VS.
EACH SIDE CAN PUT FORWARD ...
...AS MANY ENTRANTS AS IT WANTS.
AND THE LOSING SIDE HAS TO HONOR THE WINNER'S REQUEST.

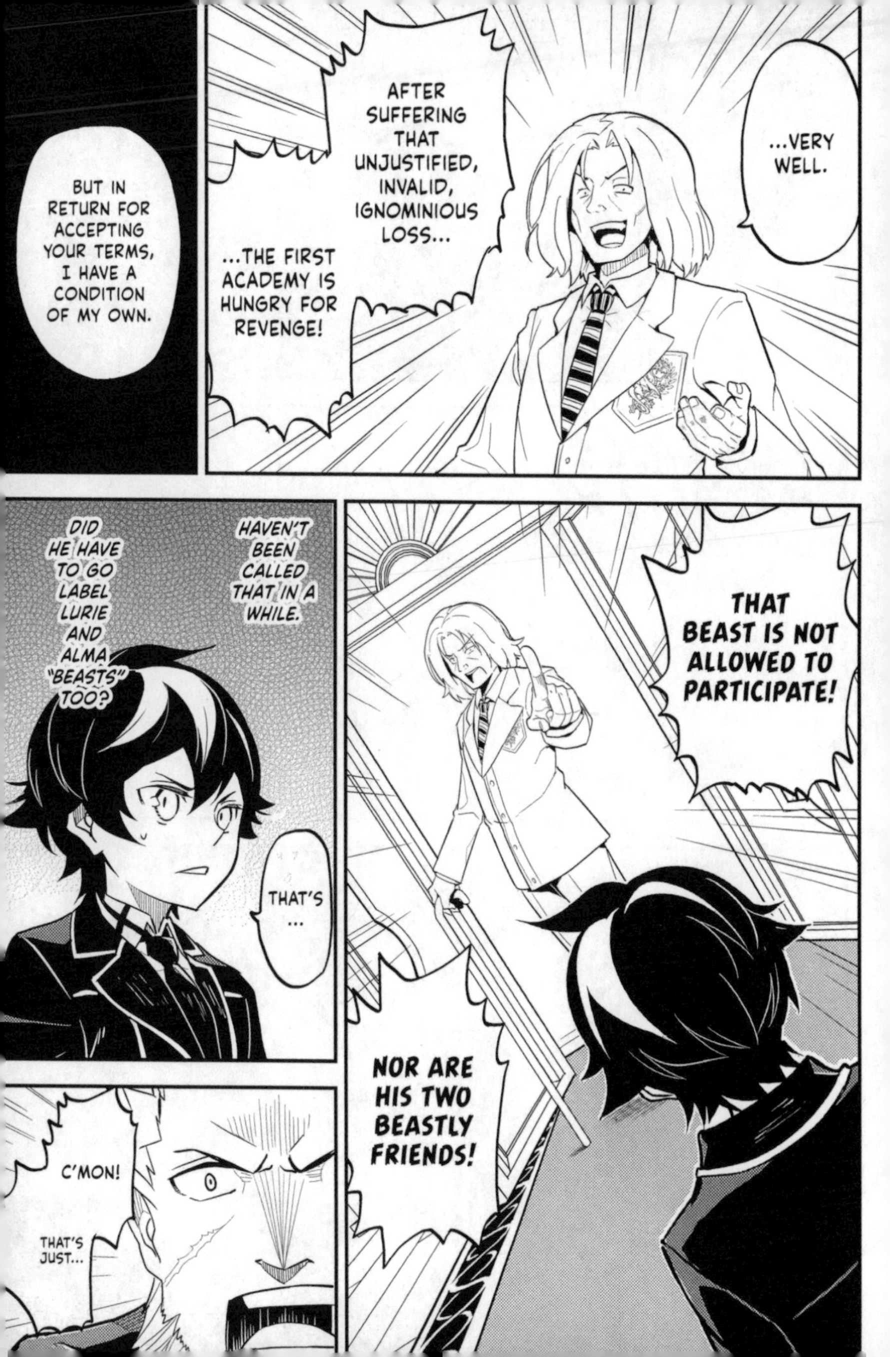
...VERY WELL.
AFTER SUFFERING THAT UNJUSTIFIED, INVALID, IGNOMINIOUS LOSS...
...THE FIRST ACADEMY IS HUNGRY FOR REVENGE!
BUT IN RETURN FOR ACCEPTING YOUR TERMS, I HAVE A CONDITION OF MY OWN.
THAT BEAST IS NOT ALLOWED TO PARTICIPATE!
NOR ARE HIS TWO BEASTLY FRIENDS!
HAVEN'T BEEN CALLED THAT IN A WHILE.
DID HE HAVE TO GO LABEL LURIE AND ALMA "BEASTS" TOO?
THAT'S ...
C'MON!
THAT'S JUST...

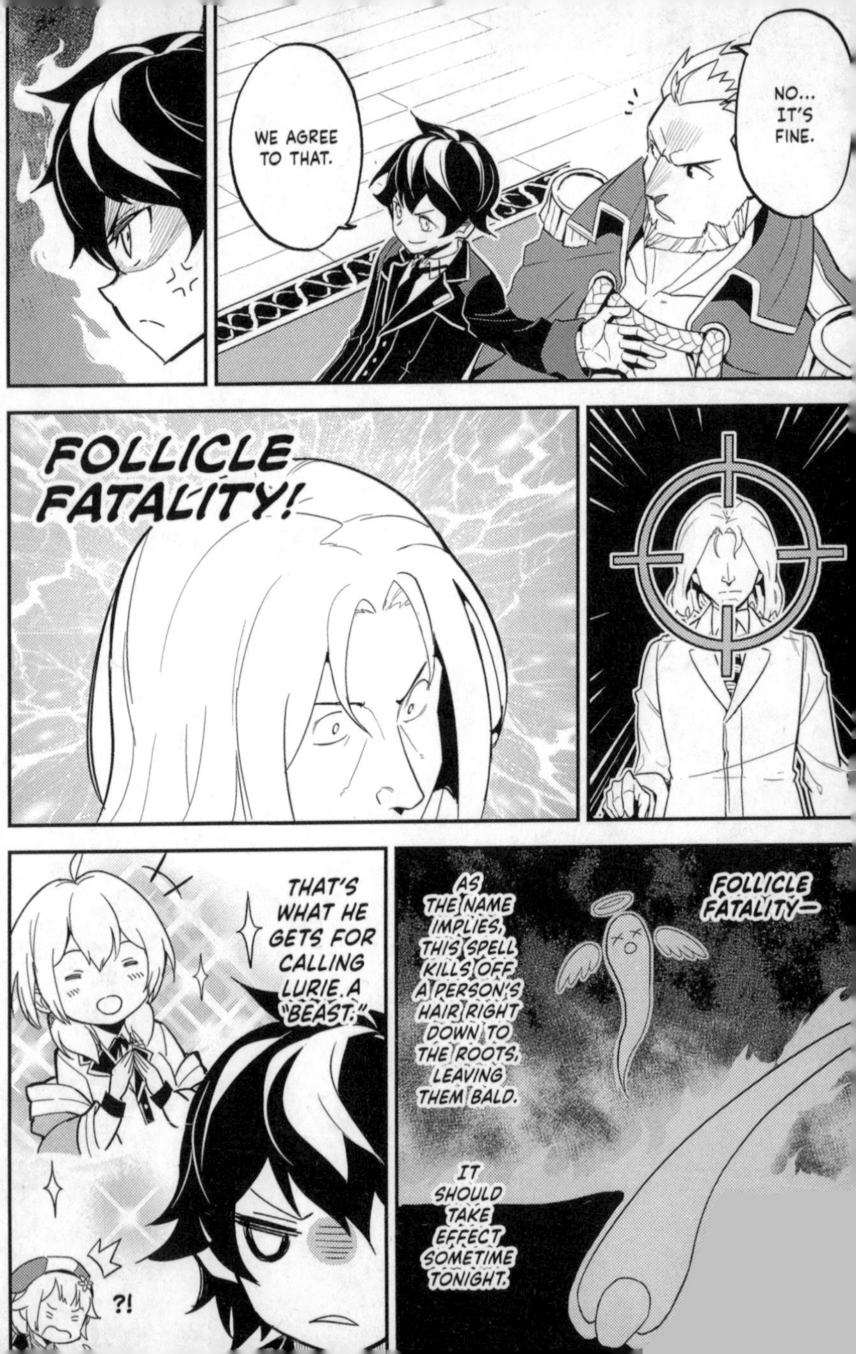
NO... IT'S FINE.
WE AGREE TO THAT.
FOLLICLE FATALITY!
FOLLICLE FATALITY—
AS THE NAME IMPLIES, THIS SPELL KILLS OFF A PERSON'S HAIR RIGHT DOWN TO THE ROOTS, LEAVING THEM BALD.
IT SHOULD TAKE EFFECT SOMETIME TONIGHT.
THAT'S WHAT HE GETS FOR CALLING LURIE A "BEAST."
?!

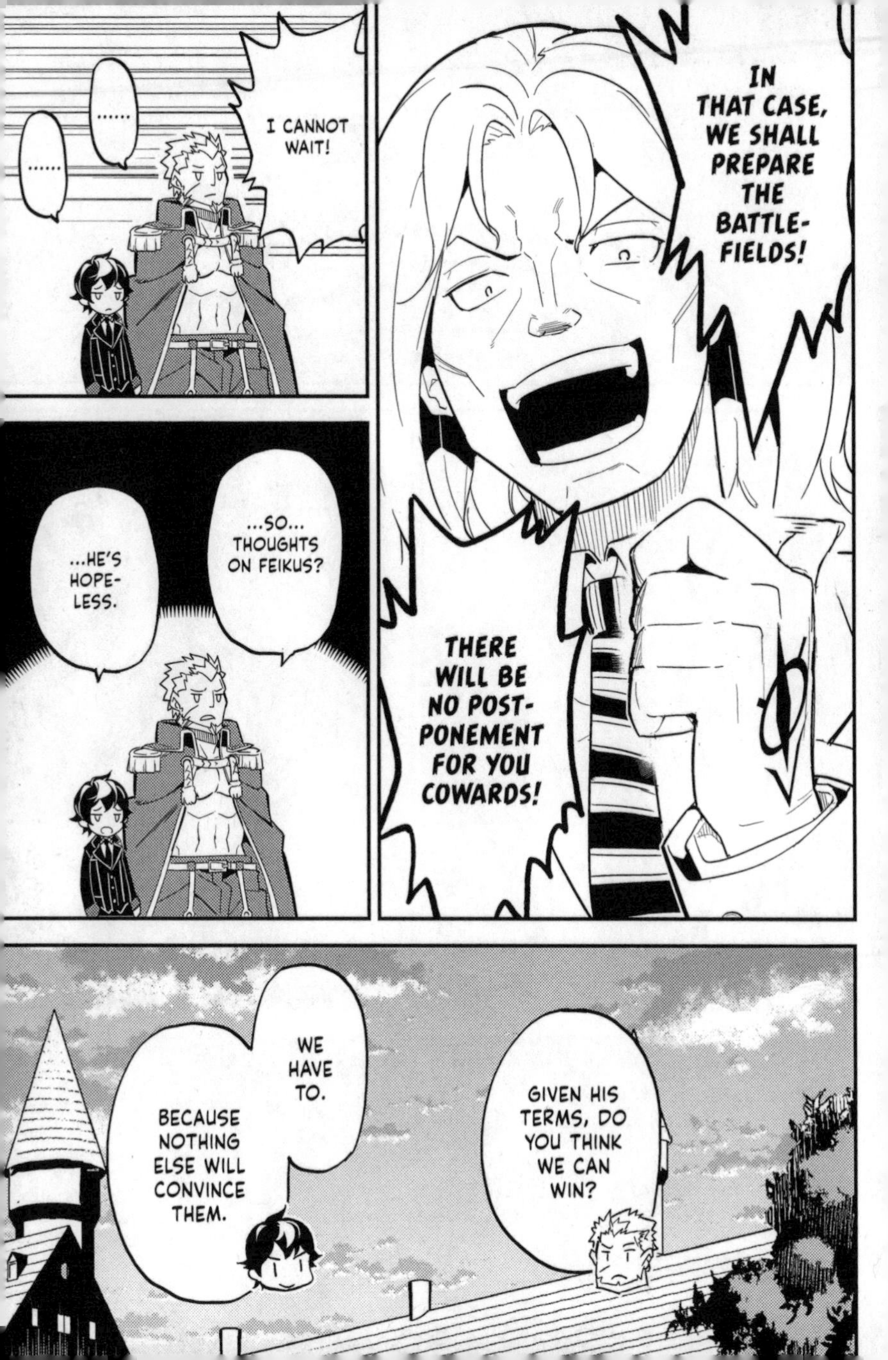
IN THAT CASE, WE SHALL PREPARE THE BATTLE-FIELDS!
THERE WILL BE NO POST-PONEMENT FOR YOU COWARDS!
I CANNOT WAIT!
......
......
...SO... THOUGHTS ON FEIKUS?
...HE'S HOPE-LESS.
GIVEN HIS TERMS, DO YOU THINK WE CAN WIN?
WE HAVE TO.
BECAUSE NOTHING ELSE WILL CONVINCE THEM.

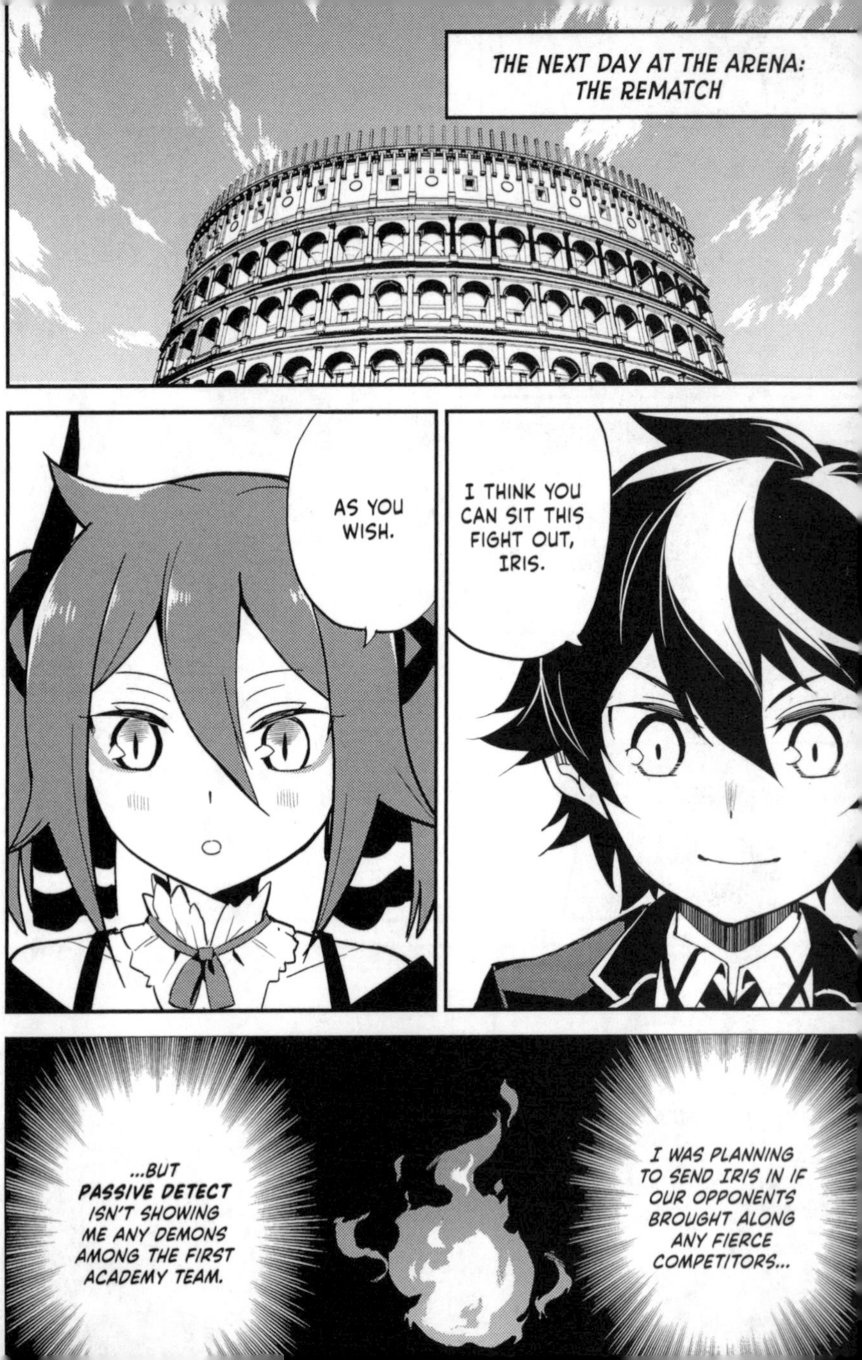
THE NEXT DAY AT THE ARENA: THE REMATCH
I THINK YOU CAN SIT THIS FIGHT OUT, IRIS.
AS YOU WISH.
I WAS PLANNING TO SEND IRIS IN IF OUR OPPONENTS BROUGHT ALONG ANY FIERCE COMPETITORS...
...BUT PASSIVE DETECT ISN'T SHOWING ME ANY DEMONS AMONG THE FIRST ACADEMY TEAM.

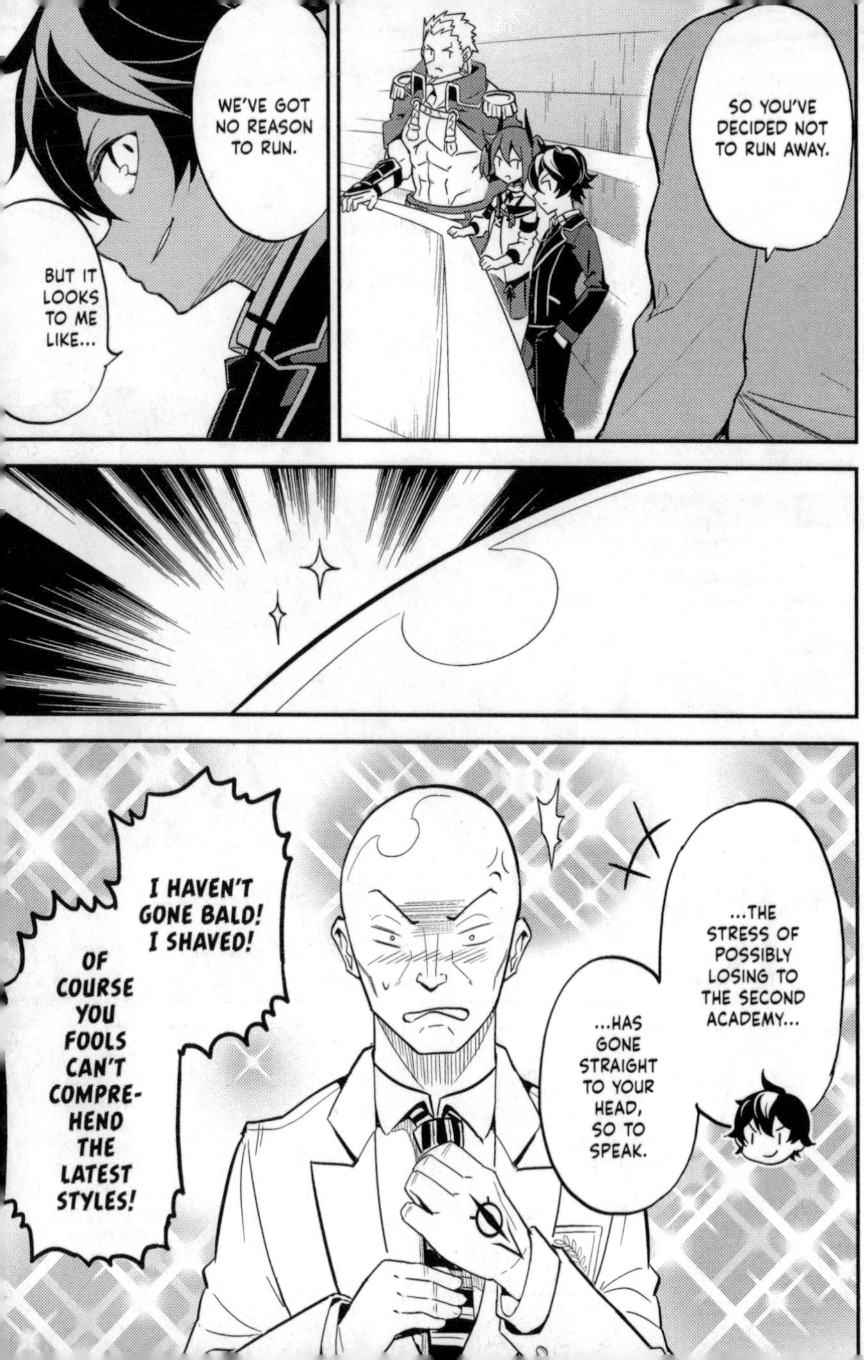
SO YOU'VE DECIDED NOT TO RUN AWAY.
WE'VE GOT NO REASON TO RUN.
BUT IT LOOKS TO ME LIKE...
...THE STRESS OF POSSIBLY LOSING TO THE SECOND ACADEMY...
...HAS GONE STRAIGHT TO YOUR HEAD, SO TO SPEAK.
I HAVEN'T GONE BALD! I SHAVED!
OF COURSE YOU FOOLS CAN'T COMPRE-HEND THE LATEST STYLES!

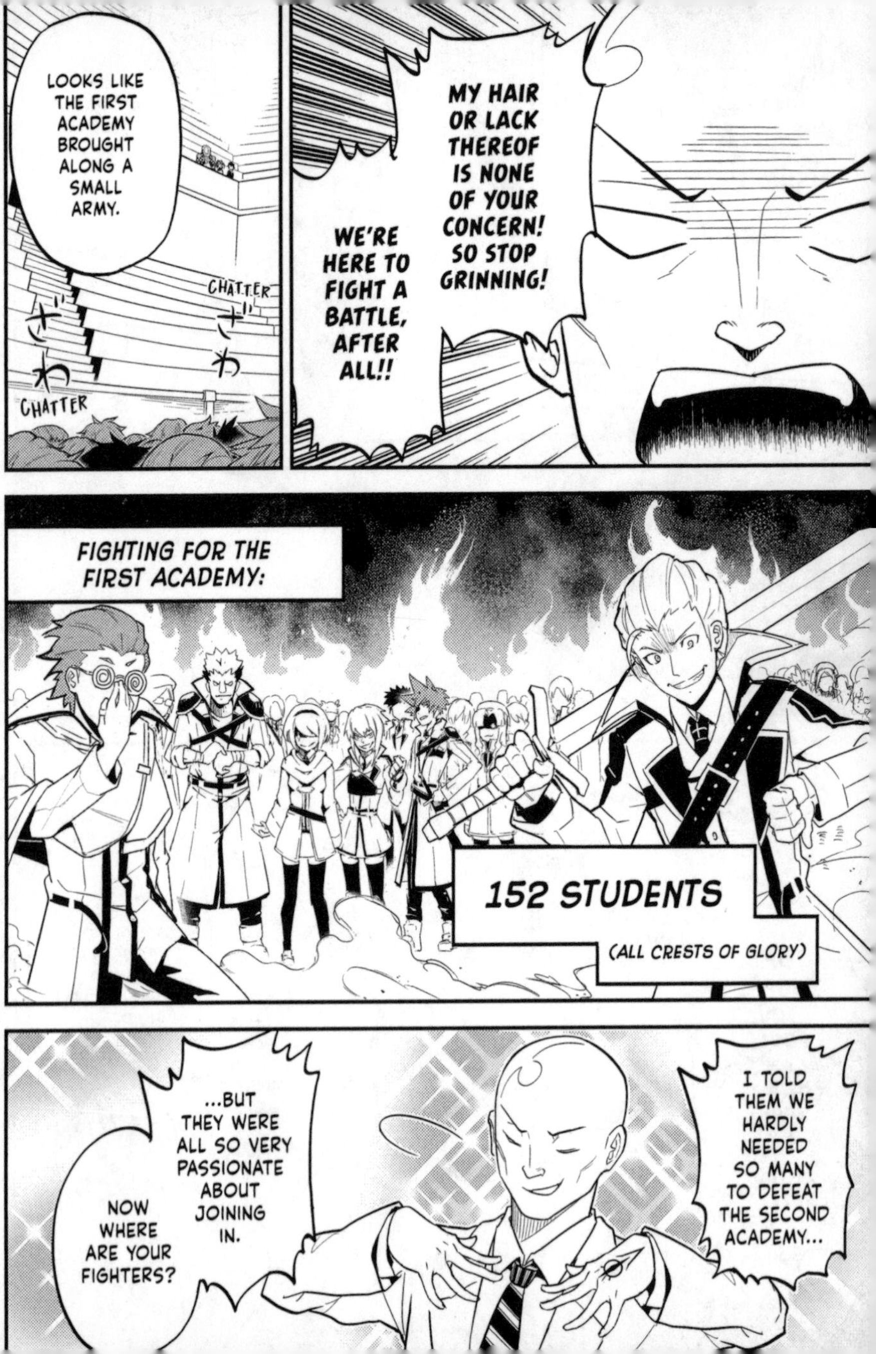
MY HAIR OR LACK THEREOF IS NONE OF YOUR CONCERN! SO STOP GRINNING!
WE'RE HERE TO FIGHT A BATTLE, AFTER ALL!!
LOOKS LIKE THE FIRST ACADEMY BROUGHT ALONG A SMALL ARMY.
CHATTER
ざわ
ざわ
CHATTER
FIGHTING FOR THE FIRST ACADEMY:
152 STUDENTS
(ALL CRESTS OF GLORY)
I TOLD THEM WE HARDLY NEEDED SO MANY TO DEFEAT THE SECOND ACADEMY...
...BUT THEY WERE ALL SO VERY PASSIONATE ABOUT JOINING IN.
NOW WHERE ARE YOUR FIGHTERS?

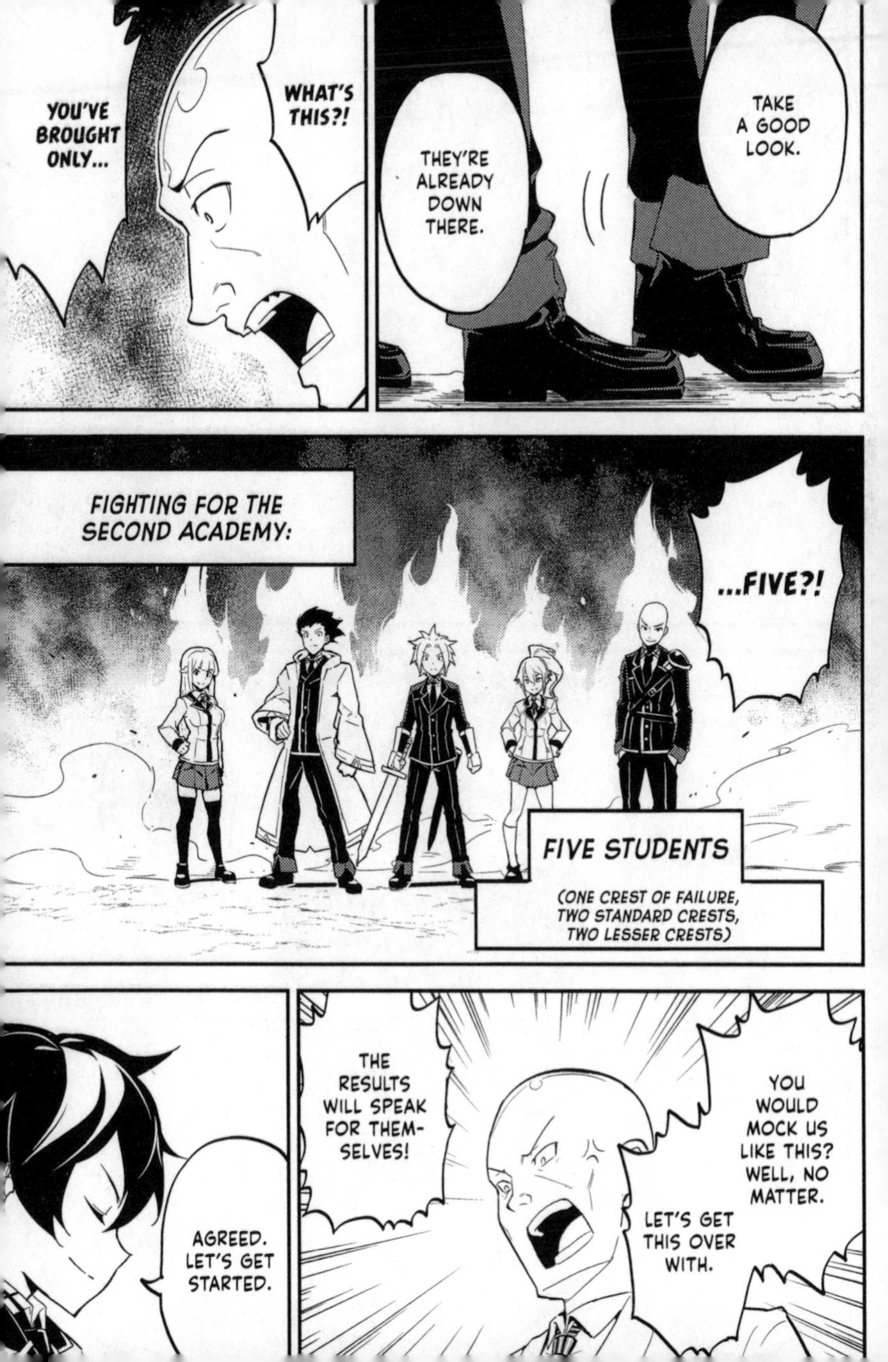

TAKE A GOOD LOOK.
THEY'RE ALREADY DOWN THERE.
WHAT'S THIS?!
YOU'VE BROUGHT ONLY...
...FIVE?!
FIGHTING FOR THE SECOND ACADEMY:
FIVE STUDENTS
(ONE CREST OF FAILURE, TWO STANDARD CRESTS, TWO LESSER CRESTS)
YOU WOULD MOCK US LIKE THIS? WELL, NO MATTER.
LET'S GET THIS OVER WITH.
THE RESULTS WILL SPEAK FOR THEM-SELVES!
AGREED. LET'S GET STARTED.

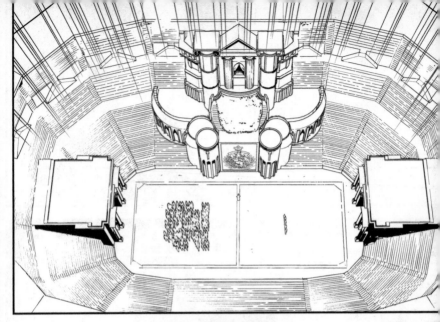

LET THE INVITATIONAL REMATCH...

SILENCE, ALL!

...BEGIN!

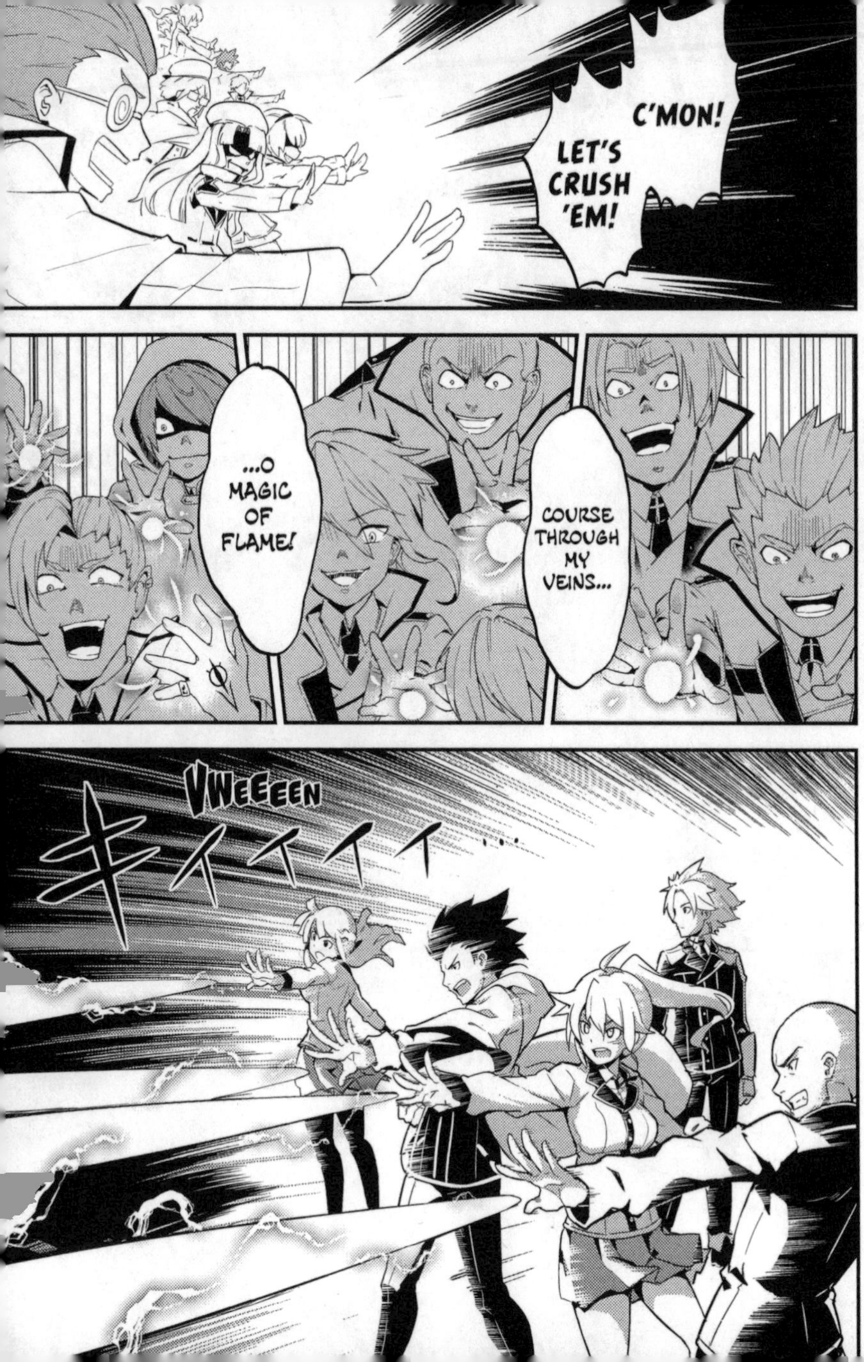
C'MON!
LET'S CRUSH 'EM!
COURSE THROUGH MY VEINS...
...O MAGIC OF FLAME!
VWEEEEN
キイイイ...

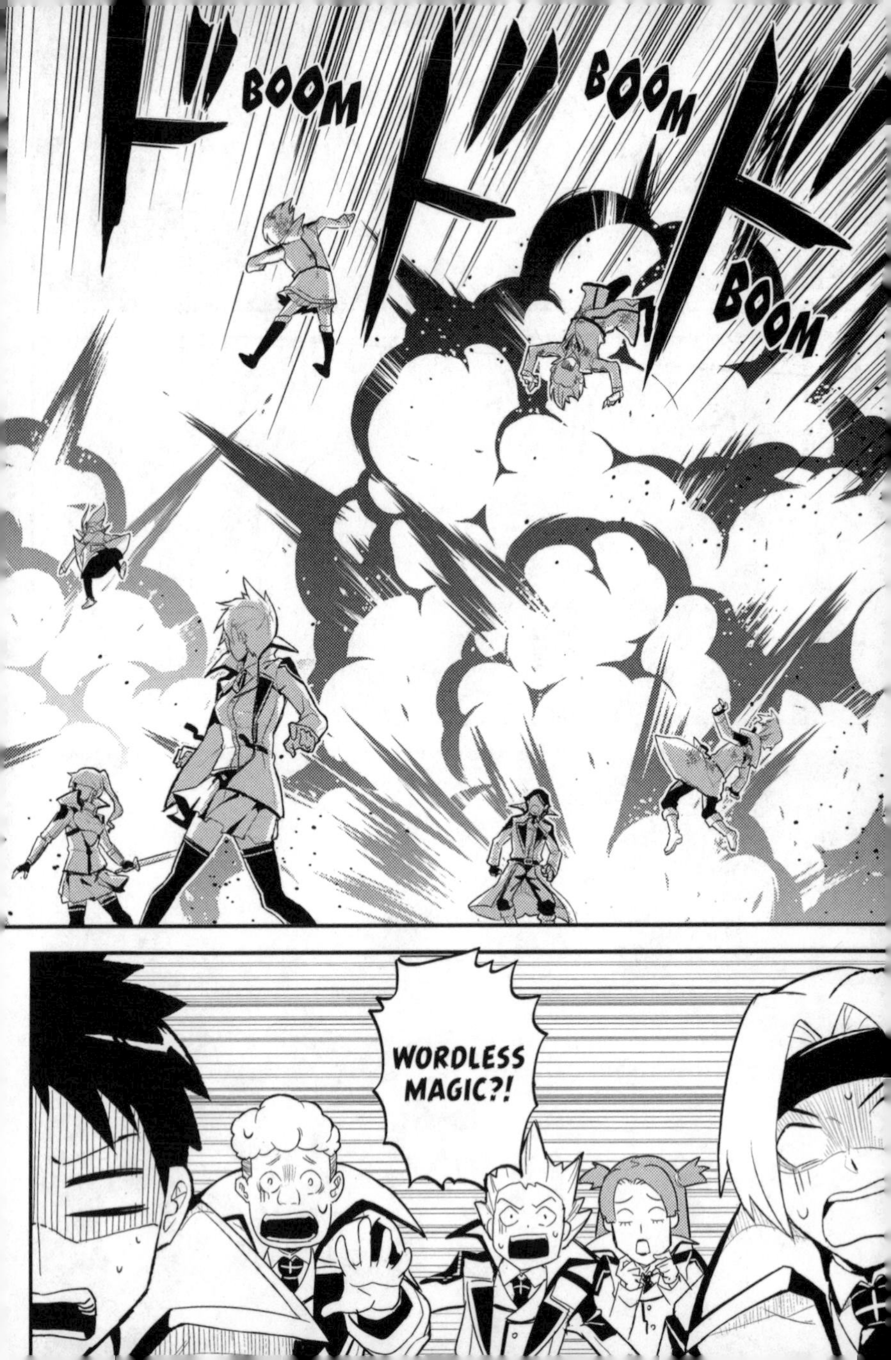
BOOM
BOOM
BOOM
WORDLESS MAGIC?!

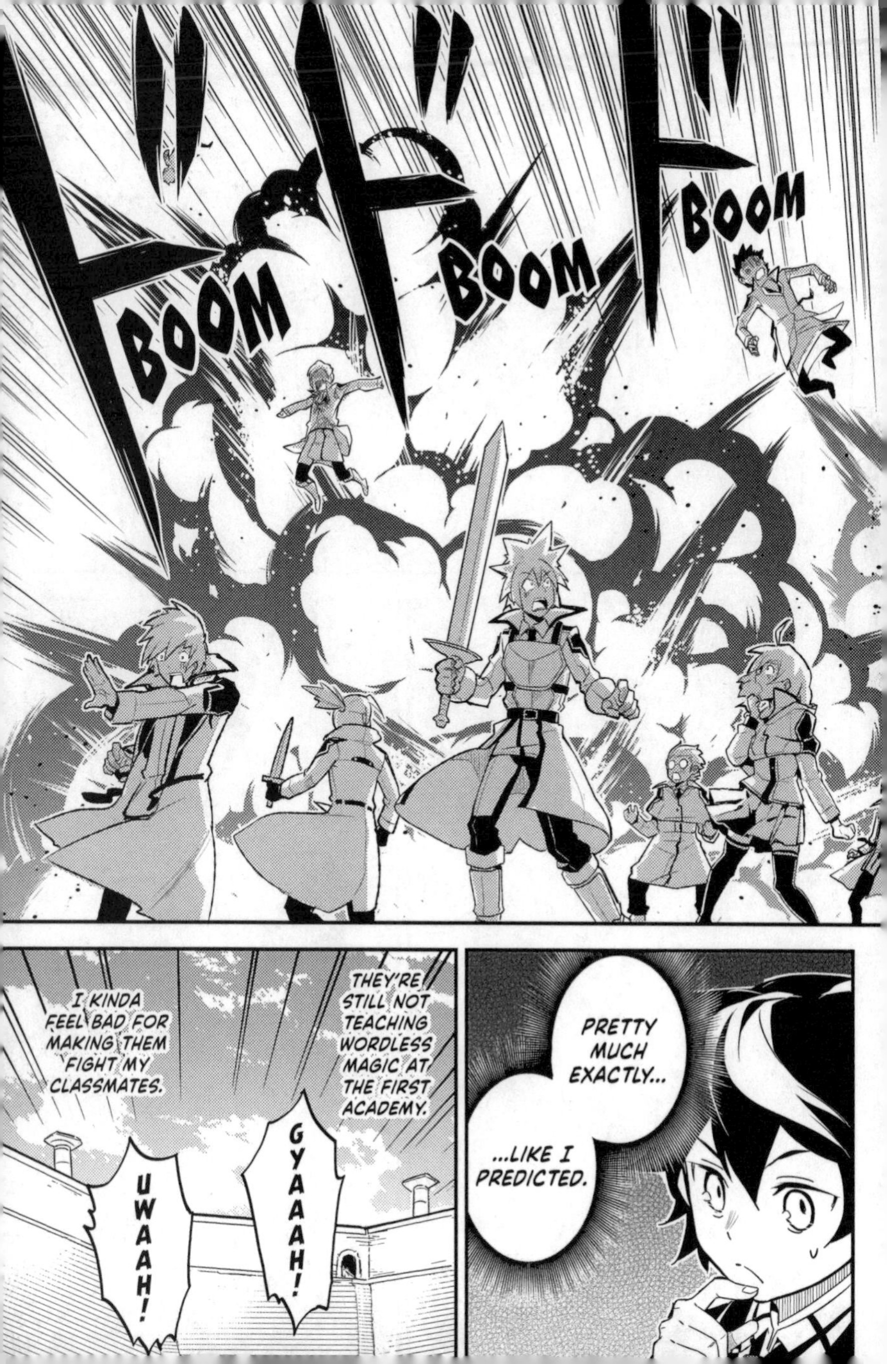
BOOM
BOOM
BOOM
PRETTY MUCH EXACTLY...
...LIKE I PREDICTED.
THEY'RE STILL NOT TEACHING WORDLESS MAGIC AT THE FIRST ACADEMY.
I KINDA FEEL BAD FOR MAKING THEM FIGHT MY CLASSMATES.
GYAAAAH!
UWAAAH!

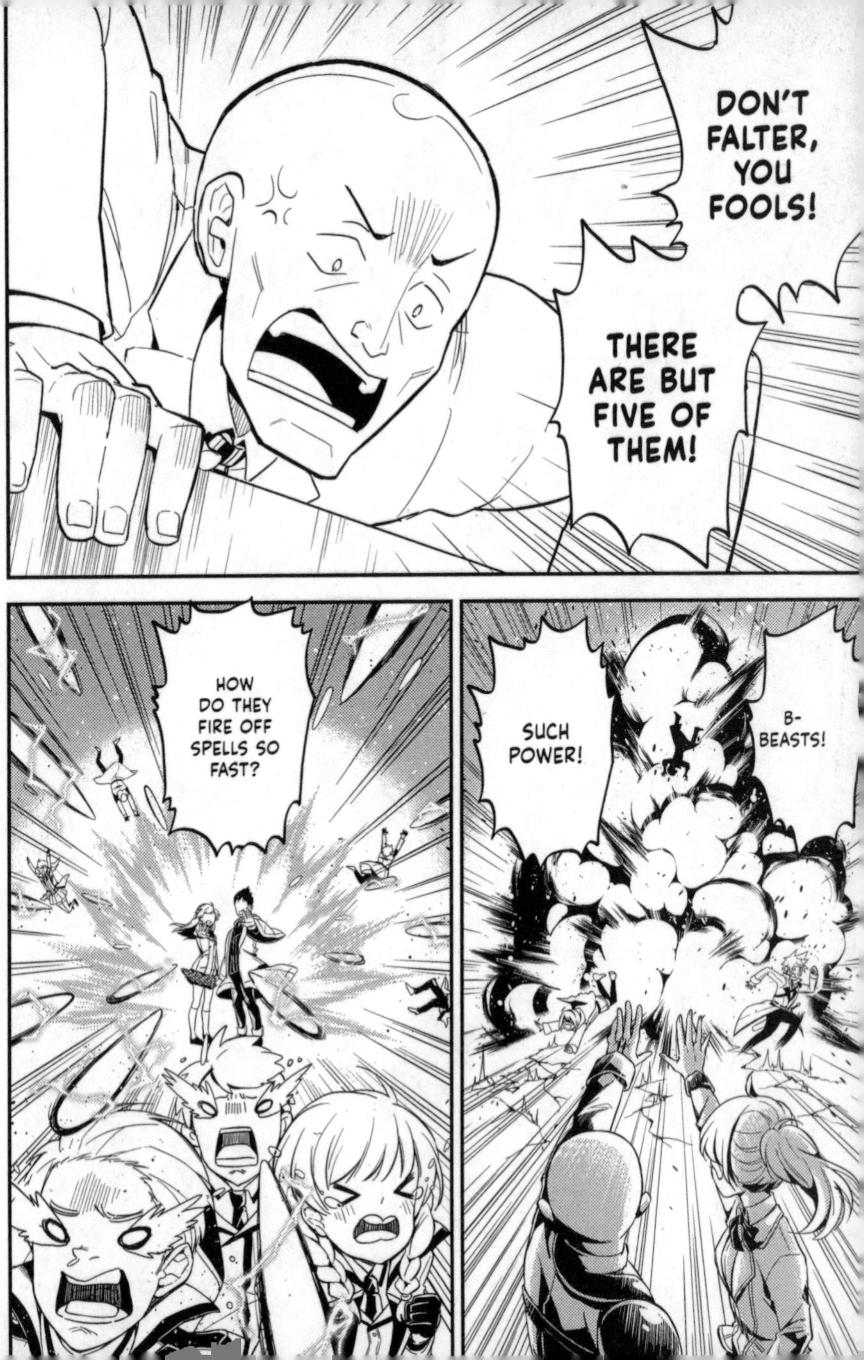
DON'T FALTER, YOU FOOLS!
THERE ARE BUT FIVE OF THEM!
B-BEASTS!
SUCH POWER!
HOW DO THEY FIRE OFF SPELLS SO FAST?

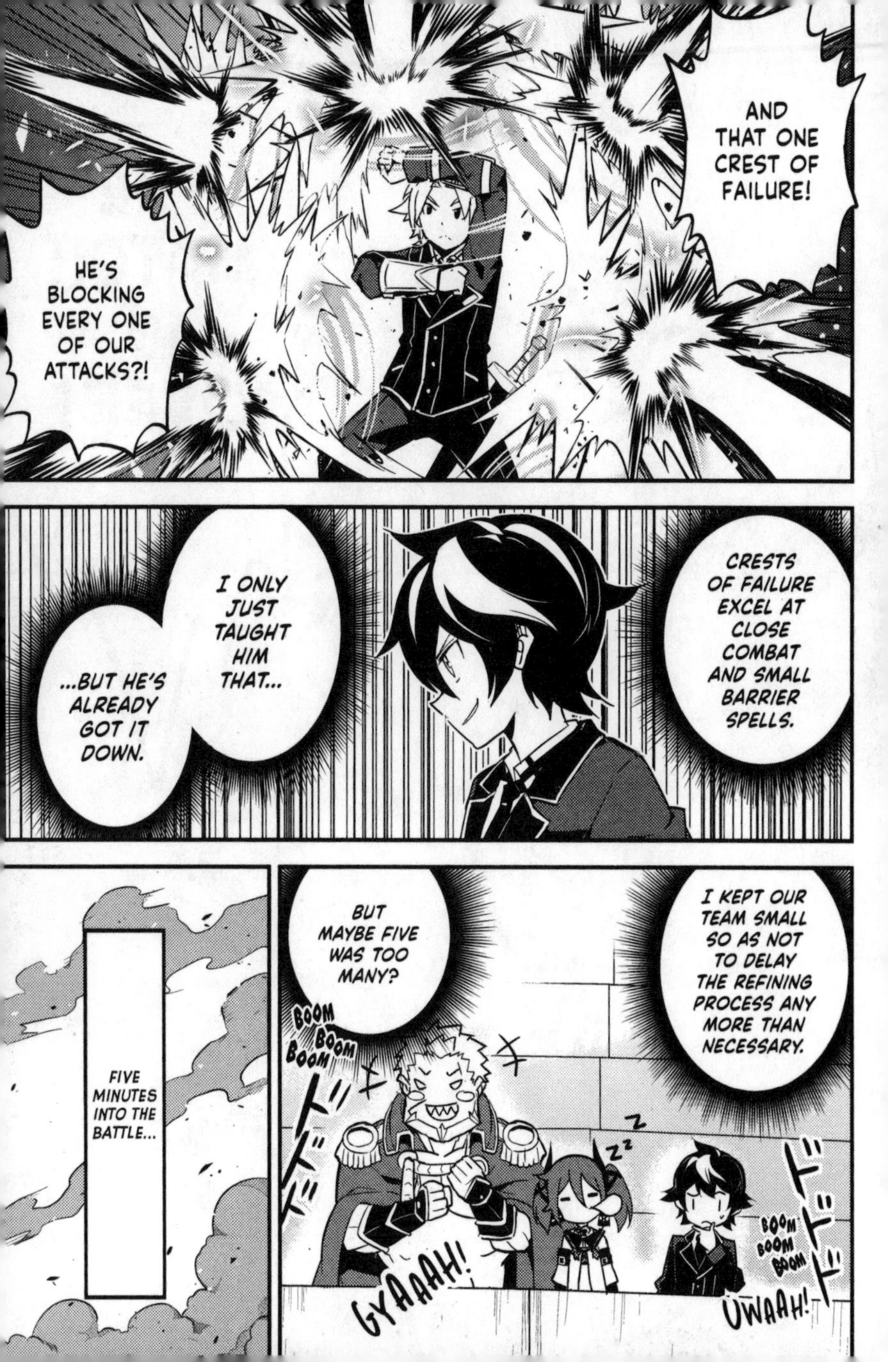
AND THAT ONE CREST OF FAILURE!
HE'S BLOCKING EVERY ONE OF OUR ATTACKS?!
CRESTS OF FAILURE EXCEL AT CLOSE COMBAT AND SMALL BARRIER SPELLS.
I ONLY JUST TAUGHT HIM THAT...
...BUT HE'S ALREADY GOT IT DOWN.
I KEPT OUR TEAM SMALL SO AS NOT TO DELAY THE REFINING PROCESS ANY MORE THAN NECESSARY.
BUT MAYBE FIVE WAS TOO MANY?
BOOM BOOM BOOM
BOOM BOOM BOOM
UWAAH!
GYAAAH!
FIVE MINUTES INTO THE BATTLE...

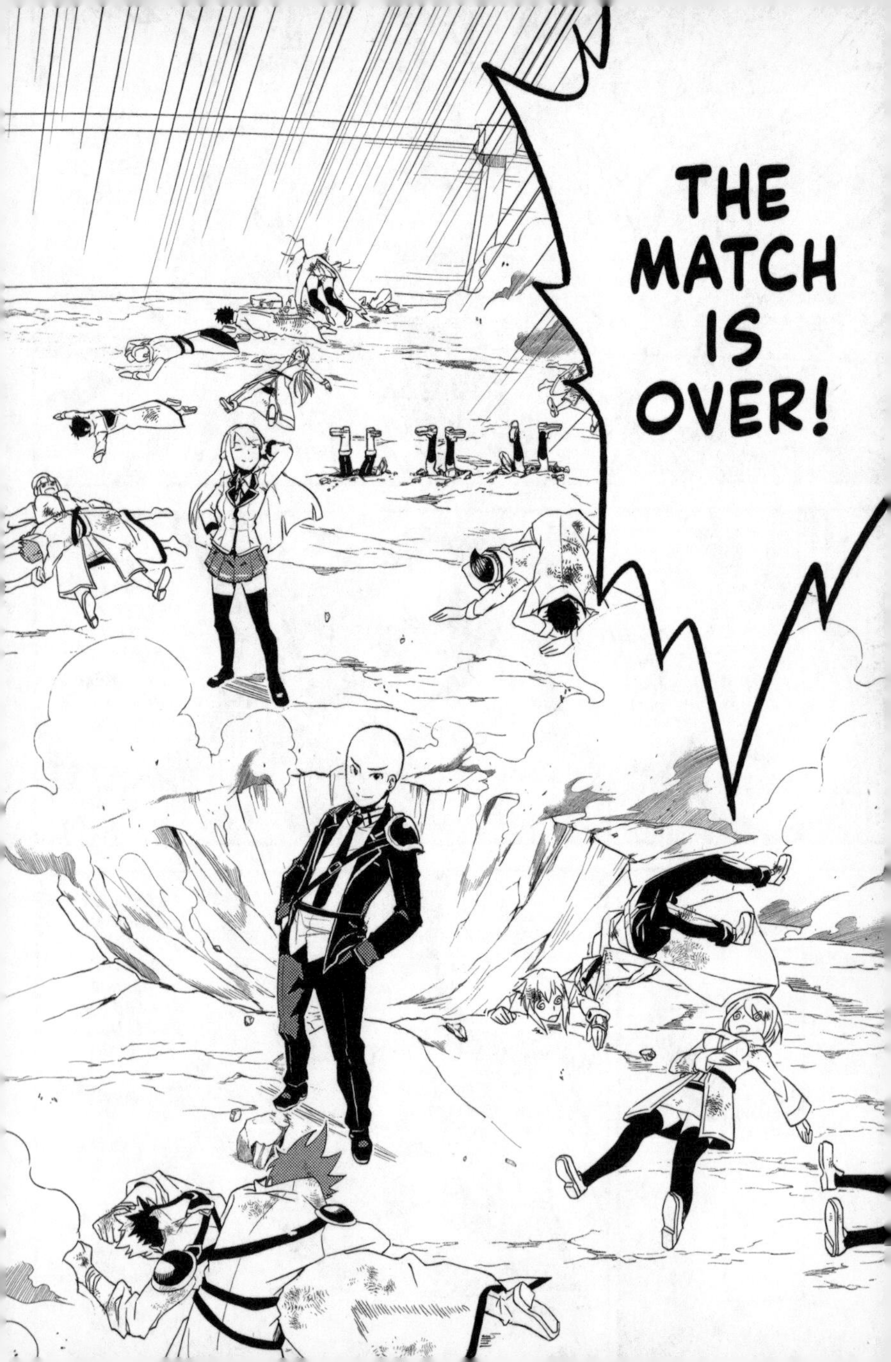
THE MATCH IS OVER!

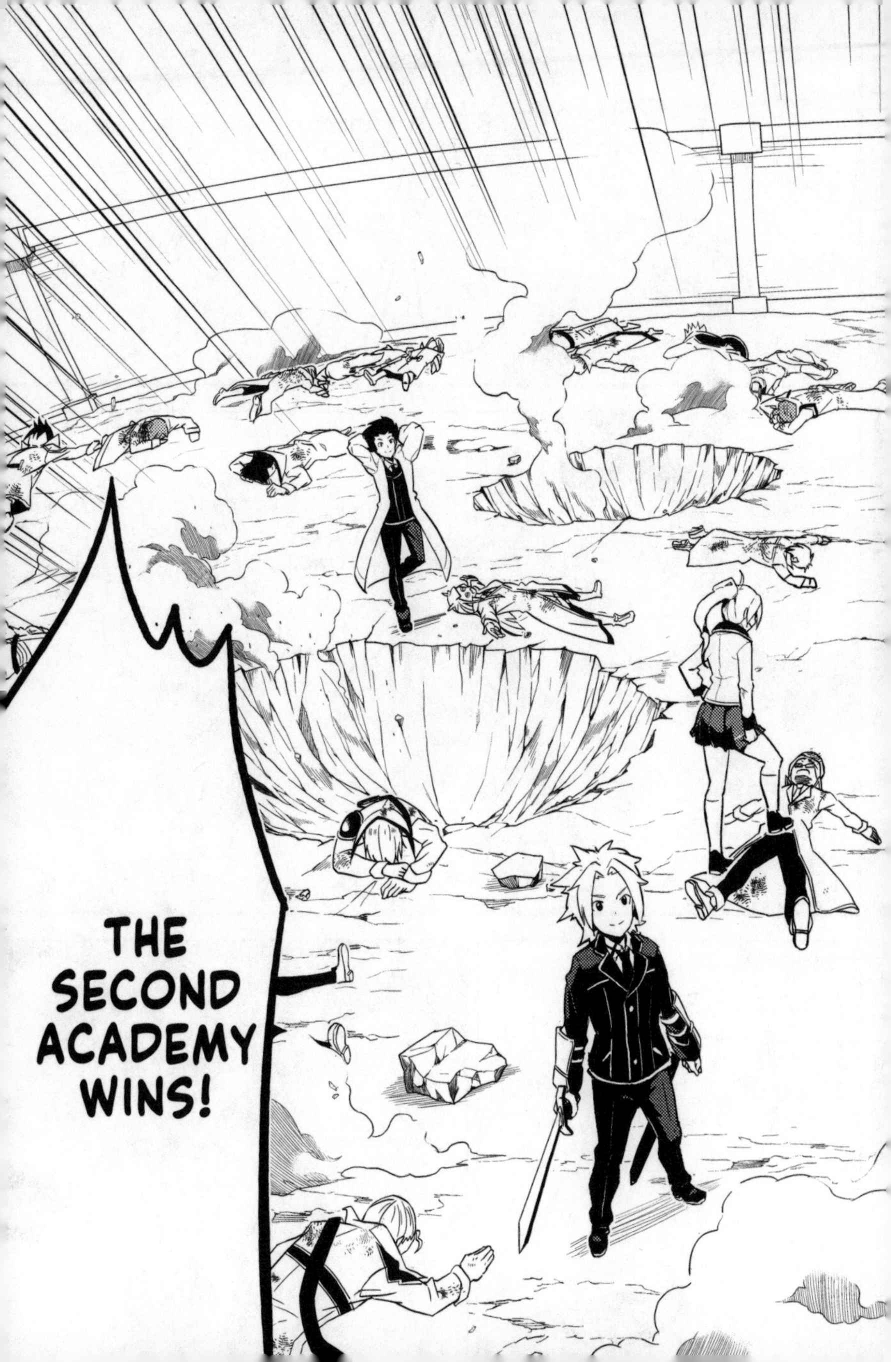
THE SECOND ACADEMY WINS!

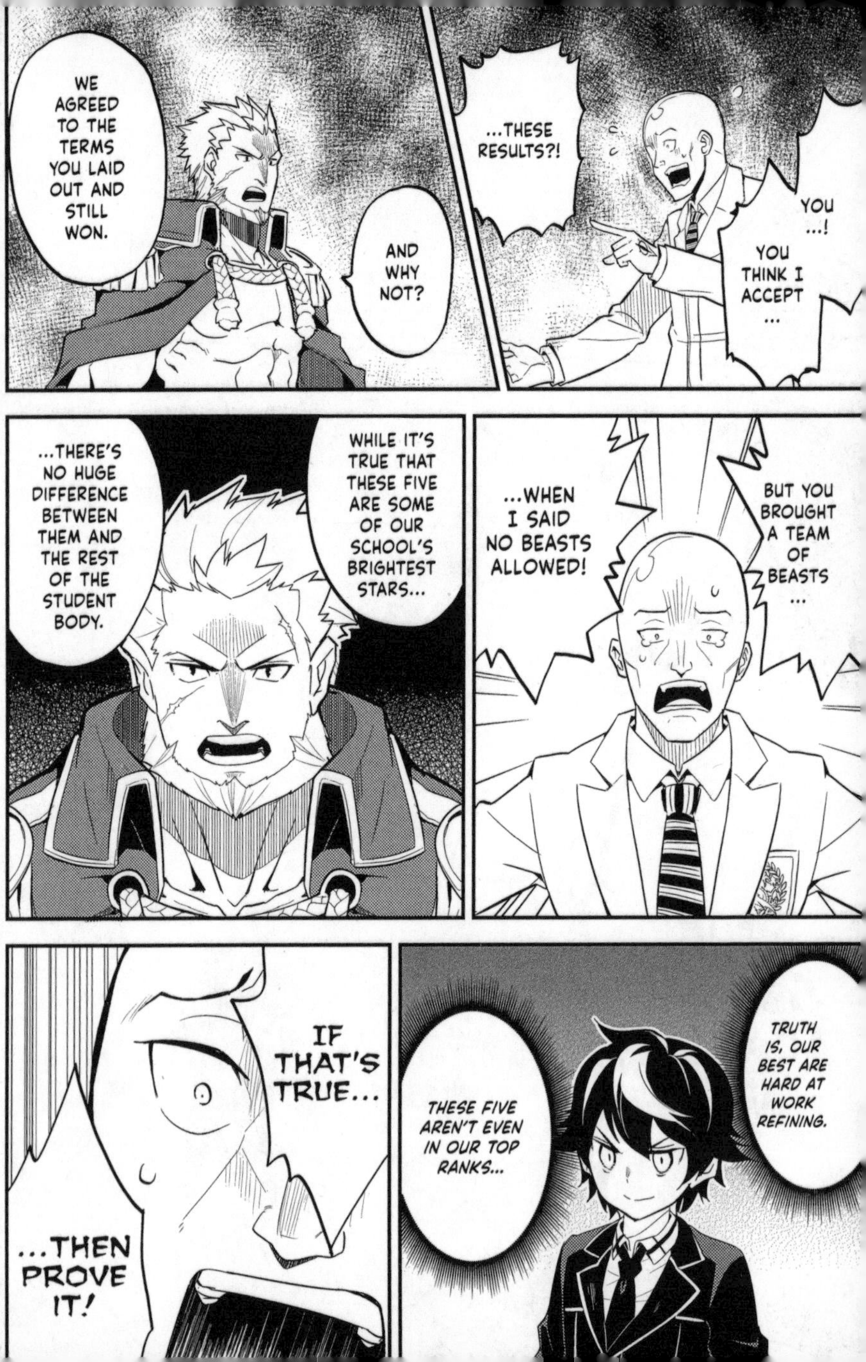
YOU ...!
YOU THINK I ACCEPT ...
...THESE RESULTS?!
AND WHY NOT?
WE AGREED TO THE TERMS YOU LAID OUT AND STILL WON.
BUT YOU BROUGHT A TEAM OF BEASTS ...
...WHEN I SAID NO BEASTS ALLOWED!
WHILE IT'S TRUE THAT THESE FIVE ARE SOME OF OUR SCHOOL'S BRIGHTEST STARS...
...THERE'S NO HUGE DIFFERENCE BETWEEN THEM AND THE REST OF THE STUDENT BODY.
TRUTH IS, OUR BEST ARE HARD AT WORK REFINING.
THESE FIVE AREN'T EVEN IN OUR TOP RANKS...
IF THAT'S TRUE...
...THEN PROVE IT!

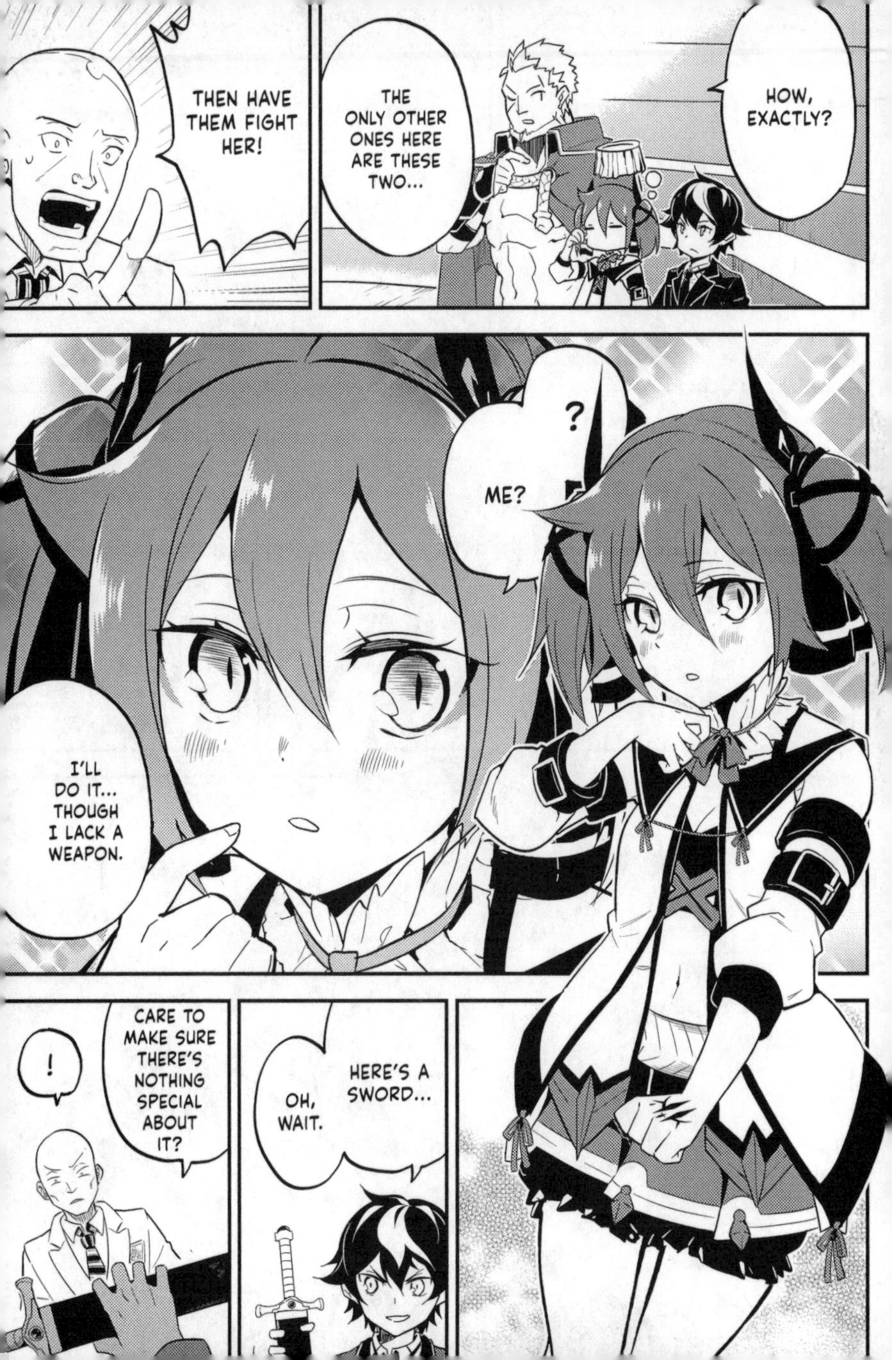
HOW, EXACTLY?
THE ONLY OTHER ONES HERE ARE THESE TWO...
THEN HAVE THEM FIGHT HER!
?
ME?
I'LL DO IT... THOUGH I LACK A WEAPON.
HERE'S A SWORD...
OH, WAIT.
CARE TO MAKE SURE THERE'S NOTHING SPECIAL ABOUT IT?
!

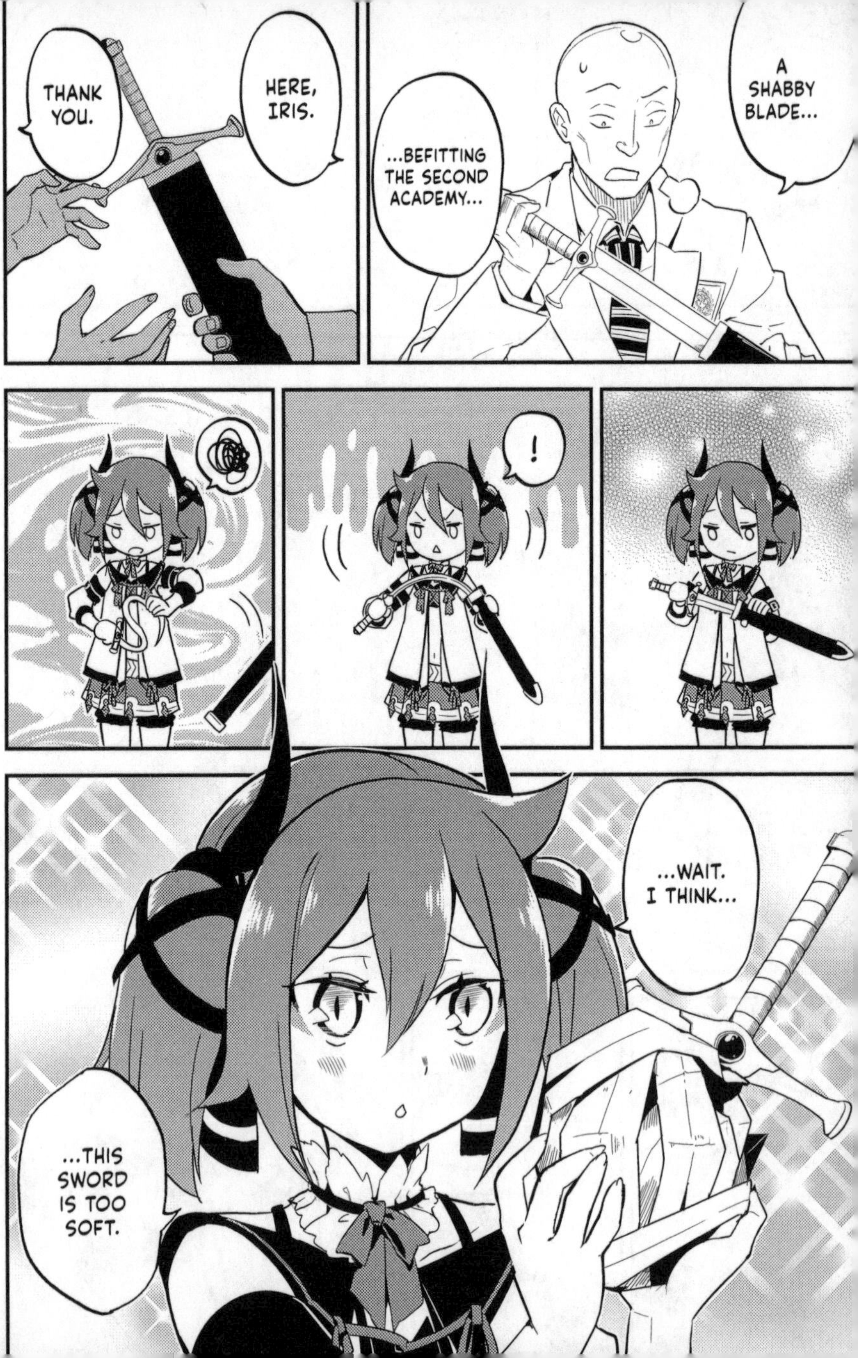
A SHABBY BLADE...
...BEFITTING THE SECOND ACADEMY...
HERE, IRIS.
THANK YOU.
!
...WAIT. I THINK...
...THIS SWORD IS TOO SOFT.

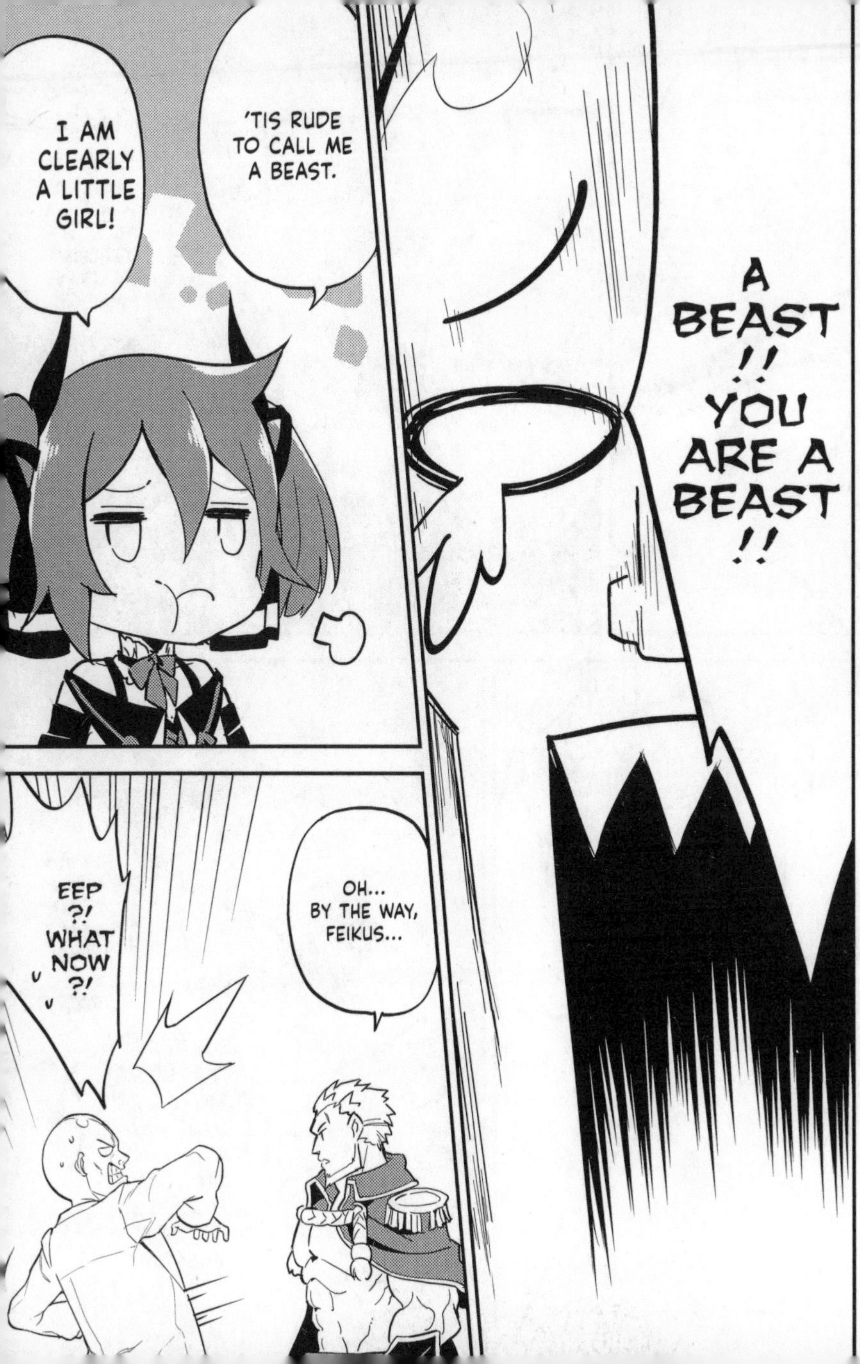
A BEAST!! YOU ARE A BEAST!!
'TIS RUDE TO CALL ME A BEAST.
I AM CLEARLY A LITTLE GIRL!
OH... BY THE WAY, FEIKUS...
EEP?! WHAT NOW?!

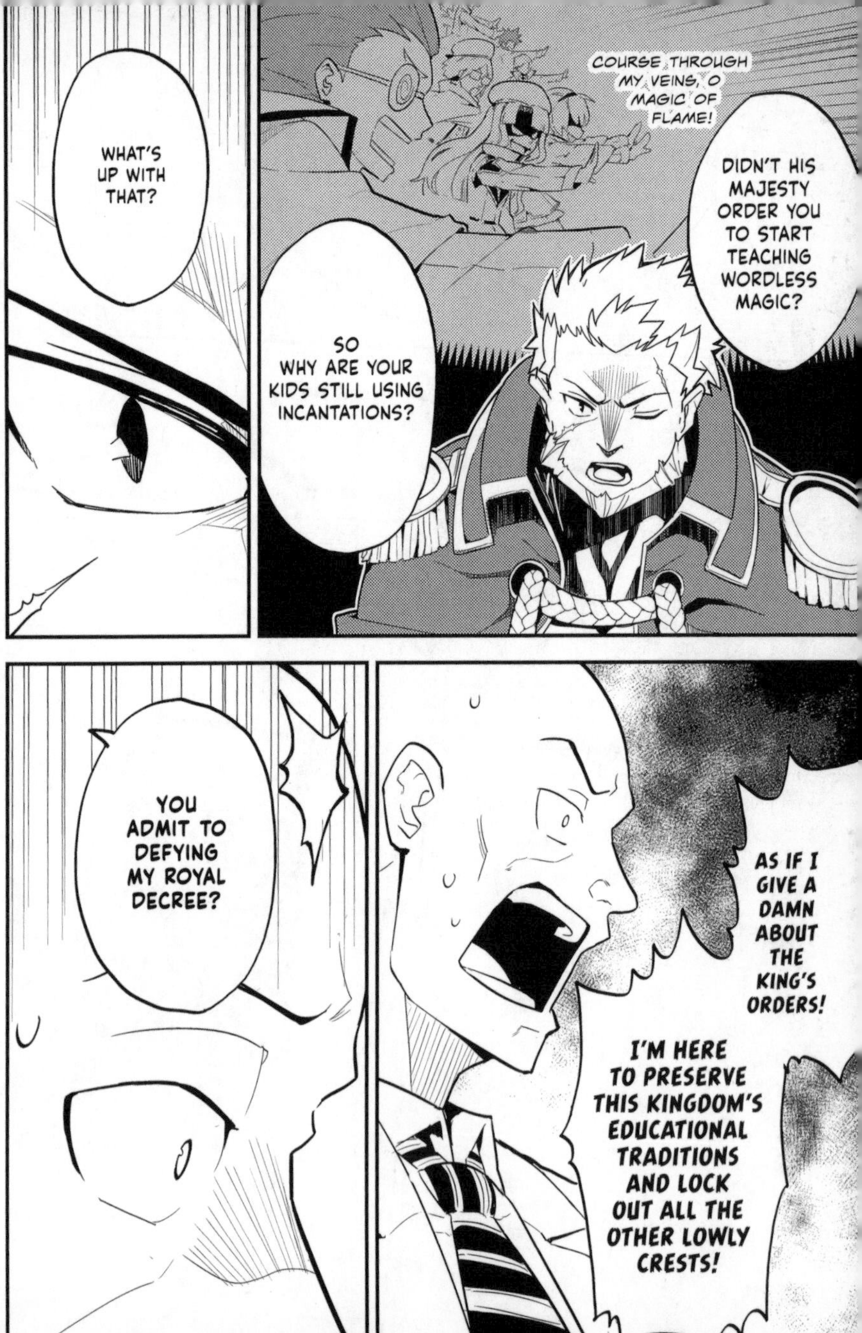
COURSE THROUGH MY VEINS, O MAGIC OF FLAME!
DIDN'T HIS MAJESTY ORDER YOU TO START TEACHING WORDLESS MAGIC?
SO WHY ARE YOUR KIDS STILL USING INCANTATIONS?
WHAT'S UP WITH THAT?
AS IF I GIVE A DAMN ABOUT THE KING'S ORDERS!
I'M HERE TO PRESERVE THIS KINGDOM'S EDUCATIONAL TRADITIONS AND LOCK OUT ALL THE OTHER LOWLY CRESTS!
YOU ADMIT TO DEFYING MY ROYAL DECREE?

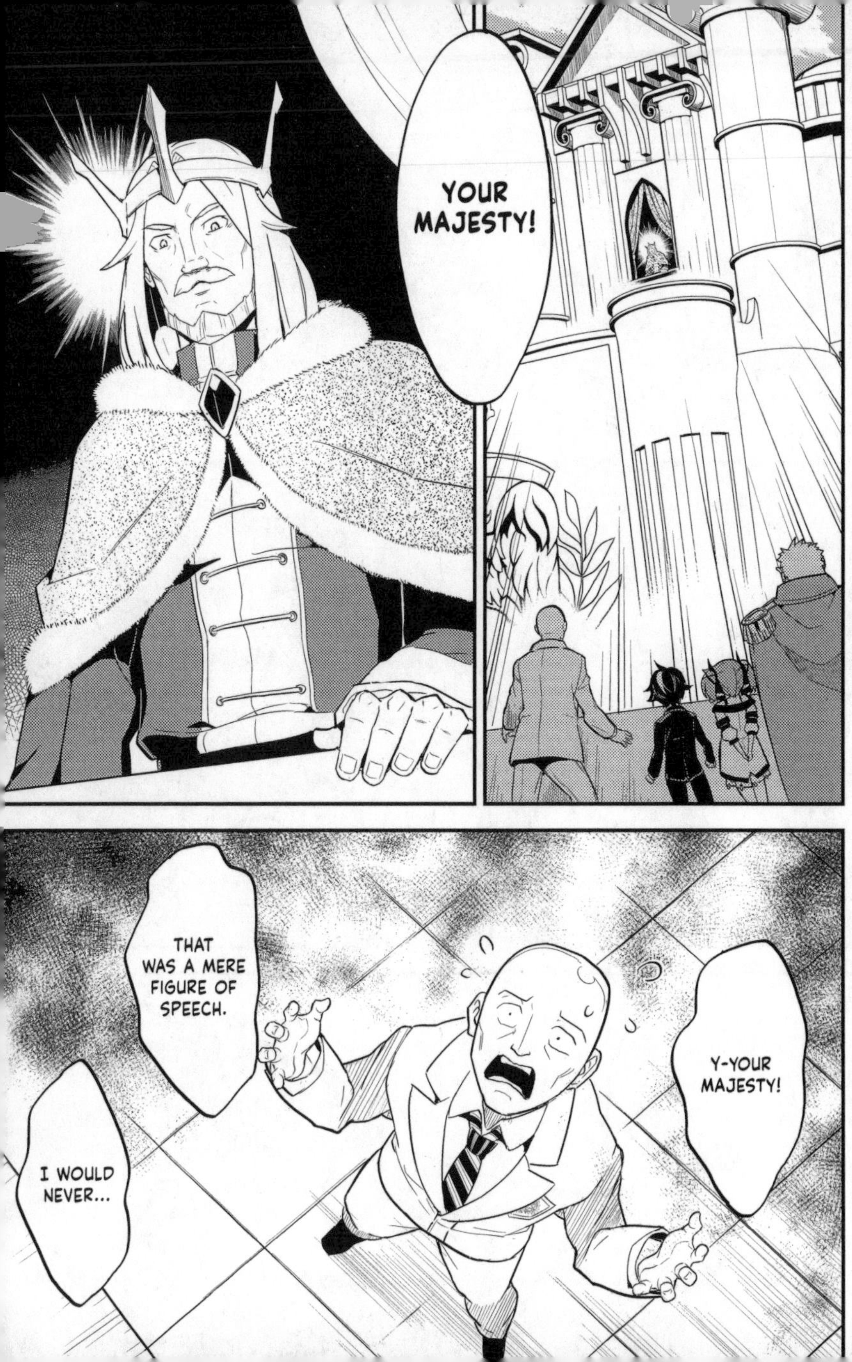
YOUR MAJESTY!
Y-YOUR MAJESTY!
THAT WAS A MERE FIGURE OF SPEECH.
I WOULD NEVER...

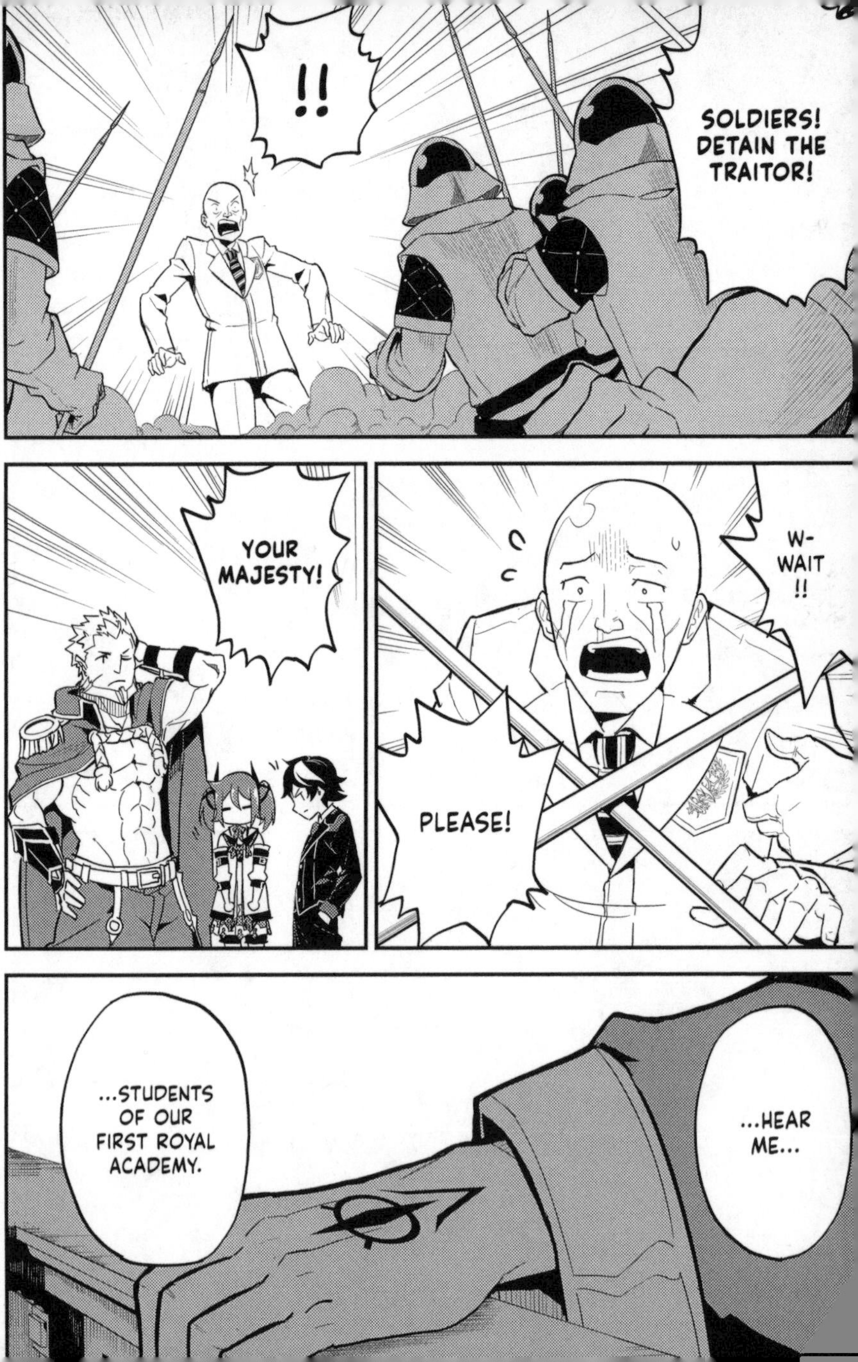
SOLDIERS! DETAIN THE TRAITOR!
!!
W-WAIT!!
PLEASE!
YOUR MAJESTY!
...HEAR ME...
...STUDENTS OF OUR FIRST ROYAL ACADEMY.

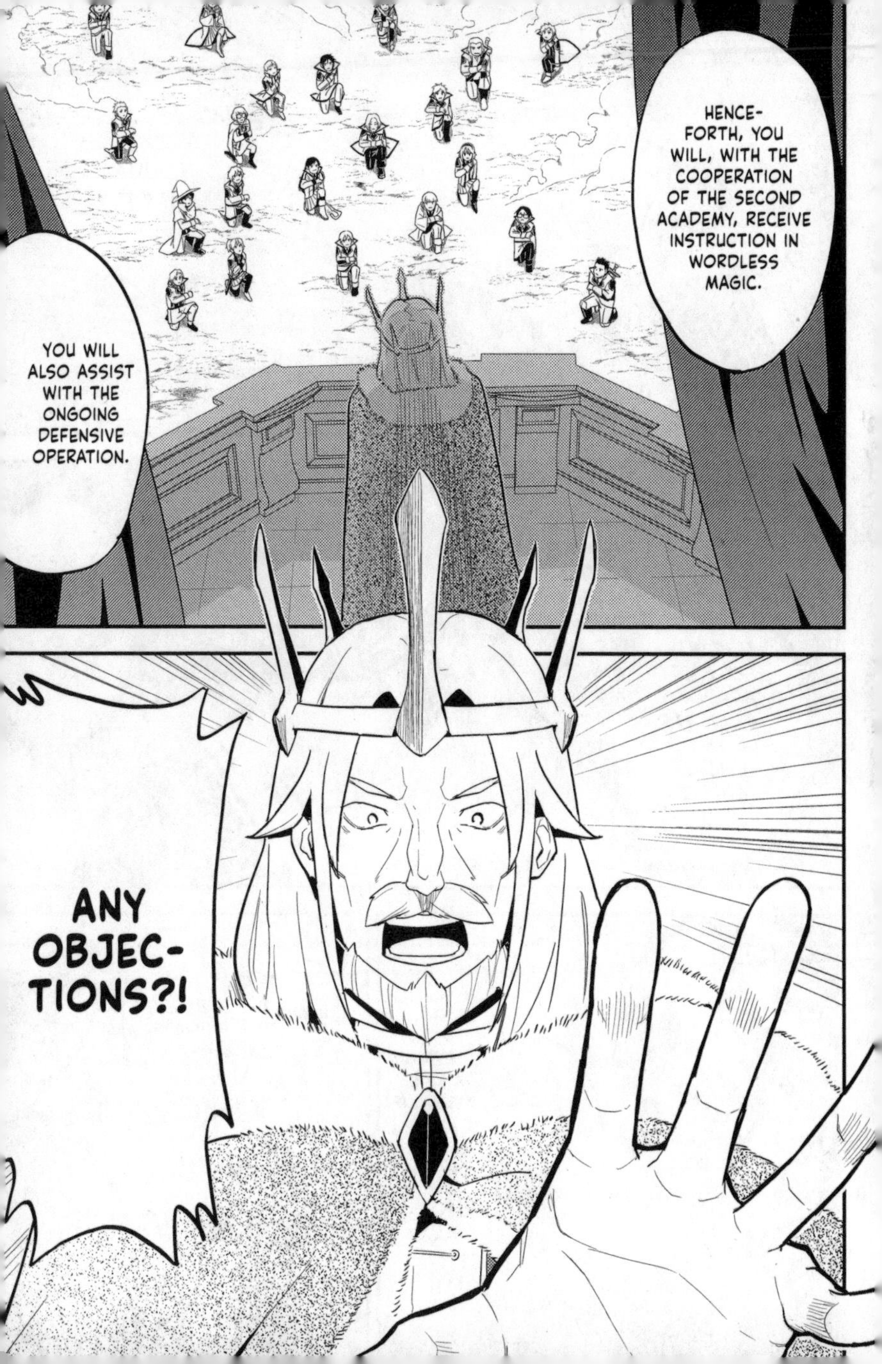
HENCE-FORTH, YOU WILL, WITH THE COOPERATION OF THE SECOND ACADEMY, RECEIVE INSTRUCTION IN WORDLESS MAGIC.
YOU WILL ALSO ASSIST WITH THE ONGOING DEFENSIVE OPERATION.
ANY OBJEC-TIONS?!

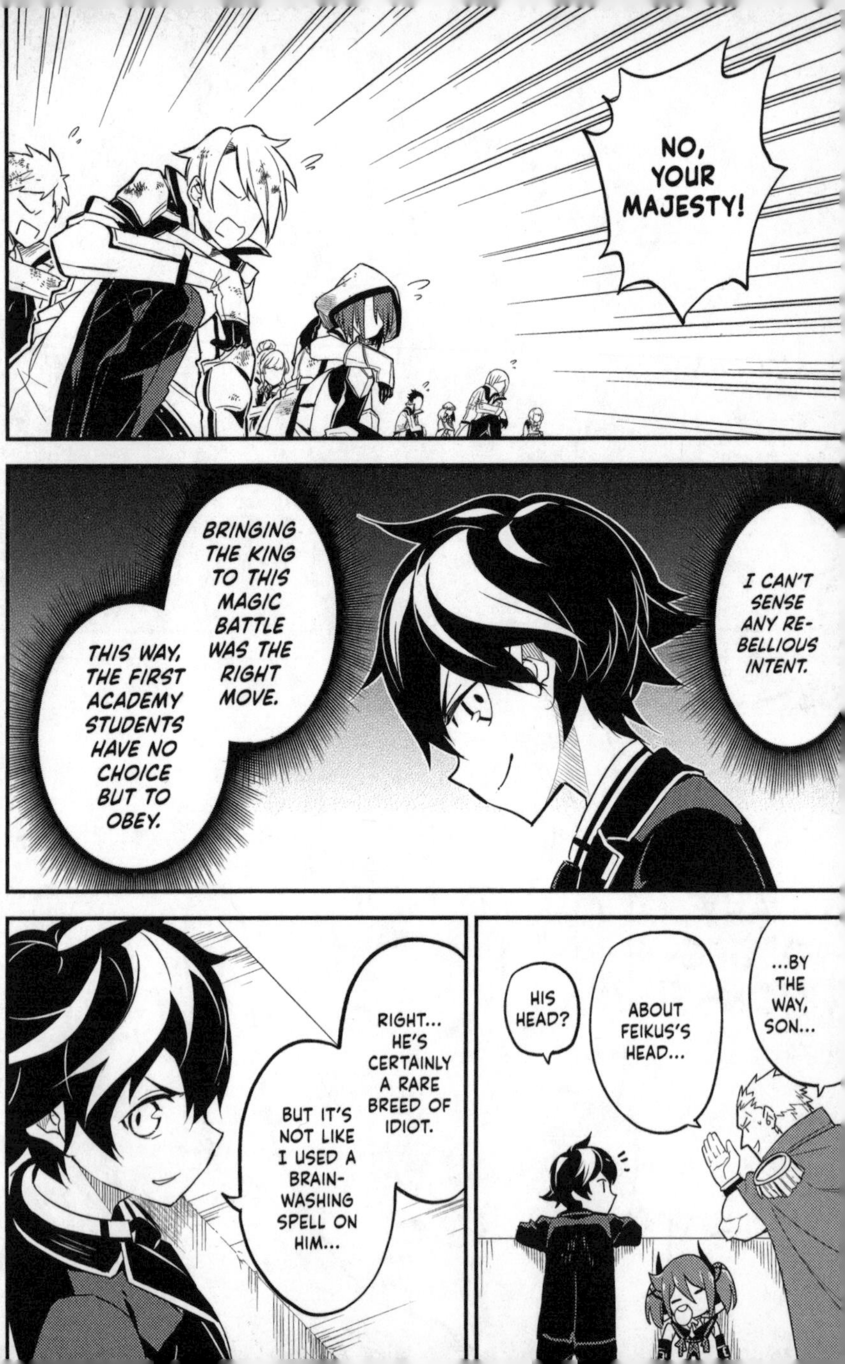
NO, YOUR MAJESTY!
I CAN'T SENSE ANY RE-BELLIOUS INTENT.
BRINGING THE KING TO THIS MAGIC BATTLE WAS THE RIGHT MOVE.
THIS WAY, THE FIRST ACADEMY STUDENTS HAVE NO CHOICE BUT TO OBEY.
...BY THE WAY, SON...
ABOUT FEIKUS'S HEAD...
HIS HEAD?
RIGHT... HE'S CERTAINLY A RARE BREED OF IDIOT.
BUT IT'S NOT LIKE I USED A BRAIN-WASHING SPELL ON HIM...

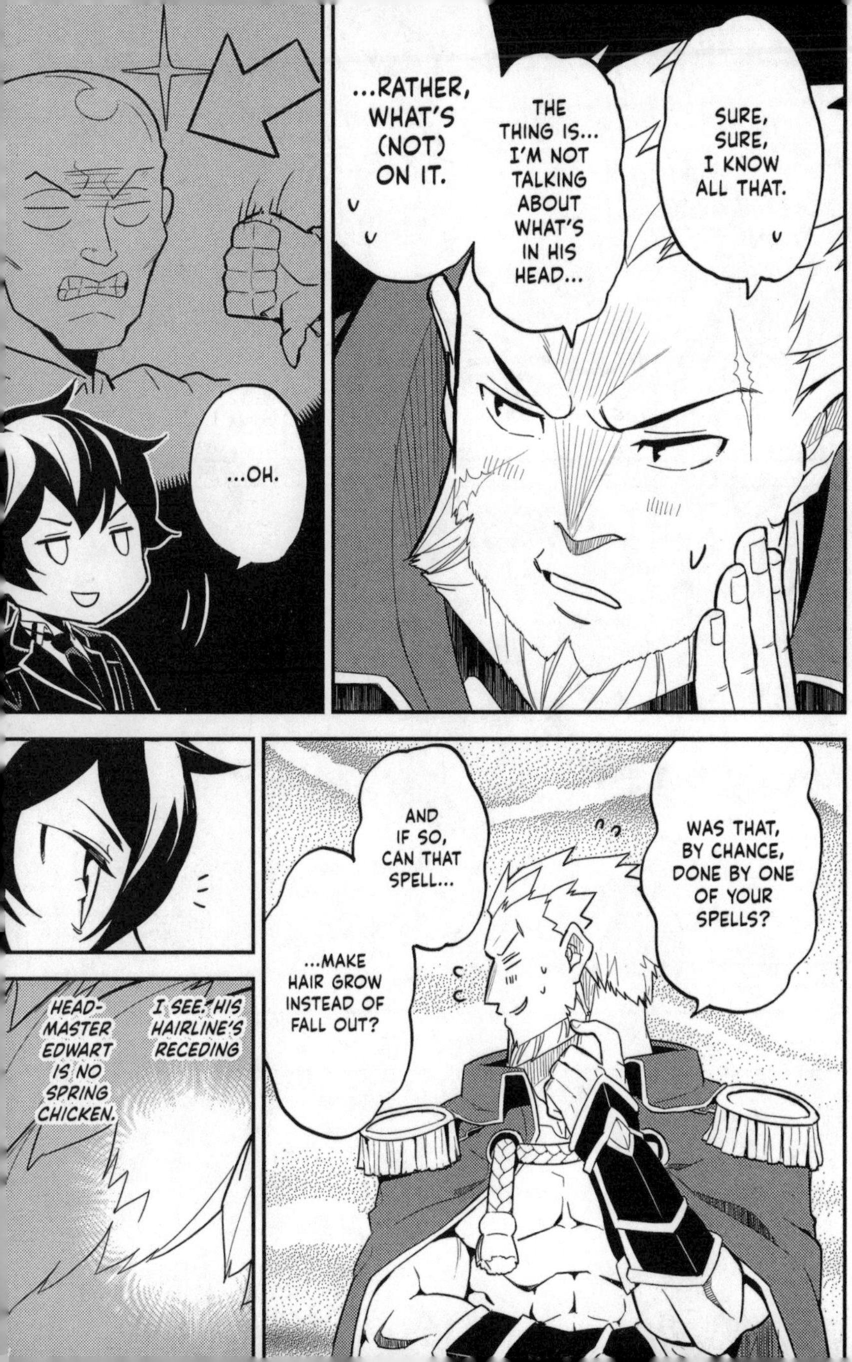
SURE, SURE, I KNOW ALL THAT.
THE THING IS... I'M NOT TALKING ABOUT WHAT'S IN HIS HEAD...
...RATHER, WHAT'S (NOT) ON IT.
...OH.
WAS THAT, BY CHANCE, DONE BY ONE OF YOUR SPELLS?
AND IF SO, CAN THAT SPELL...
...MAKE HAIR GROW INSTEAD OF FALL OUT?
I SEE. HIS HAIRLINE'S RECEDING
HEAD-MASTER EDWART IS NO SPRING CHICKEN.

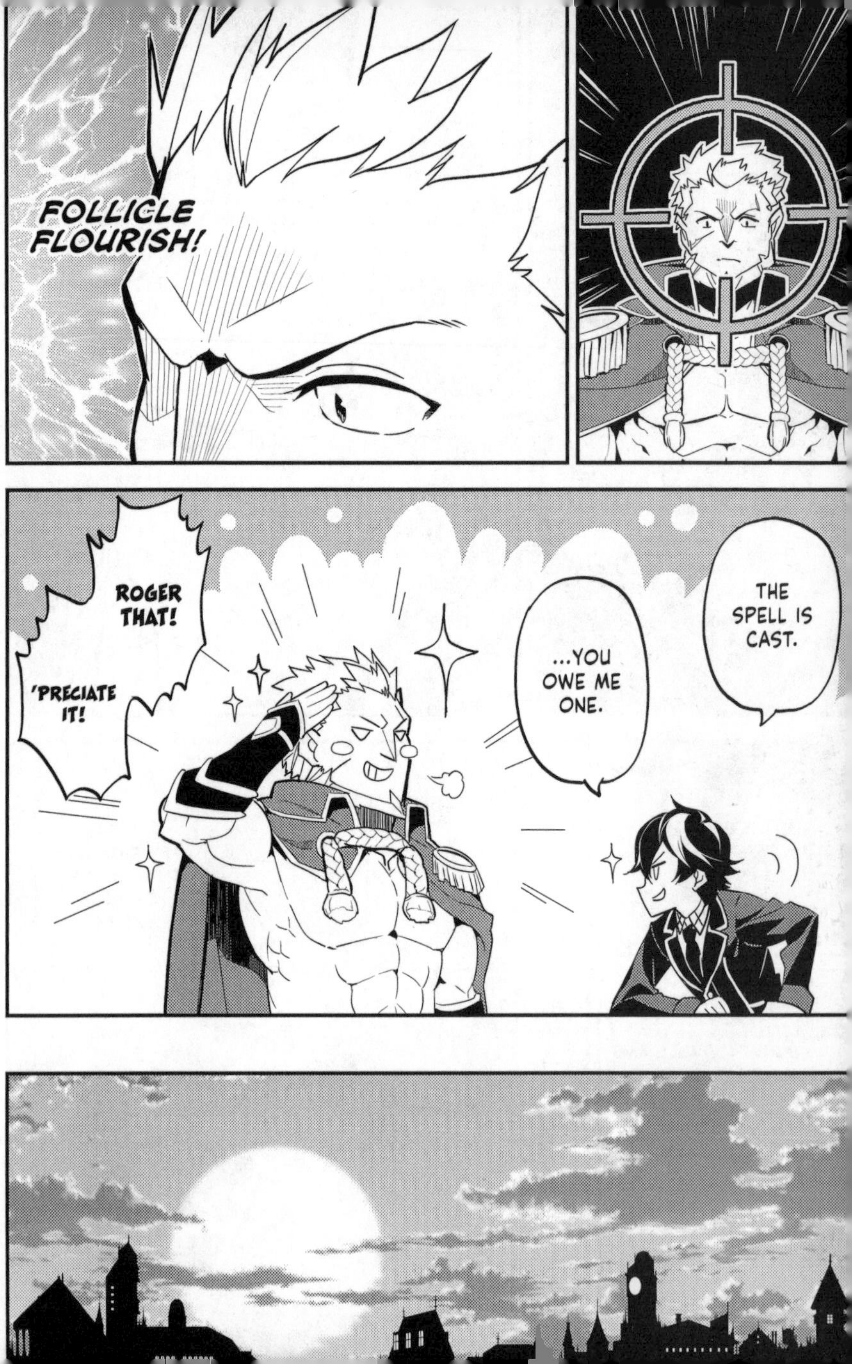
FOLLICLE FLOURISH!
THE SPELL IS CAST.
...YOU OWE ME ONE.
ROGER THAT!
'PRECIATE IT!

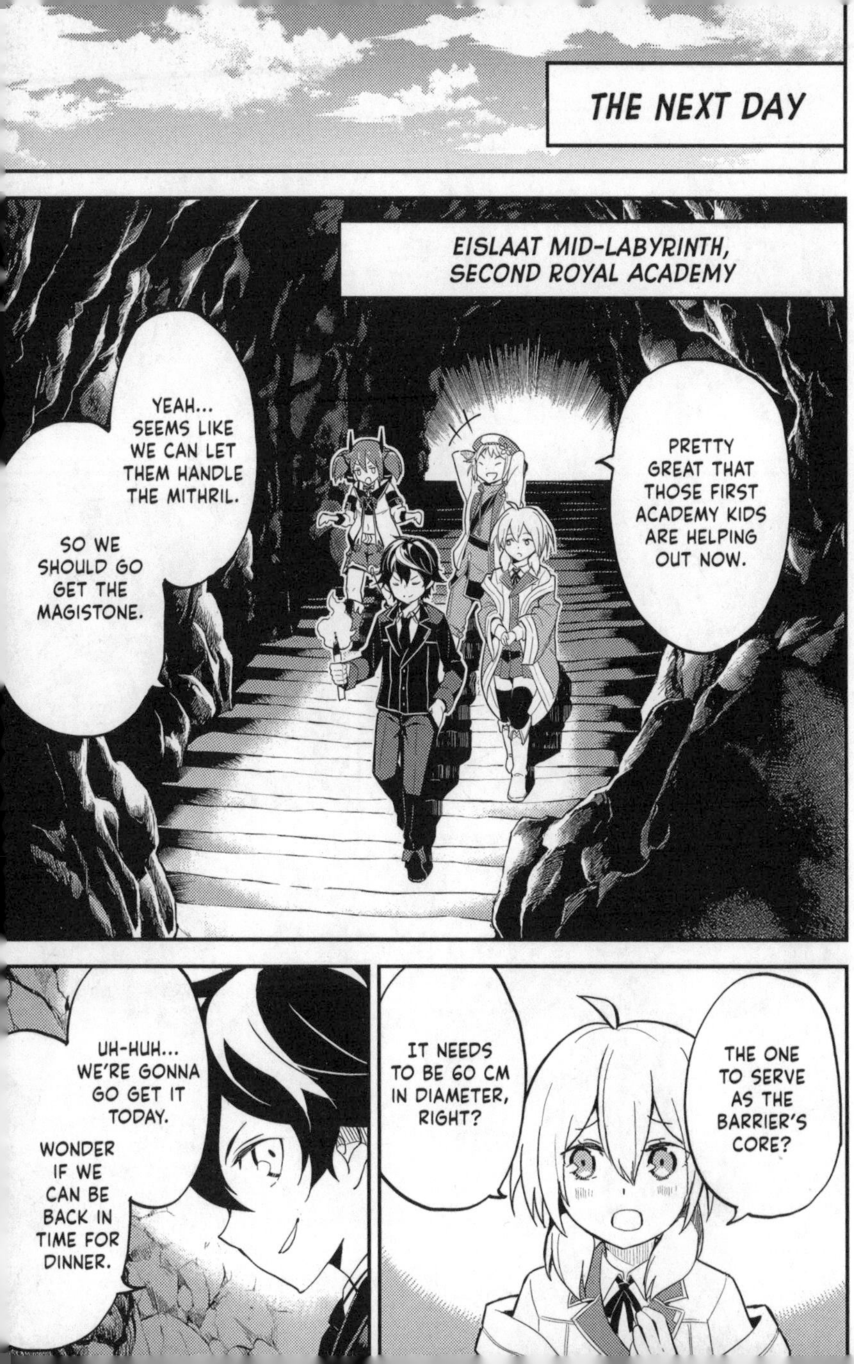
THE NEXT DAY
EISLAAT MID-LABYRINTH, SECOND ROYAL ACADEMY
PRETTY GREAT THAT THOSE FIRST ACADEMY KIDS ARE HELPING OUT NOW.
YEAH... SEEMS LIKE WE CAN LET THEM HANDLE THE MITHRIL.
SO WE SHOULD GO GET THE MAGISTONE.
THE ONE TO SERVE AS THE BARRIER'S CORE?
IT NEEDS TO BE 60 CM IN DIAMETER, RIGHT?
UH-HUH... WE'RE GONNA GO GET IT TODAY.
WONDER IF WE CAN BE BACK IN TIME FOR DINNER.

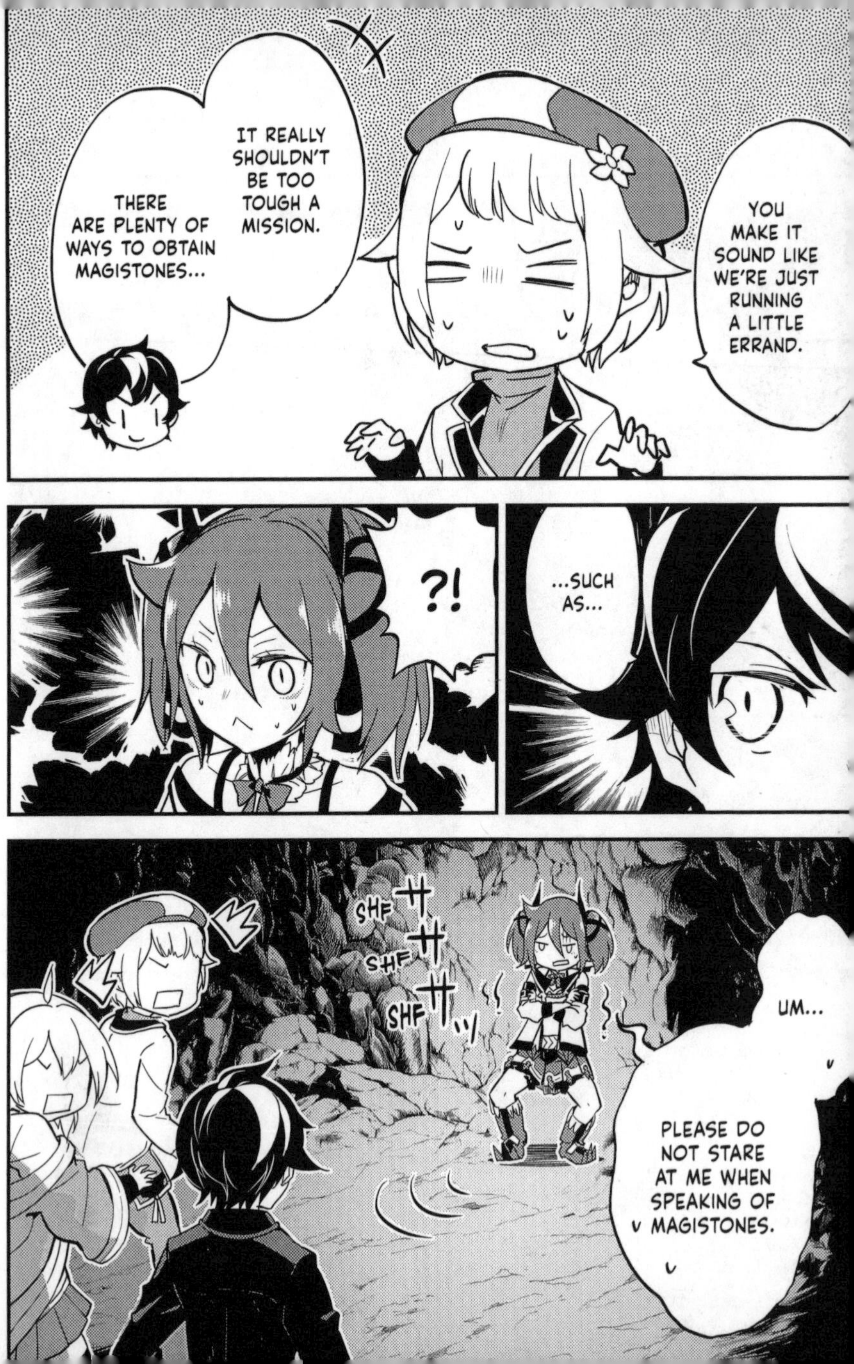
YOU MAKE IT SOUND LIKE WE'RE JUST RUNNING A LITTLE ERRAND.
IT REALLY SHOULDN'T BE TOO TOUGH A MISSION.
THERE ARE PLENTY OF WAYS TO OBTAIN MAGISTONES...
...SUCH AS...
?!
UM...
PLEASE DO NOT STARE AT ME WHEN SPEAKING OF MAGISTONES.
SHF SHF SHF

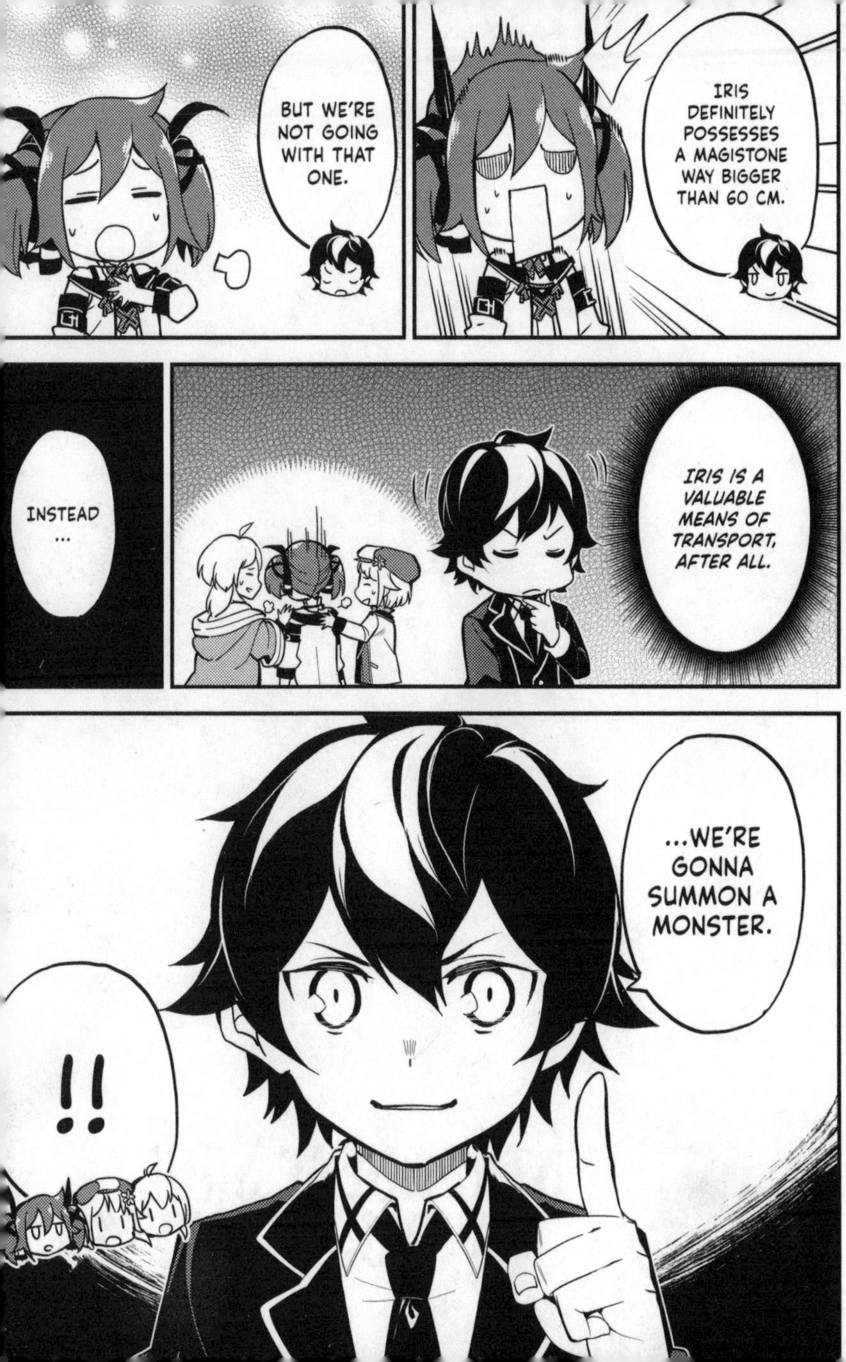
IRIS DEFINITELY POSSESSES A MAGISTONE WAY BIGGER THAN 60 CM.
BUT WE'RE NOT GOING WITH THAT ONE.
IRIS IS A VALUABLE MEANS OF TRANSPORT, AFTER ALL.
INSTEAD ...
...WE'RE GONNA SUMMON A MONSTER.
!!

THE
STRONGEST SAGE
WITH THE WEAKEST CREST

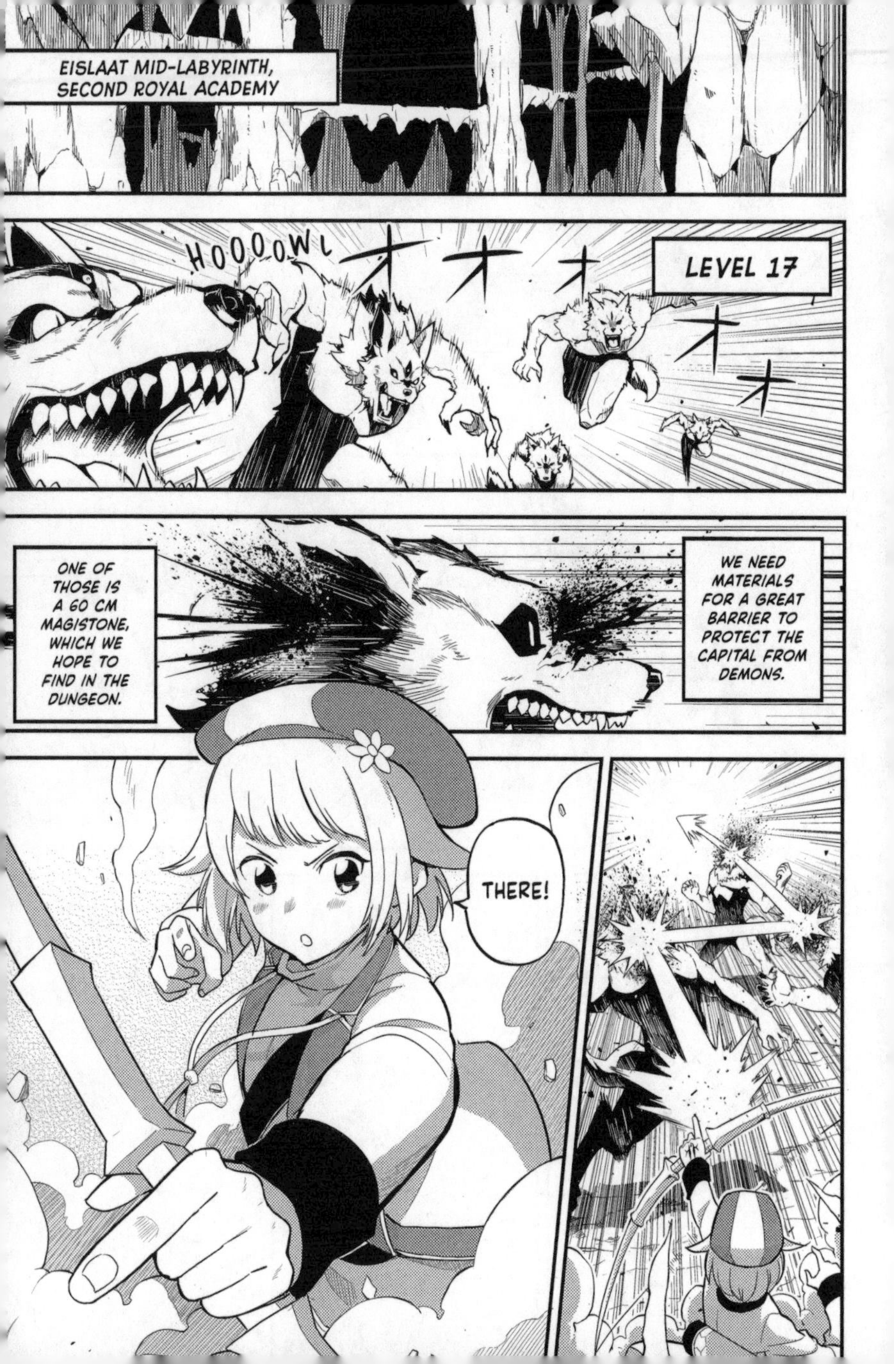
EISLAAT MID-LABYRINTH, SECOND ROYAL ACADEMY
LEVEL 17
HOOOOWL
WE NEED MATERIALS FOR A GREAT BARRIER TO PROTECT THE CAPITAL FROM DEMONS.
ONE OF THOSE IS A 60 CM MAGISTONE, WHICH WE HOPE TO FIND IN THE DUNGEON.
THERE!

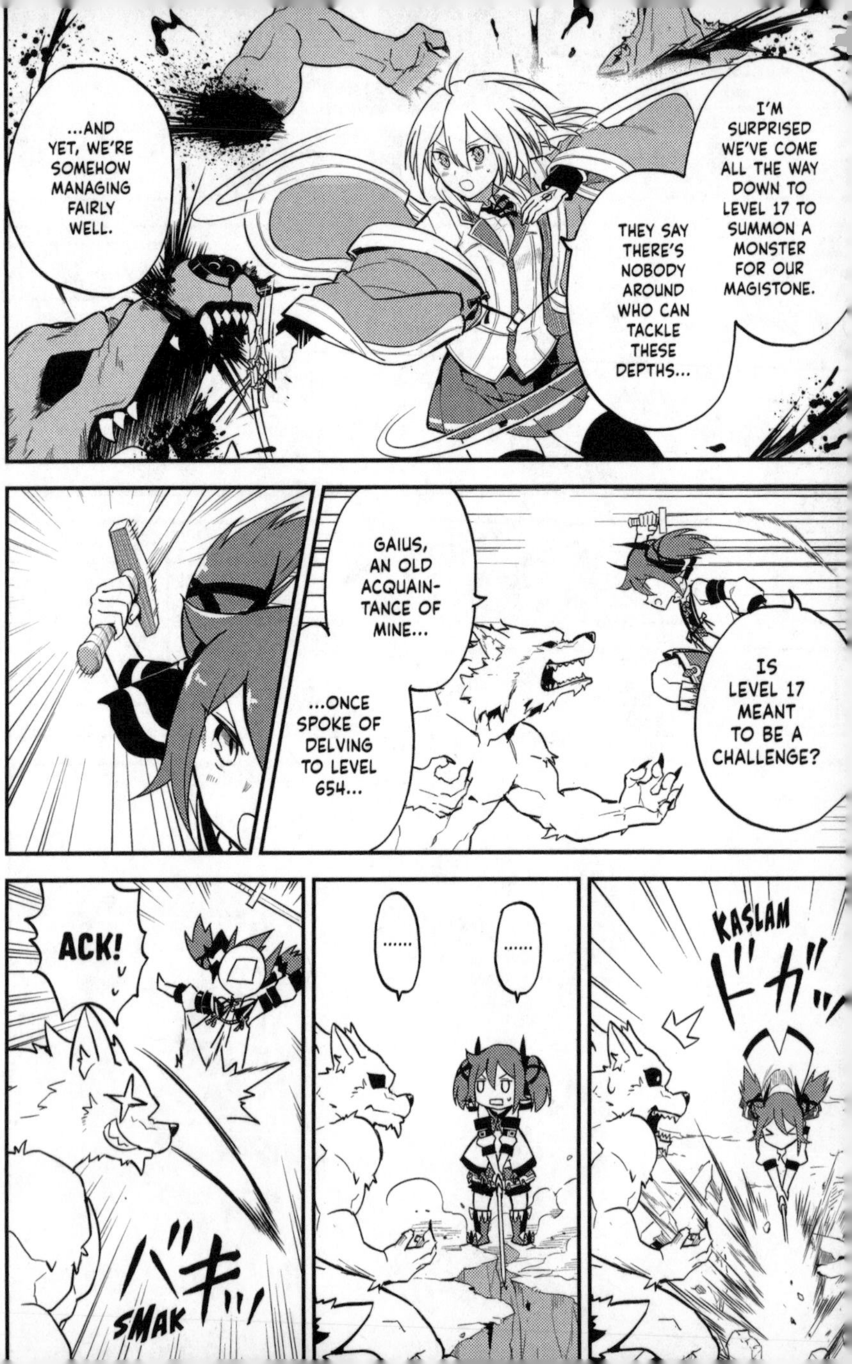
I'M SURPRISED WE'VE COME ALL THE WAY DOWN TO LEVEL 17 TO SUMMON A MONSTER FOR OUR MAGISTONE.
THEY SAY THERE'S NOBODY AROUND WHO CAN TACKLE THESE DEPTHS...
...AND YET, WE'RE SOMEHOW MANAGING FAIRLY WELL.
IS LEVEL 17 MEANT TO BE A CHALLENGE?
GAIUS, AN OLD ACQUAINTANCE OF MINE...
...ONCE SPOKE OF DELVING TO LEVEL 654...
KASLAM
ドガッ
......
......
ACK!
バキッ
SMAK

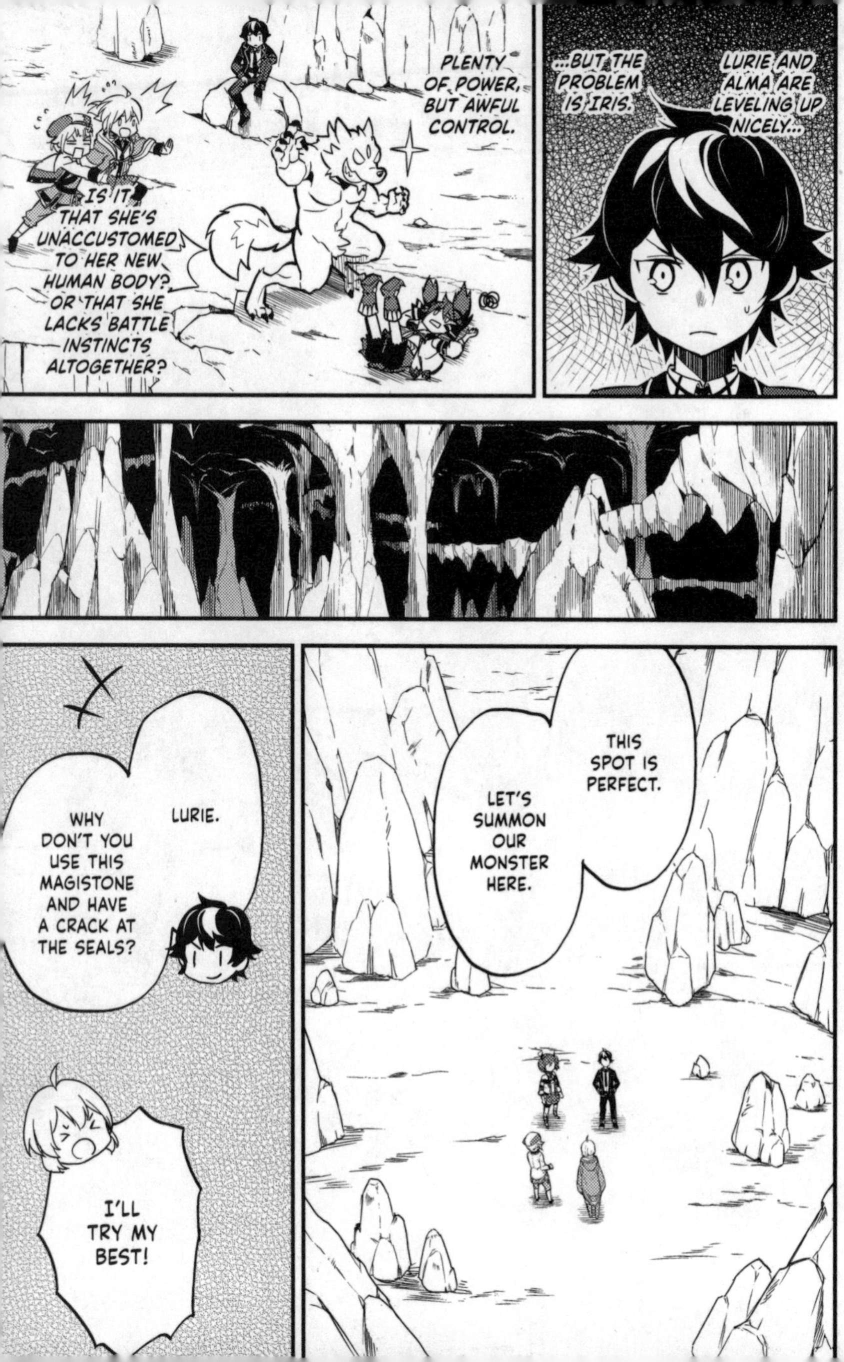
LURIE AND ALMA ARE LEVELING UP NICELY...
...BUT THE PROBLEM IS IRIS.
PLENTY OF POWER, BUT AWFUL CONTROL.
IS IT THAT SHE'S UNACCUSTOMED TO HER NEW HUMAN BODY? OR THAT SHE LACKS BATTLE INSTINCTS ALTOGETHER?
THIS SPOT IS PERFECT.
LET'S SUMMON OUR MONSTER HERE.
LURIE.
WHY DON'T YOU USE THIS MAGISTONE AND HAVE A CRACK AT THE SEALS?
I'LL TRY MY BEST!

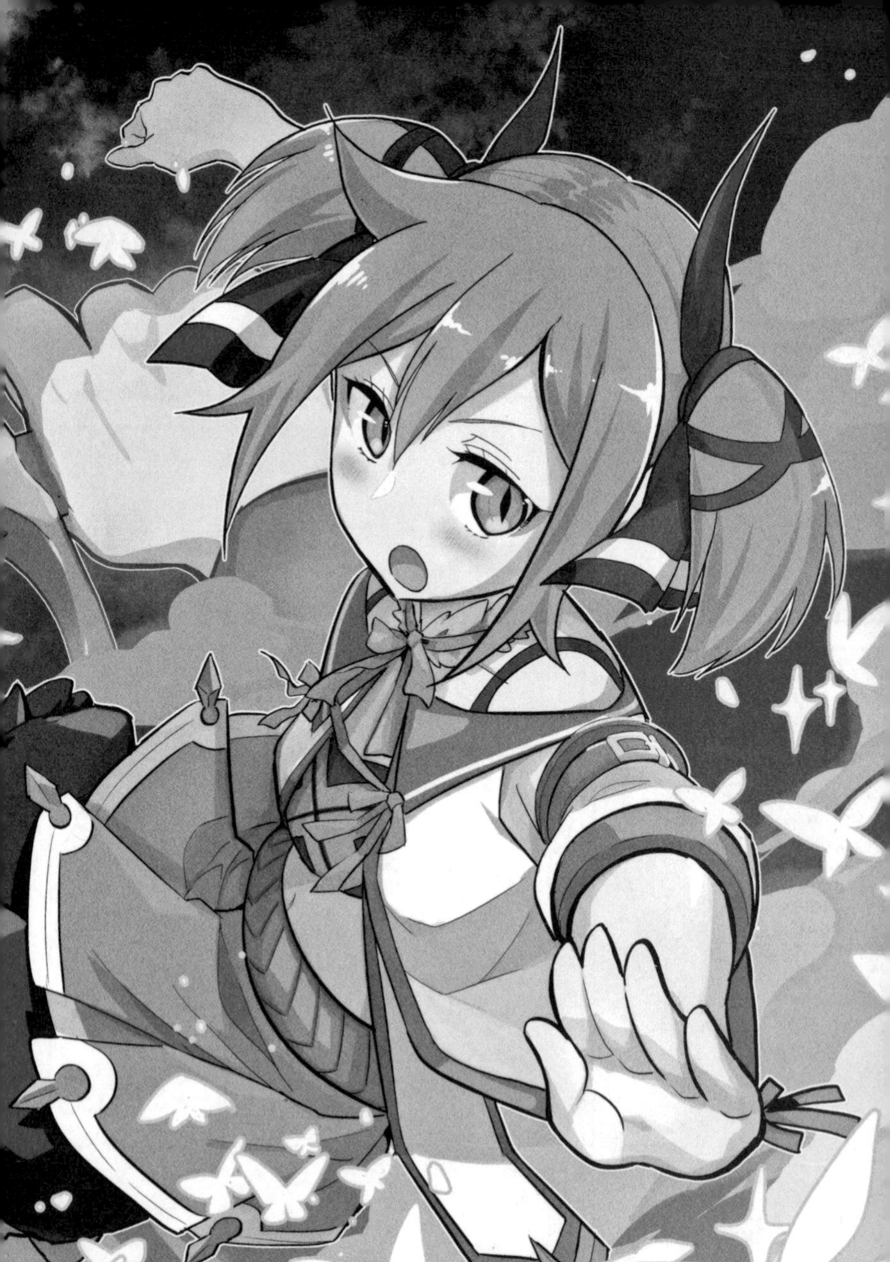

CHAPTER 17 • The Strongest Sage Acquires a Magistone

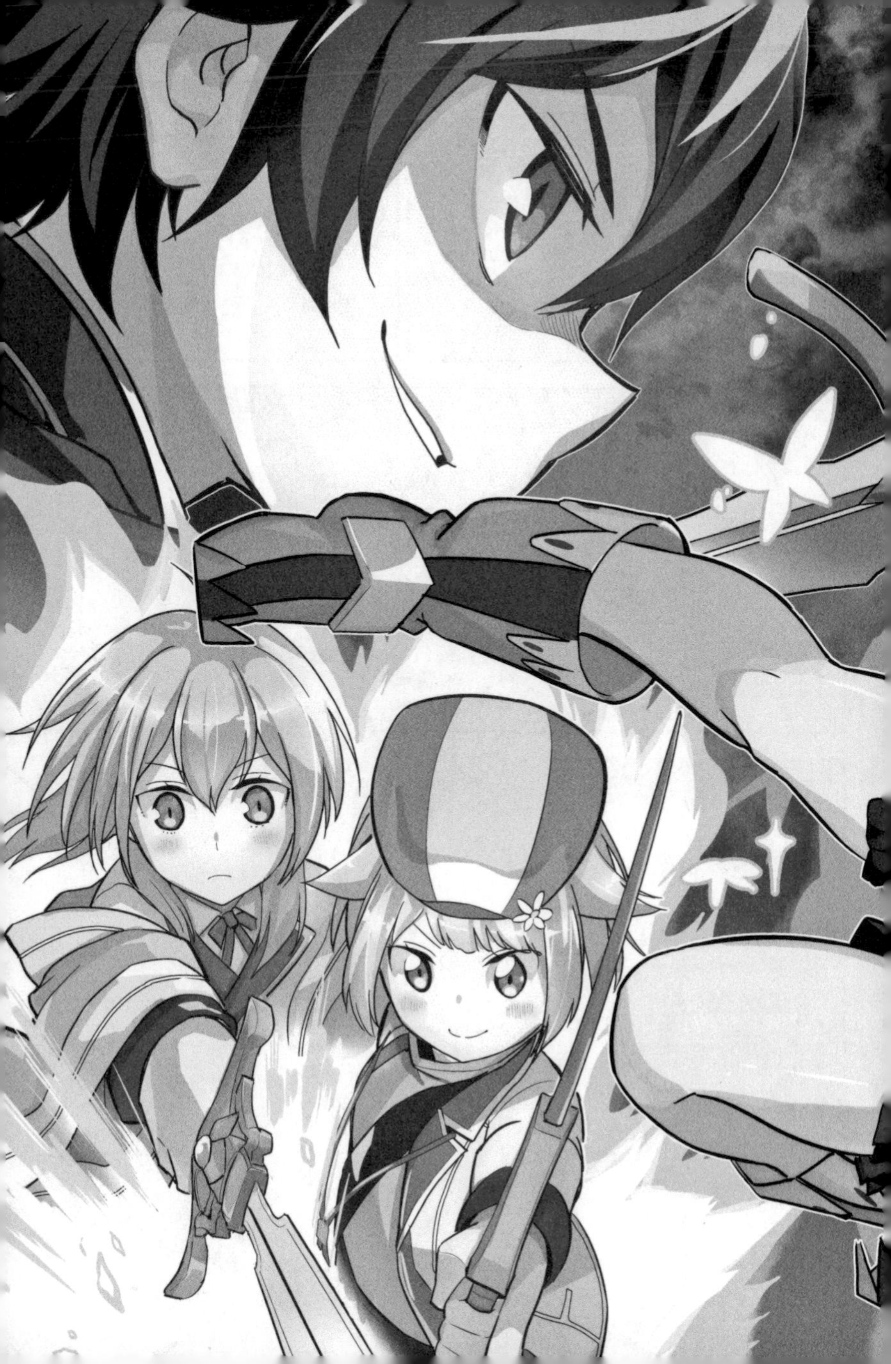

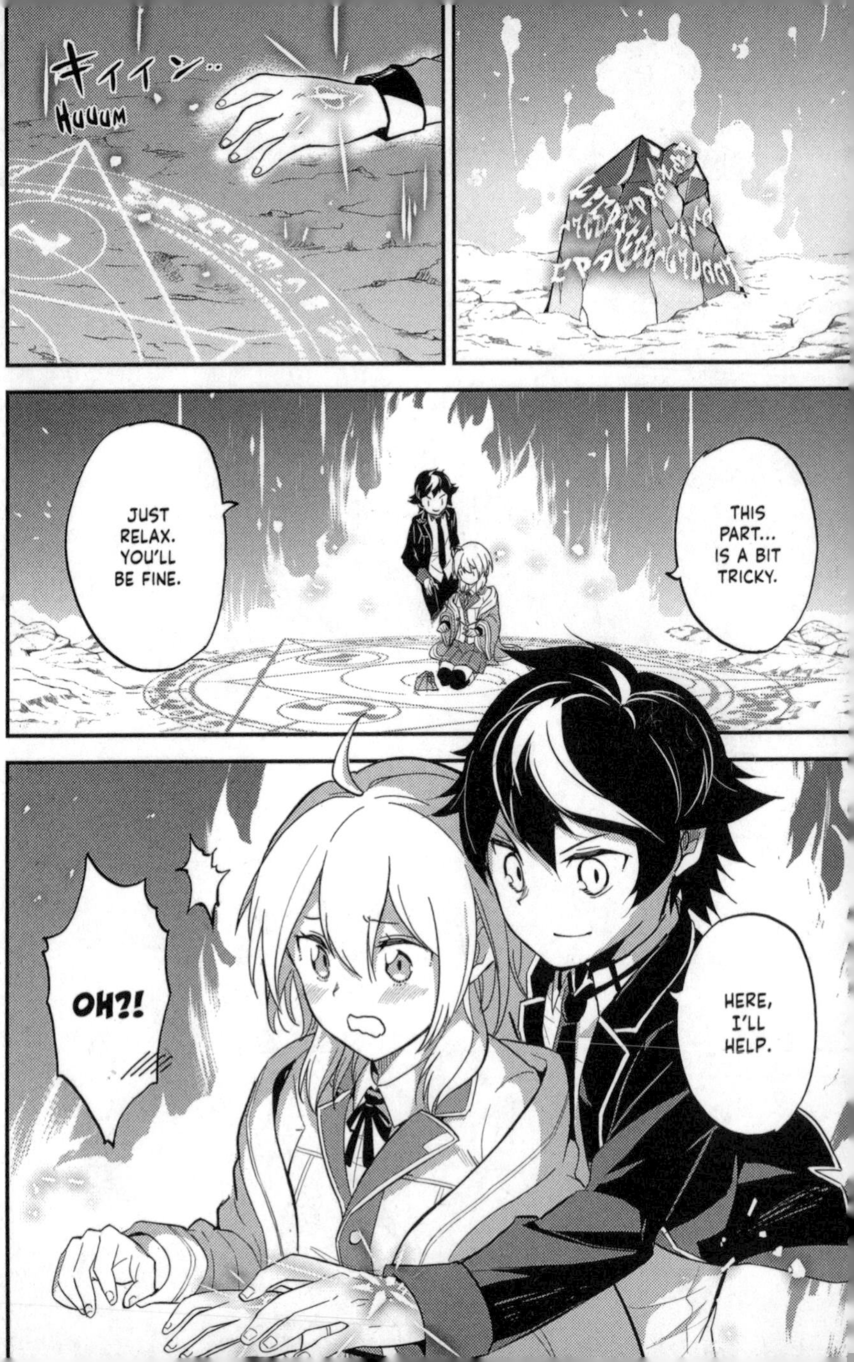
キイイン..
HUUUM
THIS PART... IS A BIT TRICKY.
JUST RELAX. YOU'LL BE FINE.
HERE, I'LL HELP.
OH?!

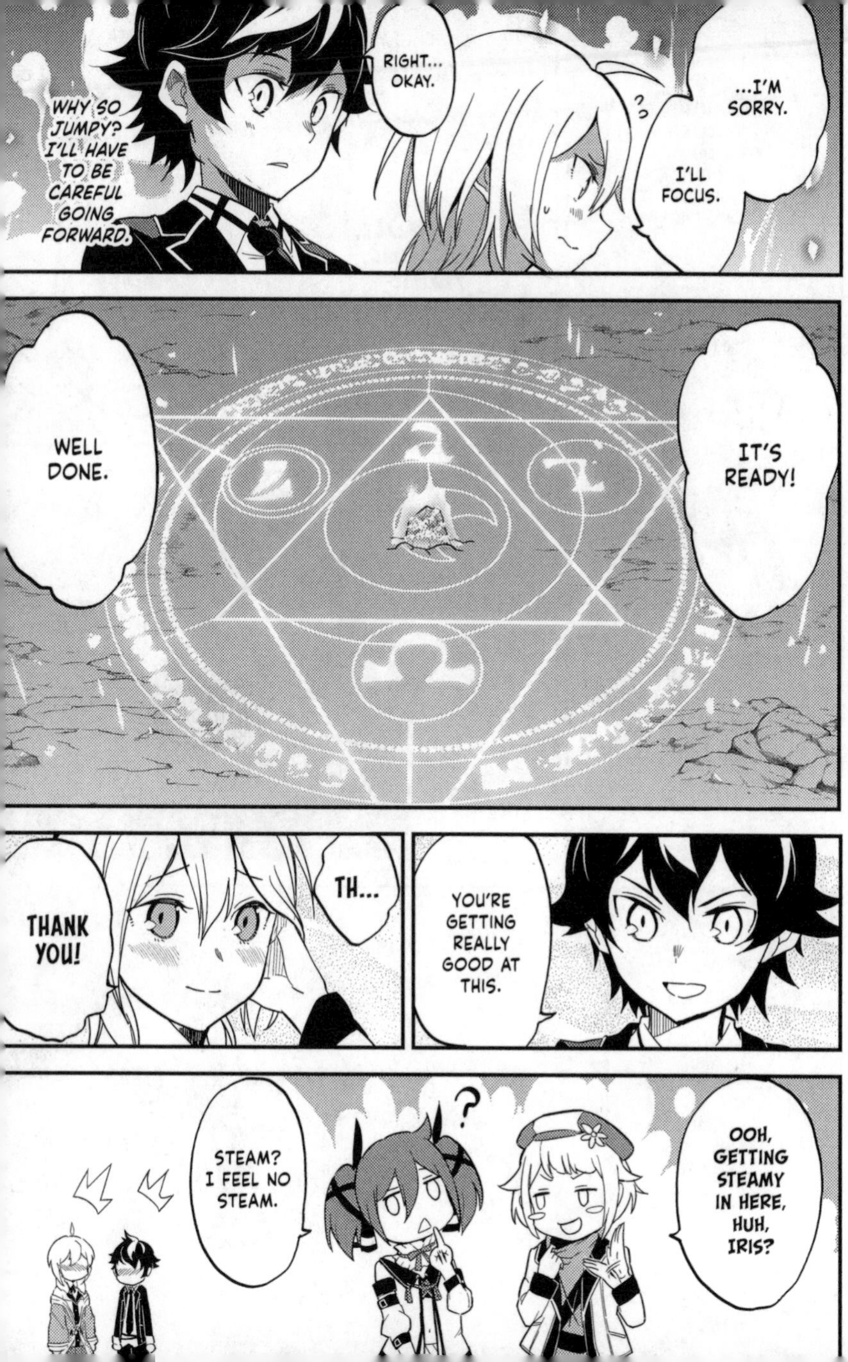
...I'M SORRY.
I'LL FOCUS.
RIGHT... OKAY.
WHY SO JUMPY? I'LL HAVE TO BE CAREFUL GOING FORWARD.
IT'S READY!
WELL DONE.
YOU'RE GETTING REALLY GOOD AT THIS.
TH...
THANK YOU!
OOH, GETTING STEAMY IN HERE, HUH, IRIS?
?
STEAM? I FEEL NO STEAM.

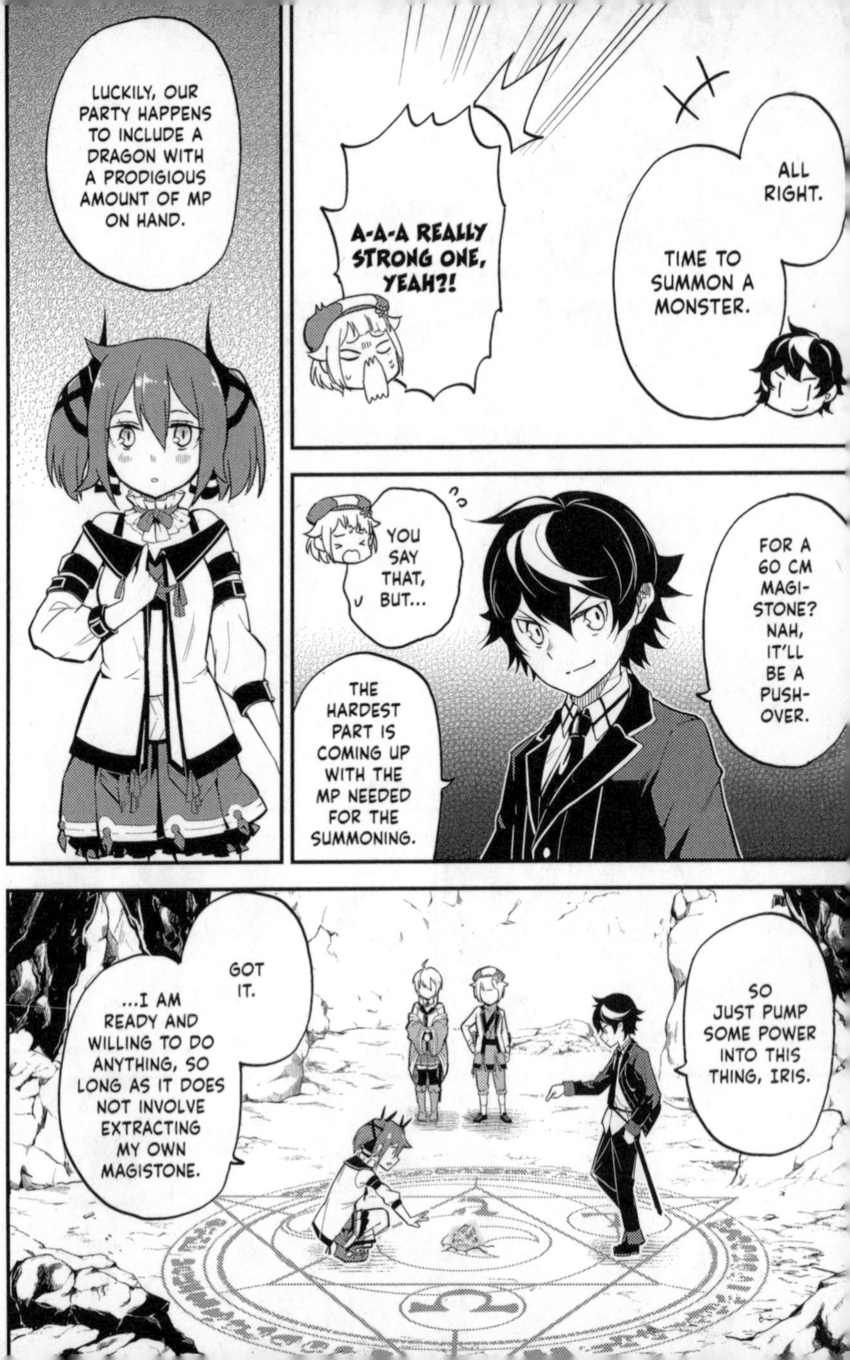
ALL RIGHT.
TIME TO SUMMON A MONSTER.
A-A-A REALLY STRONG ONE, YEAH?!
FOR A 60 CM MAGI- STONE? NAH, IT'LL BE A PUSH- OVER.
YOU SAY THAT, BUT...
THE HARDEST PART IS COMING UP WITH THE MP NEEDED FOR THE SUMMONING.
LUCKILY, OUR PARTY HAPPENS TO INCLUDE A DRAGON WITH A PRODIGIOUS AMOUNT OF MP ON HAND.
SO JUST PUMP SOME POWER INTO THIS THING, IRIS.
GOT IT.
...I AM READY AND WILLING TO DO ANYTHING, SO LONG AS IT DOES NOT INVOLVE EXTRACTING MY OWN MAGISTONE.

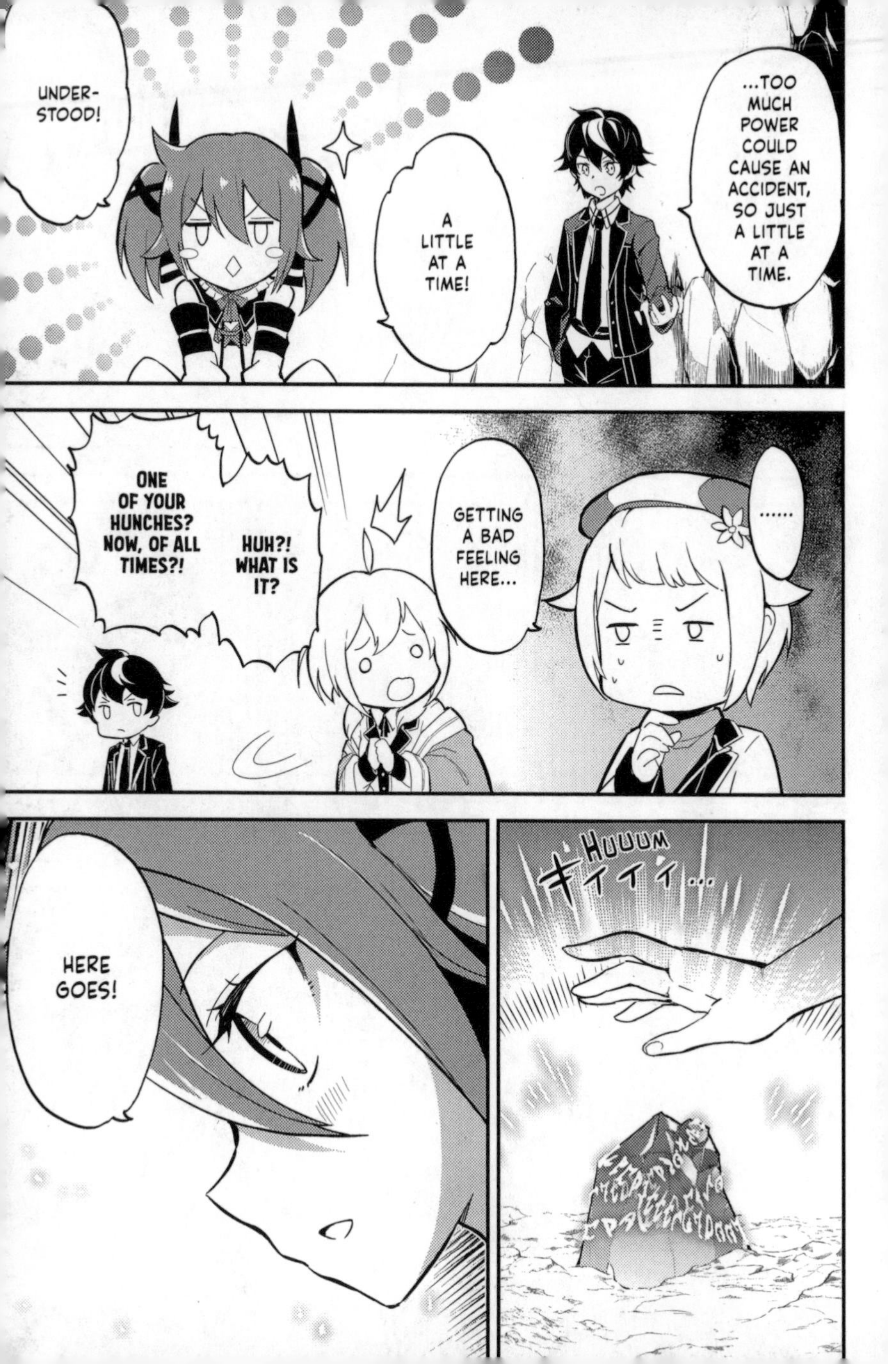
...TOO MUCH POWER COULD CAUSE AN ACCIDENT, SO JUST A LITTLE AT A TIME.
A LITTLE AT A TIME!
UNDER-STOOD!
......
GETTING A BAD FEELING HERE...
HUH?! WHAT IS IT?
ONE OF YOUR HUNCHES? NOW, OF ALL TIMES?!
HUUUM
キイイイ...
HERE GOES!

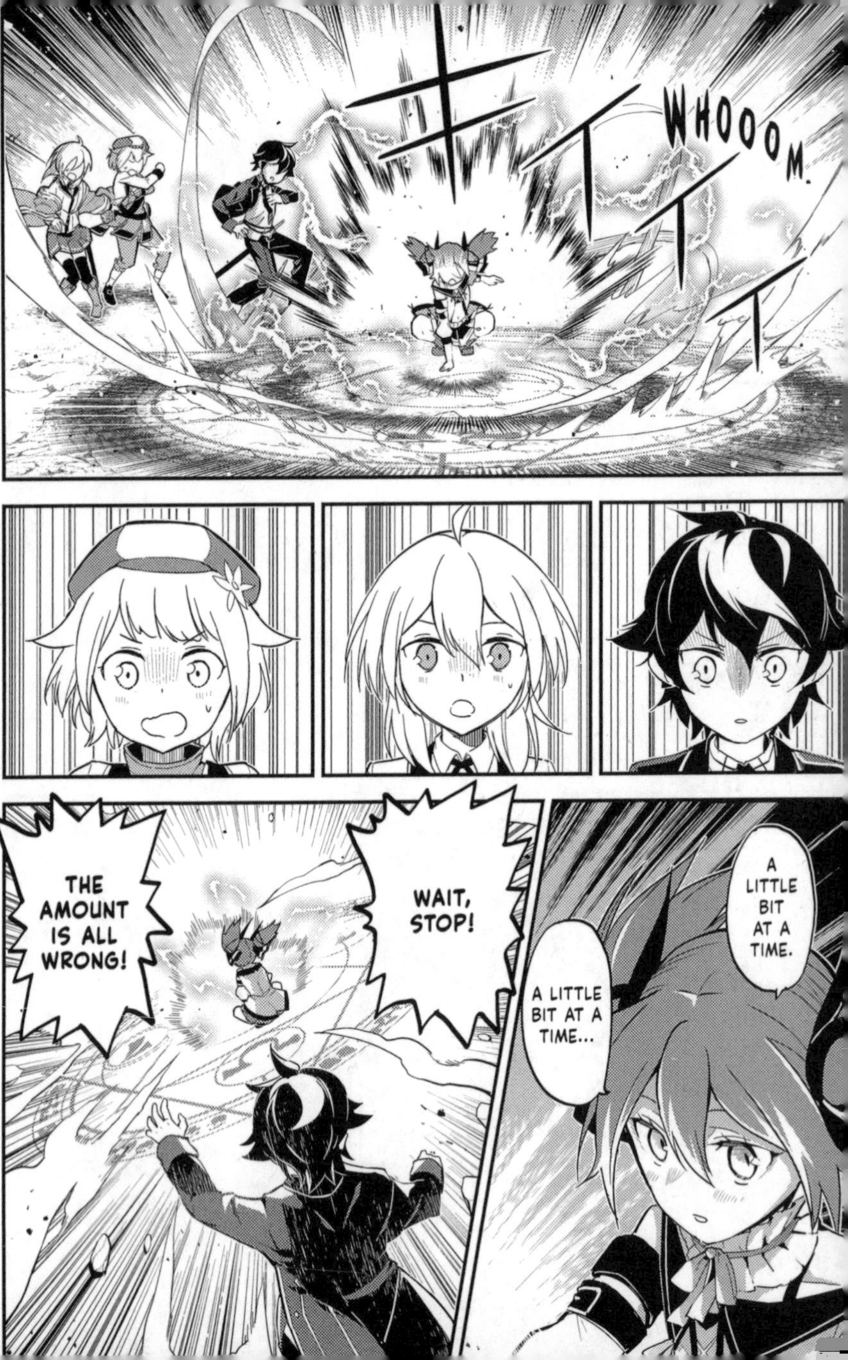
WHOOOM
A LITTLE BIT AT A TIME.
A LITTLE BIT AT A TIME...
WAIT, STOP!
THE AMOUNT IS ALL WRONG!

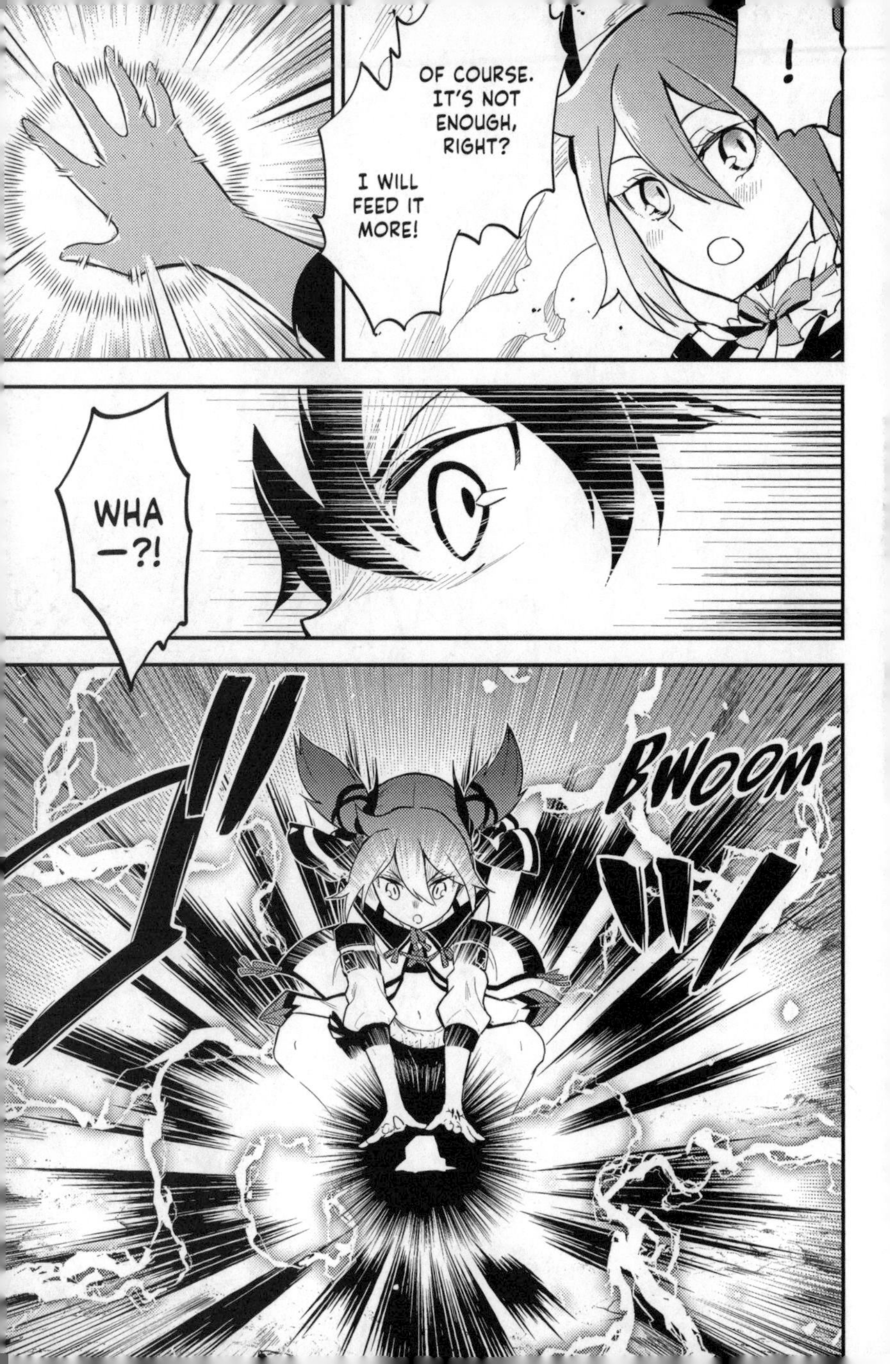
!
OF COURSE. IT'S NOT ENOUGH, RIGHT?
I WILL FEED IT MORE!
WHA —?!
BWOOM

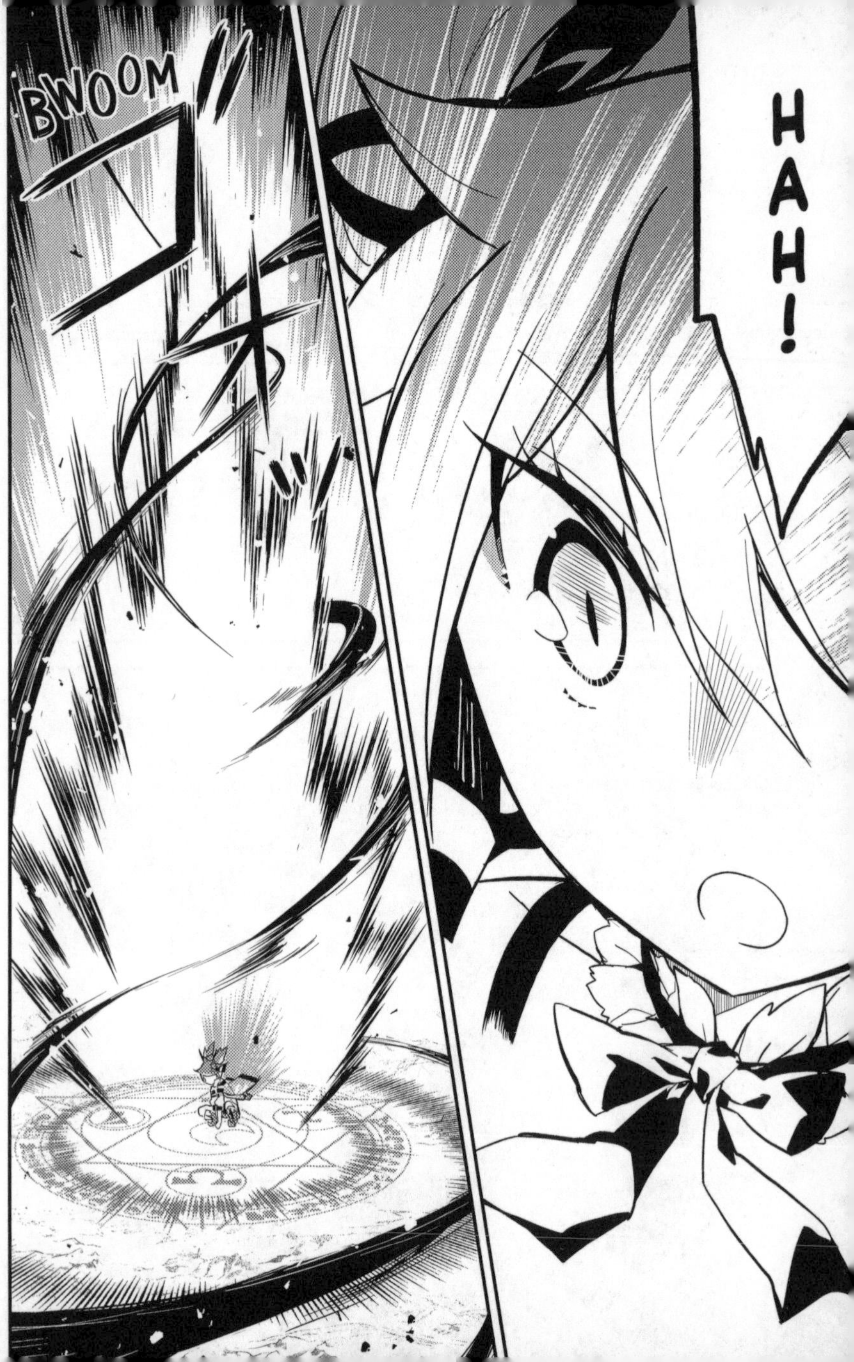
HAH!
BWOOM

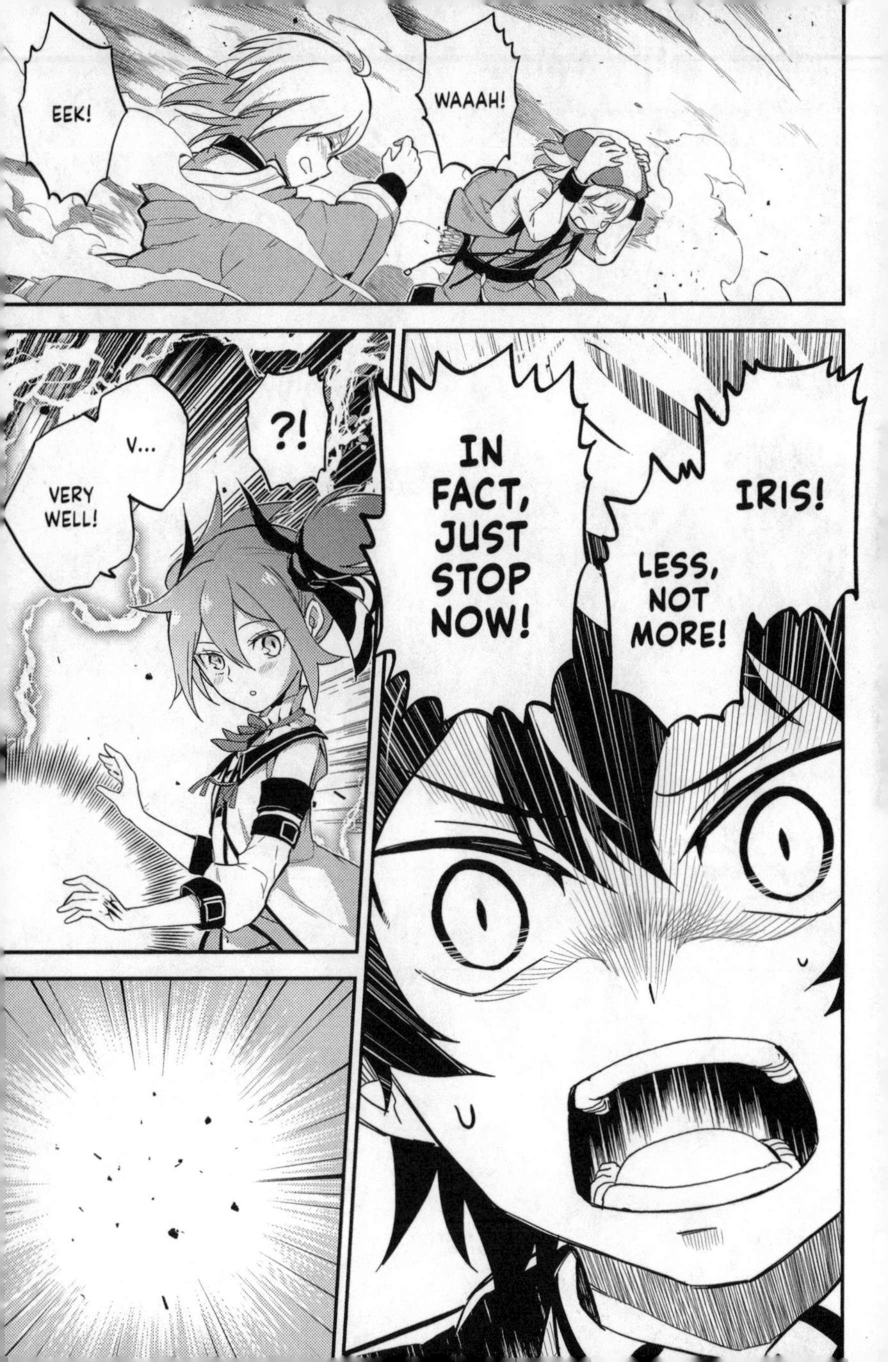
WAAAH!
EEK!
IRIS! LESS, NOT MORE!
IN FACT, JUST STOP NOW!
?!
V... VERY WELL!

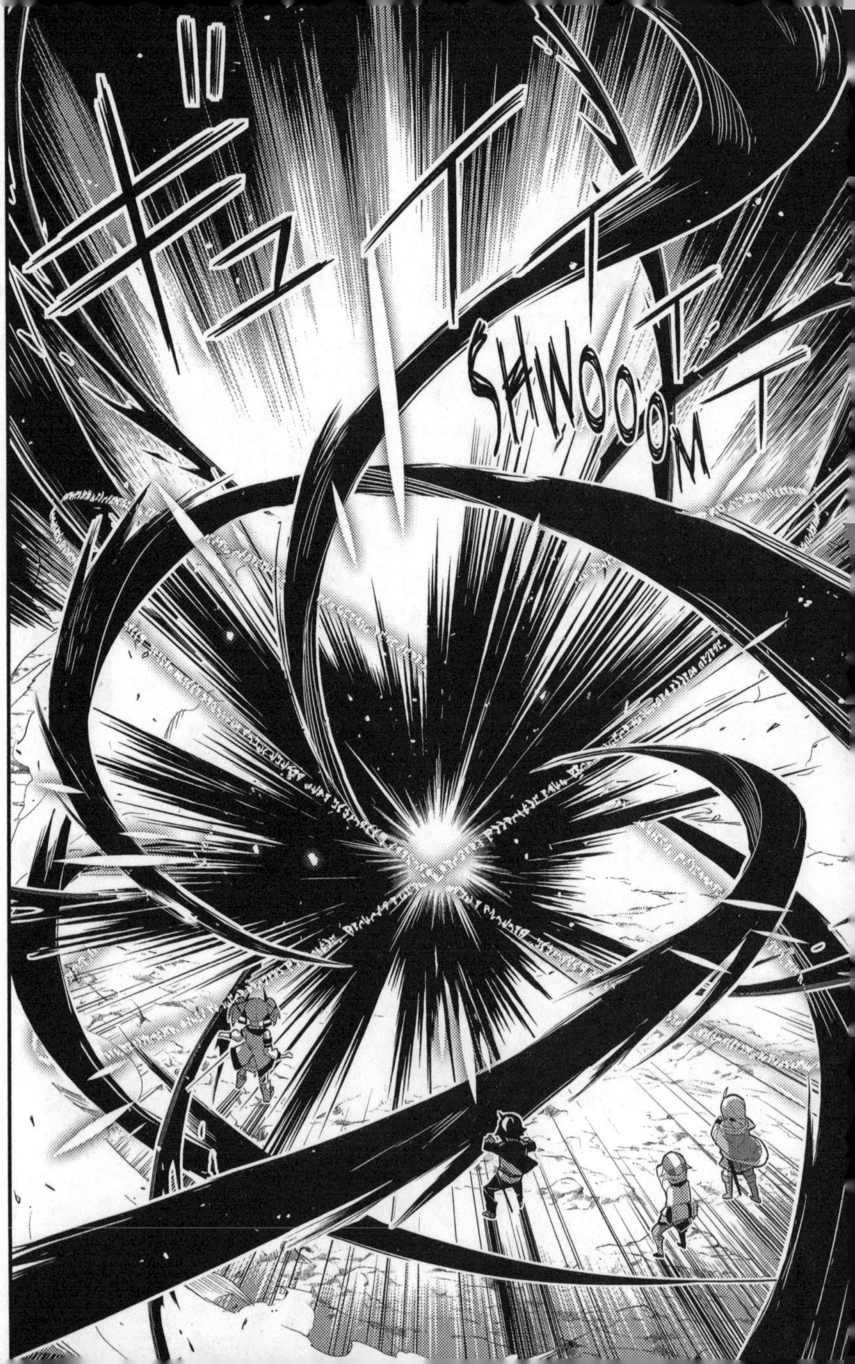
SHWOOOM

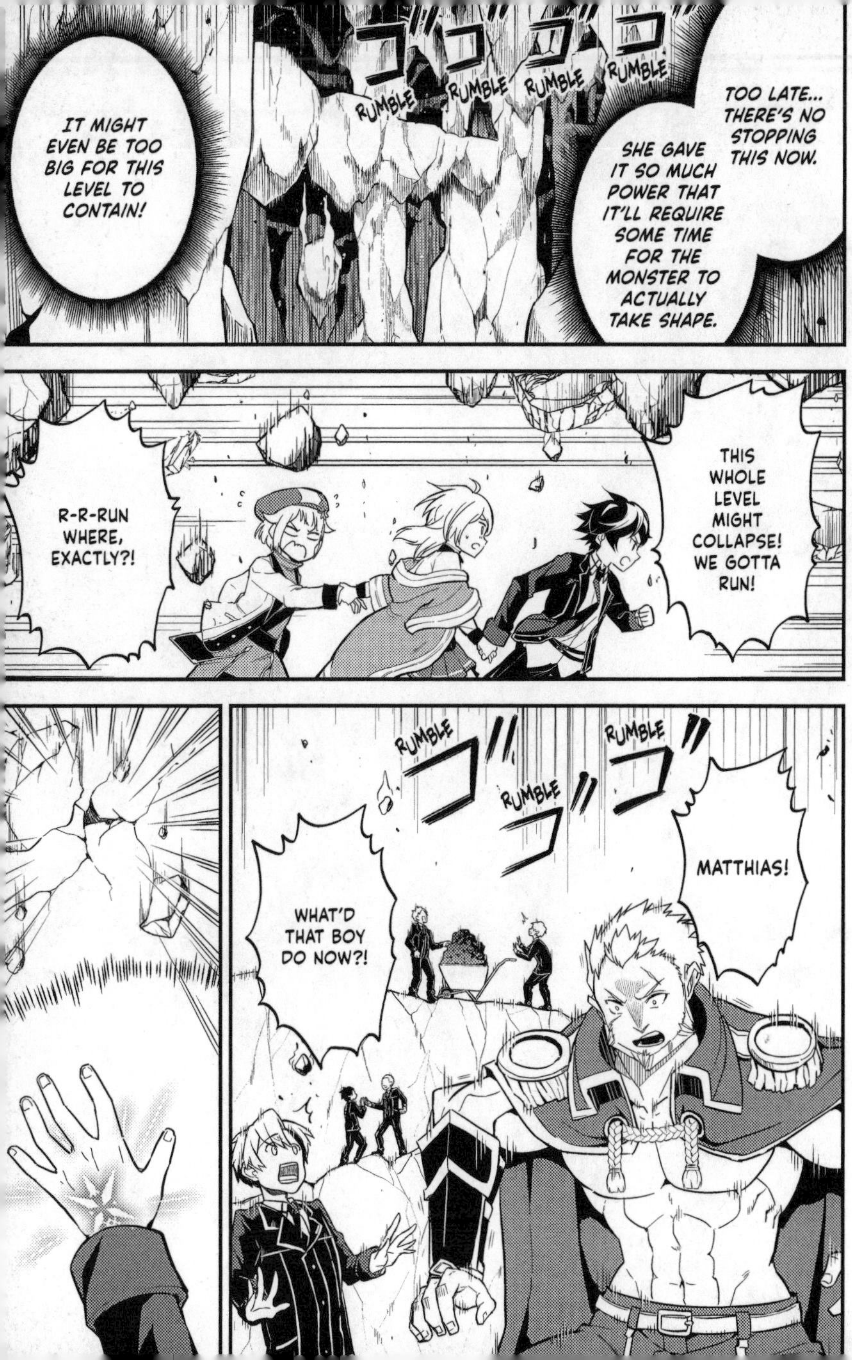
RUMBLE RUMBLE RUMBLE RUMBLE
TOO LATE... THERE'S NO STOPPING THIS NOW.
SHE GAVE IT SO MUCH POWER THAT IT'LL REQUIRE SOME TIME FOR THE MONSTER TO ACTUALLY TAKE SHAPE.
IT MIGHT EVEN BE TOO BIG FOR THIS LEVEL TO CONTAIN!
THIS WHOLE LEVEL MIGHT COLLAPSE! WE GOTTA RUN!
R-R-RUN WHERE, EXACTLY?!
RUMBLE RUMBLE RUMBLE
MATTHIAS!
WHAT'D THAT BOY DO NOW?!

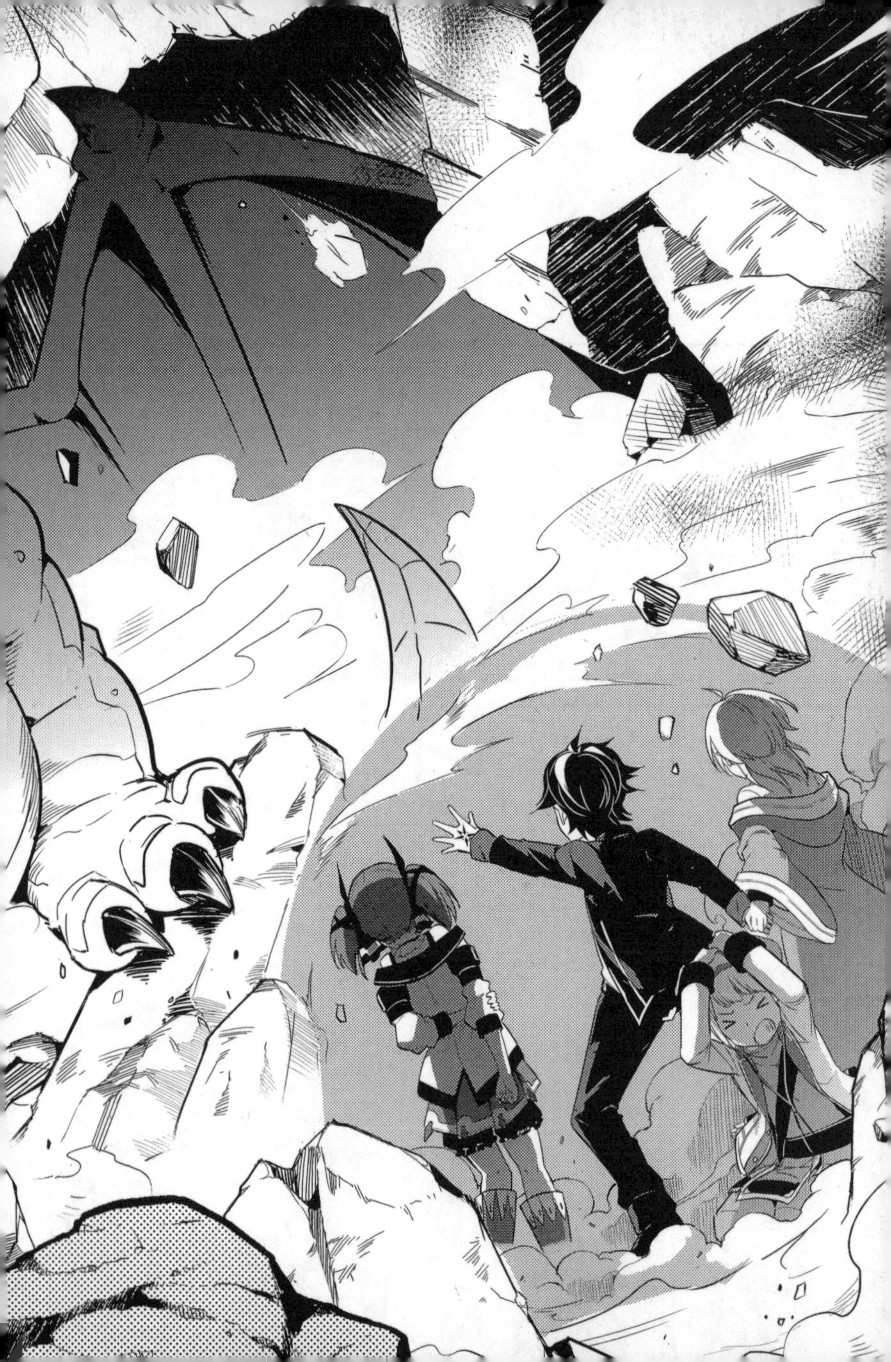

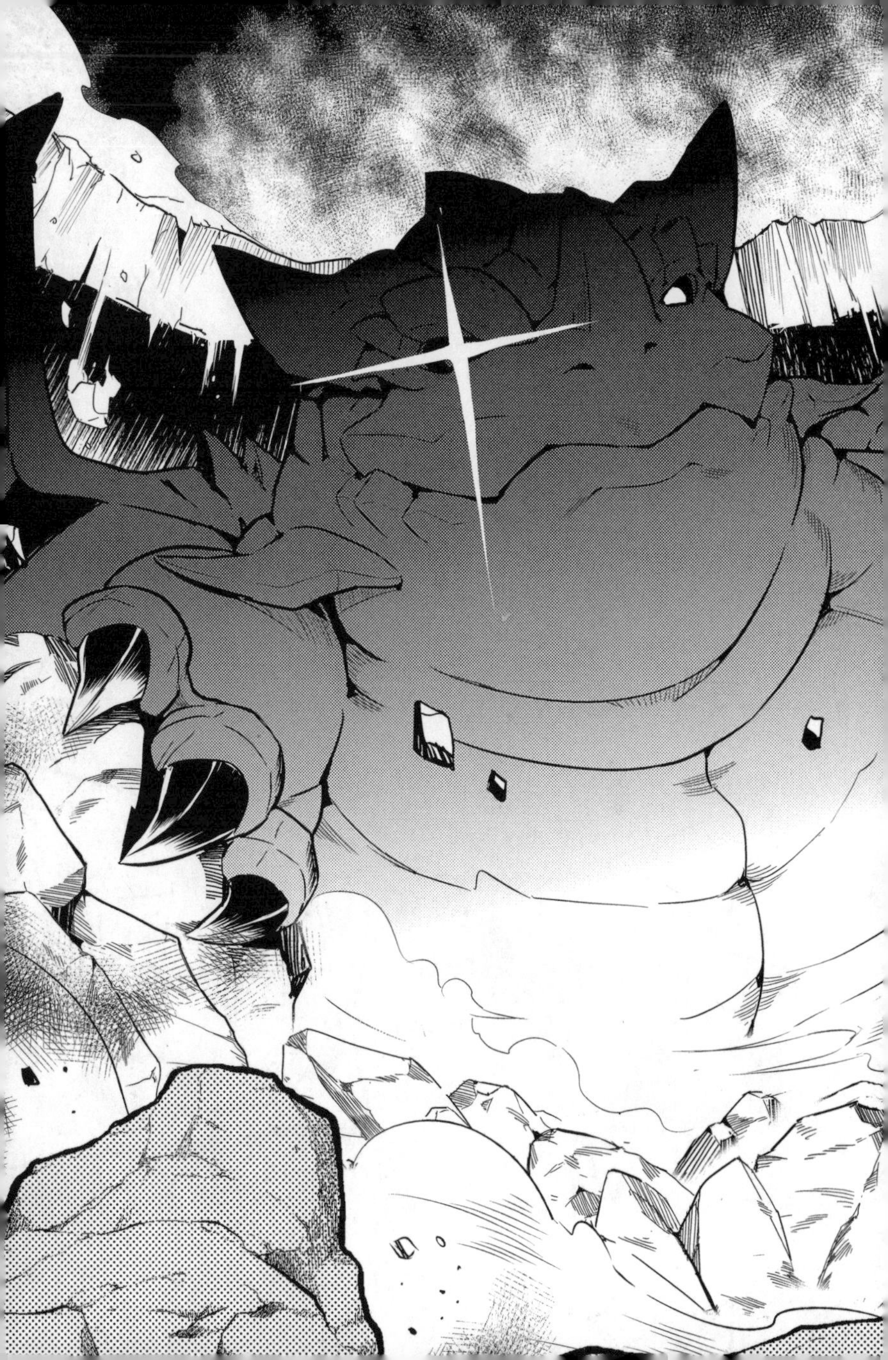

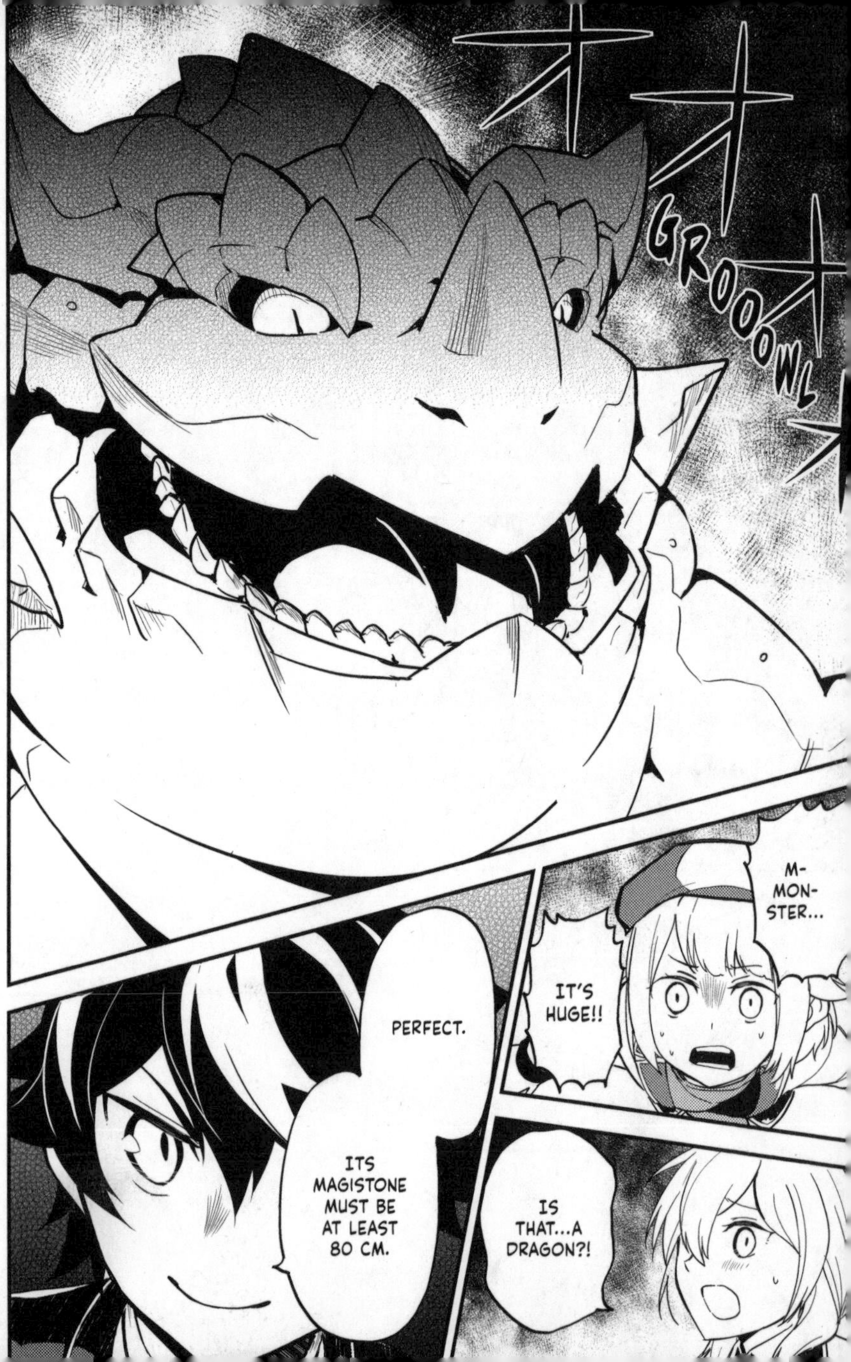
GROOOOWL
M-MONSTER...
IT'S HUGE!!
IS THAT...A DRAGON?!
PERFECT.
ITS MAGISTONE MUST BE AT LEAST 80 CM.

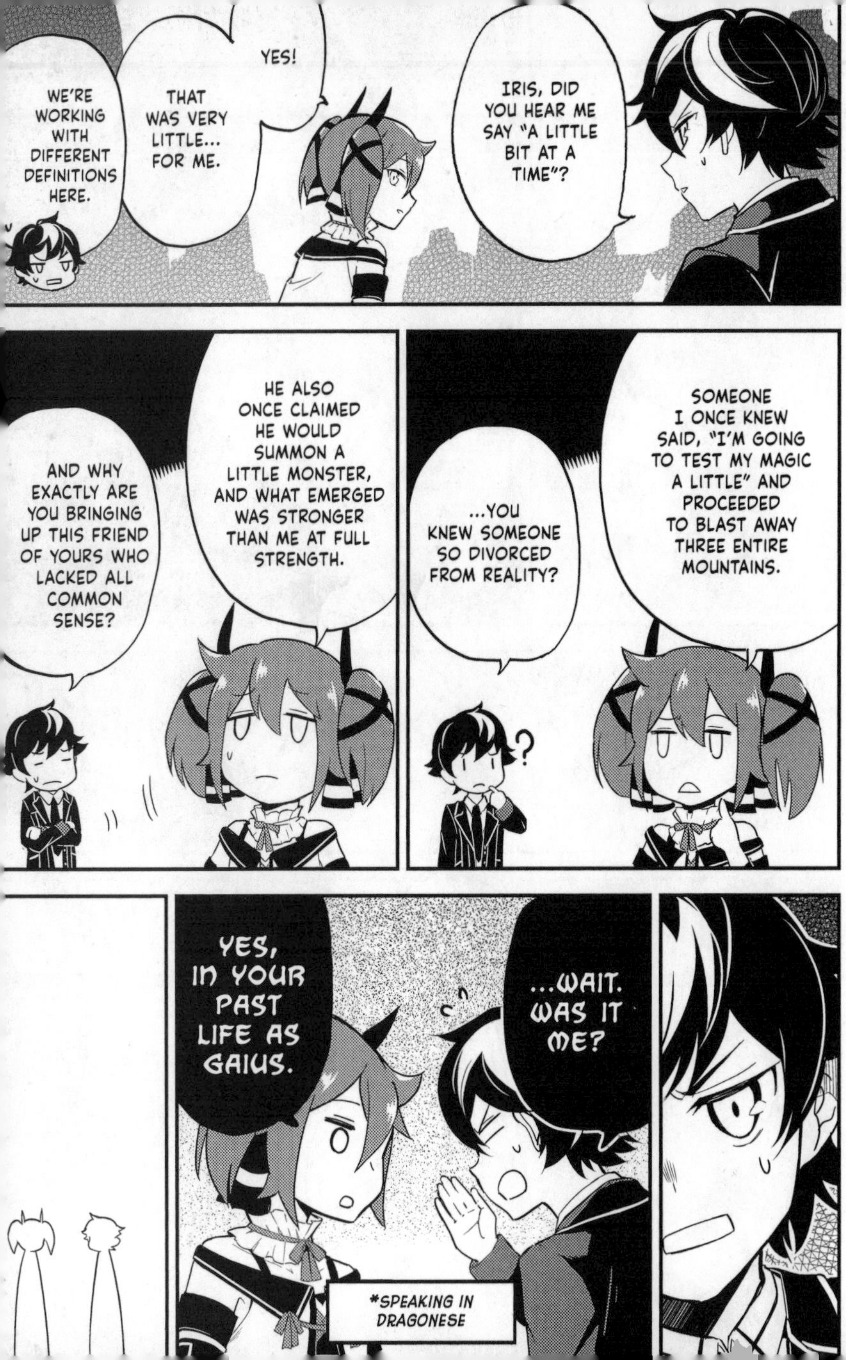
IRIS, DID YOU HEAR ME SAY "A LITTLE BIT AT A TIME"?
YES!
THAT WAS VERY LITTLE... FOR ME.
WE'RE WORKING WITH DIFFERENT DEFINITIONS HERE.
SOMEONE I ONCE KNEW SAID, "I'M GOING TO TEST MY MAGIC A LITTLE" AND PROCEEDED TO BLAST AWAY THREE ENTIRE MOUNTAINS.
...YOU KNEW SOMEONE SO DIVORCED FROM REALITY?
HE ALSO ONCE CLAIMED HE WOULD SUMMON A LITTLE MONSTER, AND WHAT EMERGED WAS STRONGER THAN ME AT FULL STRENGTH.
AND WHY EXACTLY ARE YOU BRINGING UP THIS FRIEND OF YOURS WHO LACKED ALL COMMON SENSE?
...WAIT. WAS IT ME?
YES, IN YOUR PAST LIFE AS GAIUS.
*SPEAKING IN DRAGONESE

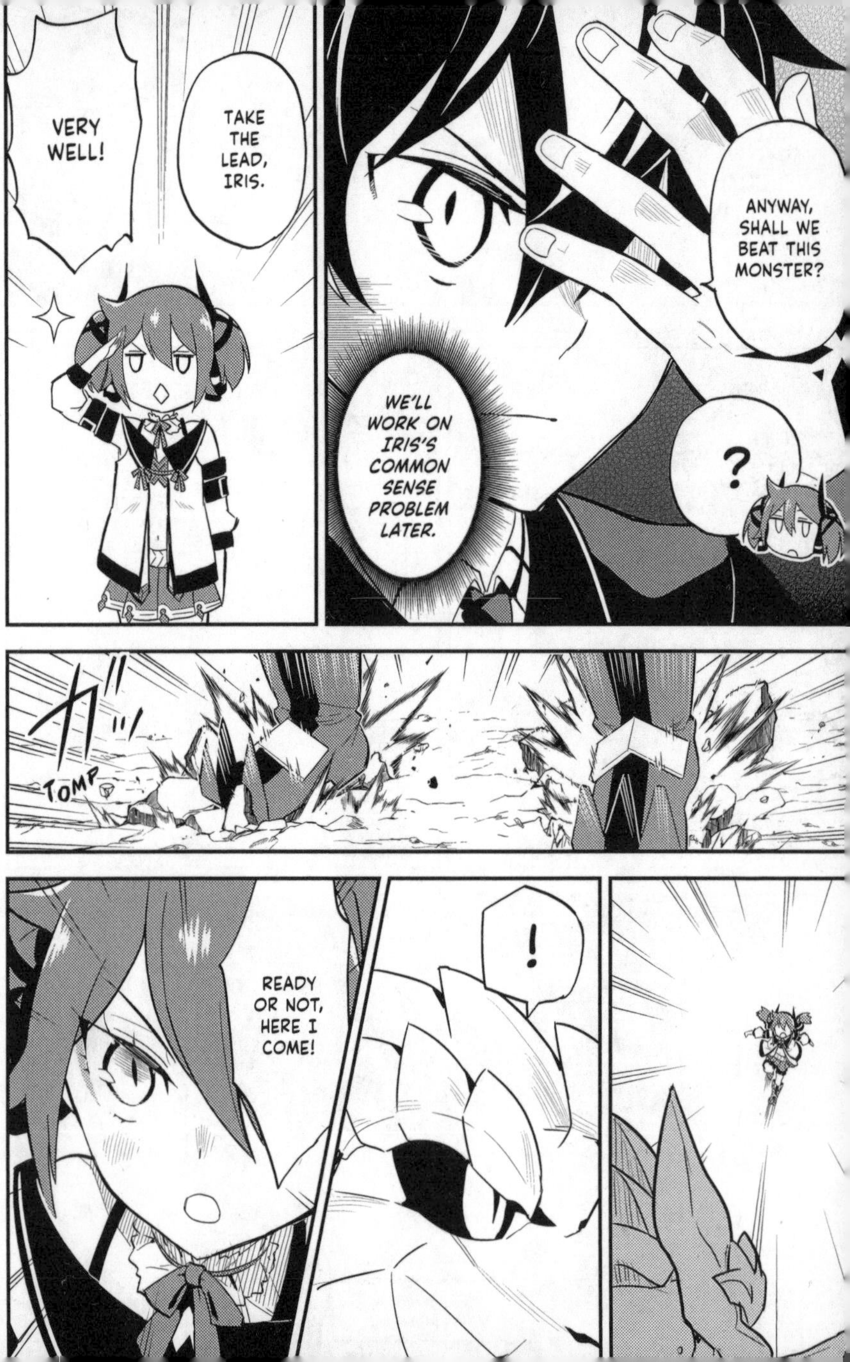
ANYWAY, SHALL WE BEAT THIS MONSTER?
WE'LL WORK ON IRIS'S COMMON SENSE PROBLEM LATER.
?
TAKE THE LEAD, IRIS.
VERY WELL!
TOMP
!
READY OR NOT, HERE I COME!

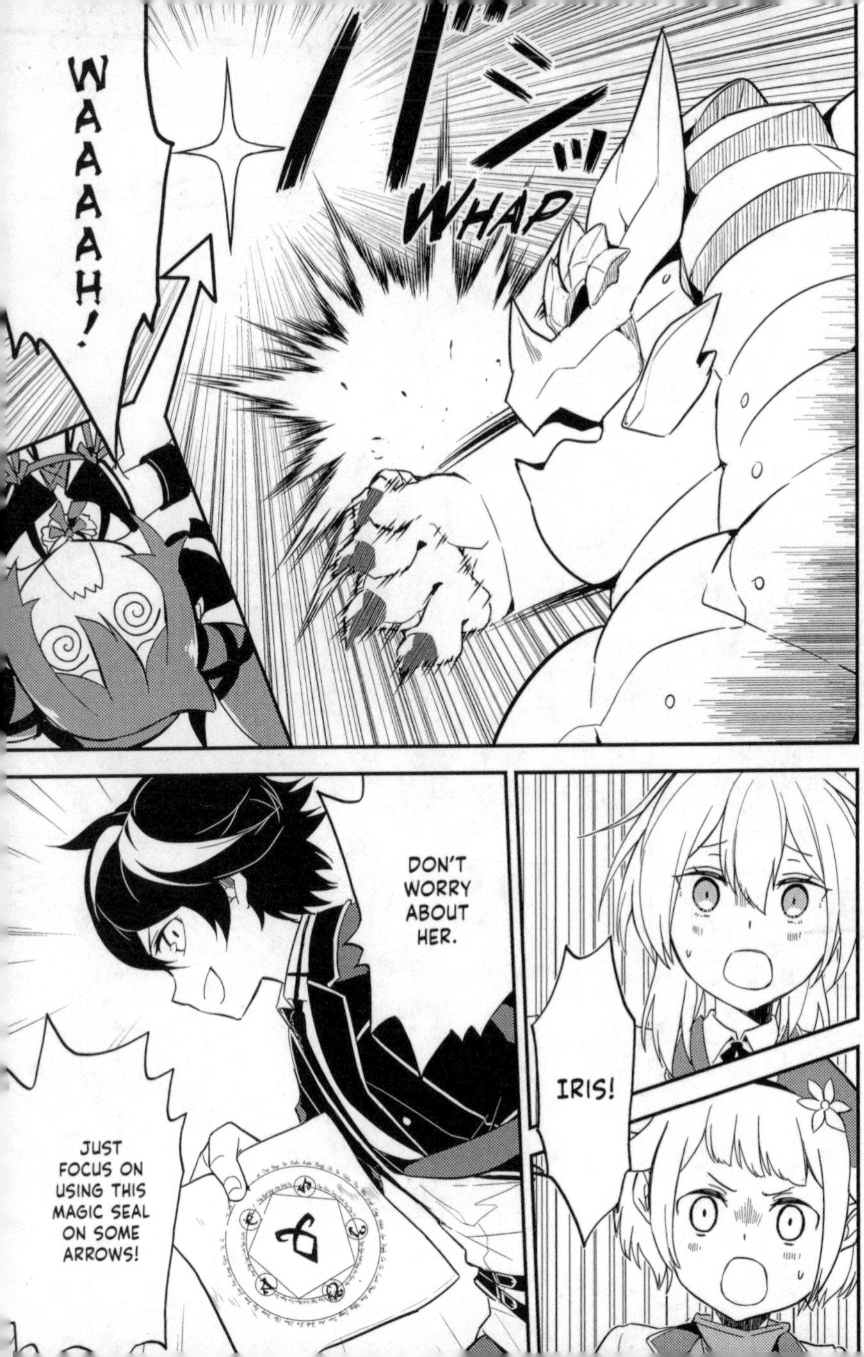
WHAP
WAAAAAH!
IRIS!
DON'T WORRY ABOUT HER.
JUST FOCUS ON USING THIS MAGIC SEAL ON SOME ARROWS!

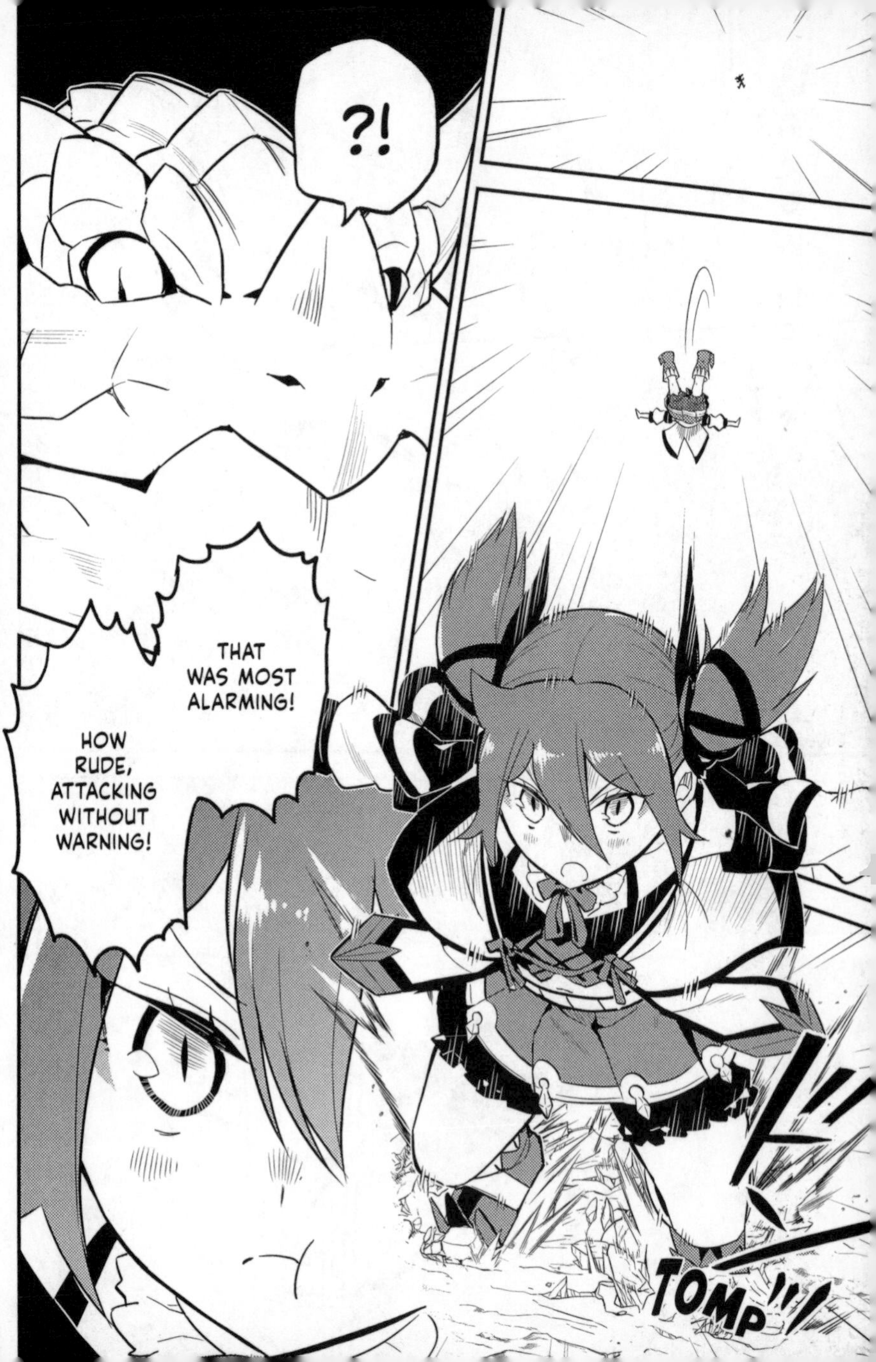
TOMP!!!
?!
THAT WAS MOST ALARMING!
HOW RUDE, ATTACKING WITHOUT WARNING!

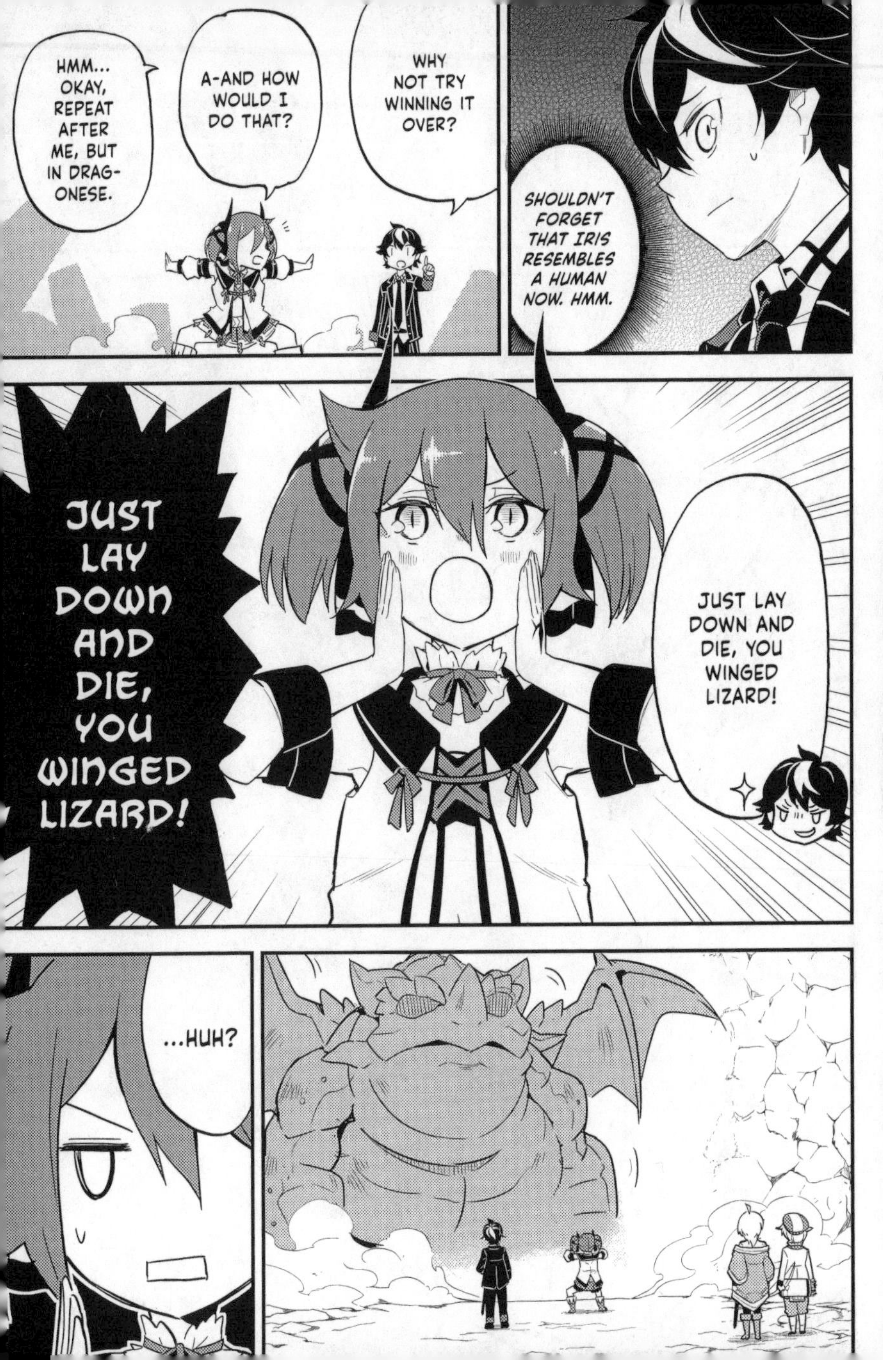
SHOULDN'T FORGET THAT IRIS RESEMBLES A HUMAN NOW. HMM.
WHY NOT TRY WINNING IT OVER?
A-AND HOW WOULD I DO THAT?
HMM... OKAY, REPEAT AFTER ME, BUT IN DRAG-ONESE.
JUST LAY DOWN AND DIE, YOU WINGED LIZARD!
JUST LAY DOWN AND DIE, YOU WINGED LIZARD!
...HUH?

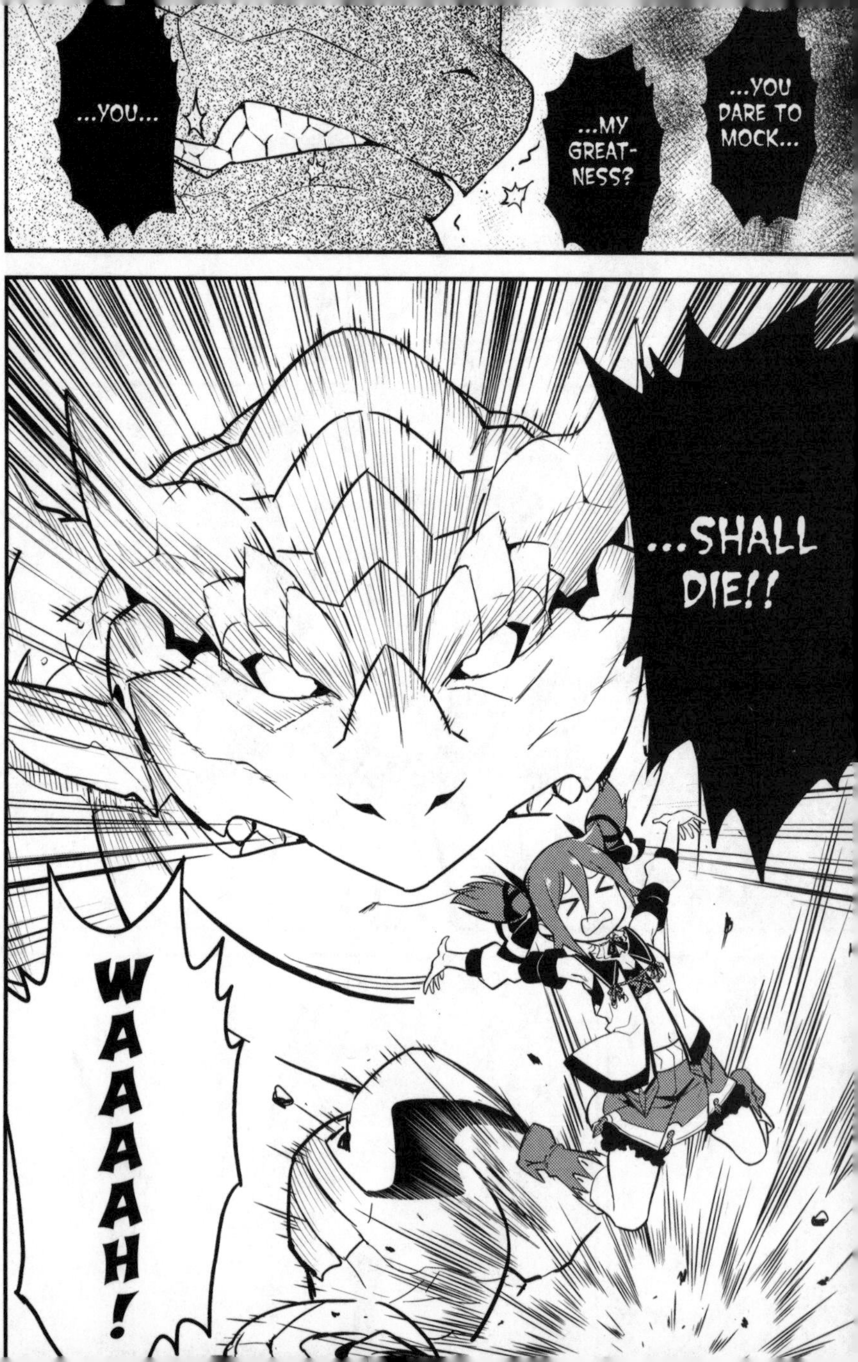
...YOU DARE TO MOCK...
...MY GREAT-NESS?
...YOU...
...SHALL DIE!!
WAAAAAH!

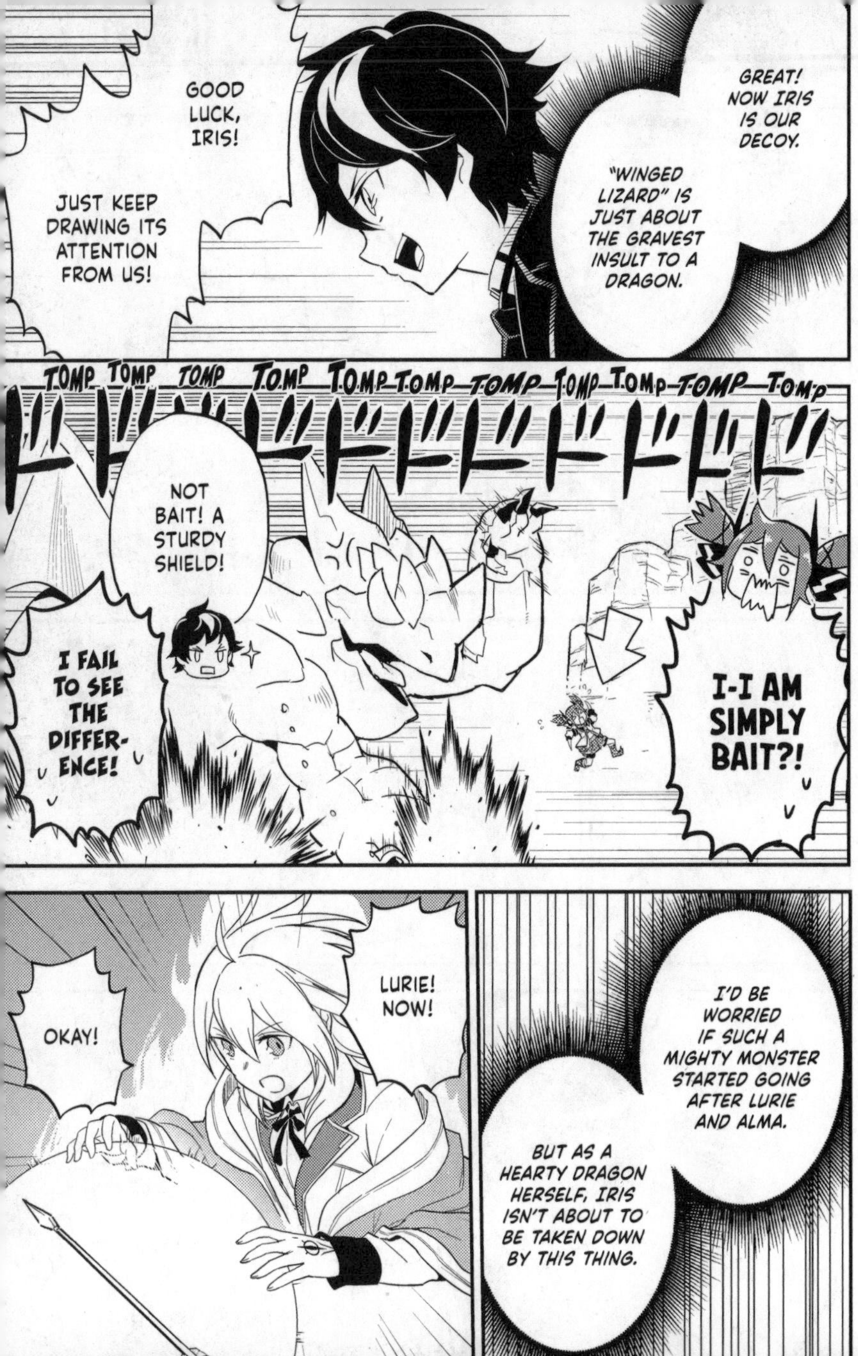
GREAT! NOW IRIS IS OUR DECOY.
"WINGED LIZARD" IS JUST ABOUT THE GRAVEST INSULT TO A DRAGON.
GOOD LUCK, IRIS!
JUST KEEP DRAWING ITS ATTENTION FROM US!
TOMP TOMP TOMP TOMP TOMP TOMP TOMP TOMP TOMP TOMP TOMP
ドドドドドドドドドド
I-I AM SIMPLY BAIT?!
NOT BAIT! A STURDY SHIELD!
I FAIL TO SEE THE DIFFER-ENCE!
I'D BE WORRIED IF SUCH A MIGHTY MONSTER STARTED GOING AFTER LURIE AND ALMA.
BUT AS A HEARTY DRAGON HERSELF, IRIS ISN'T ABOUT TO BE TAKEN DOWN BY THIS THING.
LURIE! NOW!
OKAY!

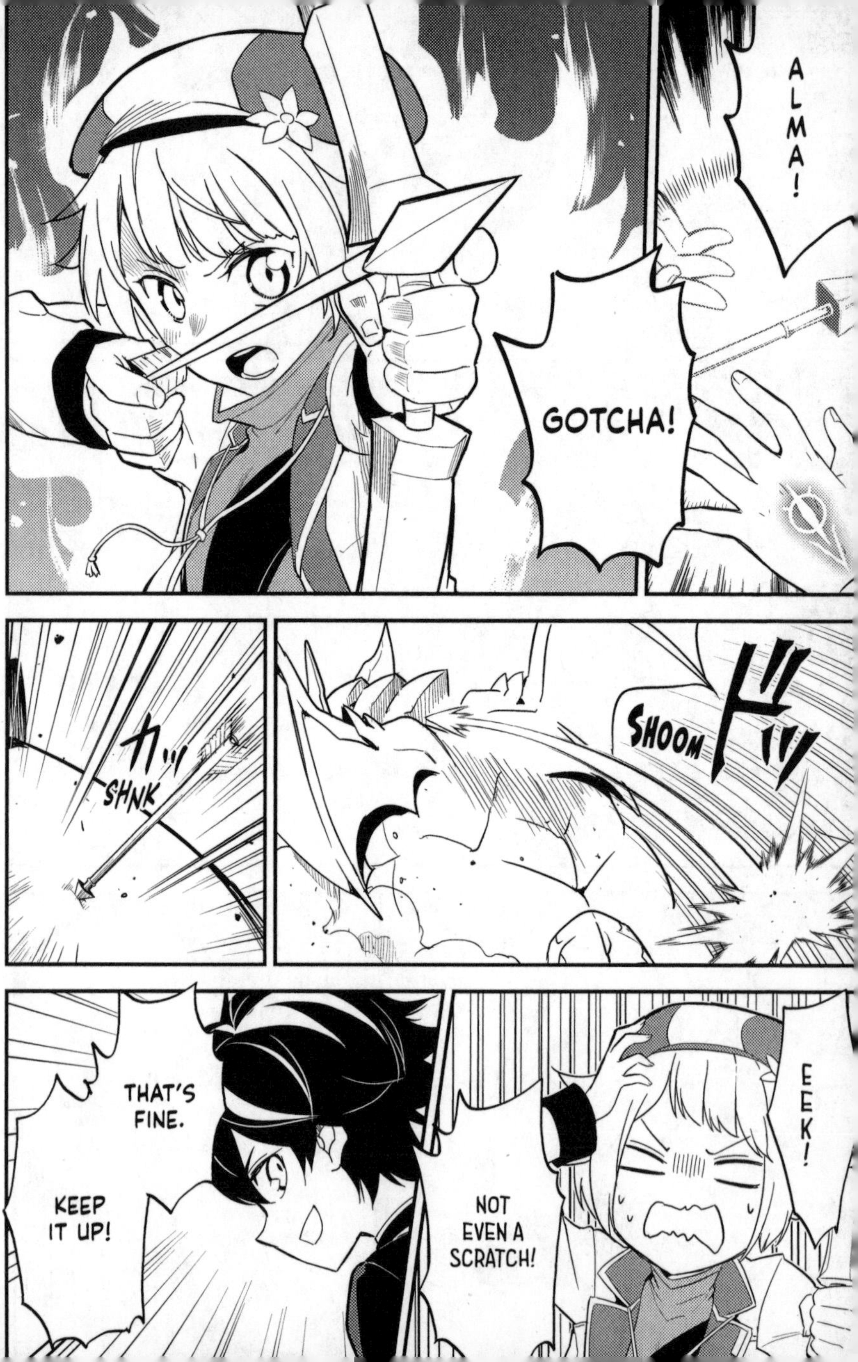
ALMA!
GOTCHA!
SHOOM
ドッ
カッ
SHNK
EEK!
NOT EVEN A SCRATCH!
THAT'S FINE.
KEEP IT UP!

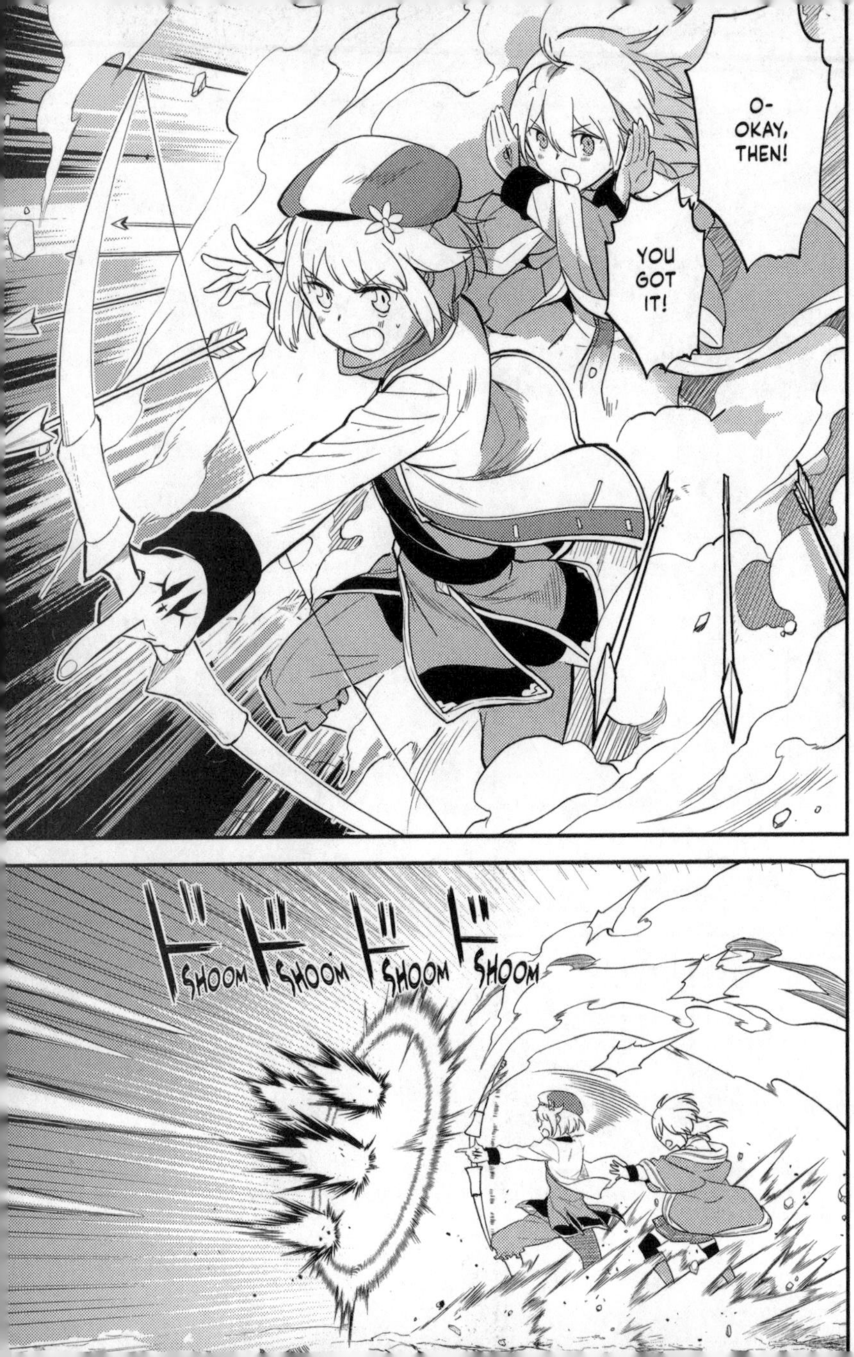
O-OKAY, THEN!
YOU GOT IT!
ドSHOOM ドSHOOM ドSHOOM ドSHOOM

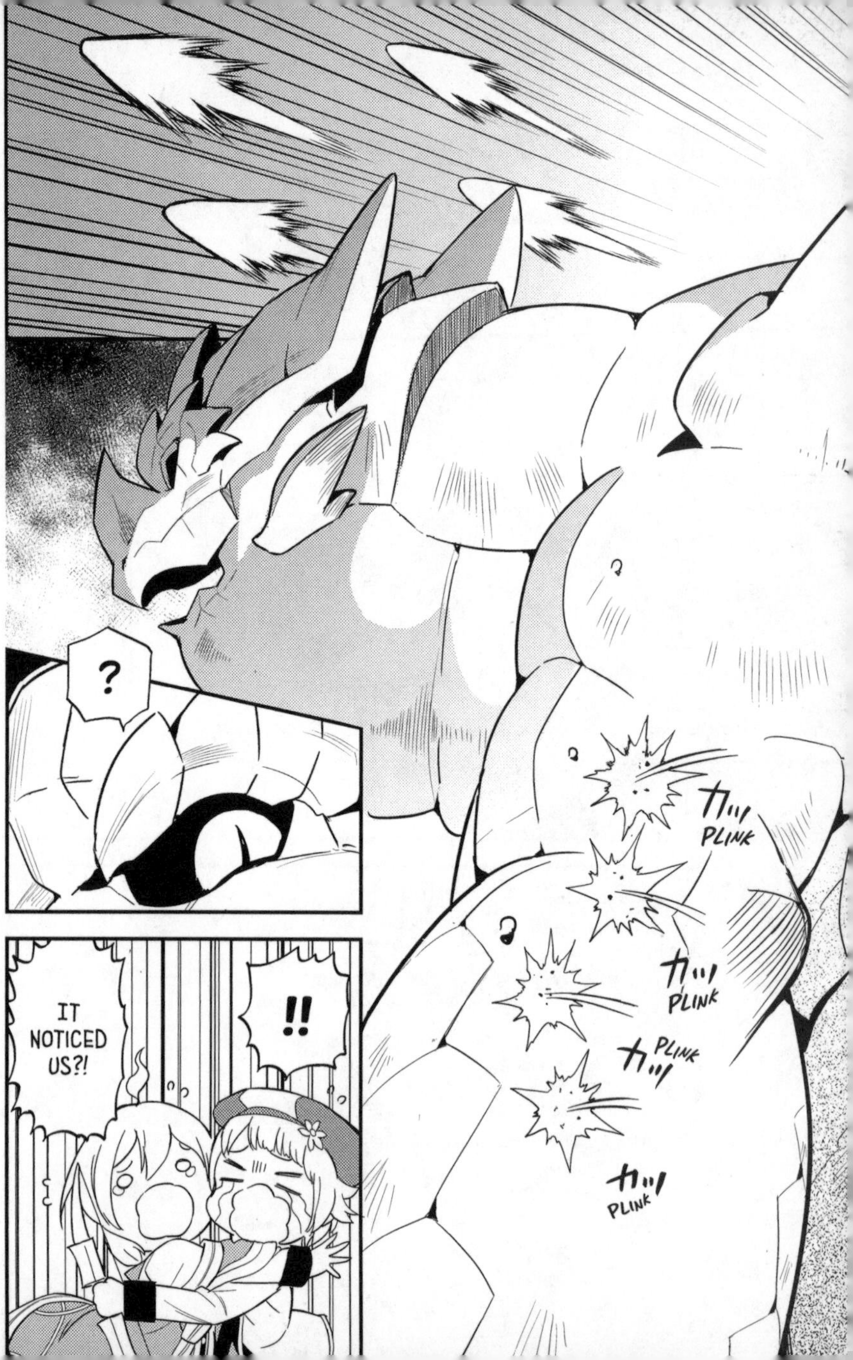
カッ PLINK
カッ PLINK
カッ PLINK
カッ PLINK
?
!!
IT NOTICED US?!

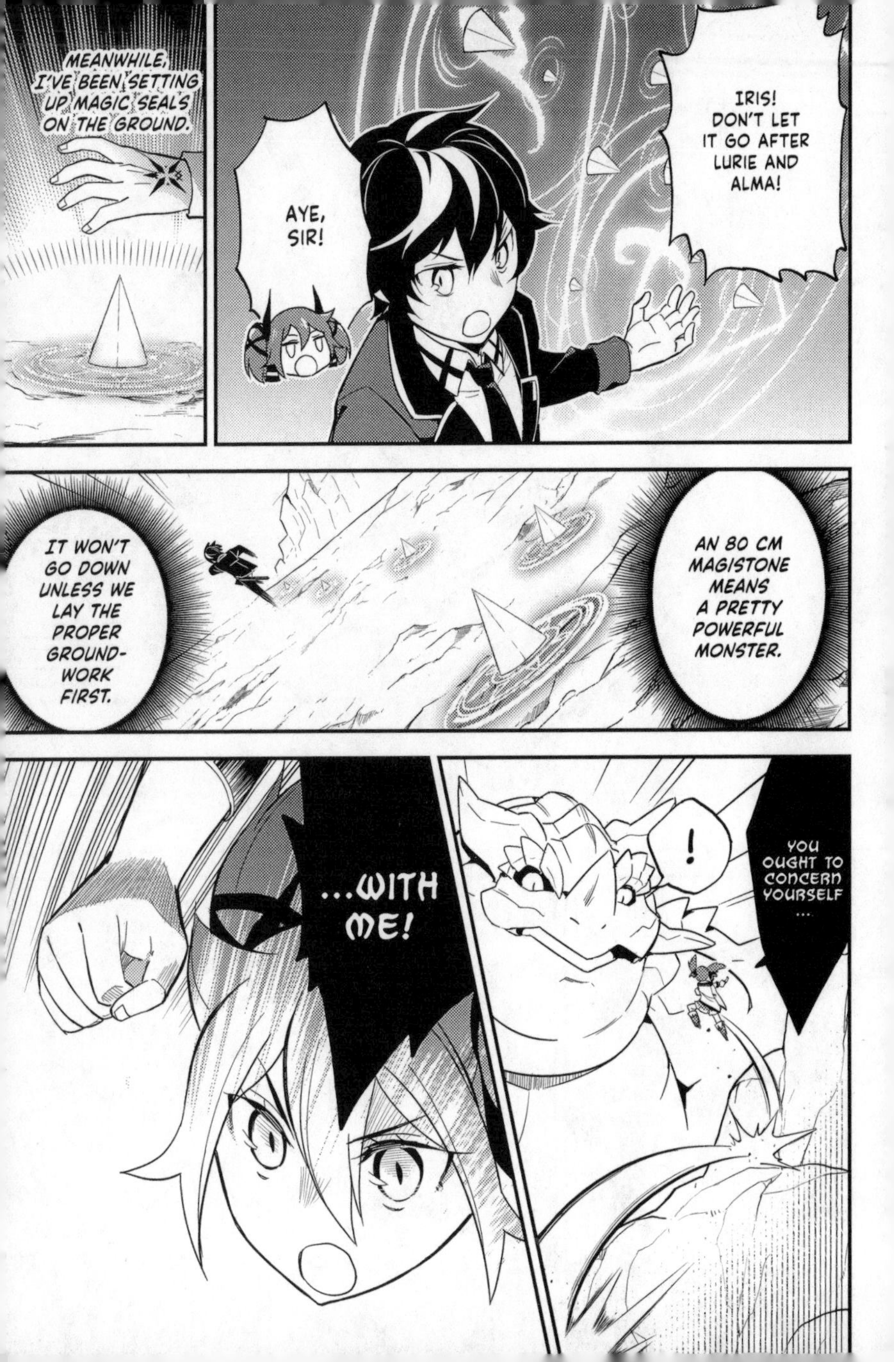
IRIS! DON'T LET IT GO AFTER LURIE AND ALMA!
AYE, SIR!
MEANWHILE, I'VE BEEN SETTING UP MAGIC SEALS ON THE GROUND.
AN 80 CM MAGISTONE MEANS A PRETTY POWERFUL MONSTER.
IT WON'T GO DOWN UNLESS WE LAY THE PROPER GROUND-WORK FIRST.
YOU OUGHT TO CONCERN YOURSELF ...
!
...WITH ME!

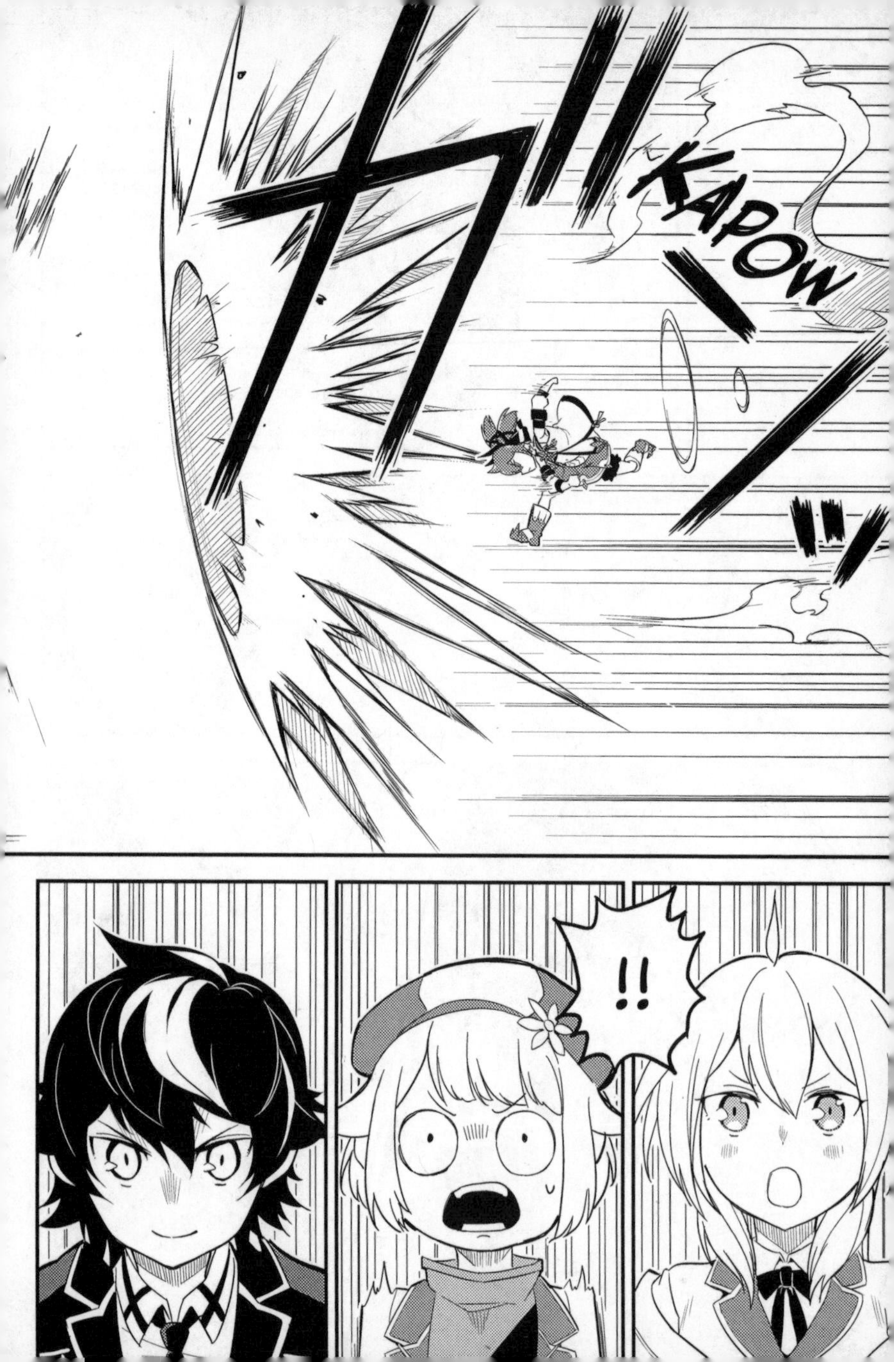
KAPOW
!!

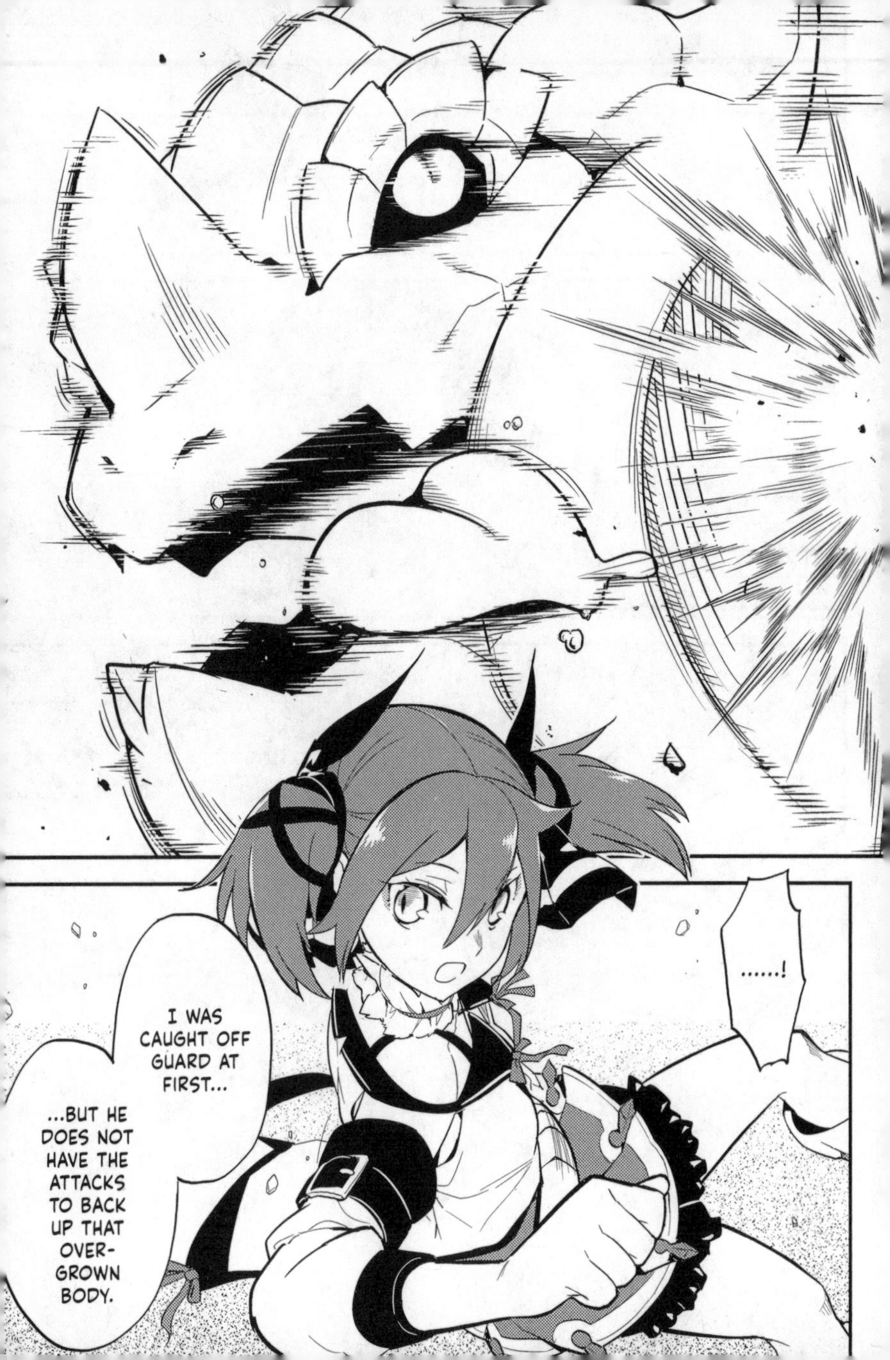
......!
I WAS CAUGHT OFF GUARD AT FIRST...
...BUT HE DOES NOT HAVE THE ATTACKS TO BACK UP THAT OVER-GROWN BODY.

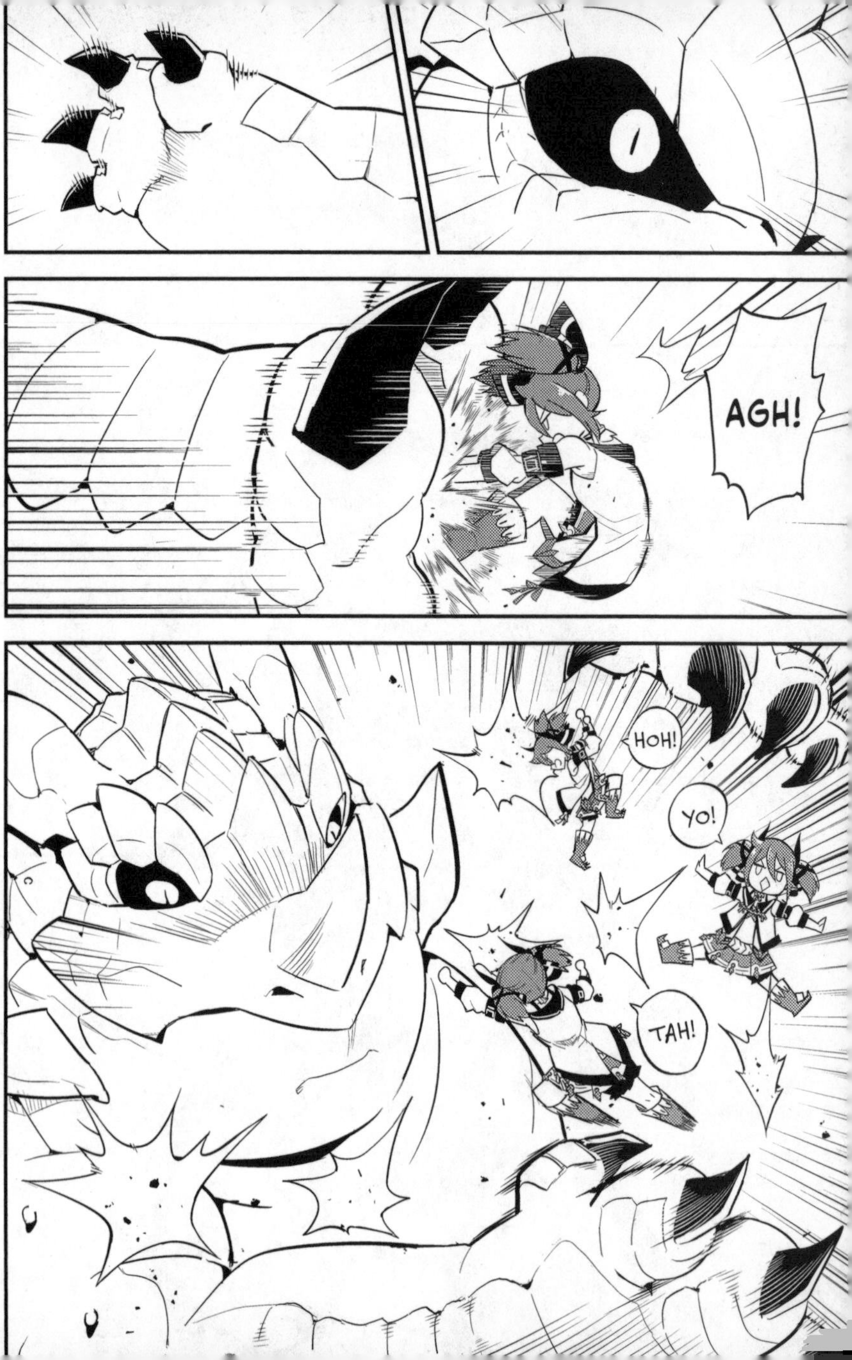
AGH!
HOH!
YO!
TAH!

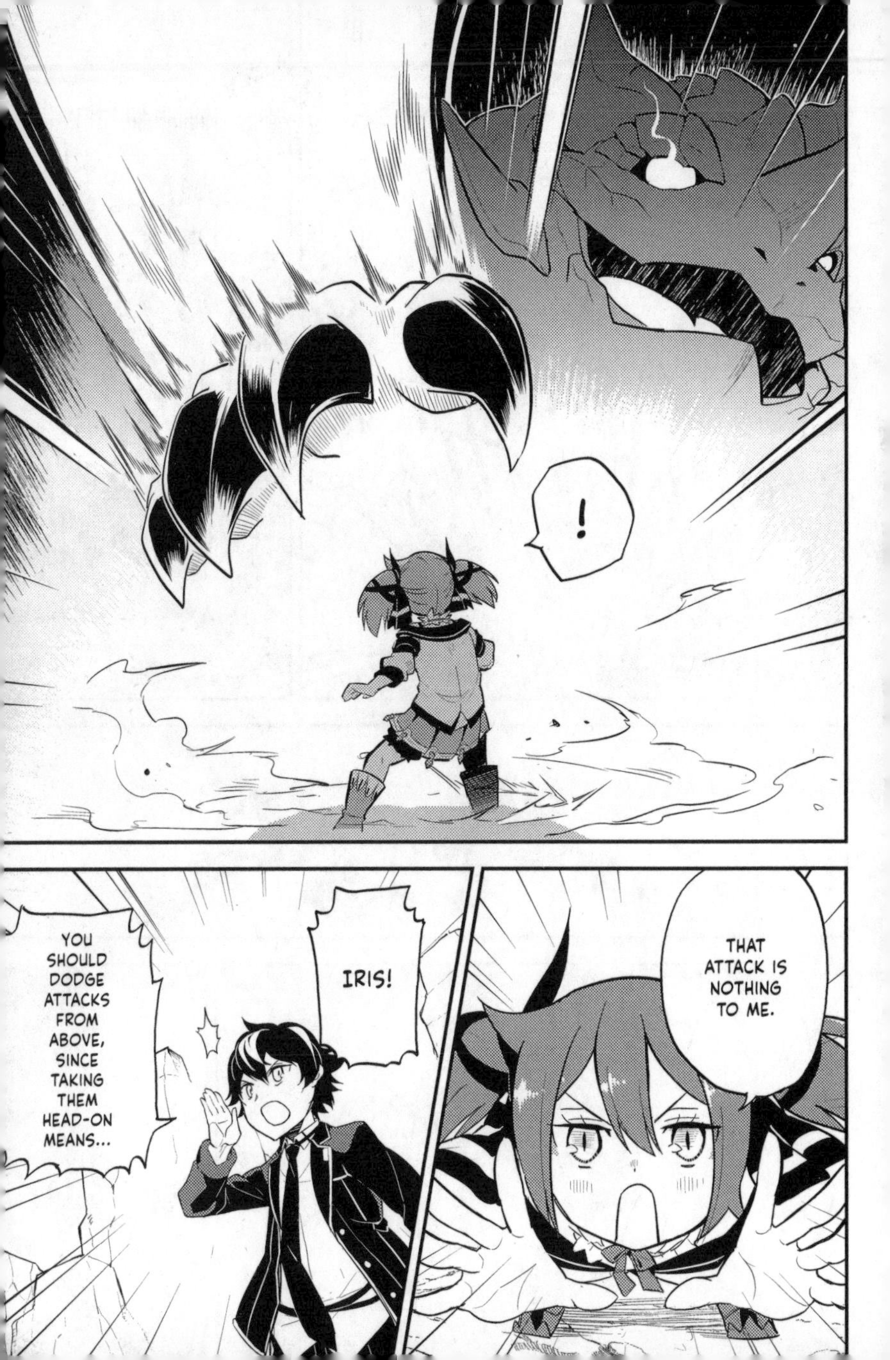
!
THAT ATTACK IS NOTHING TO ME.
IRIS!
YOU SHOULD DODGE ATTACKS FROM ABOVE, SINCE TAKING THEM HEAD-ON MEANS...

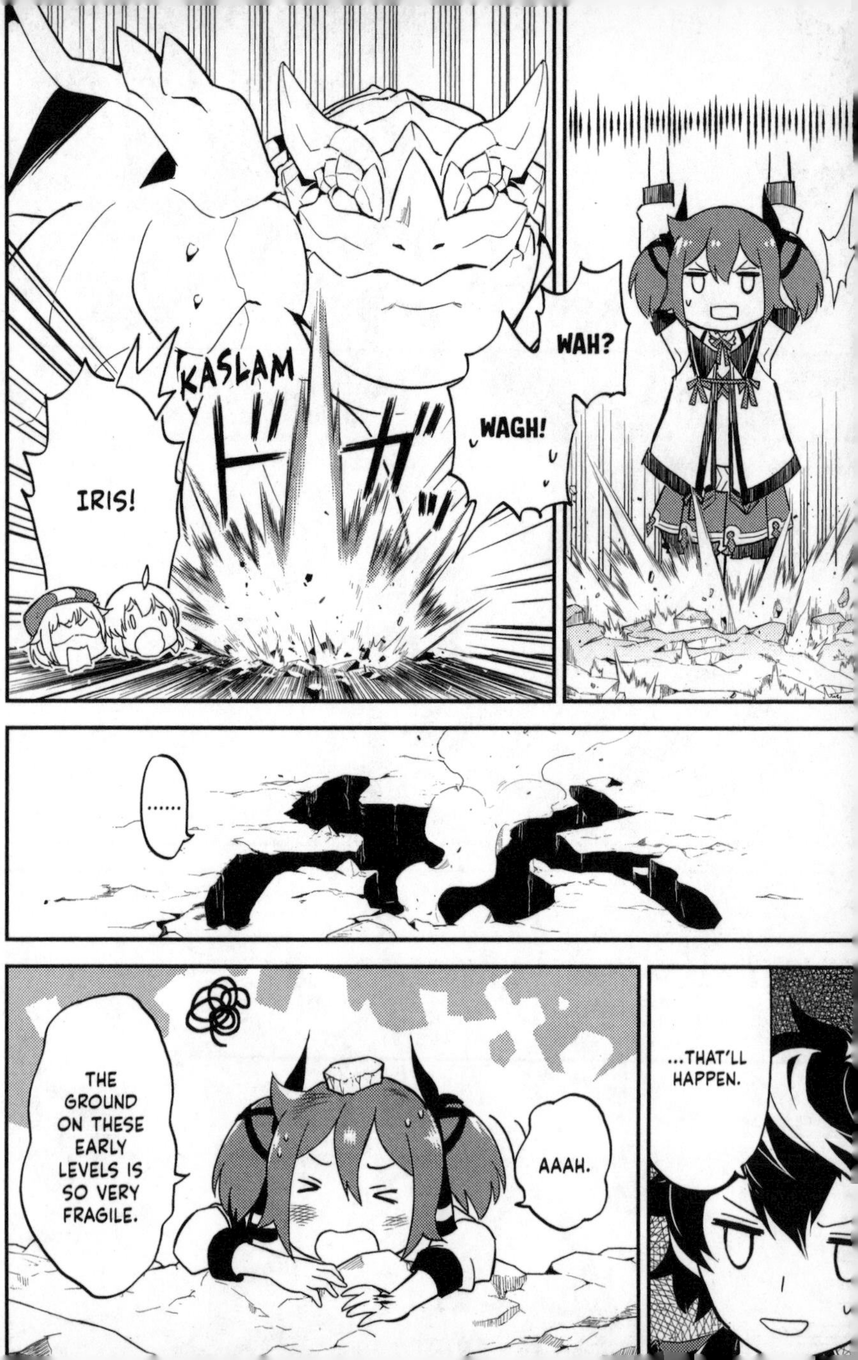

WAH?
WAGH!
KASLAM
ドガッ
IRIS!
......
...THAT'LL HAPPEN.
AAAH.
THE GROUND ON THESE EARLY LEVELS IS SO VERY FRAGILE.

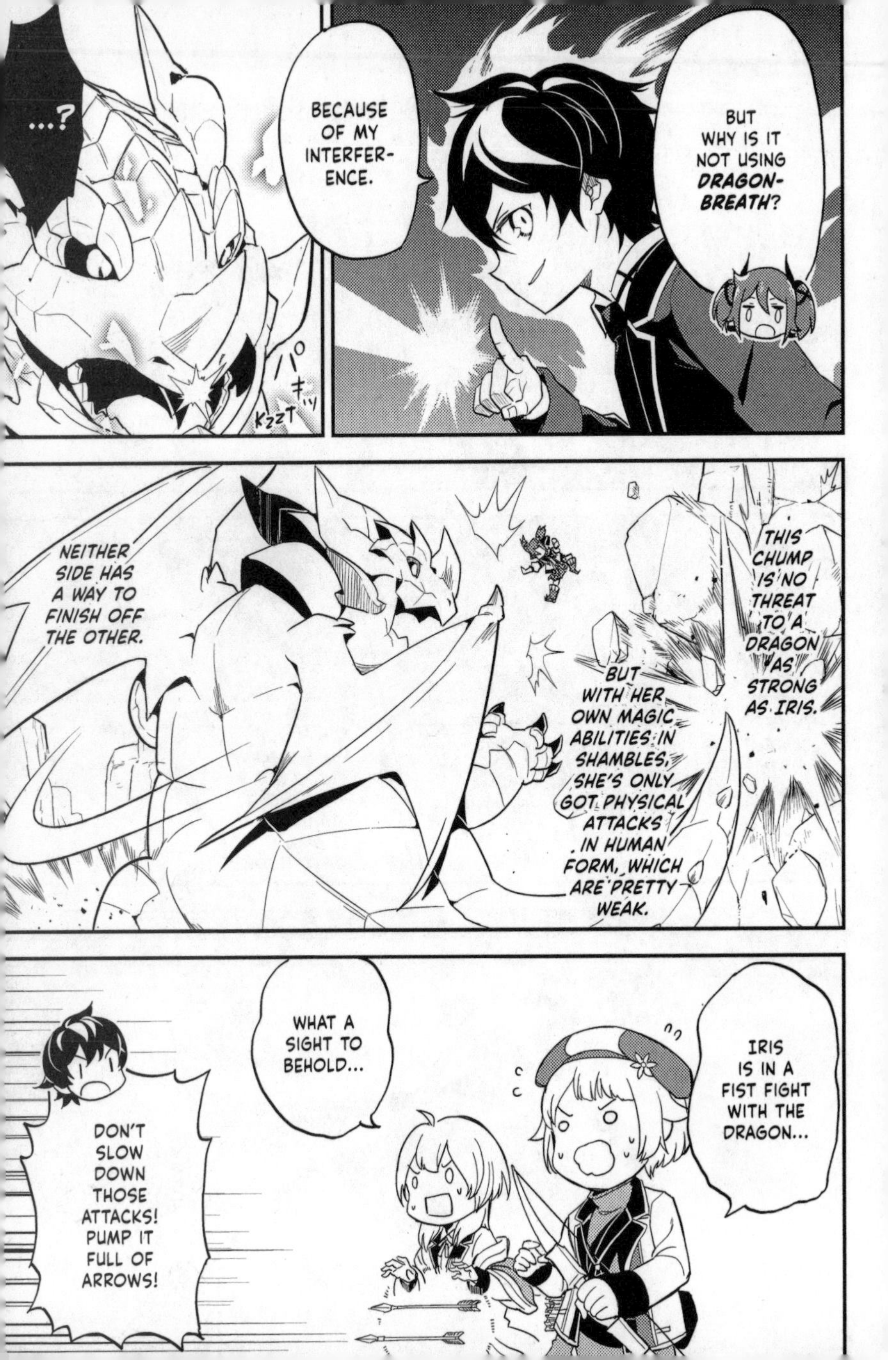
BUT WHY IS IT NOT USING DRAGON-BREATH?
BECAUSE OF MY INTERFERENCE.
...?
パキッ
KZZT
THIS CHUMP IS NO THREAT TO A DRAGON AS STRONG AS IRIS.
BUT WITH HER OWN MAGIC ABILITIES IN SHAMBLES, SHE'S ONLY GOT PHYSICAL ATTACKS IN HUMAN FORM, WHICH ARE PRETTY WEAK.
NEITHER SIDE HAS A WAY TO FINISH OFF THE OTHER.
IRIS IS IN A FIST FIGHT WITH THE DRAGON...
WHAT A SIGHT TO BEHOLD...
DON'T SLOW DOWN THOSE ATTACKS! PUMP IT FULL OF ARROWS!

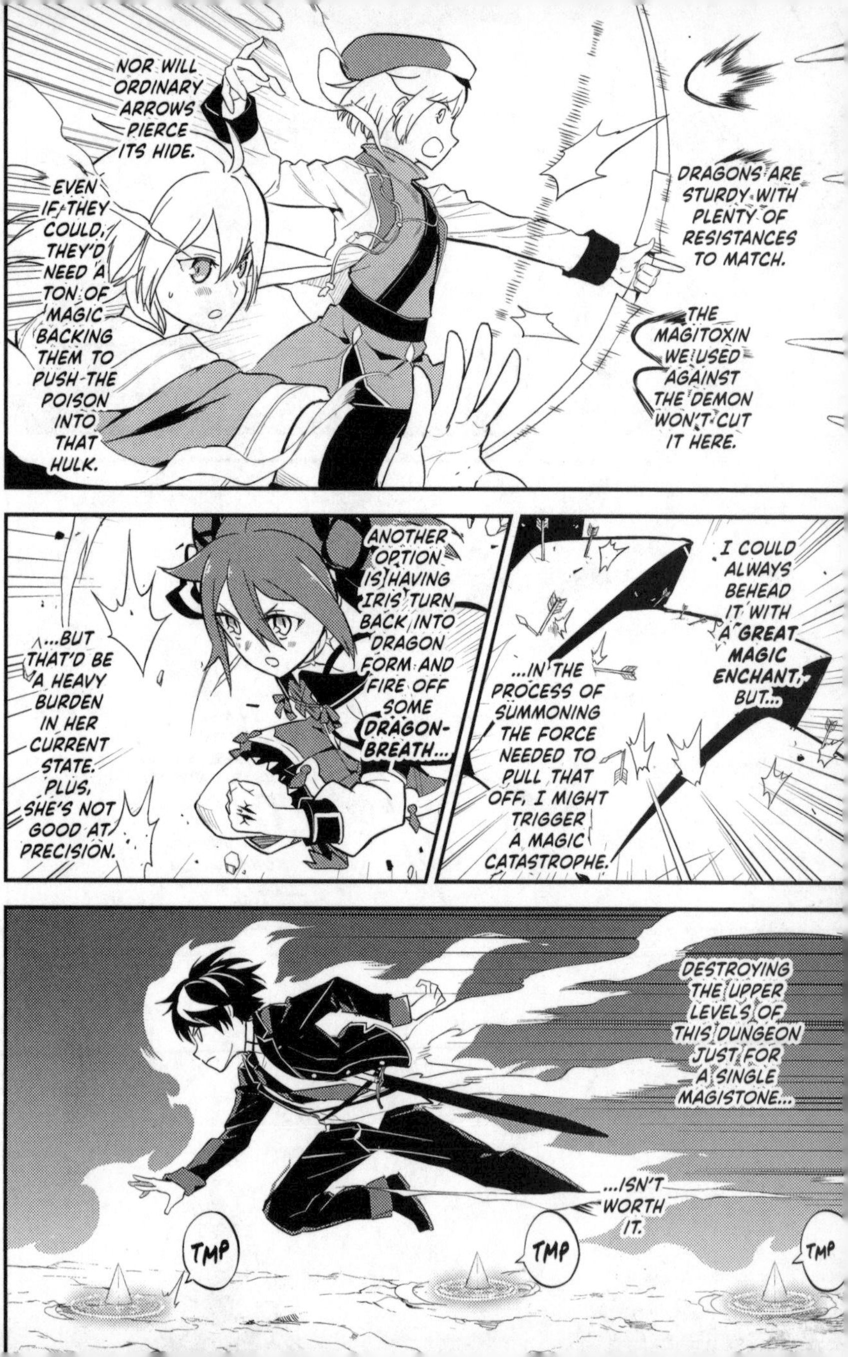

DRAGONS ARE STURDY WITH PLENTY OF RESISTANCES TO MATCH.
THE MAGITOXIN WE USED AGAINST THE DEMON WON'T CUT IT HERE.
NOR WILL ORDINARY ARROWS PIERCE ITS HIDE.
EVEN IF THEY COULD, THEY'D NEED A TON OF MAGIC BACKING THEM TO PUSH THE POISON INTO THAT HULK.
I COULD ALWAYS BEHEAD IT WITH A GREAT MAGIC ENCHANT, BUT...
...IN THE PROCESS OF SUMMONING THE FORCE NEEDED TO PULL THAT OFF, I MIGHT TRIGGER A MAGIC CATASTROPHE.
ANOTHER OPTION IS HAVING IRIS TURN BACK INTO DRAGON FORM AND FIRE OFF SOME DRAGON-BREATH...
...BUT THAT'D BE A HEAVY BURDEN IN HER CURRENT STATE. PLUS, SHE'S NOT GOOD AT PRECISION.
DESTROYING THE UPPER LEVELS OF THIS DUNGEON JUST FOR A SINGLE MAGISTONE...
...ISN'T WORTH IT.
TMP
TMP
TMP

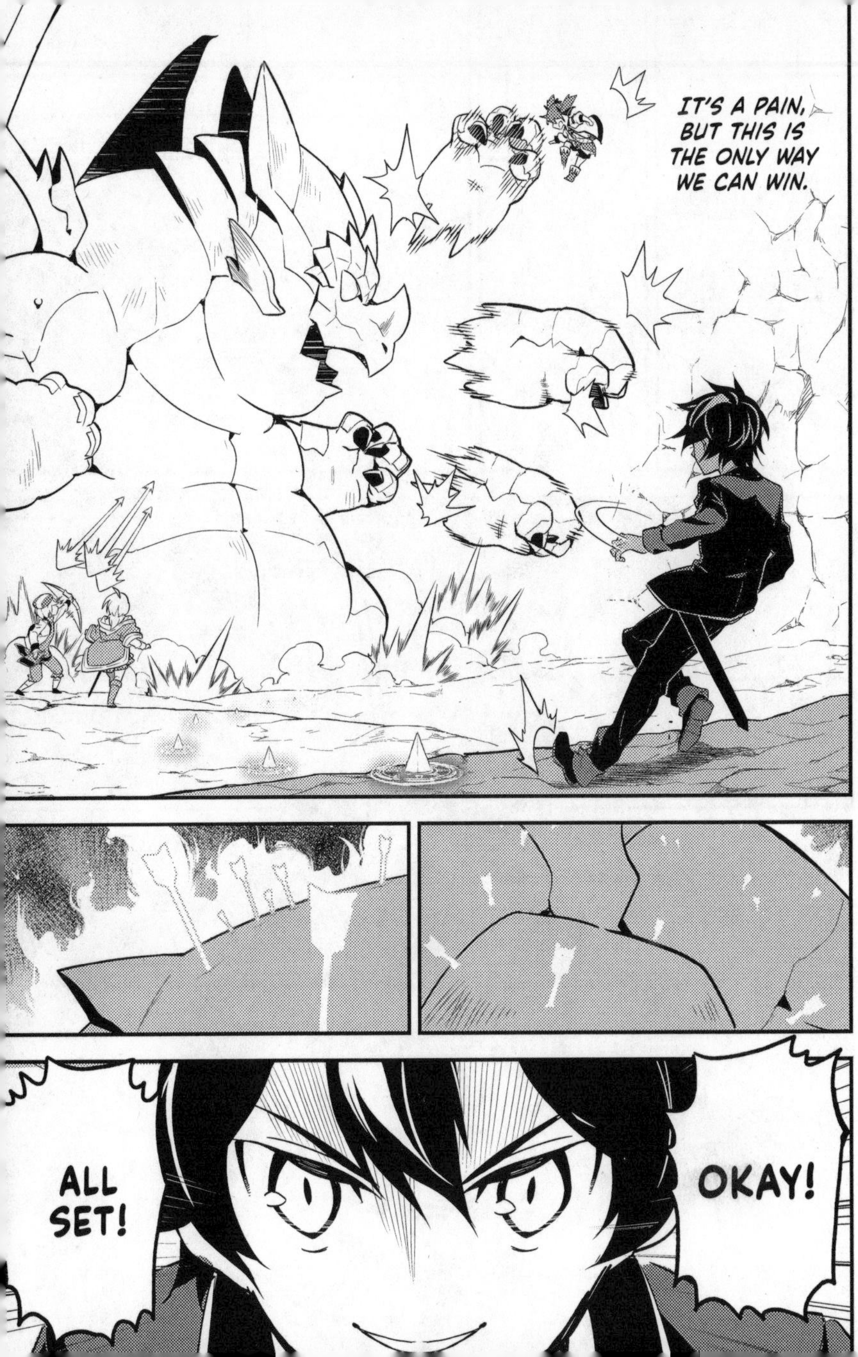
IT'S A PAIN, BUT THIS IS THE ONLY WAY WE CAN WIN.
OKAY!
ALL SET!

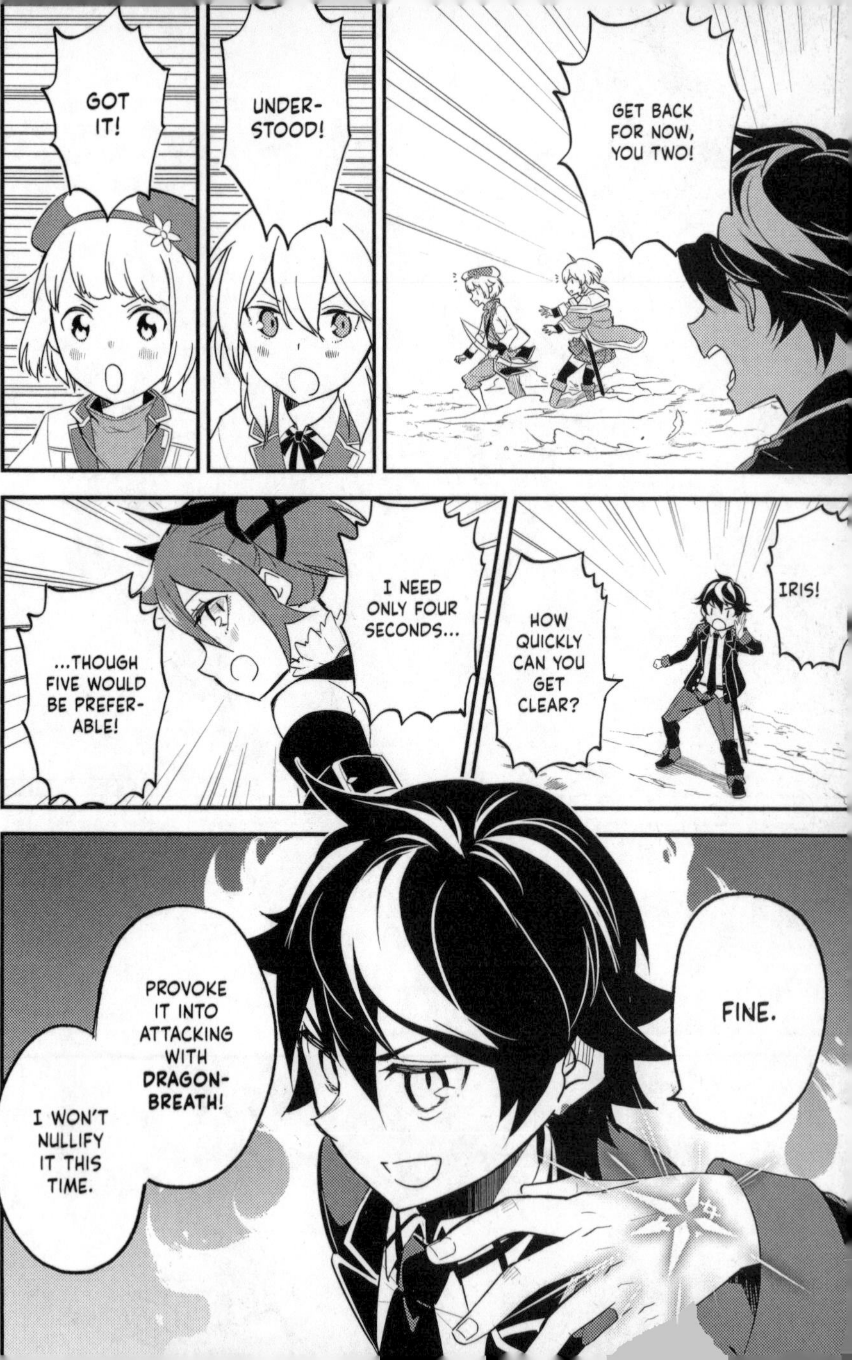
GET BACK FOR NOW, YOU TWO!
UNDER-STOOD!
GOT IT!
IRIS!
HOW QUICKLY CAN YOU GET CLEAR?
I NEED ONLY FOUR SECONDS...
...THOUGH FIVE WOULD BE PREFER-ABLE!
FINE.
PROVOKE IT INTO ATTACKING WITH DRAGON-BREATH!
I WON'T NULLIFY IT THIS TIME.

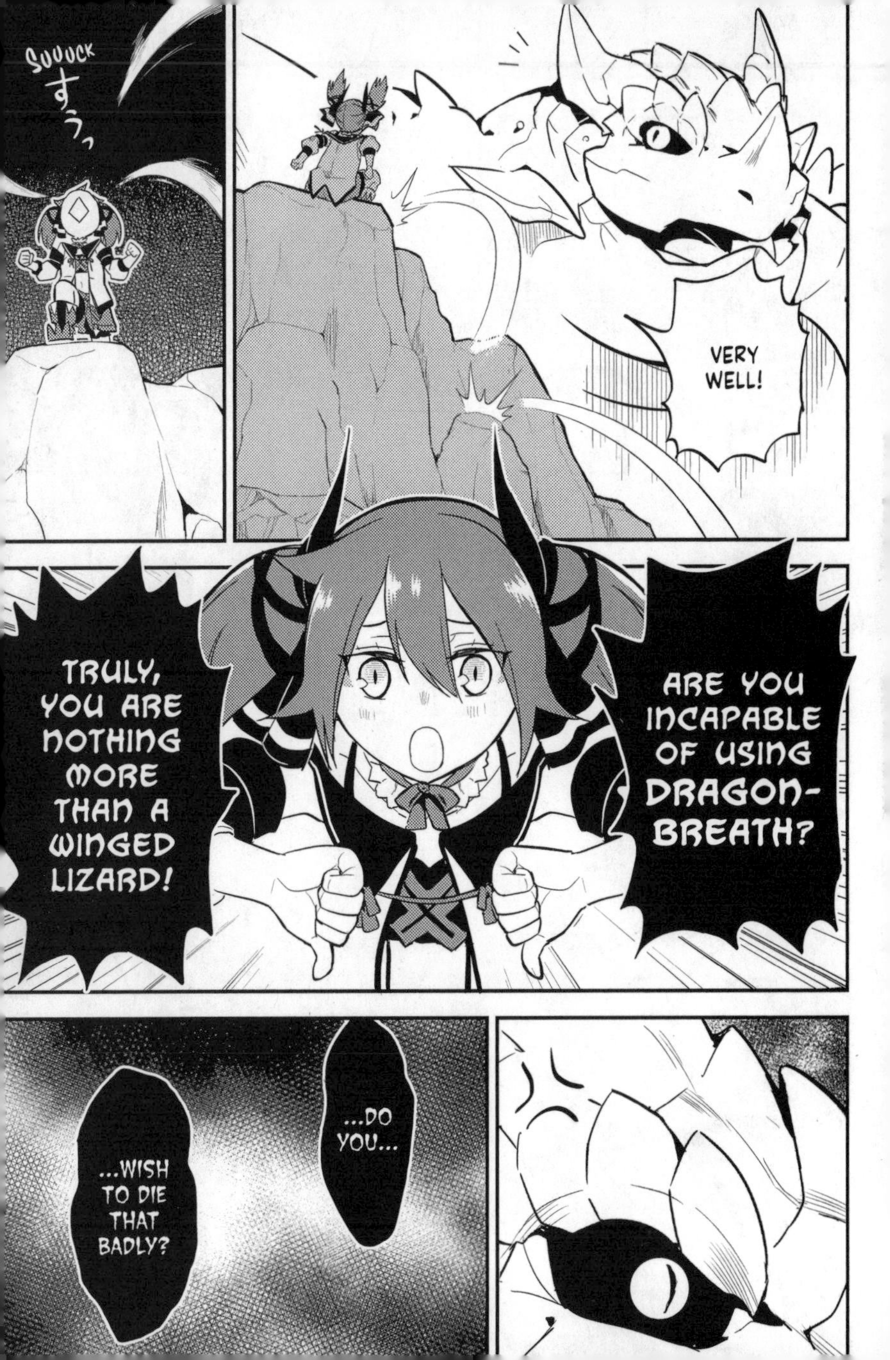
VERY WELL!
SUUUCK
すぅっ
ARE YOU INCAPABLE OF USING DRAGON-BREATH?
TRULY, YOU ARE NOTHING MORE THAN A WINGED LIZARD!
...DO YOU...
...WISH TO DIE THAT BADLY?

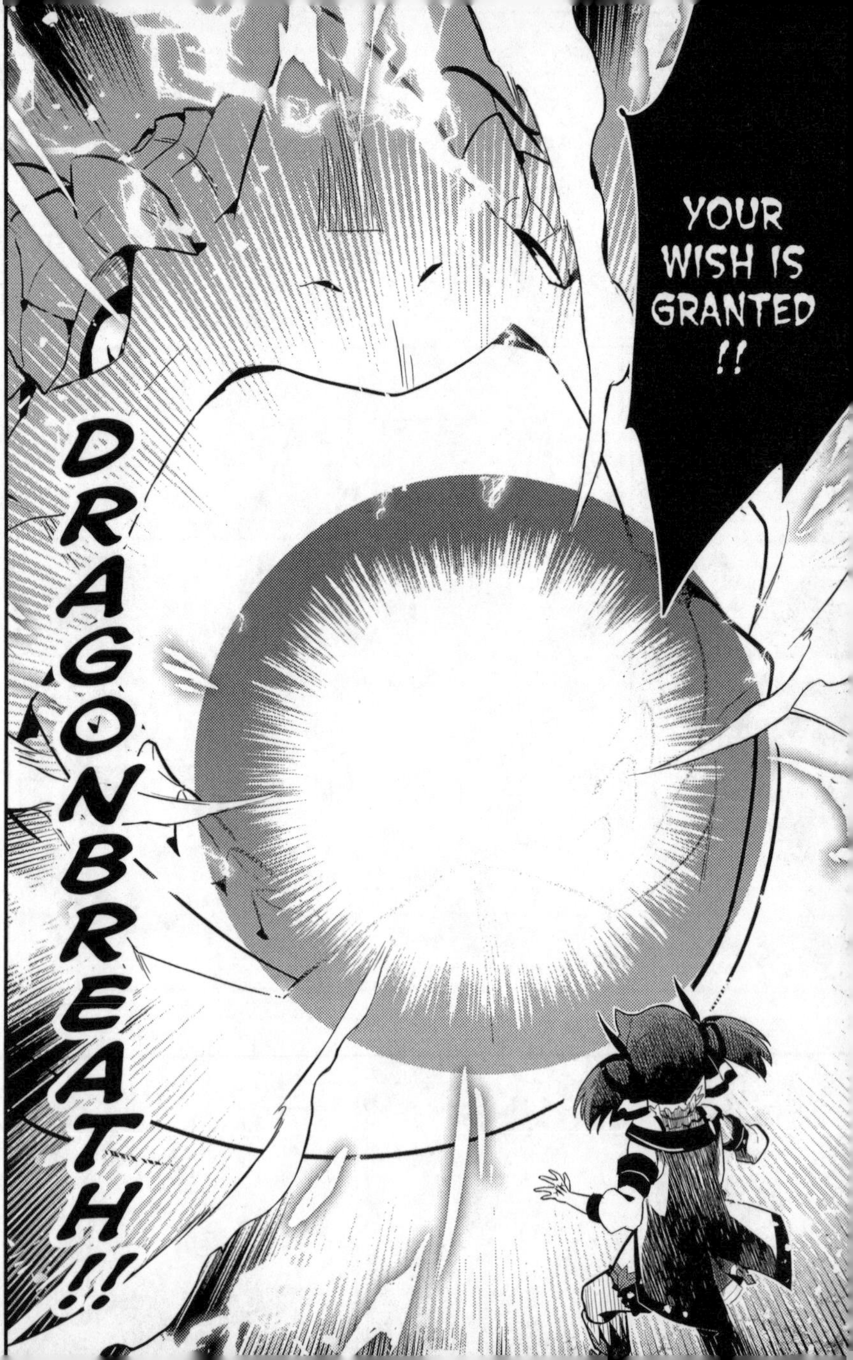
YOUR WISH IS GRANTED !!
DRAGONBREATH!!!

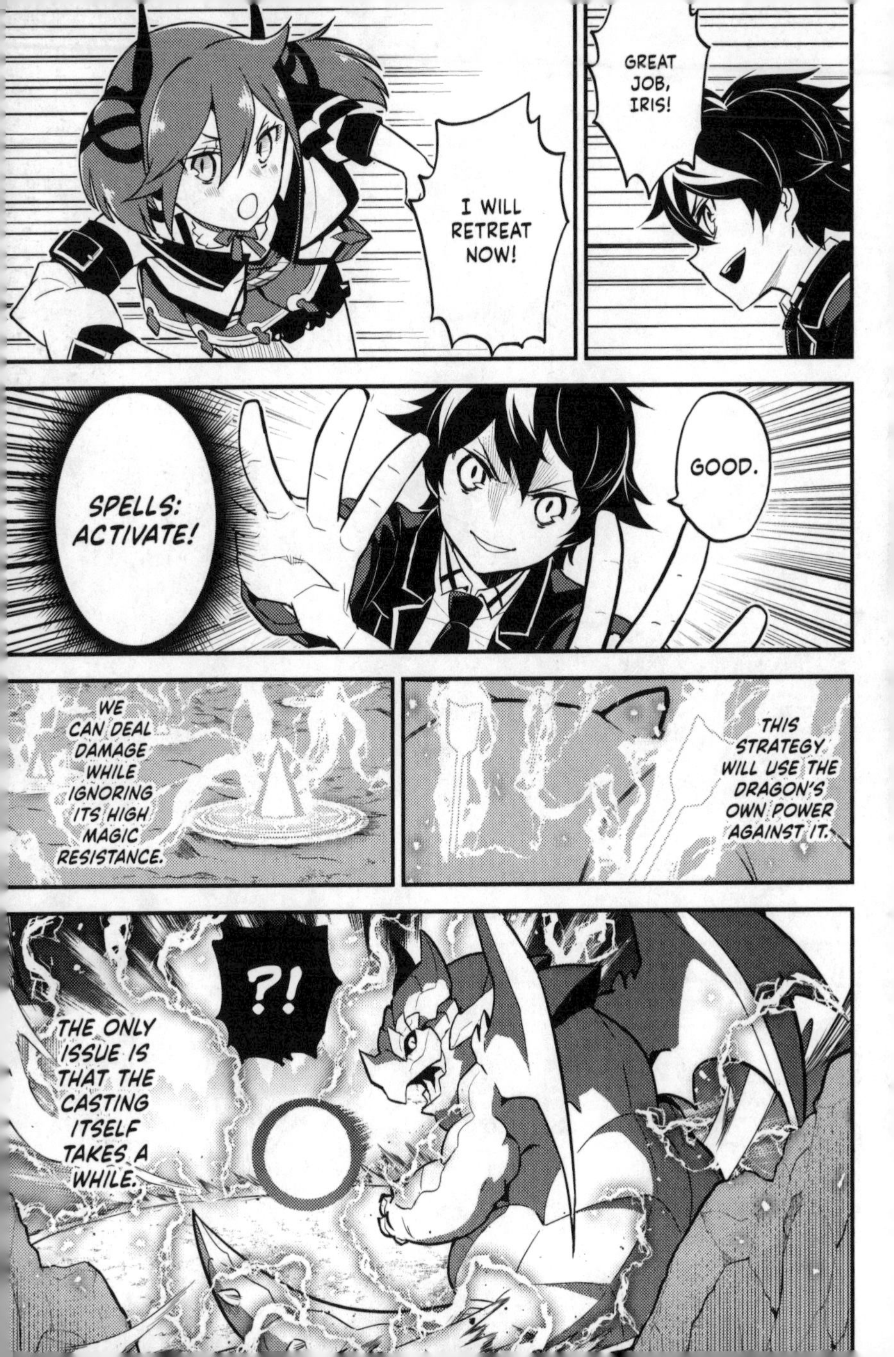
GREAT JOB, IRIS!
I WILL RETREAT NOW!
GOOD.
SPELLS: ACTIVATE!
THIS STRATEGY WILL USE THE DRAGON'S OWN POWER AGAINST IT.
WE CAN DEAL DAMAGE WHILE IGNORING ITS HIGH MAGIC RESISTANCE.
?!
THE ONLY ISSUE IS THAT THE CASTING ITSELF TAKES A WHILE.

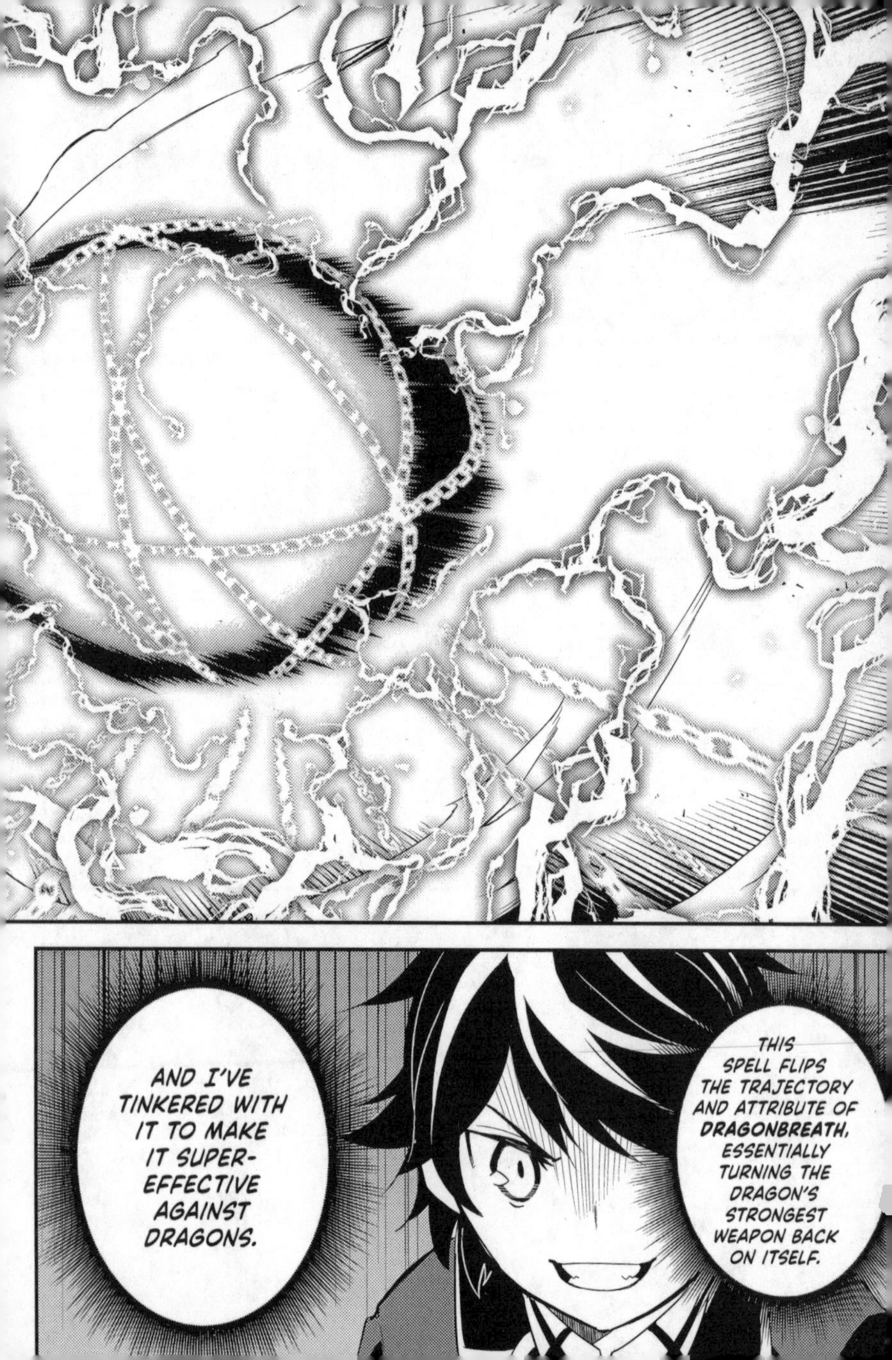
THIS SPELL FLIPS THE TRAJECTORY AND ATTRIBUTE OF DRAGONBREATH, ESSENTIALLY TURNING THE DRAGON'S STRONGEST WEAPON BACK ON ITSELF.
AND I'VE TINKERED WITH IT TO MAKE IT SUPER-EFFECTIVE AGAINST DRAGONS.

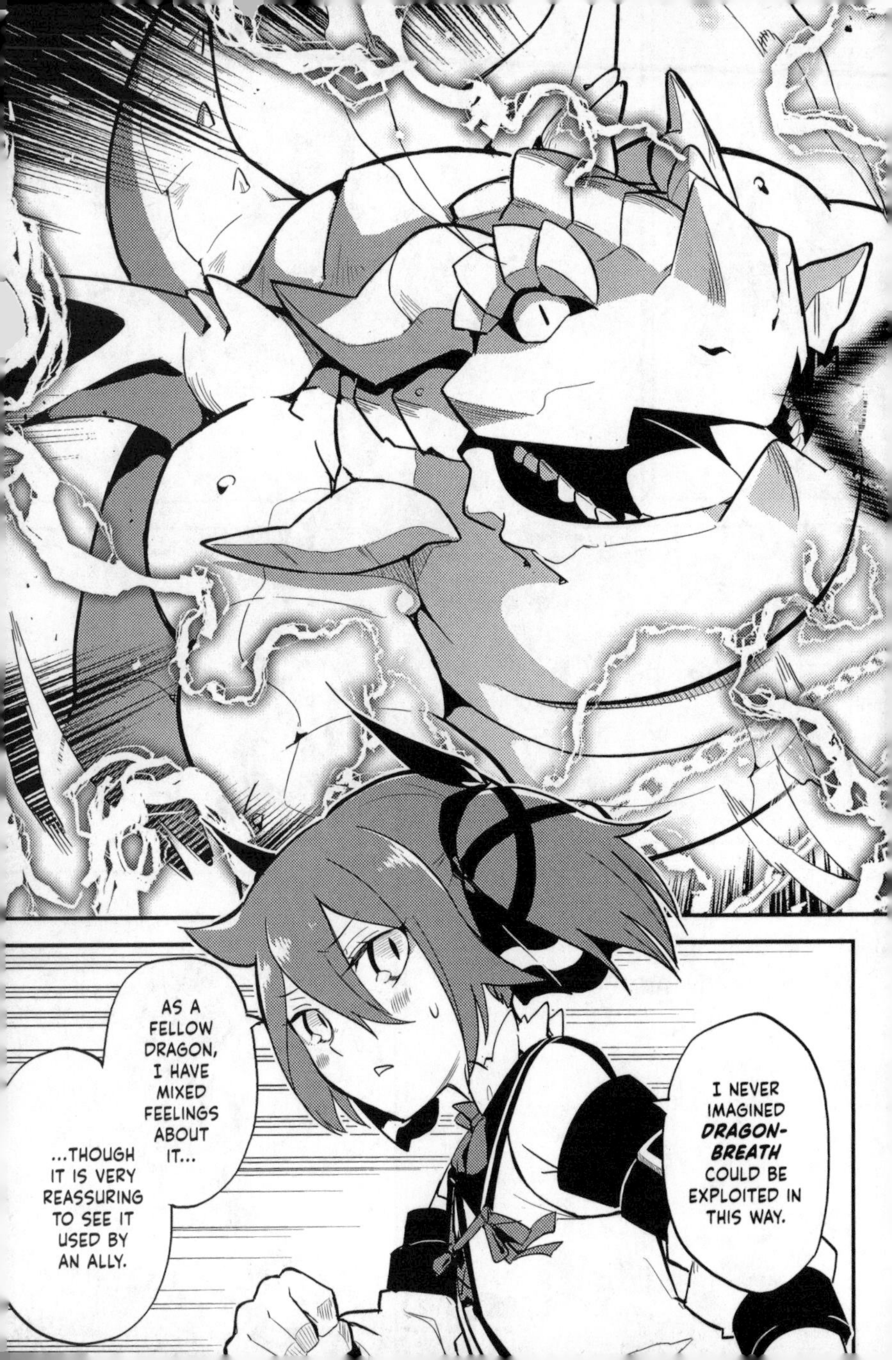
I NEVER IMAGINED DRAGON-BREATH COULD BE EXPLOITED IN THIS WAY.
AS A FELLOW DRAGON, I HAVE MIXED FEELINGS ABOUT IT...
...THOUGH IT IS VERY REASSURING TO SEE IT USED BY AN ALLY.

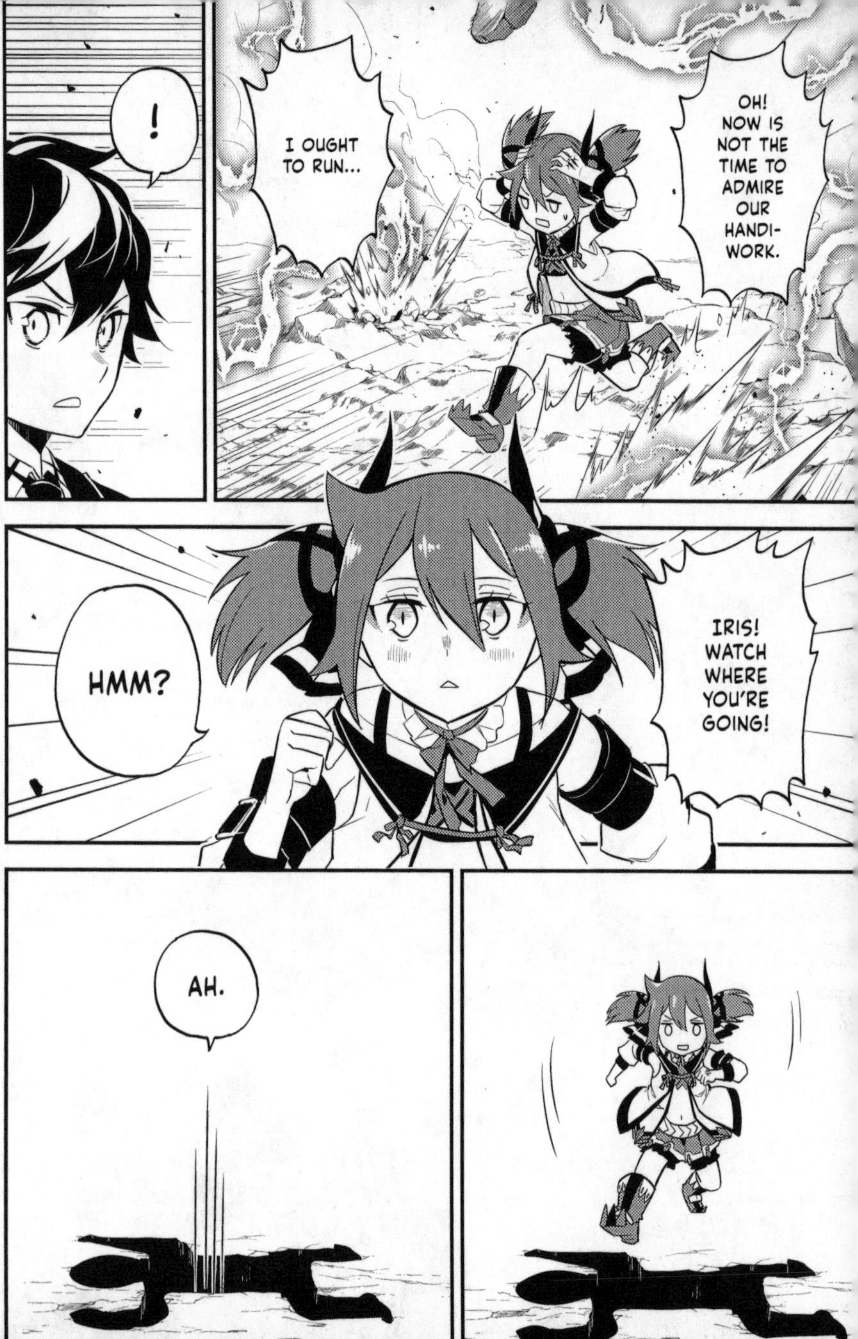
OH! NOW IS NOT THE TIME TO ADMIRE OUR HANDI-WORK.
I OUGHT TO RUN...
!
IRIS! WATCH WHERE YOU'RE GOING!
HMM?
AH.

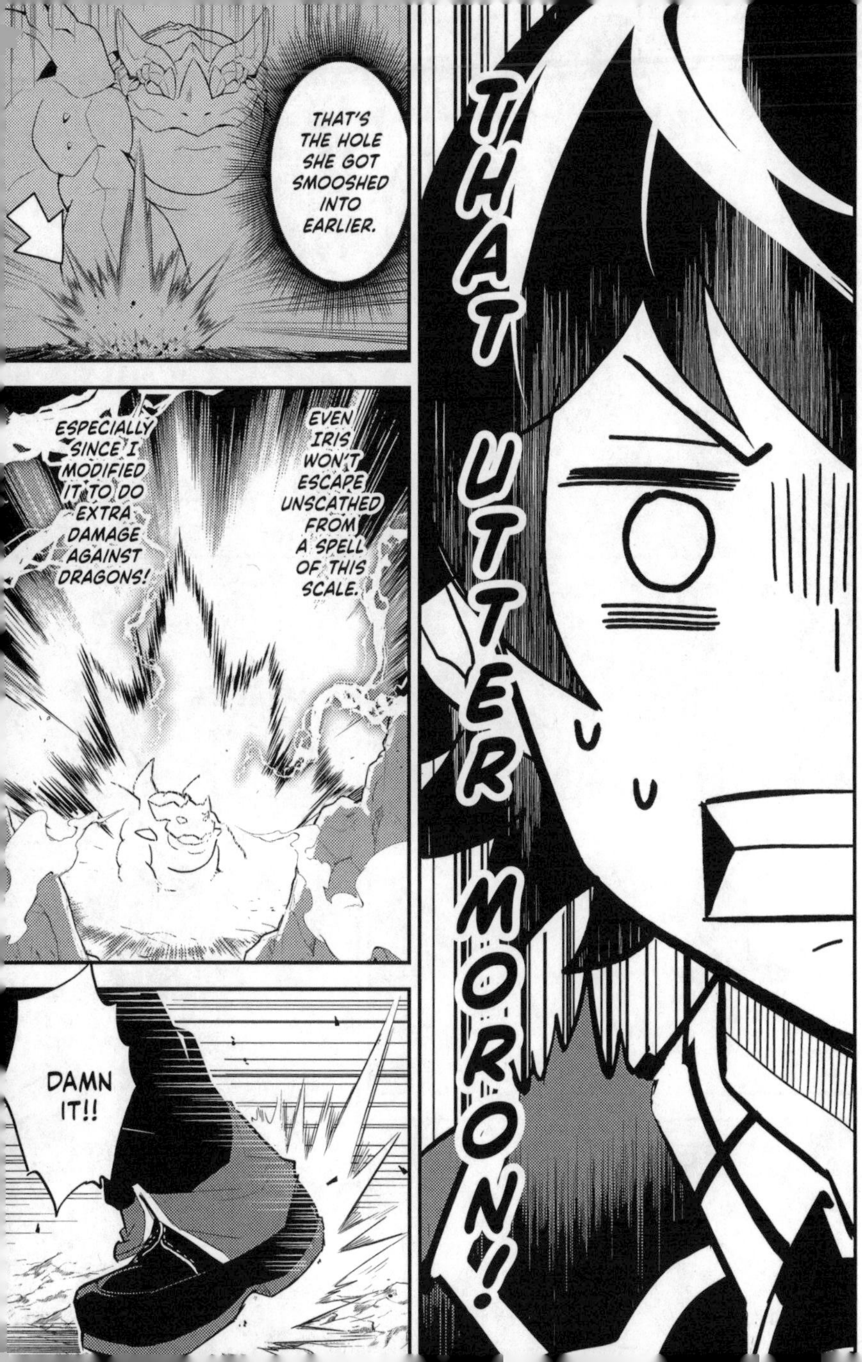
THAT UTTER MORON!
THAT'S THE HOLE SHE GOT SMOOSHED INTO EARLIER.
EVEN IRIS WON'T ESCAPE UNSCATHED FROM A SPELL OF THIS SCALE.
ESPECIALLY SINCE I MODIFIED IT TO DO EXTRA DAMAGE AGAINST DRAGONS!
DAMN IT!!

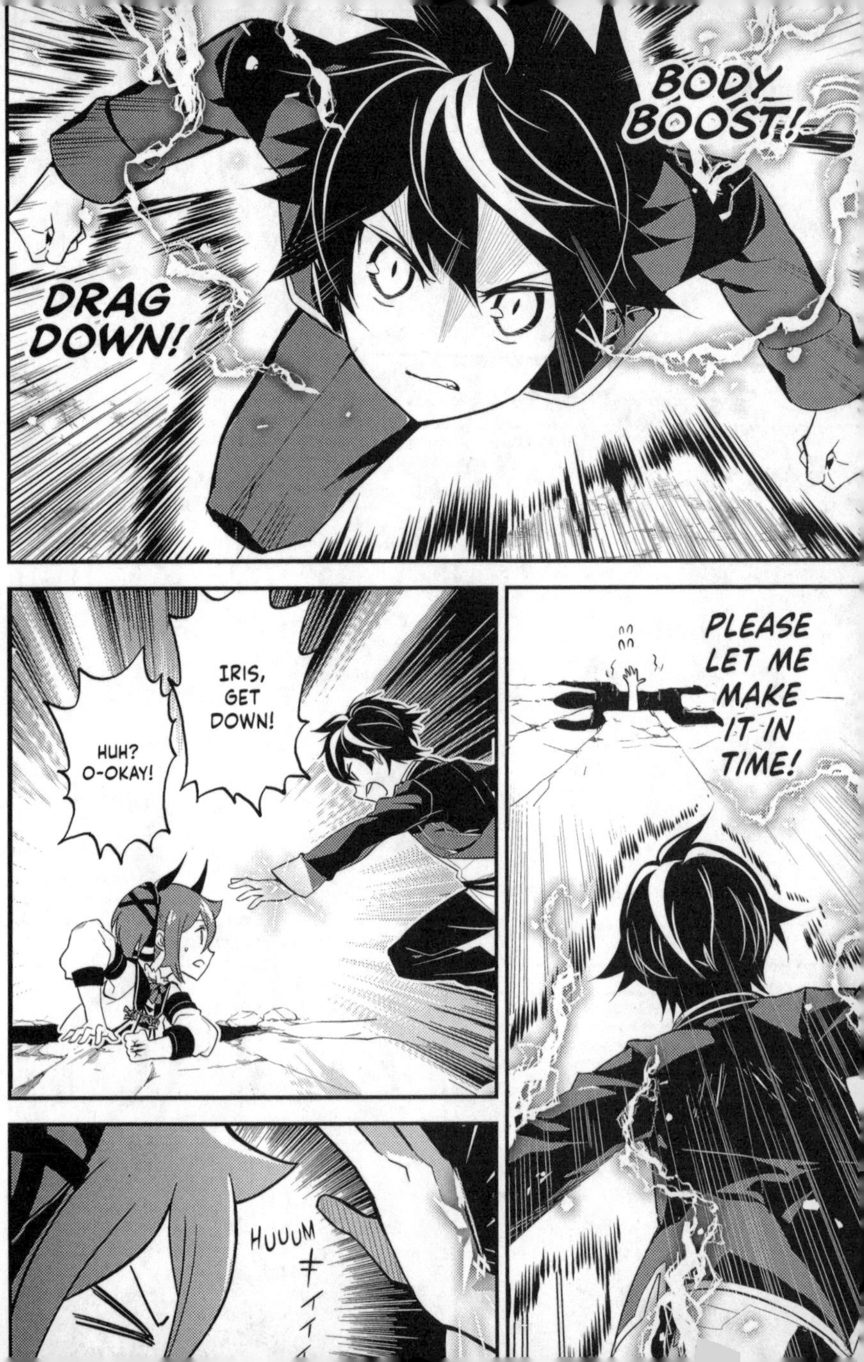
BODY BOOST!
DRAG DOWN!
PLEASE LET ME MAKE IT IN TIME!
IRIS, GET DOWN!
HUH? O-OKAY!
HUUUM

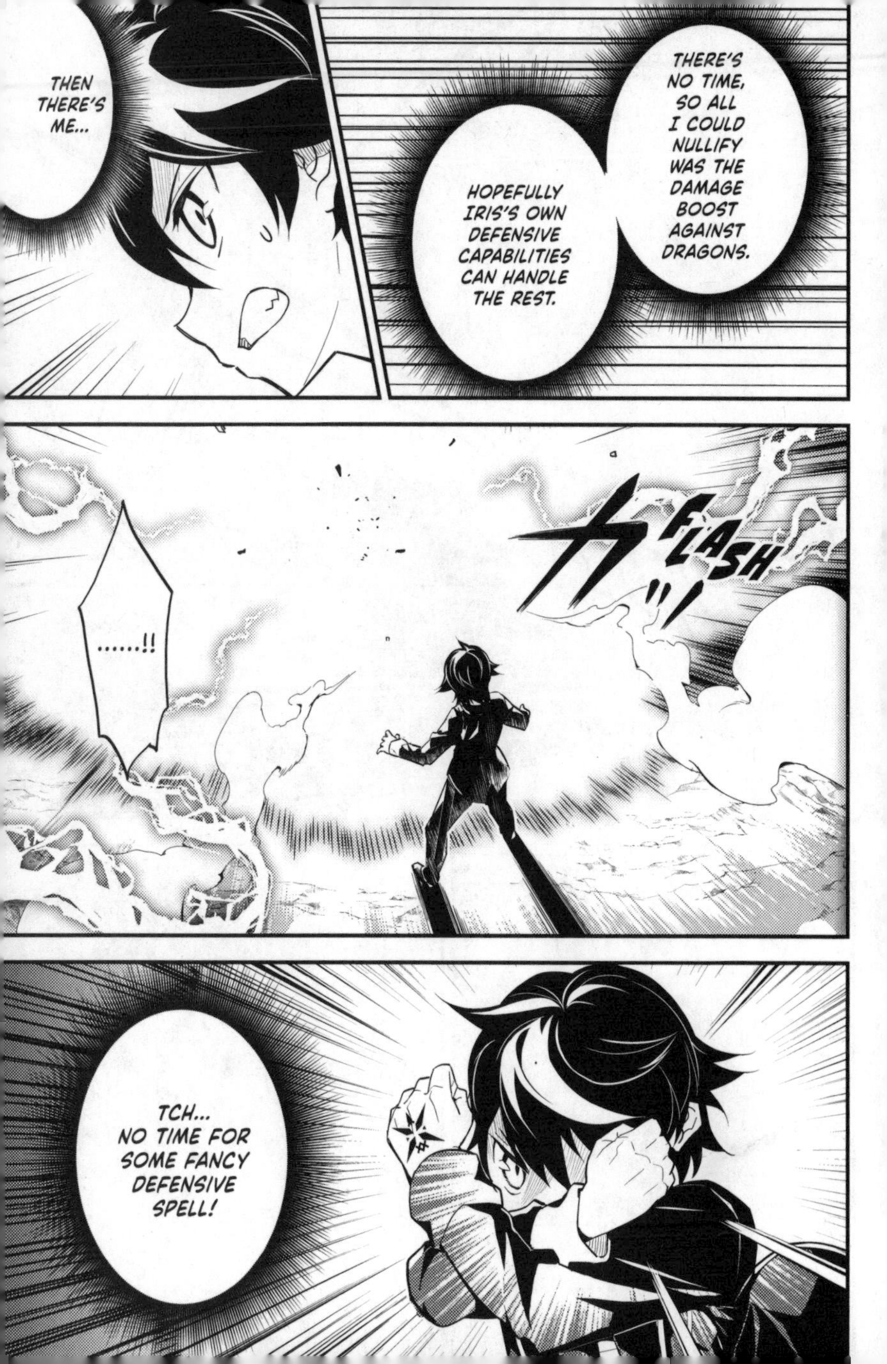
THERE'S NO TIME, SO ALL I COULD NULLIFY WAS THE DAMAGE BOOST AGAINST DRAGONS.
HOPEFULLY IRIS'S OWN DEFENSIVE CAPABILITIES CAN HANDLE THE REST.
THEN THERE'S ME...
FLASH
......!!
TCH... NO TIME FOR SOME FANCY DEFENSIVE SPELL!

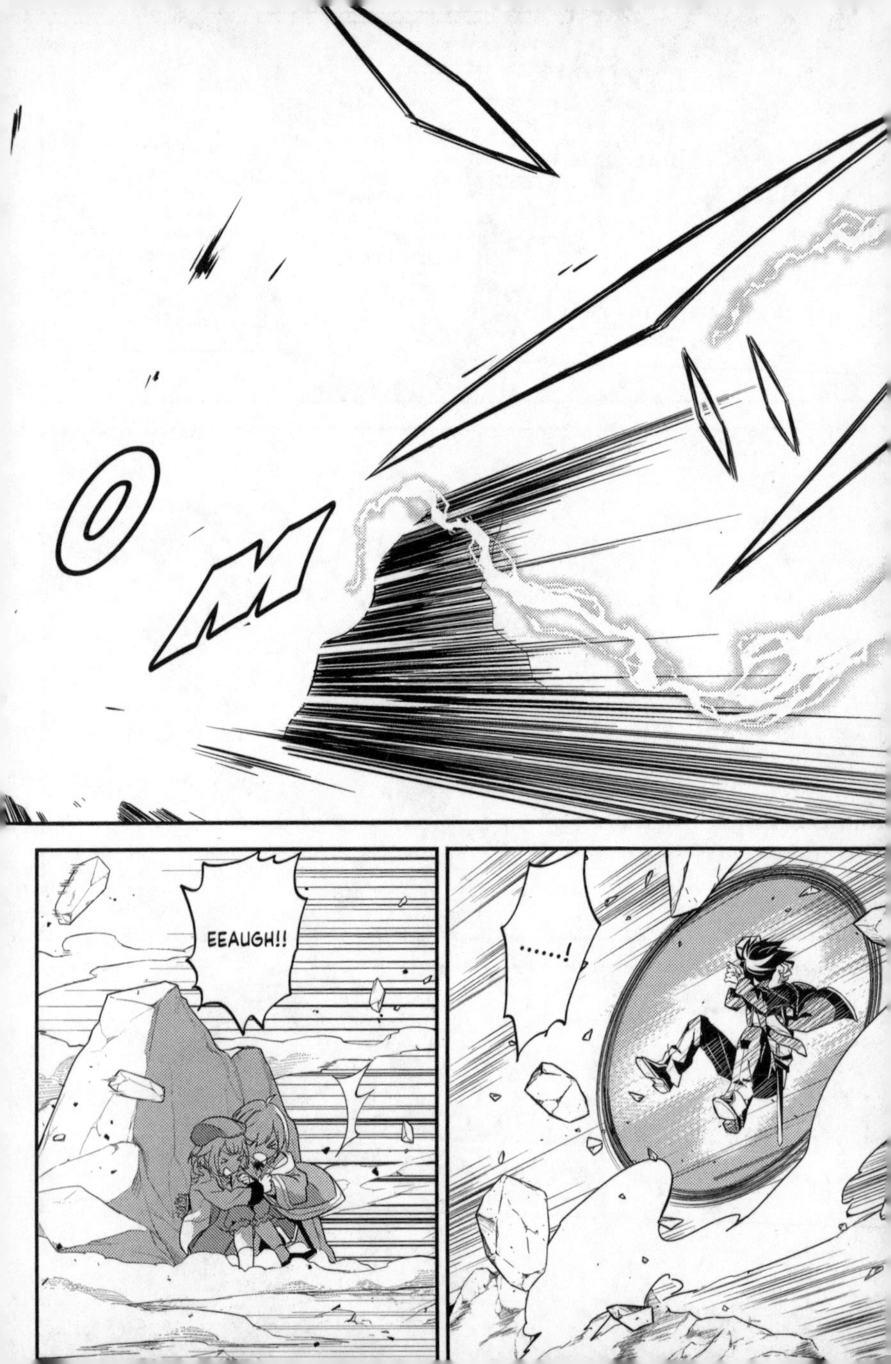
OM
......!
EEAUGH!!

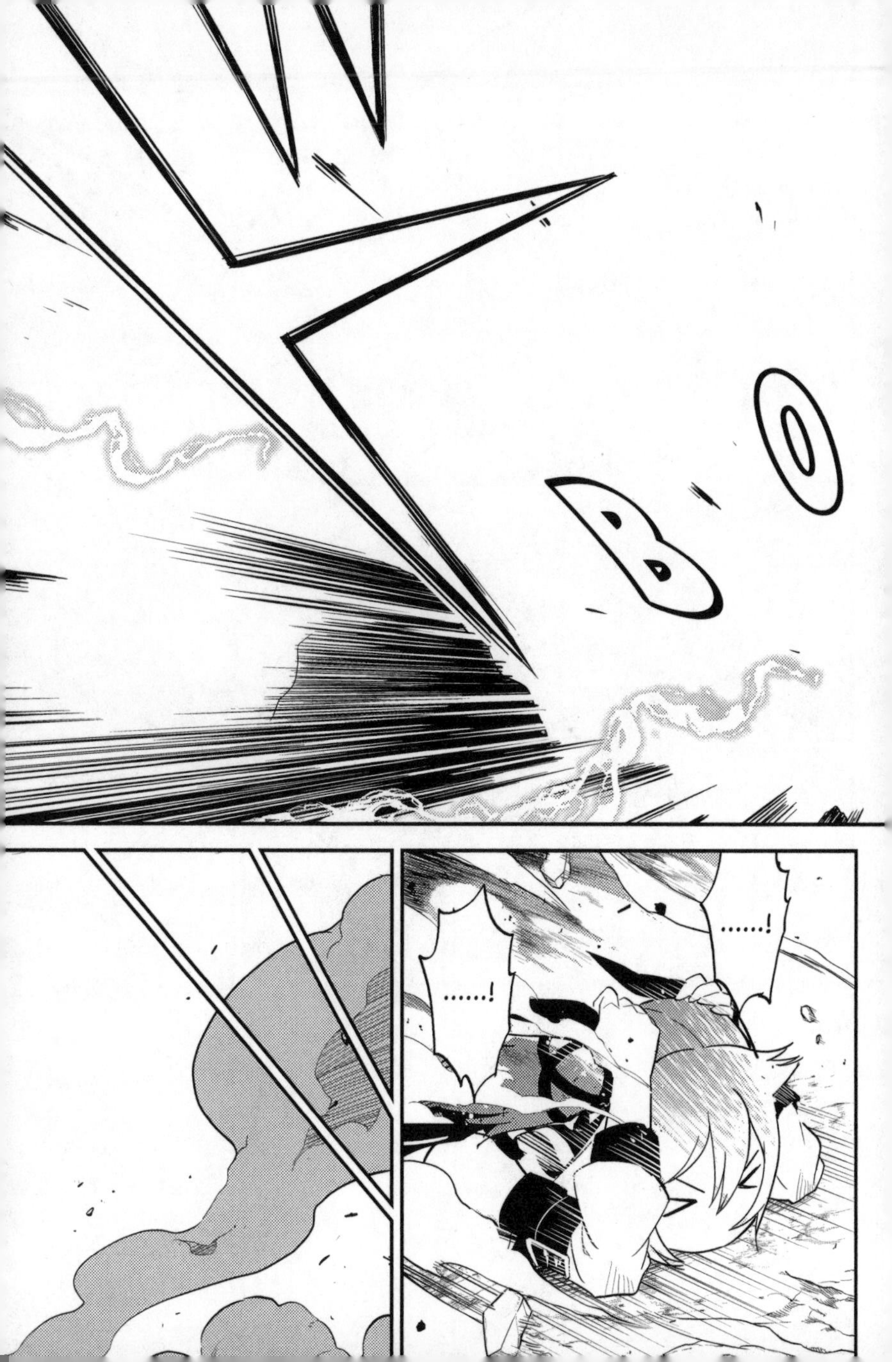
BO
......!
......!

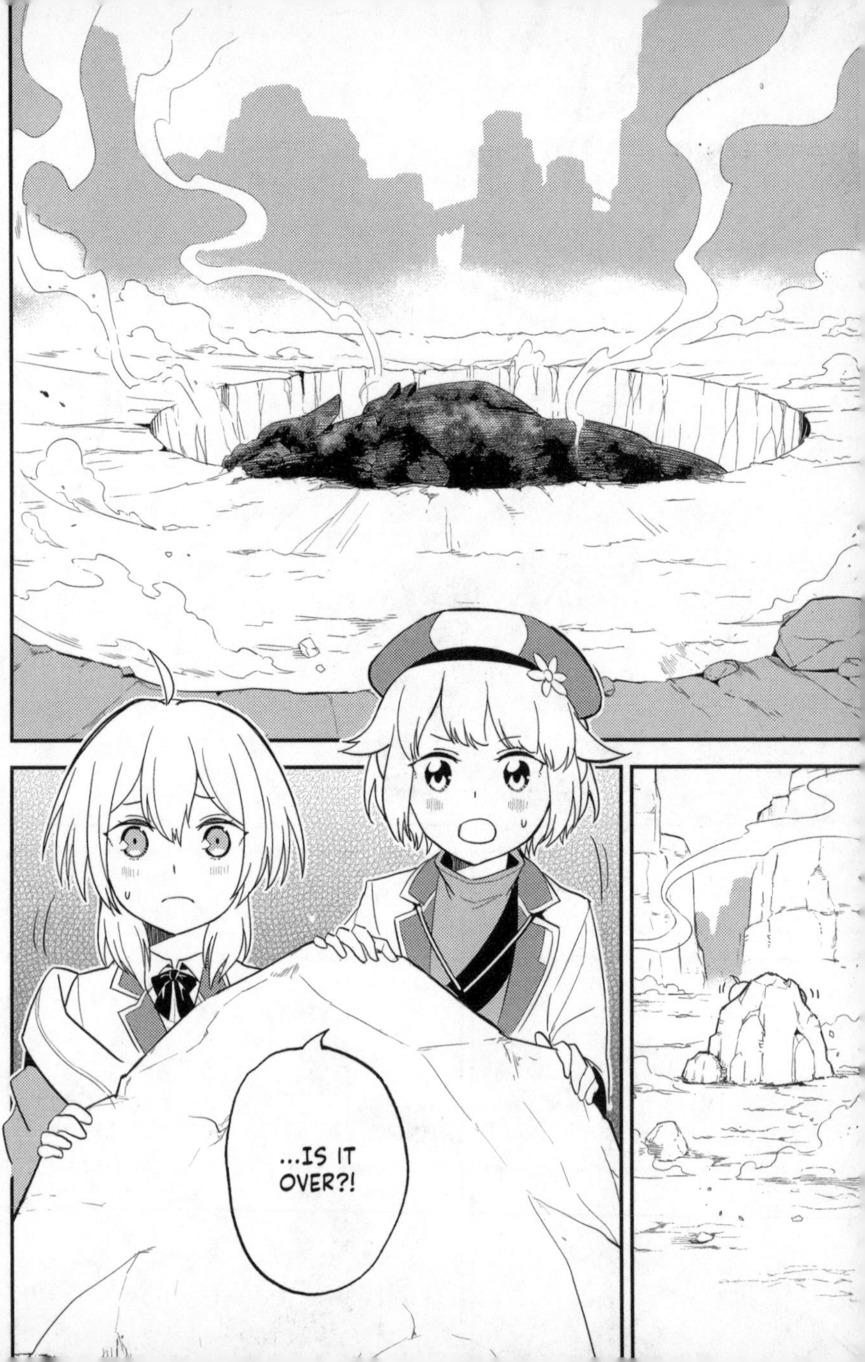
...IS IT
OVER?!

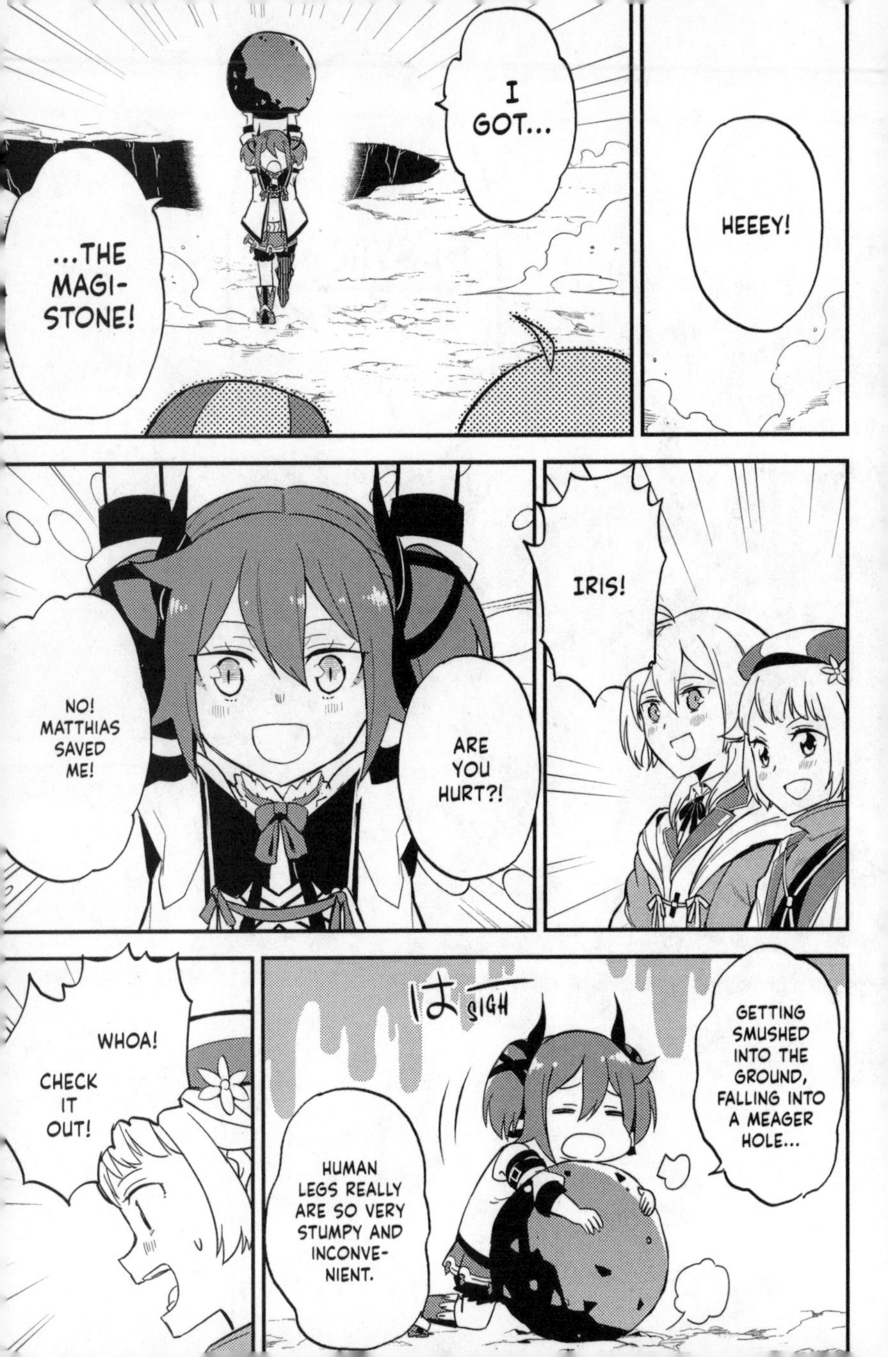
HEEEY!
I GOT...
...THE MAGI-STONE!
IRIS!
ARE YOU HURT?!
NO! MATTHIAS SAVED ME!
GETTING SMUSHED INTO THE GROUND, FALLING INTO A MEAGER HOLE...
は SIGH
HUMAN LEGS REALLY ARE SO VERY STUMPY AND INCONVE-NIENT.
WHOA!
CHECK IT OUT!

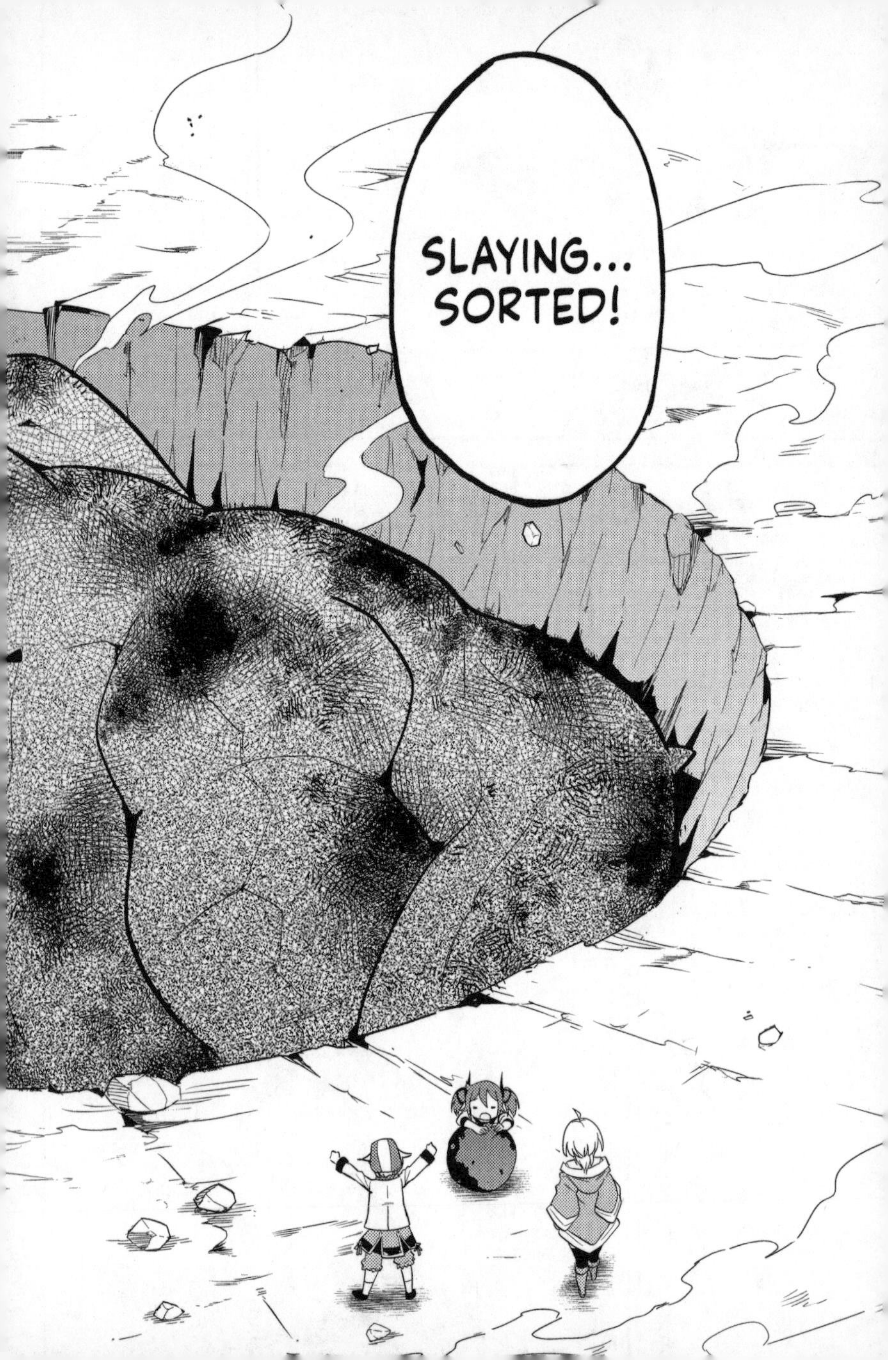
SLAYING... SORTED!

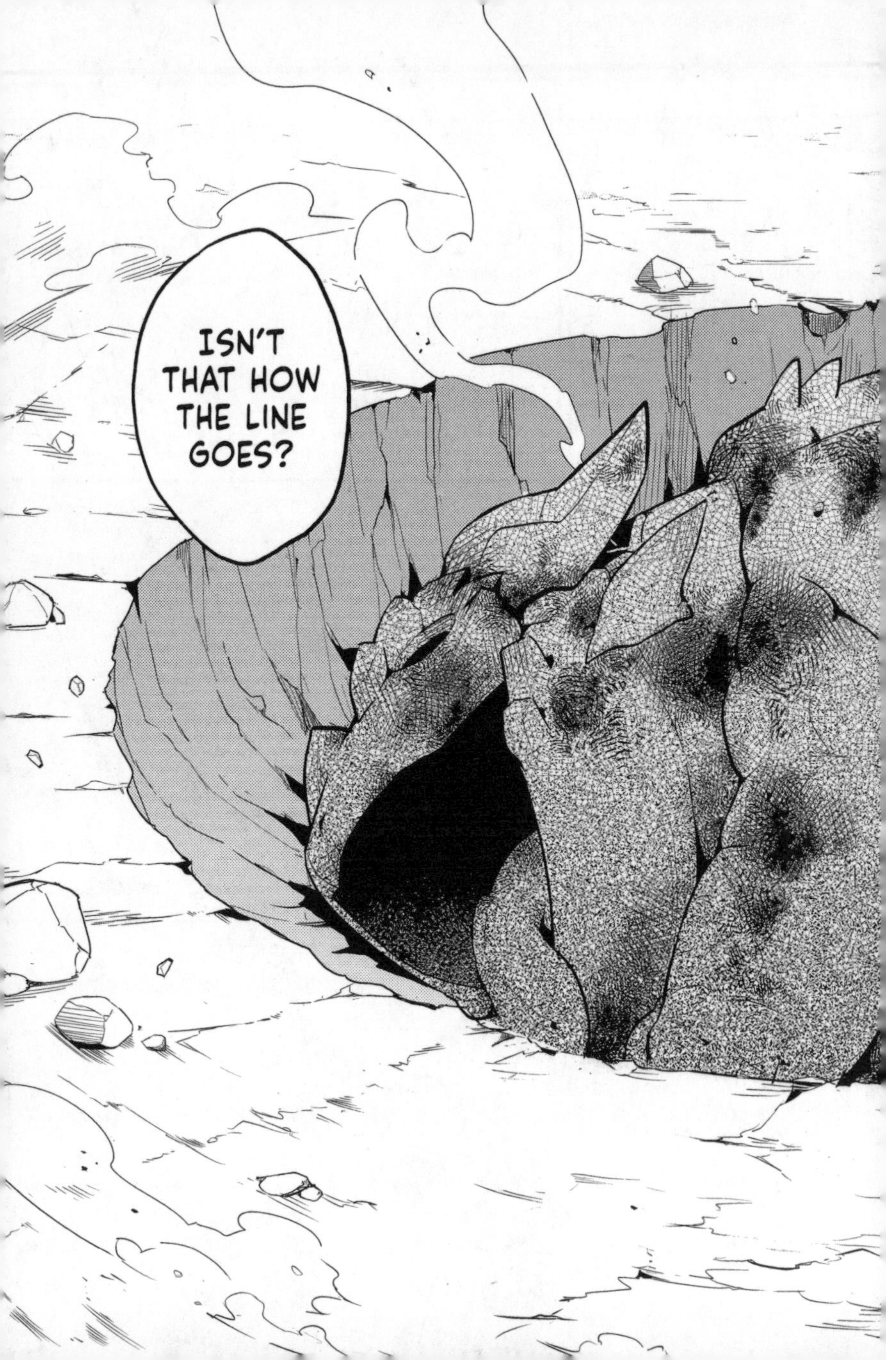
ISN'T THAT HOW THE LINE GOES?

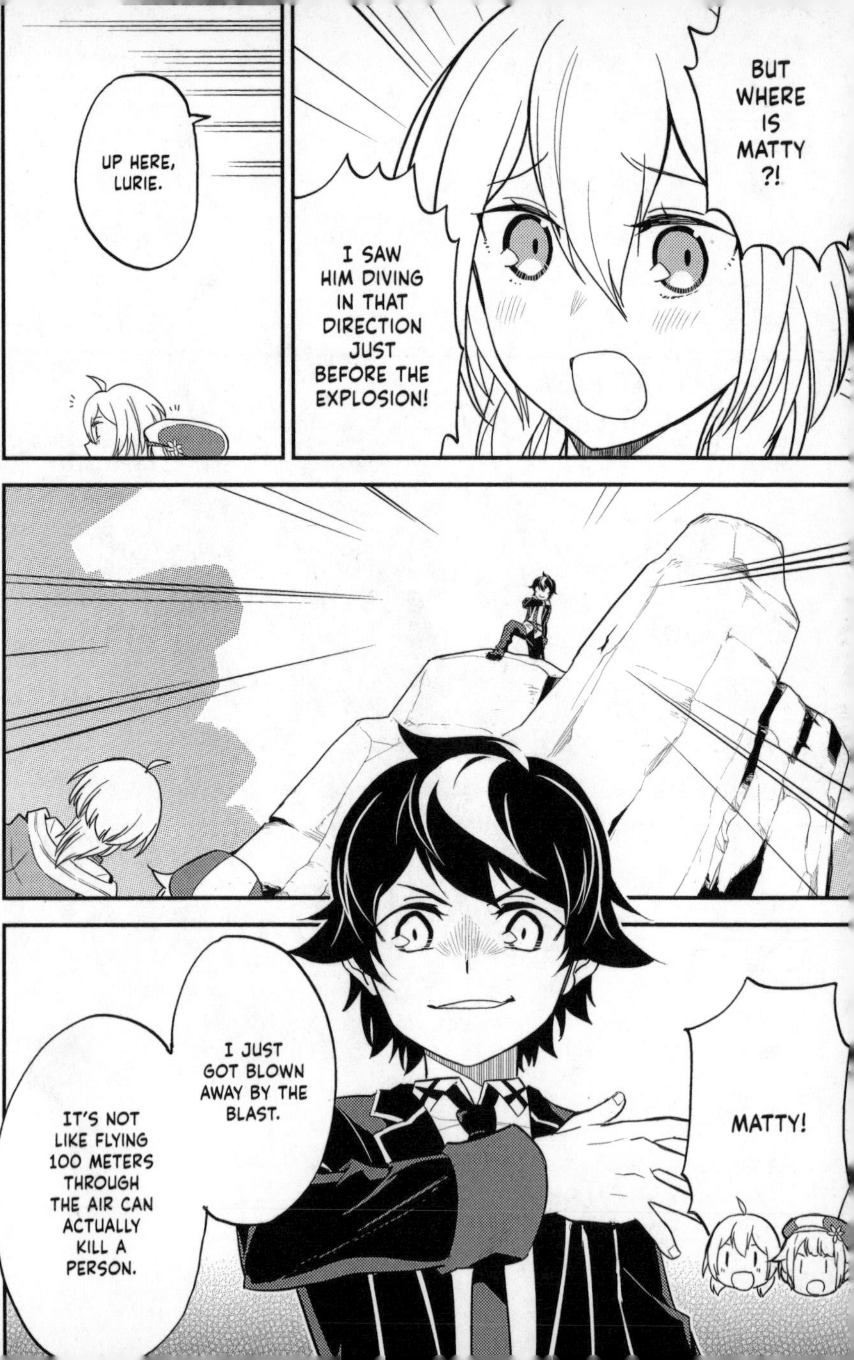
BUT WHERE IS MATTY?!
I SAW HIM DIVING IN THAT DIRECTION JUST BEFORE THE EXPLOSION!
UP HERE, LURIE.
MATTY!
I JUST GOT BLOWN AWAY BY THE BLAST.
IT'S NOT LIKE FLYING 100 METERS THROUGH THE AIR CAN ACTUALLY KILL A PERSON.

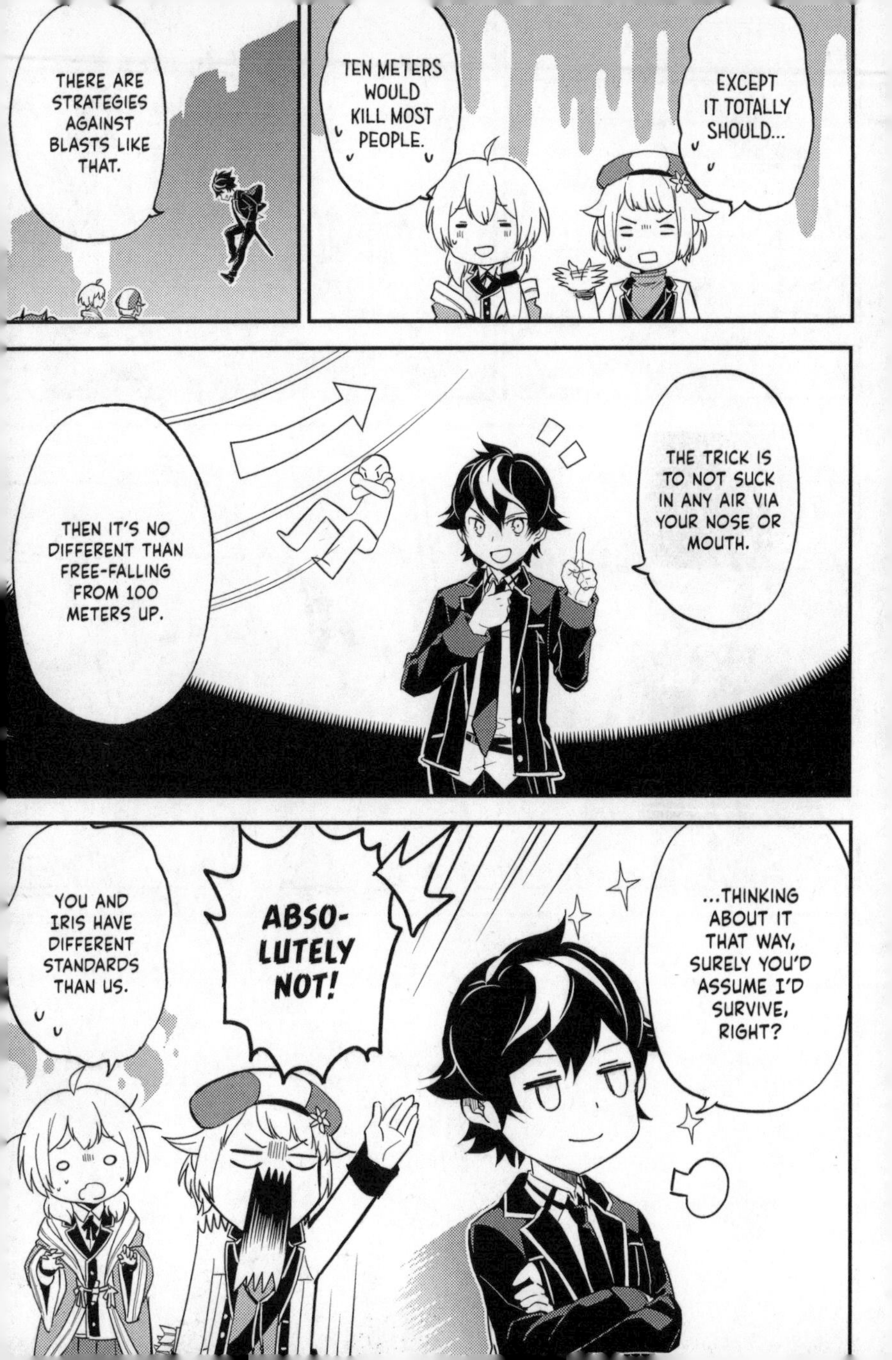
EXCEPT IT TOTALLY SHOULD...
TEN METERS WOULD KILL MOST PEOPLE.
THERE ARE STRATEGIES AGAINST BLASTS LIKE THAT.
THE TRICK IS TO NOT SUCK IN ANY AIR VIA YOUR NOSE OR MOUTH.
THEN IT'S NO DIFFERENT THAN FREE-FALLING FROM 100 METERS UP.
...THINKING ABOUT IT THAT WAY, SURELY YOU'D ASSUME I'D SURVIVE, RIGHT?
ABSO-LUTELY NOT!
YOU AND IRIS HAVE DIFFERENT STANDARDS THAN US.

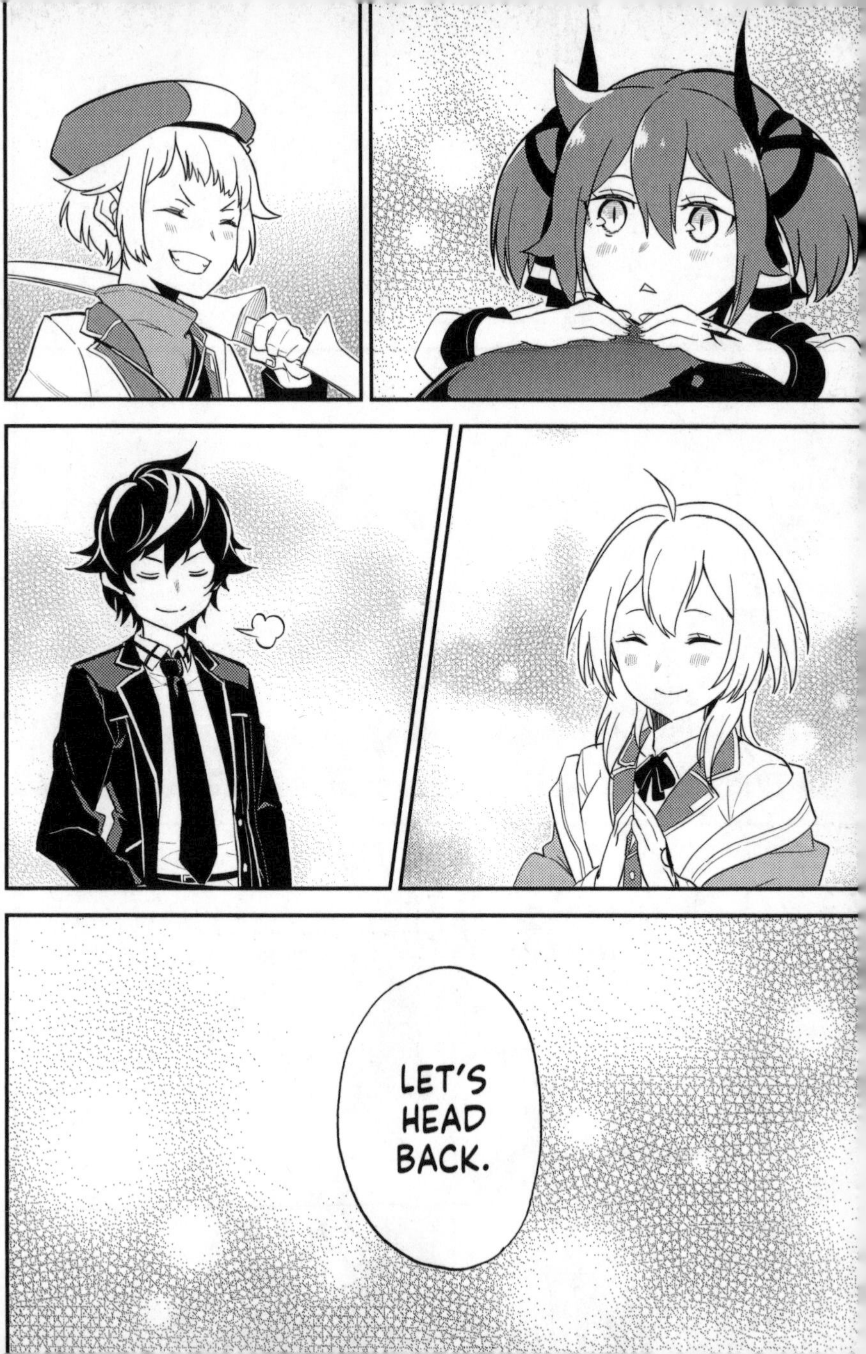
LET'S HEAD BACK.

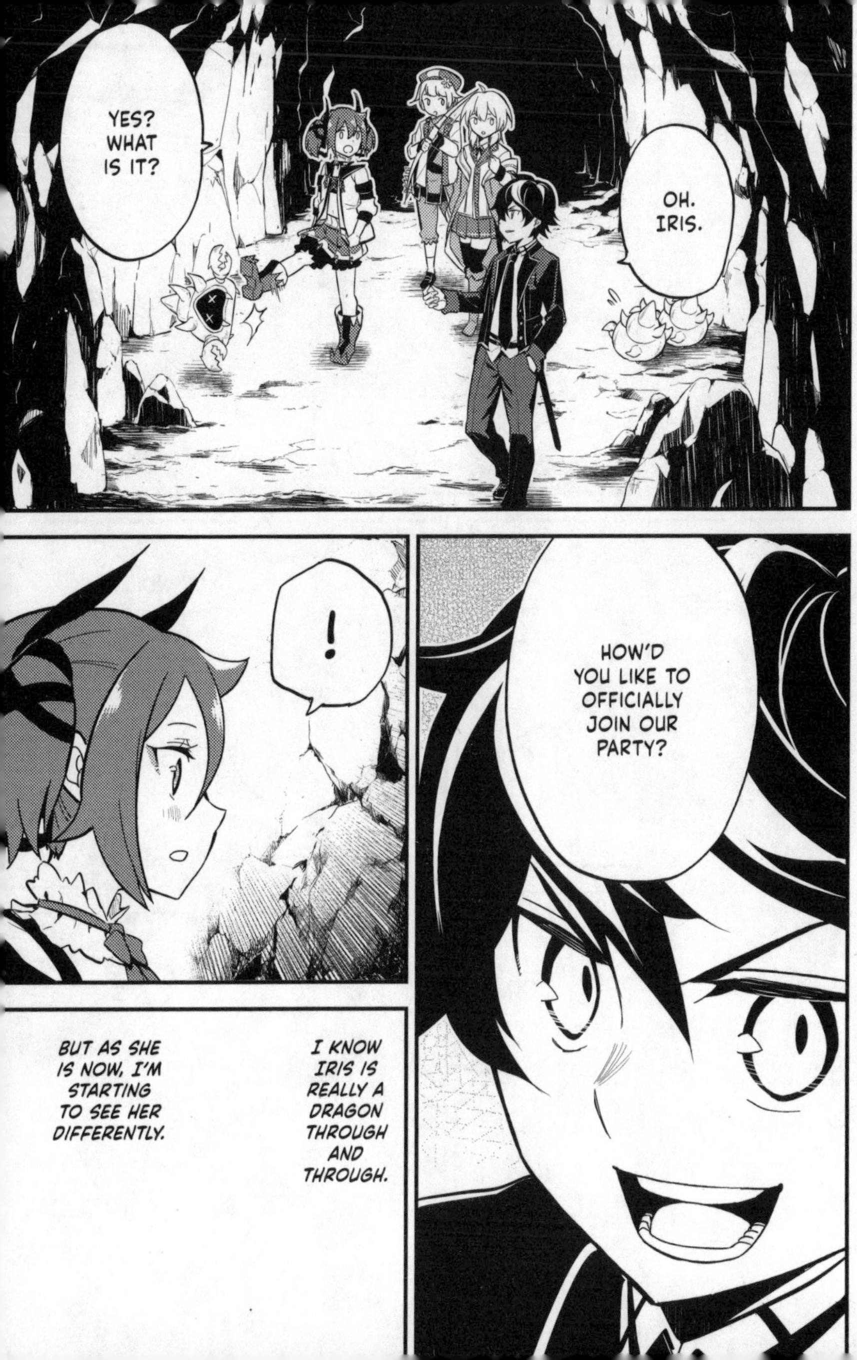
OH. IRIS.
YES? WHAT IS IT?
HOW'D YOU LIKE TO OFFICIALLY JOIN OUR PARTY?
!
I KNOW IRIS IS REALLY A DRAGON THROUGH AND THROUGH.
BUT AS SHE IS NOW, I'M STARTING TO SEE HER DIFFERENTLY.

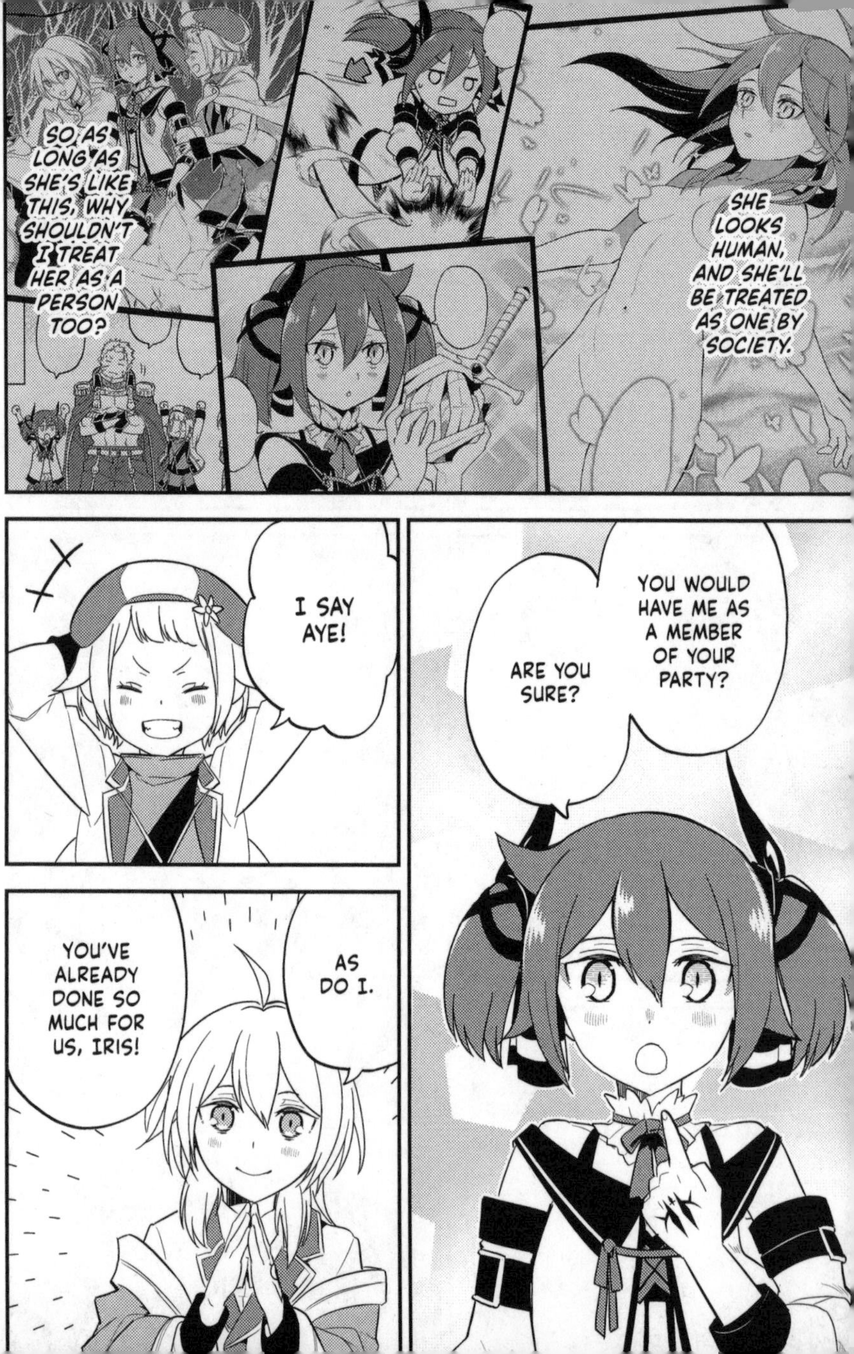
SHE LOOKS HUMAN, AND SHE'LL BE TREATED AS ONE BY SOCIETY.
SO AS LONG AS SHE'S LIKE THIS, WHY SHOULDN'T I TREAT HER AS A PERSON TOO?
YOU WOULD HAVE ME AS A MEMBER OF YOUR PARTY?
ARE YOU SURE?
I SAY AYE!
AS DO I.
YOU'VE ALREADY DONE SO MUCH FOR US, IRIS!

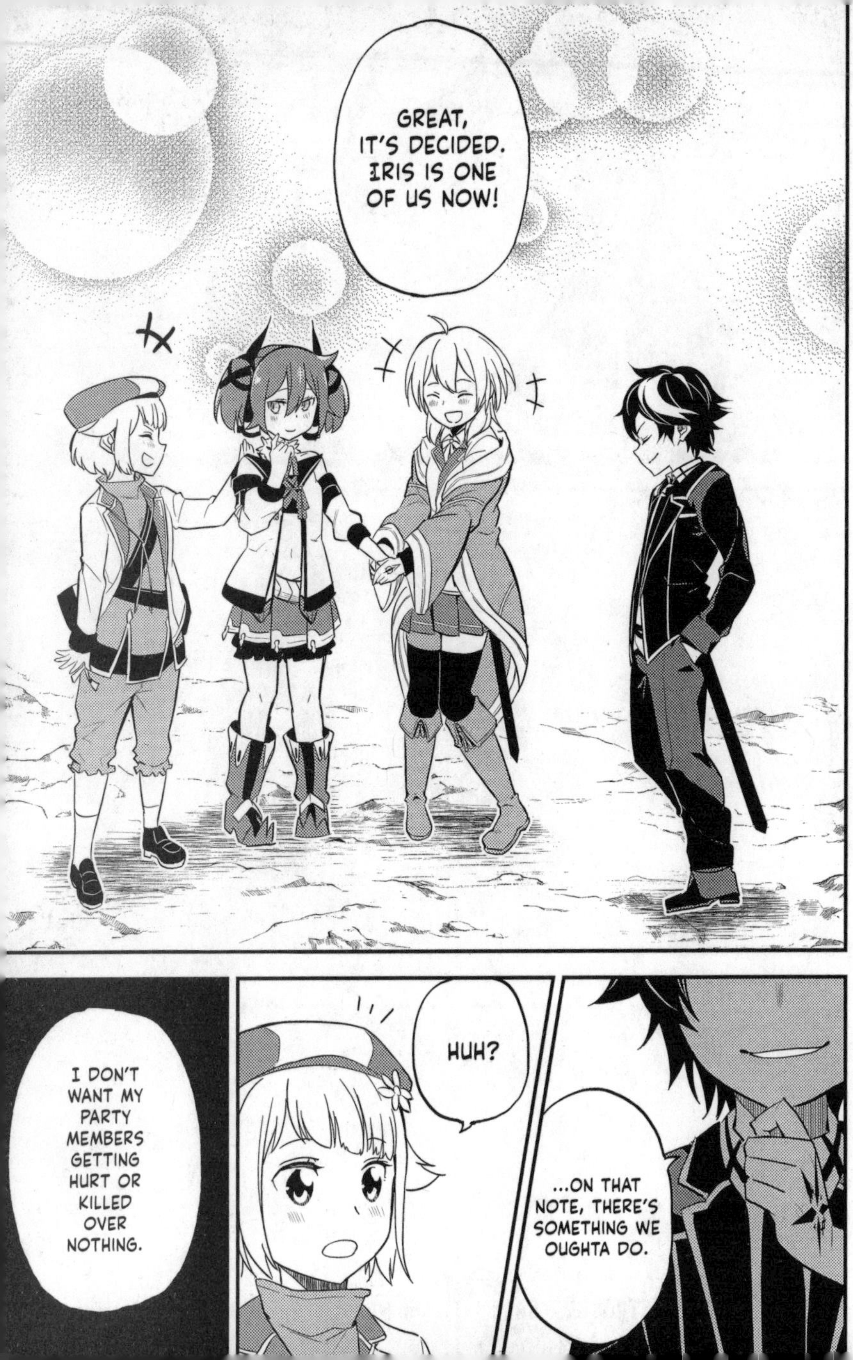
GREAT, IT'S DECIDED. IRIS IS ONE OF US NOW!
...ON THAT NOTE, THERE'S SOMETHING WE OUGHTA DO.
HUH?
I DON'T WANT MY PARTY MEMBERS GETTING HURT OR KILLED OVER NOTHING.

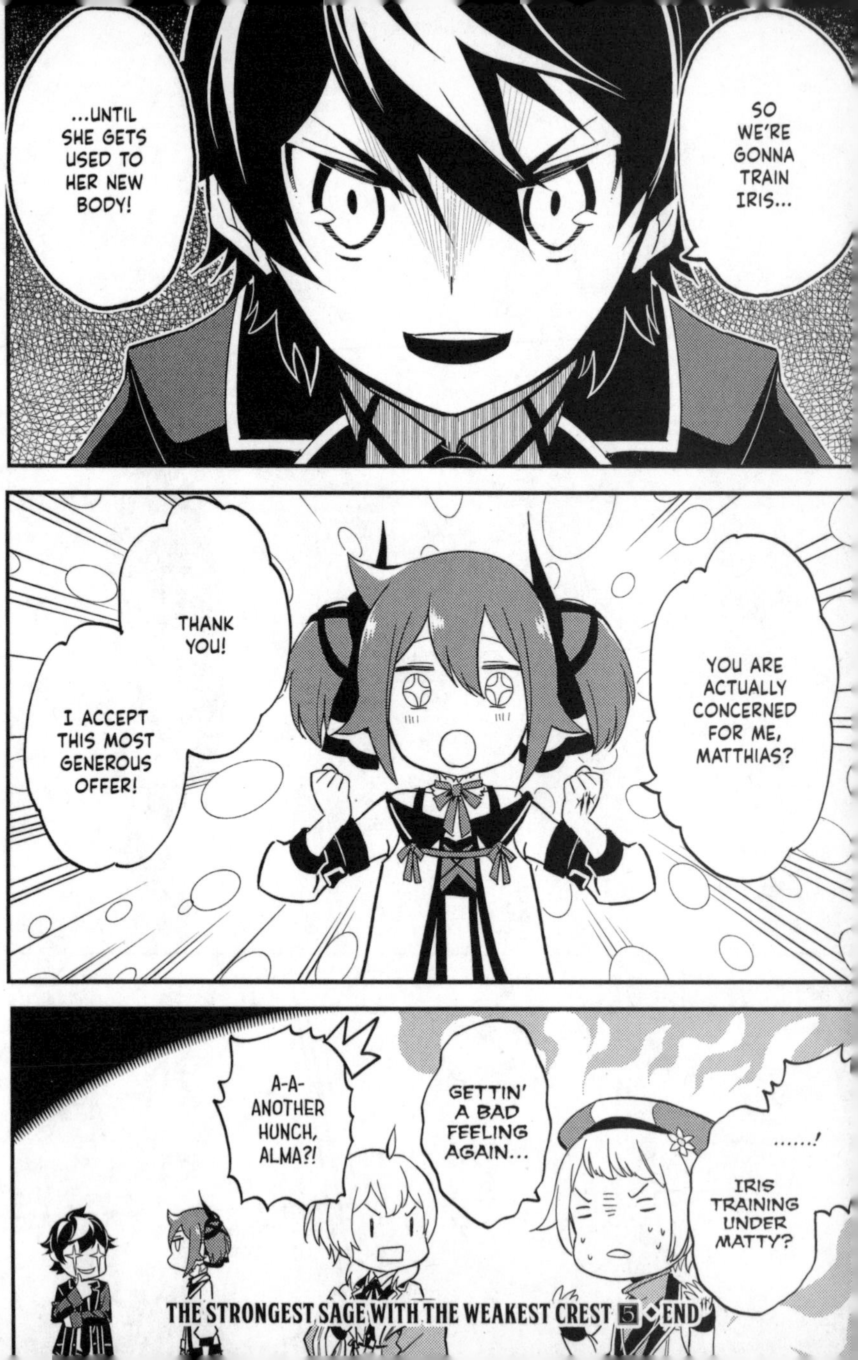
SO WE'RE GONNA TRAIN IRIS...
...UNTIL SHE GETS USED TO HER NEW BODY!
YOU ARE ACTUALLY CONCERNED FOR ME, MATTHIAS?
THANK YOU!
I ACCEPT THIS MOST GENEROUS OFFER!
......!
IRIS TRAINING UNDER MATTY?
GETTIN' A BAD FEELING AGAIN...
A-A-ANOTHER HUNCH, ALMA?!
THE STRONGEST SAGE WITH THE WEAKEST CREST 5 ◆ END

THE STRONGEST SAGE WITH THE WEAKEST CREST

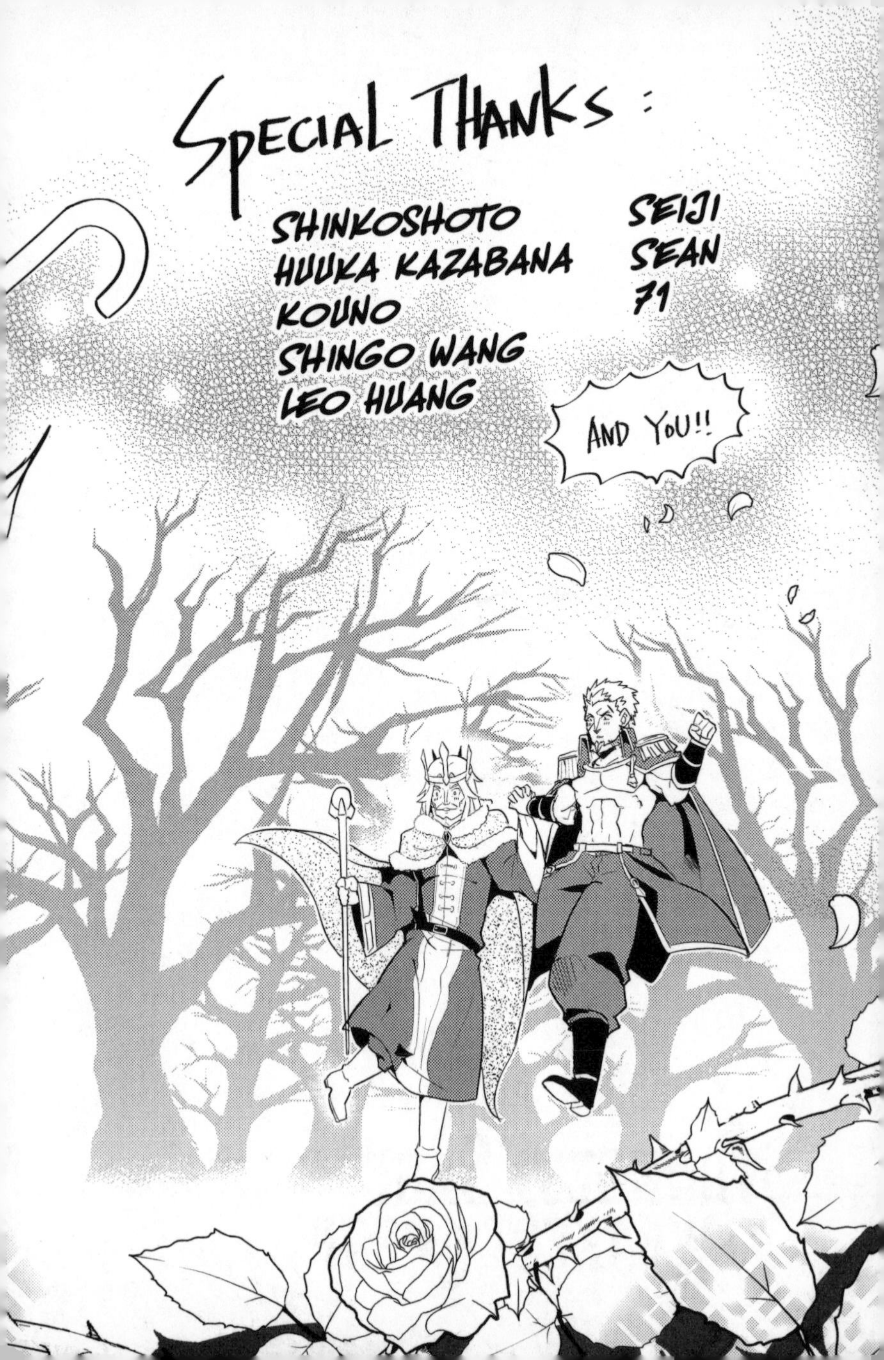
SPECIAL THANKS:
SHINKOSHOTO
HUUKA KAZABANA
KOUNO
SHINGO WANG
LEO HUANG
SEIJI
SEAN
71
AND YOU!!

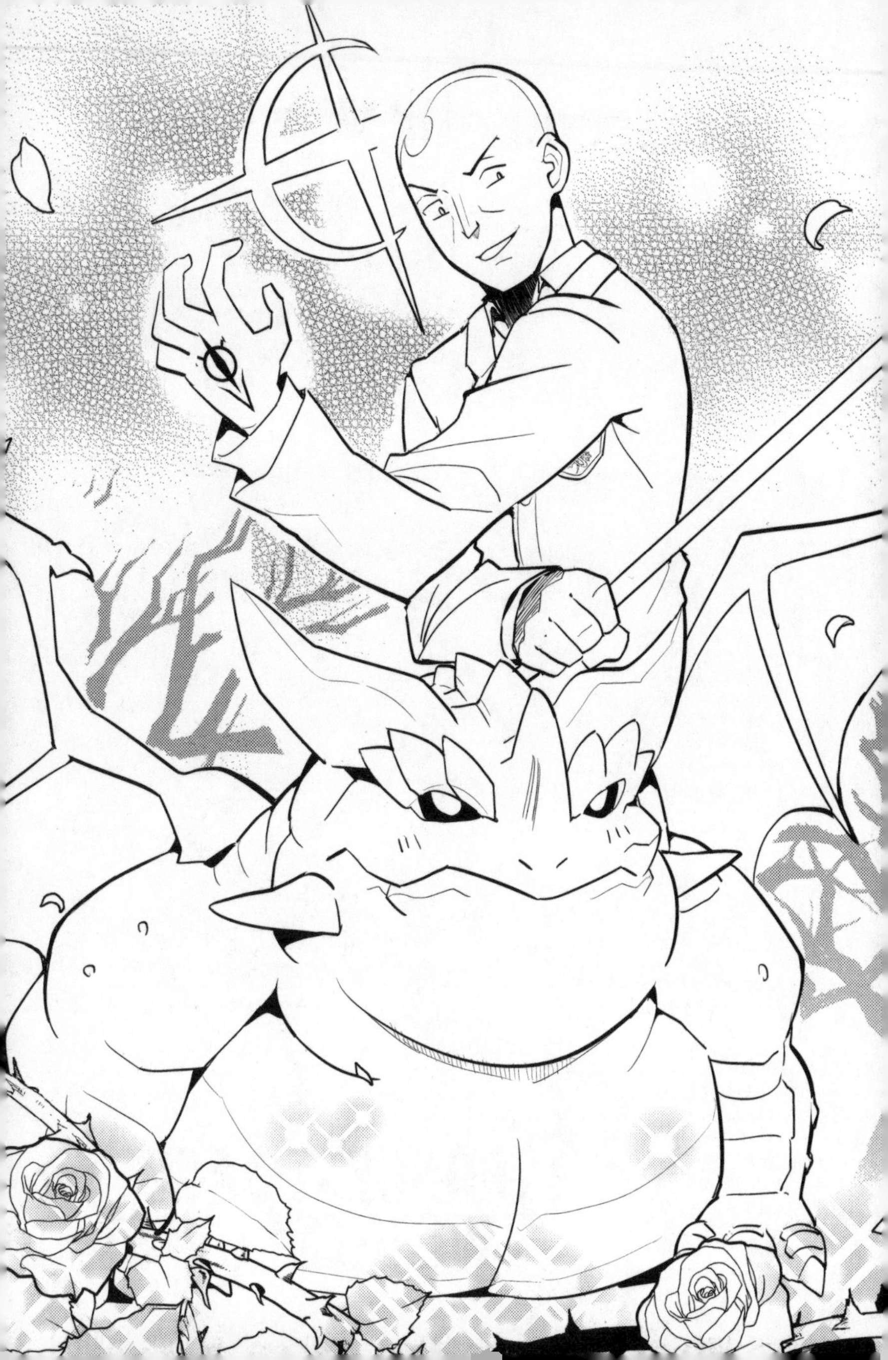

THE
STRONGEST SAGE
WITH THE WEAKEST CREST

To read a
brand-new
short story by
Shinkoshoto,
the author of
*The Strongest
Sage with the
Weakest Crest*,
please turn to
page 194 of this
book, where
you'll find the
story presented
in left-to-right
reading order!!

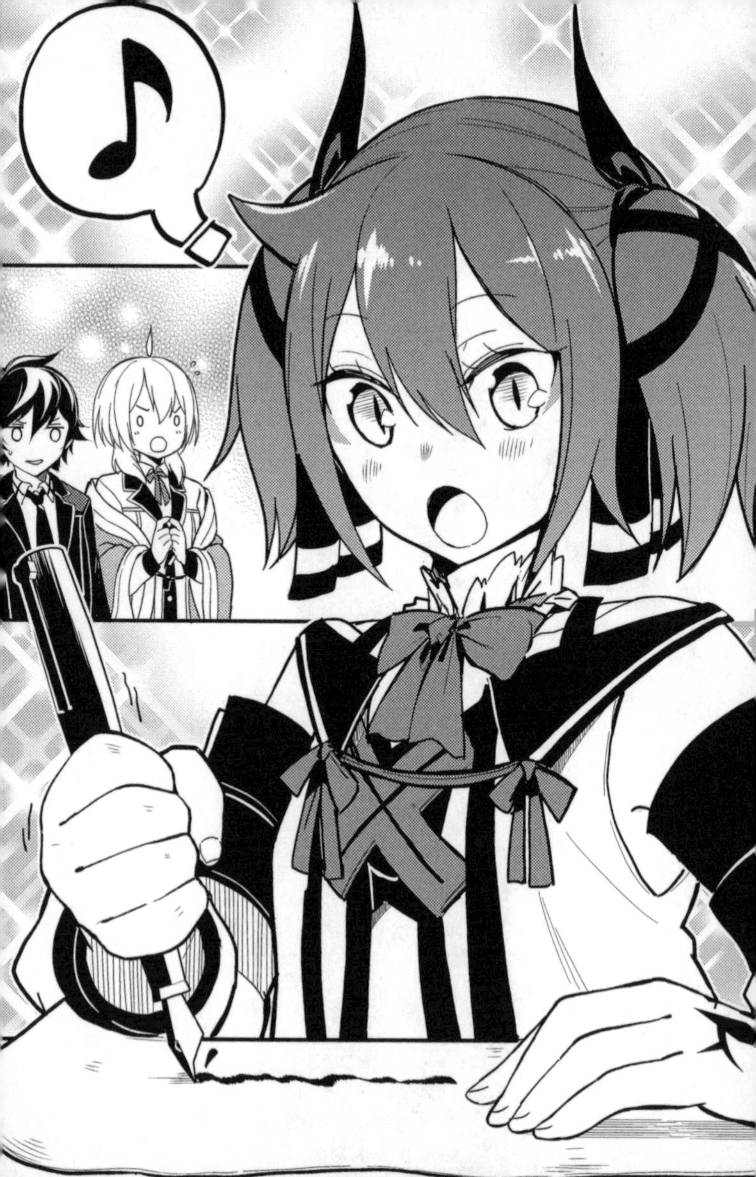

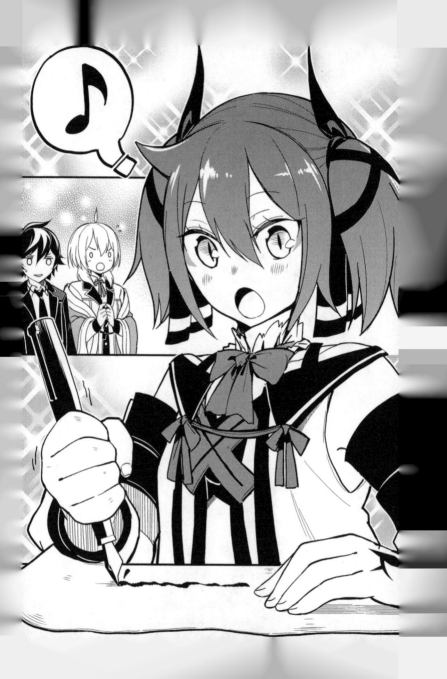

"Very well!" said Iris, determined to try again.

"Wait just a second," I said the moment before the pen hit paper.

I then cast a strengthening spell on the paper itself. Such spells are, for the most part, outside the purview of those bearing the Crest of Failure, but toughening up a piece of paper wasn't beyond my abilities.

"Okay, go ahead."

"Here I go!"

Iris was practically trembling as the pen touched the page. It didn't break, though, and she drew a straight line.

"Oh! Unbreakable, as you said!" she exclaimed, beaming at her freshly drawn line. Finally, Iris could actually start book-learning. But first, one more thing.

"Iris, try flipping the paper over."

"If you insist."

As Iris grabbed the paper to turn it, the force of her hand crumpled the desk itself inward, roughly along the line she had drawn.

How careless of me. Rather than an ordinary desk pad, my dragon friend would need an iron slab under her writing paper in future.

THE END

"I've got plans for a new writing implement here, Lurie. Could you try making it?" I asked, showing her the blueprint.

"A writing implement, you say? Fascinating," said Lurie. But upon seeing the plans, she tilted her head in confusion.

"Won't this be exceedingly heavy?" she asked.

"Yeah, but it's meant for Iris."

"That makes perfect sense! I'll give it a shot!"

With that, Lurie began refining the necessary steel and mithril. While an ordinary fountain pen would be tough to construct, my design featured a magic tool on the inside, thereby simplifying the process. It also had to eschew any dainty or delicate touches, lest it succumb to Iris's brute strength.

"It's finished!" declared Lurie, having transformed the lumps of metal into a full-fledged fountain pen in the blink of an eye.

"What a strange design, though... Can it really write?"

"Shall we try it out?"

"Okay!"

I handed Lurie an ink jar, and she began scribbling.

"Despite the heft, it writes so very smoothly!" she said, sounding shocked. "I've never seen this style of pen before!"

"It can be made much lighter, depending on the materials," I said.

It seemed the pen was a success.

"But I wonder if Iris will really be able to use it..." said Lurie.

"You and me both," I said, grabbing the pen before heading back to Iris.

"Use as little pressure as possible and give it a try," I said.

"That is a lesson I have learned. It is bitter and distinctly not tasty," said Iris.

Great. I'm glad you understand.

"Go ahead and try writing. You won't learn a thing here if you can't even use a quill," I said.

"Very well!"

Iris plunged the implement into the ink, submerging it far past the tip.

Fine. Could be worse.

But as she pressed pen to paper, I heard a dry snap.

"Huh?"

Iris stared dumbfounded at the quill whose tip had snapped clean off.

"These quill pens require utmost delicacy, I suppose. I have no choice but to endeavor!" she mumbled with grim determination.

The particular quill she'd just broken was made from a monster feather and had to be the sturdiest pen this side of the kingdom. How sturdy? Rumor spoke of a student who once slayed monsters using this very quill as a weapon.

But okay, sure. Quills wouldn't work with Iris.

"No choice, then," I said. "I'll get Lurie to whip up an unbreakable pen for you."

"An unbreakable pen?" asked Iris.

"Yup."

With that, I drew up a blueprint for Iris's personal pen—a design that I called a "fountain pen" in my previous life. Ordinarily, the fountain pen would be wooden from the tip up, but Iris's would have to be solid, nicely rounded steel with a mithril tip to keep her from snapping it like a twig.

THE STRONGEST SAGE PREPS A PEN

by **Shinkoshoto**

"Matthias, please teach me how to study!"

Iris had just gained admittance to the Second Academy the previous day. Dissatisfied with her own inability to keep up during her first day of classes, she came to me with this request. Unfortunately, she was starting from square negative-one.

"Sure. First, you've got to learn to write with a quill pen," I said, producing an ink jar and a quill.

Naturally, Iris had never had occasion to use stationery before today. She'd scored an astounding zero points on the written portion of her transfer exam, in part because she broke her quill before even writing her name at the top of the page. By the end, her test paper was a ripped, crumpled mess, which left me with a bit of egg on my face, given that I was the one who'd put her forward for consideration.

"Just dip the tip of the quill into the ink and start writing. I should mention—the ink is not for drinking," I explained.

THE
STRONGEST SAGE
WITH THE WEAKEST CREST

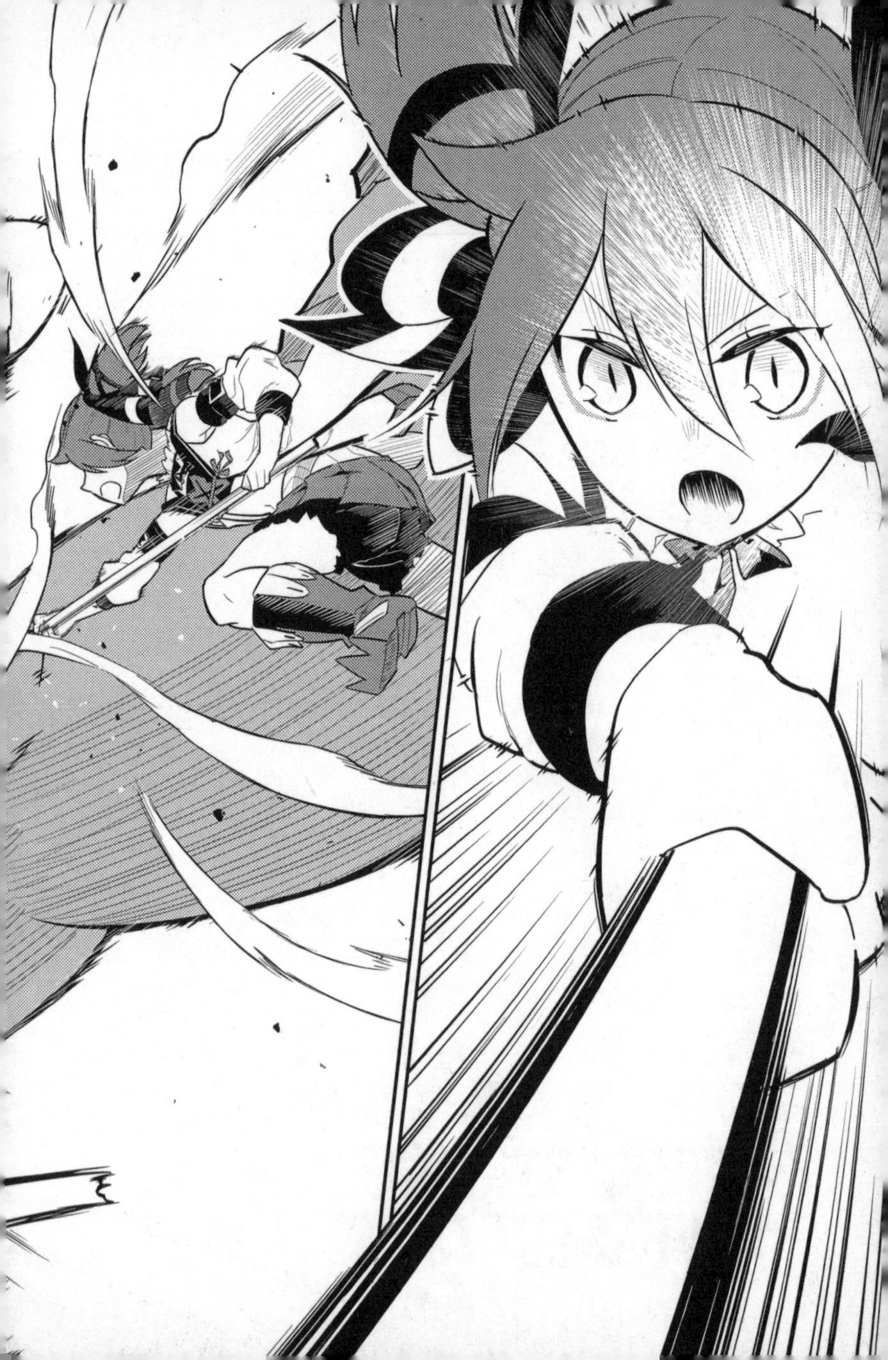

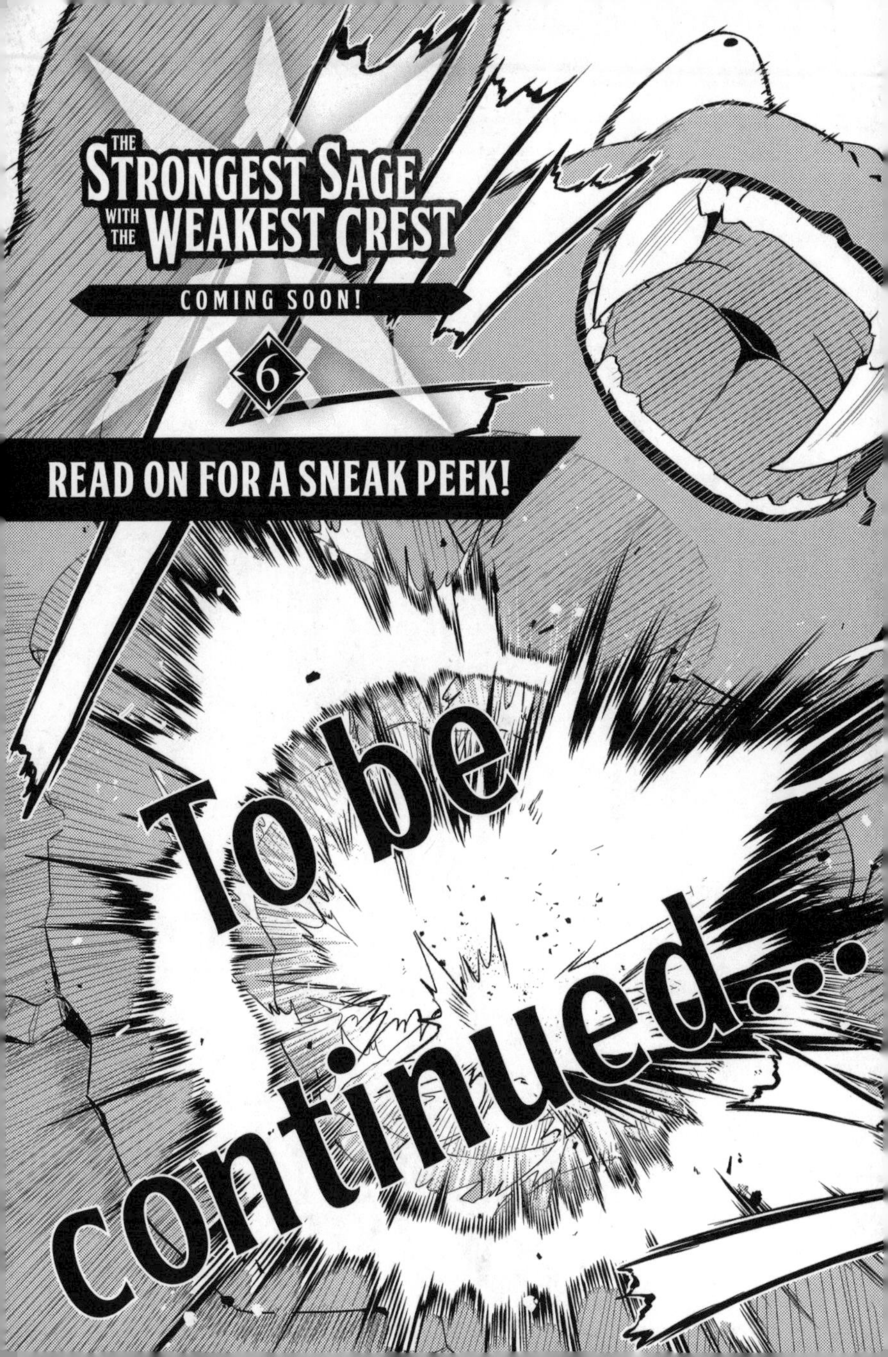
THE STRONGEST SAGE WITH THE WEAKEST CREST
COMING SOON!
6
READ ON FOR A SNEAK PEEK!
To be continued...

THE
STRONGEST SAGE
WITH THE WEAKEST CREST

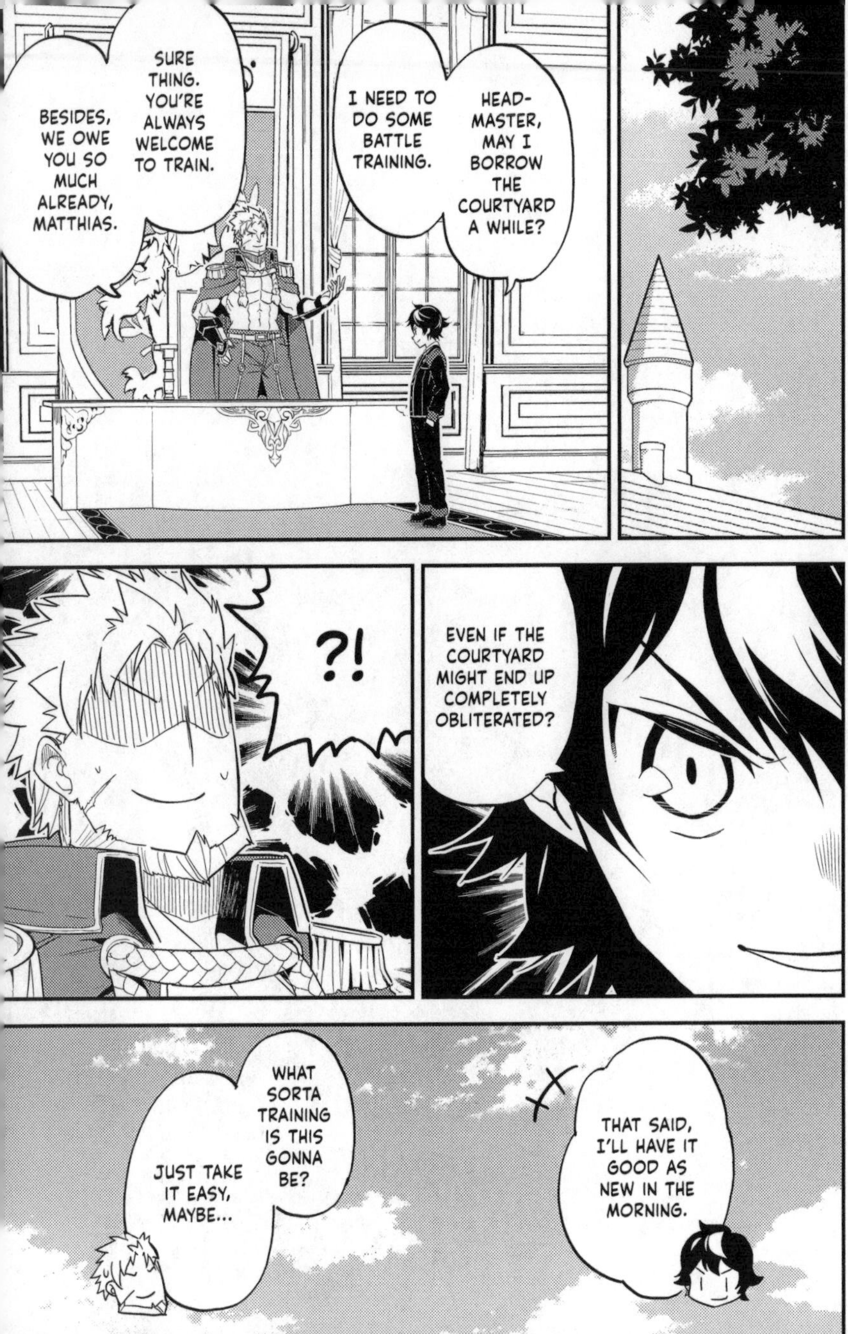
HEAD-MASTER, MAY I BORROW THE COURTYARD A WHILE?
I NEED TO DO SOME BATTLE TRAINING.
SURE THING. YOU'RE ALWAYS WELCOME TO TRAIN.
BESIDES, WE OWE YOU SO MUCH ALREADY, MATTHIAS.
EVEN IF THE COURTYARD MIGHT END UP COMPLETELY OBLITERATED?
?!
THAT SAID, I'LL HAVE IT GOOD AS NEW IN THE MORNING.
WHAT SORTA TRAINING IS THIS GONNA BE?
JUST TAKE IT EASY, MAYBE...

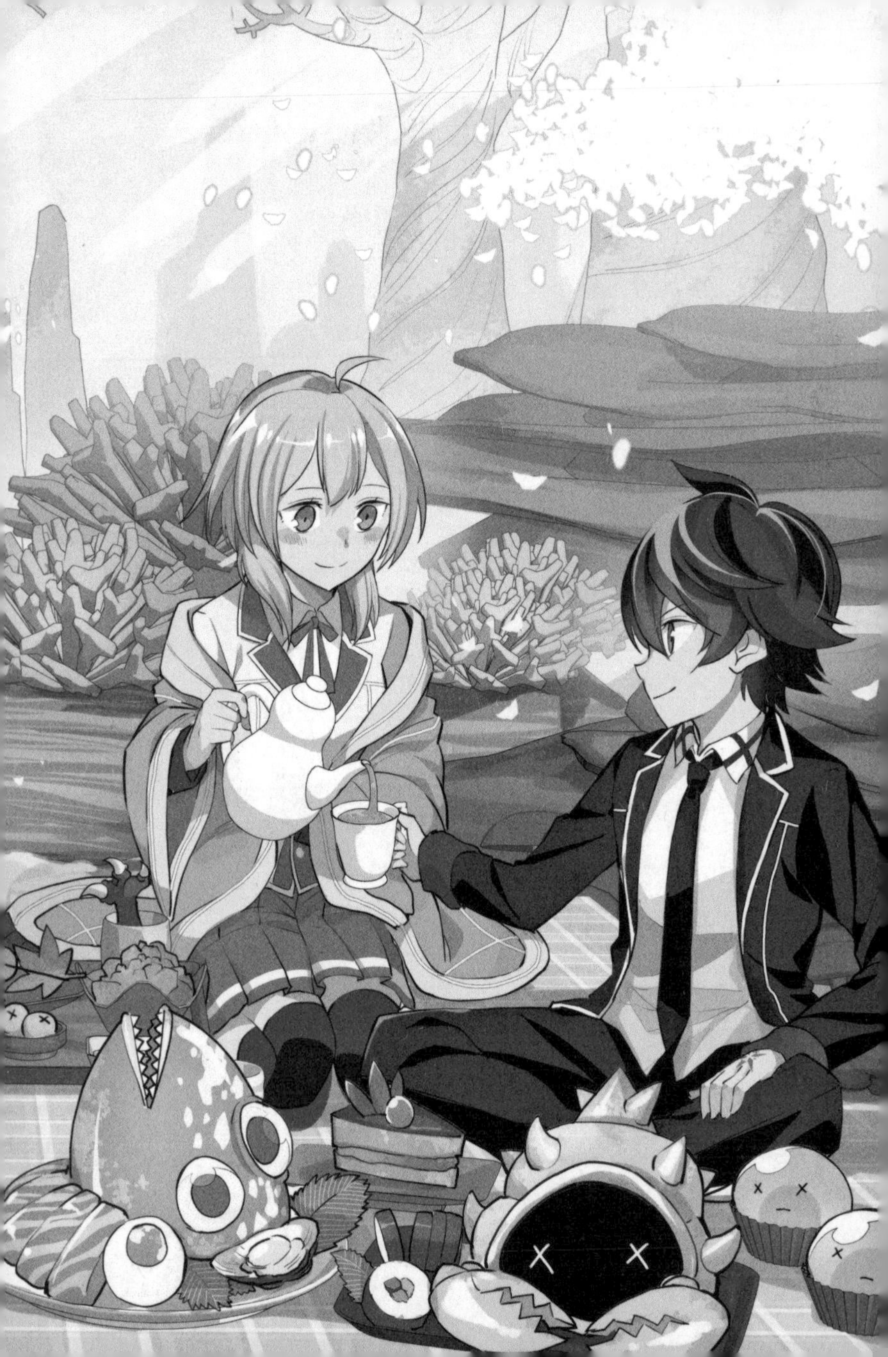

CHAPTER 18 ◆
The Strongest Sage Grinds His Party (Again)

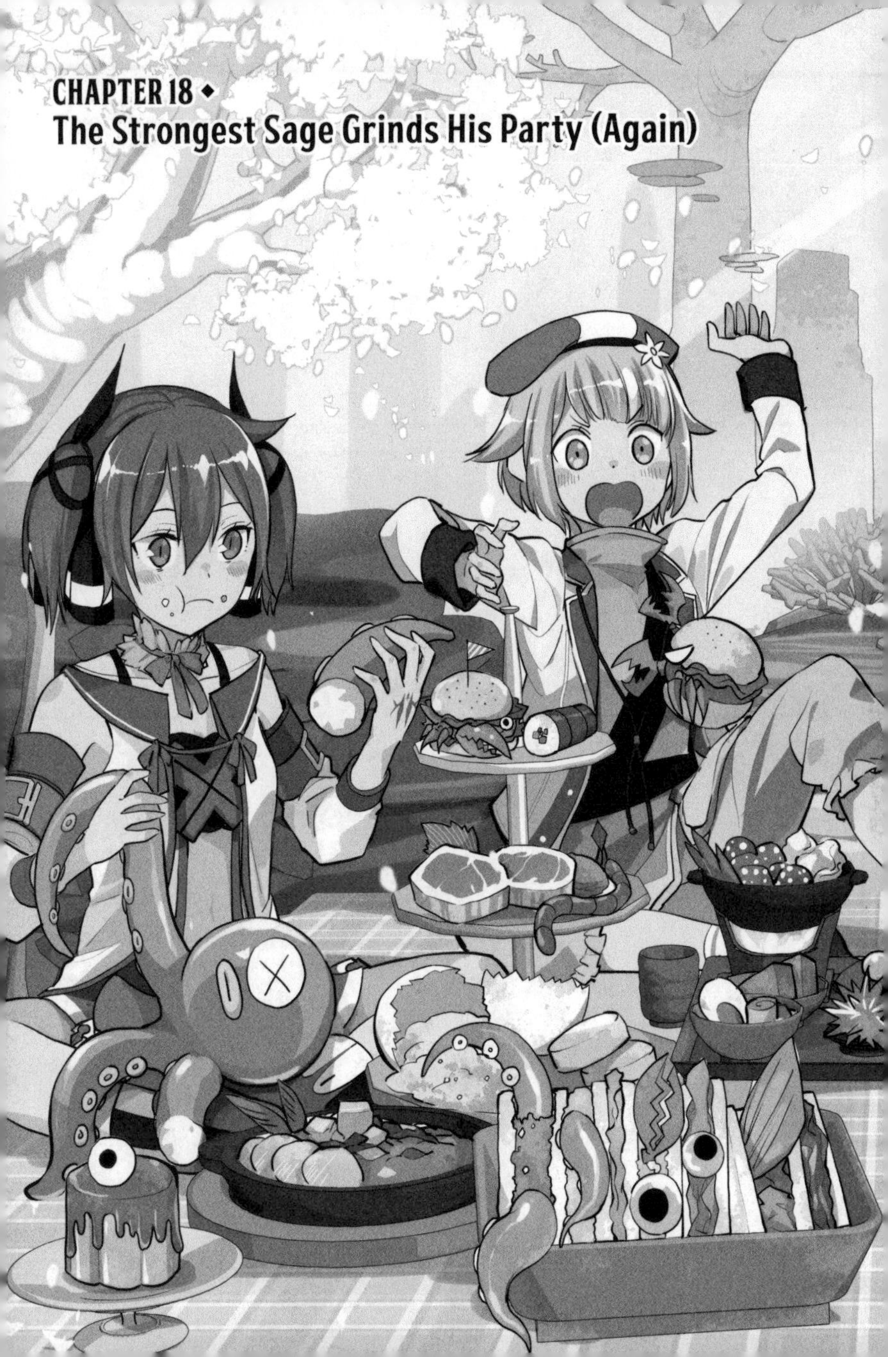

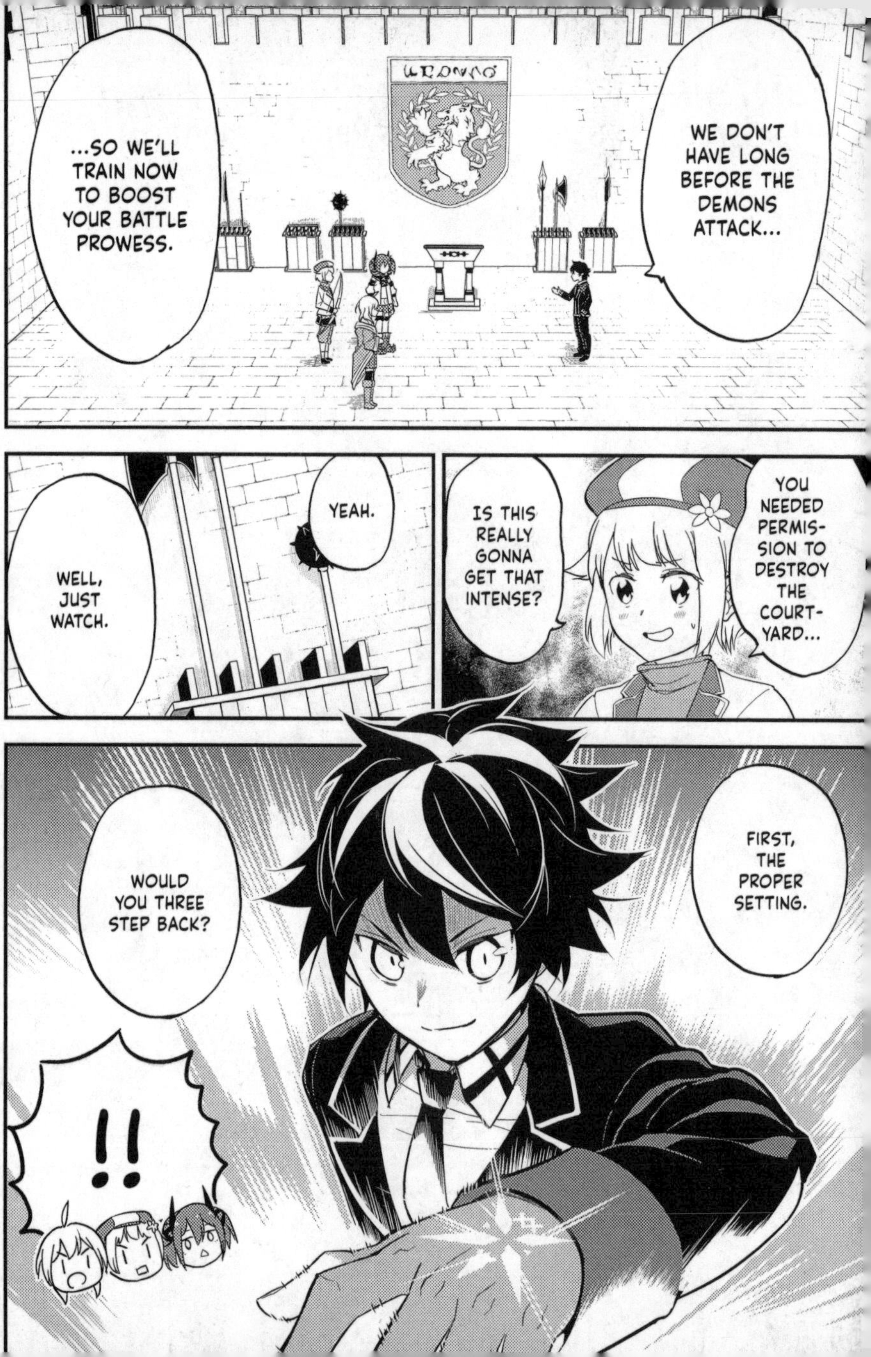
WE DON'T HAVE LONG BEFORE THE DEMONS ATTACK...
...SO WE'LL TRAIN NOW TO BOOST YOUR BATTLE PROWESS.
YOU NEEDED PERMIS-SION TO DESTROY THE COURT-YARD...
IS THIS REALLY GONNA GET THAT INTENSE?
YEAH.
WELL, JUST WATCH.
FIRST, THE PROPER SETTING.
WOULD YOU THREE STEP BACK?
!!

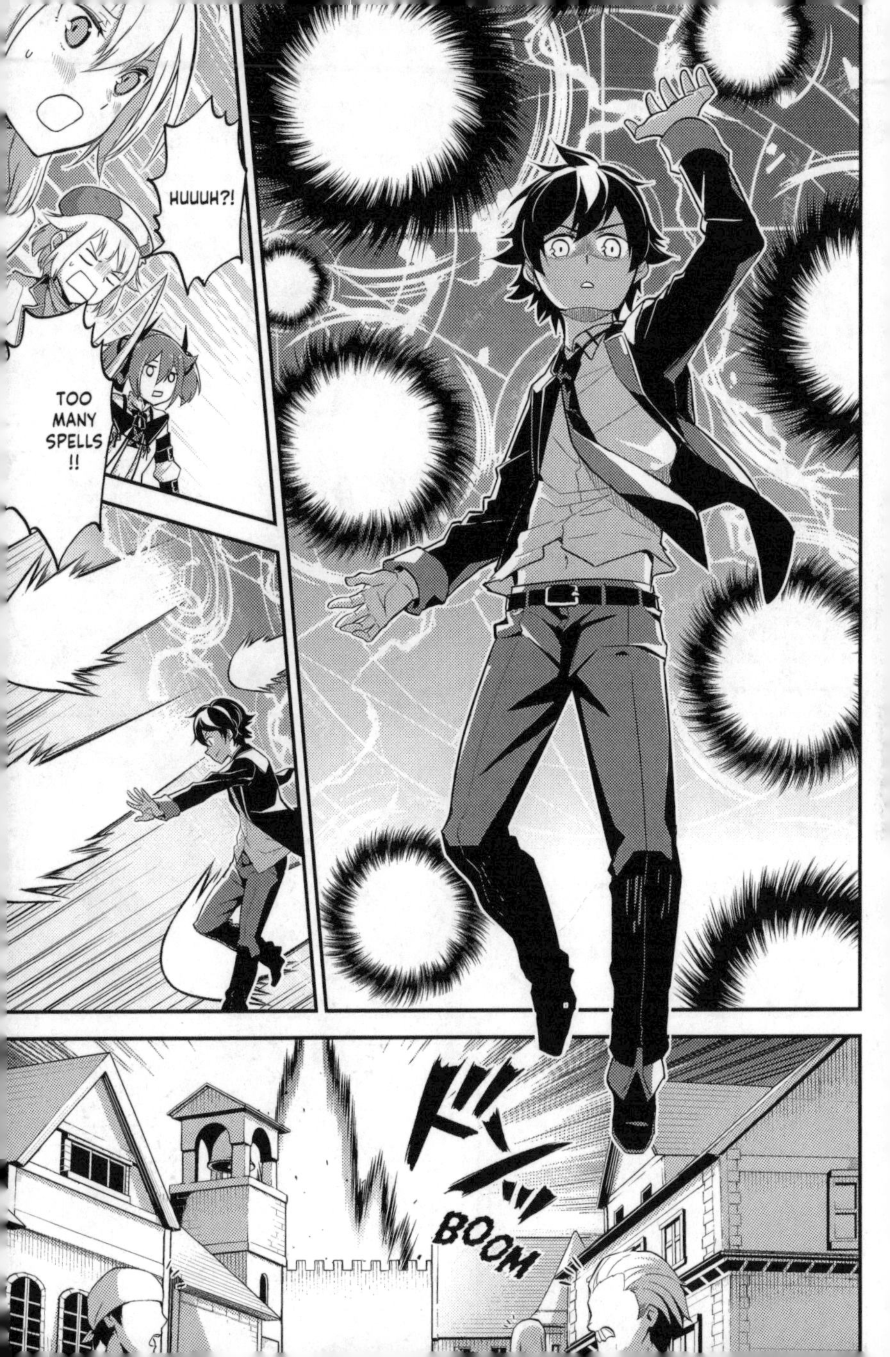
HUUUH?!
TOO MANY SPELLS !!
BOOM

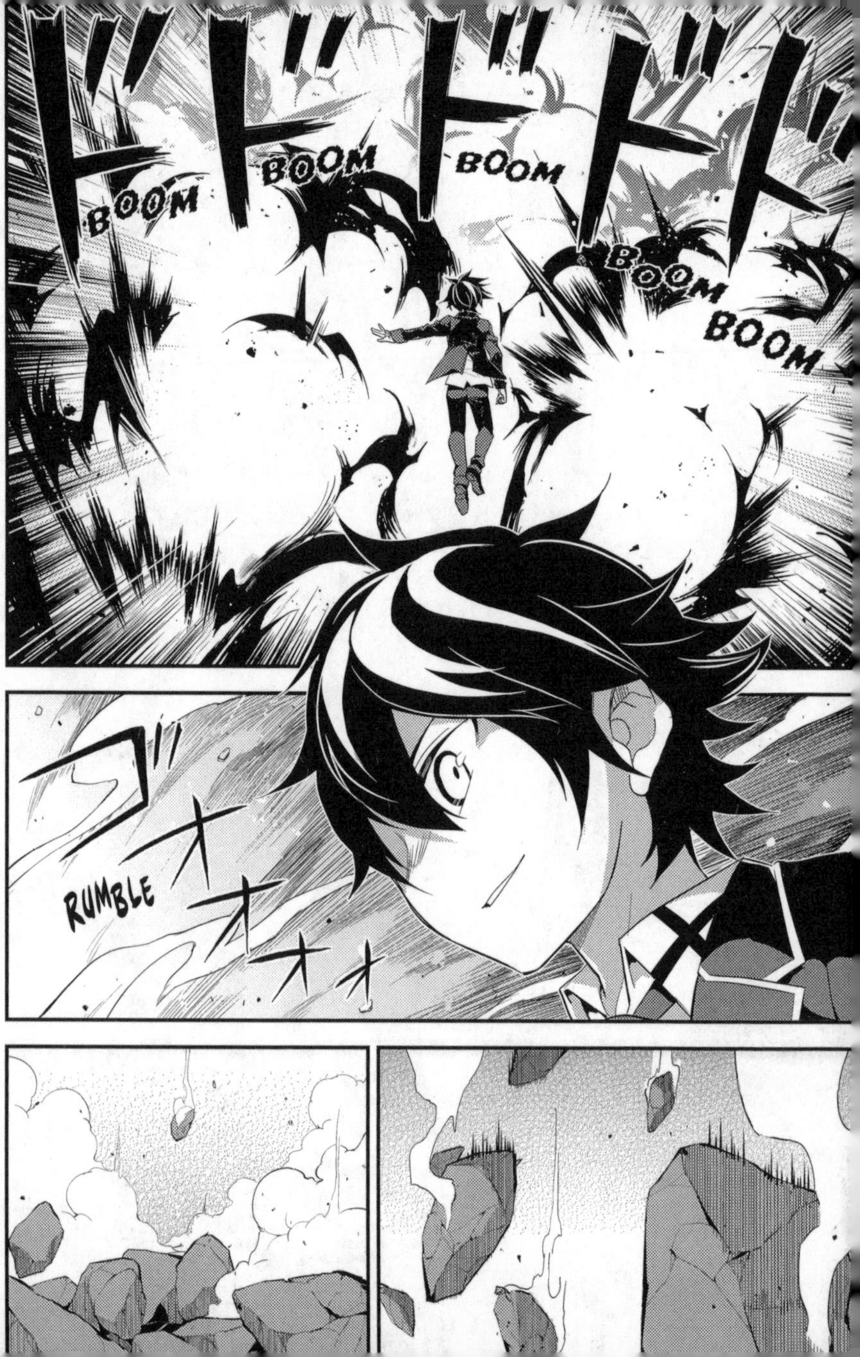
BOOM
BOOM
BOOM
BOOM
BOOM
BOOM
RUMBLE

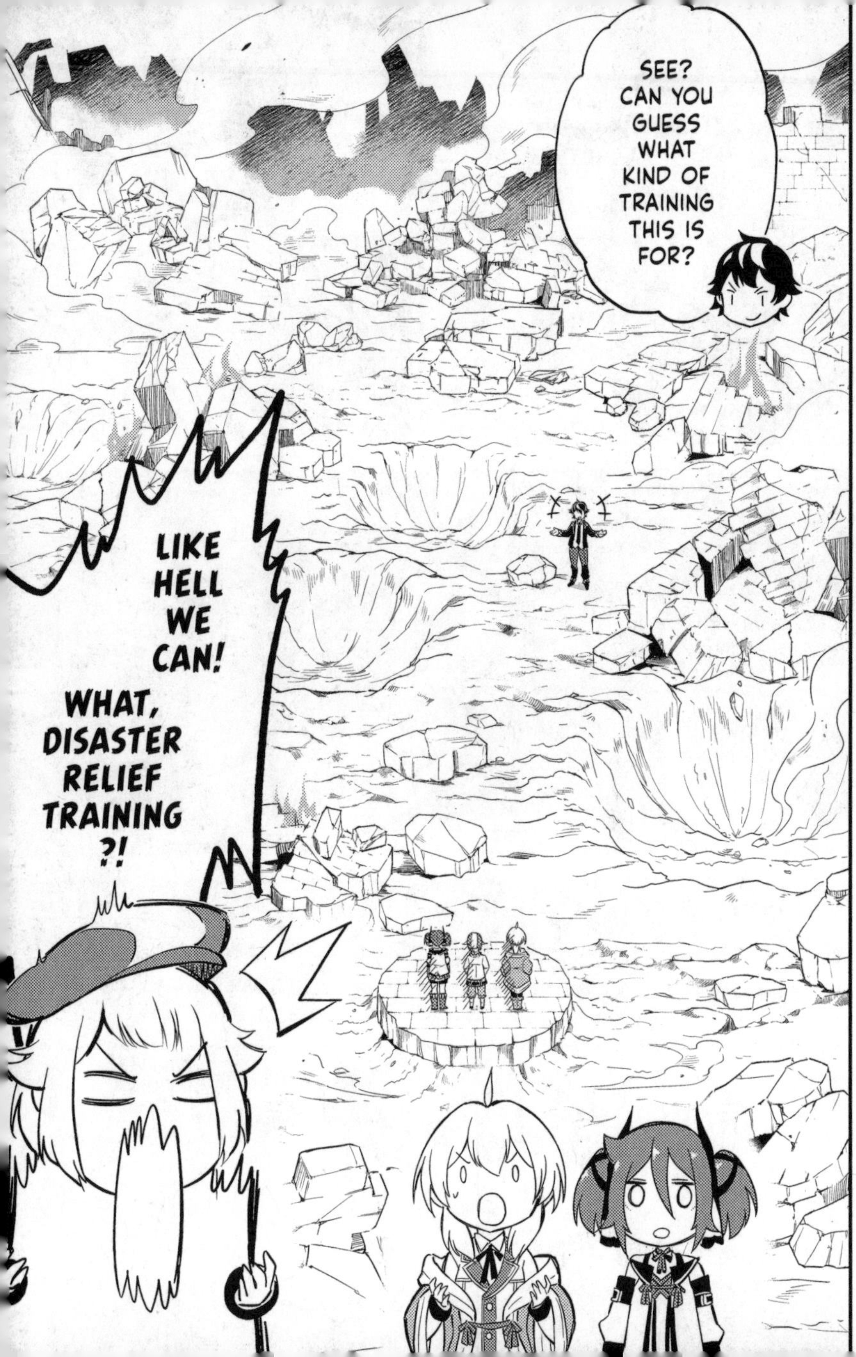
SEE? CAN YOU GUESS WHAT KIND OF TRAINING THIS IS FOR?
LIKE HELL WE CAN!
WHAT, DISASTER RELIEF TRAINING ?!

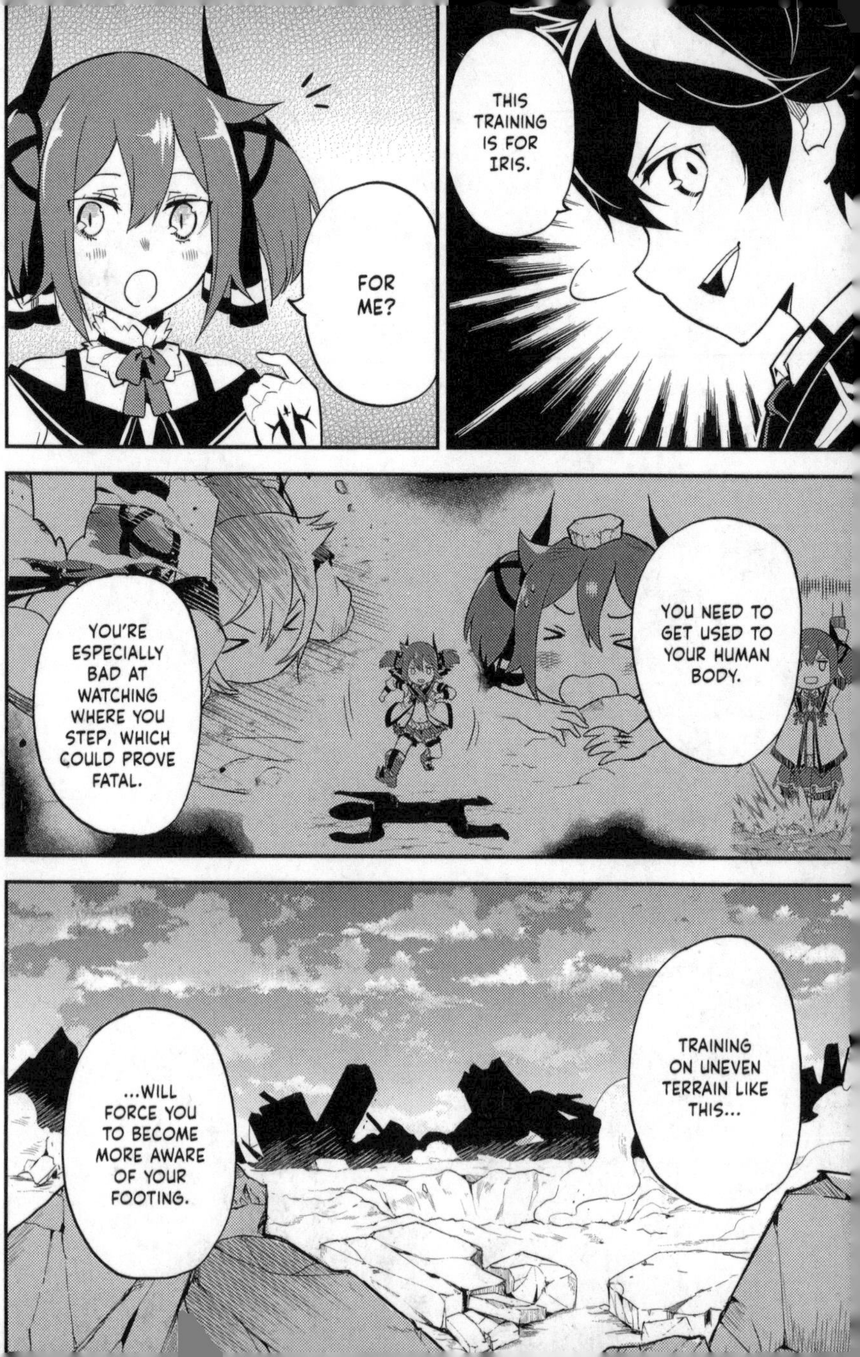
THIS TRAINING IS FOR IRIS.
FOR ME?
YOU NEED TO GET USED TO YOUR HUMAN BODY.
YOU'RE ESPECIALLY BAD AT WATCHING WHERE YOU STEP, WHICH COULD PROVE FATAL.
TRAINING ON UNEVEN TERRAIN LIKE THIS...
...WILL FORCE YOU TO BECOME MORE AWARE OF YOUR FOOTING.

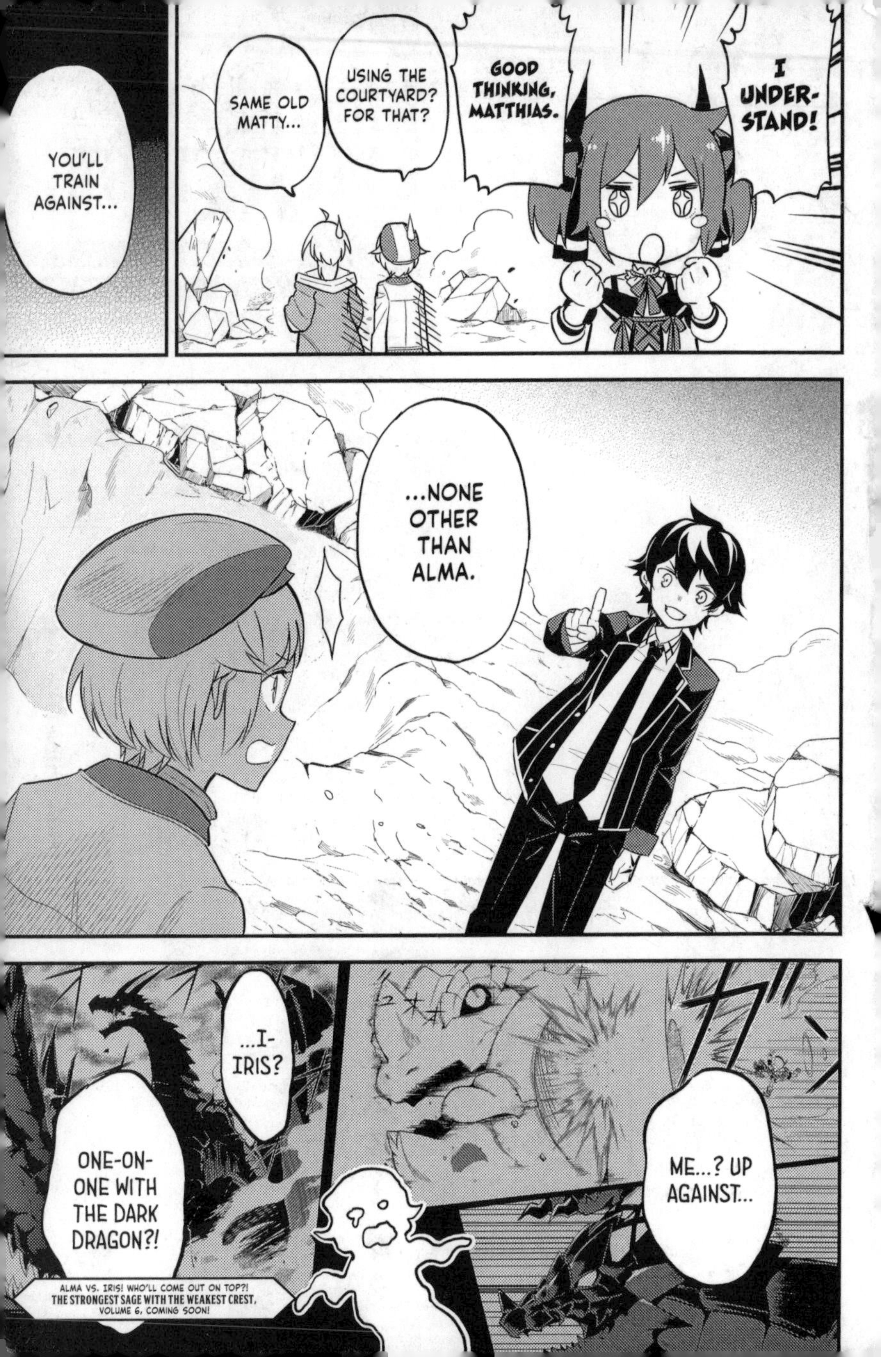
I UNDERSTAND!
GOOD THINKING, MATTHIAS.
USING THE COURTYARD? FOR THAT?
SAME OLD MATTY...
YOU'LL TRAIN AGAINST...
...NONE OTHER THAN ALMA.
ME...? UP AGAINST...
...I- IRIS?
ONE-ON-ONE WITH THE DARK DRAGON?!
ALMA VS. IRIS! WHO'LL COME OUT ON TOP?! THE STRONGEST SAGE WITH THE WEAKEST CREST, VOLUME 6, COMING SOON!

THE STRONGEST SAGE WITH THE WEAKEST CREST

Story | **Shinkoshoto**

Art | **Liver Jam & POPO** (Friendly Land)

Character Design | Huuka Kazabana

Translation: Caleb D. Cook
Lettering: Ken Kamura
Cover Design: Phil Balsman
Editors: David Yoo, Tania Biswas

SHIKKAKUMON NO SAIKYOKENJA Volume 5
©Shinkoshoto/SB Creative Corp.
Original Character Designs:©Huuka Kazabana/SB Creative Corp.
©Friendly Land/SQUARE ENIX CO., LTD.
First published in Japan in 2018 by SQUARE ENIX CO., LTD.
English translation rights arranged with SQUARE ENIX
CO., LTD. and SQUARE ENIX, INC.
English translation © 2021 by SQUARE ENIX CO., LTD.

ISBN: 978-1-64609-047-1

Library of Congress Cataloging-in-Publication
Data is on file with the publisher.

Printed in the U.S.A.
First printing, September 2021
10 9 8 7 6 5 4 3 2 1

SQUARE ENIX
MANGA & BOOKS
www.square-enix-books.com